Contemporary Russian Myths

Cover Illustration:
Poet Velimir Khlebnikov by Yuri Annenkov, 1916. From Korney Chukovsky Museum, Moscow.
Nikolay Gogol by Anatoly Zverev, 1983. From Yuri Drizhnikov's personal archive.
Alexander Kuprin and Leo Tolstoy by cartoonist P. Troyanovsky. Russian satirical magazine "Sery volk," 1908.

CONTEMPORARY RUSSIAN MYTHS
A SKEPTICAL VIEW OF THE LITERARY PAST

Yuri Druzhnikov

Studies in Slavic Languages and Literature
Volume 14

The Edwin Mellen Press
Lewiston•Queenston•Lampeter

Library of Congress Cataloging-in-Publication Data

Druzhnikov, I︠U︡riĭ, 1933-
   Contemporary Russian myths : a skeptical view of the literary past
/ Yuri Druzhnikov.
      p. cm.-- (Studies in Slavic languages and literature ; v. 14)
   Includes bibliographical references and index.
   ISBN 0-7734-8161-3 (hardcover)
   1. Russian literature--20th century--History and criticism.
2. Russia--In literature. 3. Soviet Union--In literature.
4. History in literature. I. Title. II. Series.
PG3026.H57D78   1999
891.709--dc21   99-25319
                                                                                    CIP

This is volume 14 in the continuing series
Studies in Slavic Languages & Literature
Volume 14 ISBN 0-7734-8161-3
SSLL Series ISBN 0-88946-290-9

A CIP catalog record for this book is available from the British Library.

Copyright © 1999 Yuri Druzhnikov

All rights reserved. For information contact

        The Edwin Mellen Press   The Edwin Mellen Press
                Box 450   Box 67
            Lewiston, New York   Queenston, Ontario
             USA 14092-0450   CANADA L0S 1L0

                       The Edwin Mellen Press, Ltd.
                      Lampeter, Ceredigion, Wales
                   UNITED KINGDOM SA48 8LT

                Printed in the United States of America

Contents

Foreword by Victor Terras
iii
A Word to the Reader
1
Pushkin, Stalin, and Other Poets
5
"Hitting It Off With Pushkin"
31
The Poet's 113th Love
53
A Divorce for Pushkin's Tatyana, *née* Larina
99
Pushkin's Hallowed Nurse
131
The Dangerous Jests of Albert Robida
165
The Overt and Covert Lives of Konstantin Ventzel
183
Alexander Kuprin: From Midden to Mantlepiece
217
Visiting Stalin's, Uninvited
239
The Ruchyi Churchyard Mystery
269
Trifonov's Fate: or, A Good Writer in a Bad Time
295
Notes
333
Bibliography
349
Index
359

Foreword
by Victor Terras
Henry Ledyard Goddard University Professor Emeritus of Slavic languages and comparative literature at Brown University

A nation is defined by its mythology, among other things. Russia, like other nations, has had an official and an unofficial branch of its national mythology, although the subjects of both are often the same. Professor Druzhnikov has made it his concern to look for the authentic facts behind both, though his main interest is in the official mythology ground out by the propaganda machine of the Soviet period. His study *Informer 001, or the Myth of Pavlik Morozov*, shows in meticulous detail how the heroic image of a child-martyr was fabricated and made a part of the Soviet official mythology. The present collection of essays, while it presents a miscellany of myths from different periods and walks of life, follows an identical paradigm: The reality of Russian life is a travesty, both cruel and banal, of Russia's national mythology, official or unofficial.

Alexander Pushkin is perhaps the only genuine culture hero (to use Carlyle's term) of Russia. He was declared to be Russia's national poet, while still alive, by Gogol, a younger contemporary, and glorified as the supreme and prophetic bearer of Russia's mission to all humanity in Dostoyevsky's celebrated *Discourse on Pushkin* (1880). This—unofficial—myth was made into an official one during the Soviet period. Druzhnikov's essay "Pushkin, Stalin, and Other Poets" gives an equally sad and amusing account of the transformation of Pushkin into a symbol of all that Stalin, that "great leader and teacher," thought to be essential to his rule. By the way, Vladimir Mayakovsky had anticipated this development in a poem occasioned by the 125th anniversary of Pushkin's birth (1924), where he hustles Pushkin off his pedestal for a friendly chat at his own flat and compliments him for having the stuff to have been a competent editor of *Left Front*, Mayakovsky's journal. After the demise of the Soviet regime, the Dostoyevskian version of the myth seems to have made a spectacular return. In a recent article, Professor Andrzej Lazari quotes from the publications of a whole range of Russian scholars and critics who second Dostoyevsky's prophetic vision of Pushkin as a symbol of Russian *narodnost* (national spirit), bearing the seeds of *vsechelovechnost* (universal humanity, literally "all-humanity"), the point being that it is Russia that determines the spirit of humanity, and not vice versa, as would be the case if the term *obshchechelovechnost* (common humanity) were to be used (Andrzej Lazari, "Dostoyevsky kak ideologicheskiy avtoritet v politicheskoy bor'be nashikh dney," in *Dostoevsky Studies*, New Series, vol.2, 1998, No.1, pp.104-13).

Ivan the Terrible and Peter the Great, bloody despots who were successful in augmenting their empire by conquest, left a conflicting memory in the minds of the Russian people, surprisingly positive the former, mostly negative the latter. The official mythology stressed the positive accomplishments under these Tsars and, after only a brief reversal, returned to an ever-more idealized image of both, as Stalin personally identified with them. Lenin and Stalin were, like these Tsars, official heroes, celebrated in poetry, fiction, drama, film, and every other art form. Yuri Druzhnikov is able to bring them down to concrete reality, which is, alas, almost always banal. His essay "The Dangerous Jests of Albert Robida" makes it plausible that Robida (1848-1926), a French artist and writer of science fiction, was responsible for some of the most significant ideas of Vladimir Ulyanov, alias Lenin, rather than Marx and Engels. As for Stalin, "Visiting Stalin's, Uninvited" scores the point that the many scenes in every conceivable art form under the common title of "Stalin, in the Kremlin, cares about everything" have it all wrong: Stalin did not actually live in the Kremlin, but in a suburban house which was kept secret from everybody.

Mythology is not limited to great poets, generals, and heads of state, particularly in Russia, where the Orthodox Church has nurtured a culture of kenotic apophatism: the naysaying to power, glory, learning, and common virtues; tender attention to the meek, the poor, the foolish, and humble sinners. The tremendous amount of literature devoted to the illiterate serf-woman who was Pushkin's nurse may be an expression of this attitude. Yuri Druzhnikov's carefully researched article "Pushkin's Hallowed Nurse" shows how the poet's genuine affection for his nurse and later housekeeper at the Pushkins' Mikhaylovskoye estate was built up into mythologies that suited the political ideologies of Slavophiles, Populists, and Soviet Communists, who all sought to prove that Arina Rodionovna taught Russia's national poet the real truth known only to the Russian people. Once more an episode from the life of an individual is raised to the level of national and "all-human" importance.

Russia's poets tend to have had short and troubled lives. Yet nowhere in the world have poets contributed so much to their national mythology as in Russia, where the poet's creations and his personal life are much more likely to be in the public eye than in the West—since Byron, Goethe, and Victor Hugo, one should add. Druzhnikov tells the story of a great poet who, in spite of his extraordinary originality and fantastic biography, never became a mythical figure. Velimir Khlebnikov (1888-1922), the founder of Russian Futurism (he wrote futurist poems years before the news of Filippo Marinetti's Futurist manifesto reached Russia) and without a doubt the boldest innovator and experimenter of all Russian poets, led a truly "romantic" life.

Khlebnikov moved restlessly from place to place all his life, had no permanent residence during the last ten years when he spent time in hospitals and insane asylums, Red as well as White prisons, but mostly wandering about Mother Russia. Khlebnikov was decidedly "of the people" and could feel with them. His poems occasioned by the terrible famine on the Volga in 1920-21 are far more impressive than those of Vladimir Mayakovsky, who was declared the foremost Soviet poet by Stalin himself. Yet Khlebnikov, who died essentially of starvation, never received more than lukewarm and quasi-professional recognition from his peers, and never found a way to the popular consciousness—as did Mayakovsky and some other contemporaries of his. Druzhnikov follows the trail of Khlebnikov's last months and establishes, among other things, that the body that was eventually buried in Moscow was not Khlebnikov's, who still lies buried in an unmarked grave in a village near Novgorod.

A myth that has dominated Russian thought for a long time, sometimes called "The Russian Idea," perceives Russia as an organic and indivisible subject: the Russian God, the Tsar, and his people were *one*, as were Stalin, the Party, and the people. They were united with Russia's historical destiny by common values—religious under the Tsars, ideological under Communism. Russian literature sustained this myth.

The Soviet period, which raised the myth to a dogma, saw it put to a crucial test. The story of Yuri Trifonov (1925-81), which is a chapter in Druzhnikov's book, shows the myth in action. Having known Trifonov personally, Druzhnikov believes that Trifonov was an honest and decent man. How does this square with his biography and the fact that he was sent to the U. S. in 1977 on a lecture tour essentially to advertise the myth of free creativity in Brezhnev's Soviet Union?

Trifonov was the son of an old Bolshevik who was purged by Stalin in 1937. Yet he managed to enter the Gorky Literary Institute, which produced an amazing share of prominent Soviet writers, and won a Stalin Prize with his first novel, *Students* (1950), a conventional piece of Stalinist Socialist Realism. *Quenching Thirst* (1963), a novel that deals with the construction of an irrigation channel in Turkmenia, is well within the limits of post-Thaw standards, still solidly socialist-realist. But in the late 1960s, Trifonov developed a new manner in works like *The Exchange* and *The House on the Quay*. Characters are no longer presented marked "positive" or "negative." They pursue their personal goals without any explicit reference to official values or goals, either on their part of the narrator's. Nevertheless, there is still a distinct subtext letting the reader know that a single-minded pursuit of material values is wrong. It is only in some late works, such as *Time and Place* (published posthumously), that Trifonov allows literature almost to become an end in itself, with private experience no longer integrated with history, and an interest in psychology displacing morality.

Thus, Trifonov finally was about to arrive at a point where the myth of the organic unity of the individual and society, of private life and history, and of personal morals and ideology, is beginning to fade away. It happened not by any supreme fiat, with no coercion or revolutionary fanfare. It simply was abandoned by a writer who was a conformist by nature—never a rebel, only a talented prosaist.

I hope that my remarks correctly reflect the gist of Yuri Druzhnikov's book. At any rate, my remarks, those of a generalist and theorist, should stay in the background behind the living literature of Druzhnikov, who is not only a scholar, but a creative writer.

A Word to the Reader

Before you is a book of my doubts, the result of accumulated disbelief in the facts that we Russians were made to learn from childhood. From infancy we were schooled to consider the tales in newspapers to be the truth, and punished for any doubts; so these myths are in our blood. The idea for *Russian Myths* came to me as a persistent aspiration, lasting a decade, to check and see if things were really the way they had been written up in thousands of publications, and the desire to share these doubts and their investigation with the reader.

In primordial consciousness, mythology stood for religion and the entire culture in general. By some wondrous means, that consciousness came to the fore again in the 20th century on that one-sixth of the earth's land mass known as the Soviet Union. For three quarters of a century, not only politics, but economy, history, philosophy, and even the exact sciences were subordinate to a myth, and literature itself acquired the role of herald to mythological successes. This book is about those literary illusions that have been preserved in Russia and are still spreading over the world.

Russian history and literature live mythologically to this day, although the themes change. Of course other countries, too, are full of myths, but theirs are not so stagnant, not so coercive, and have a larger dose of humor and pragmatism. And, in contrast with Russia, if there is any doubt about the myths, the opportunity is there to point a finger calmly at them. The specific character of Russian myths is their traditional untouchability. Criticizing them is permitted only when they have already expired, and even then, not always. Isn't that why they have become a customary part of the Russians themselves?

Certain myths were formed by accident, from ignorance of the truth, others were a result of voluntary illusions, and still others were created for a set purpose, to add luster to the biography of a man or the life of the whole country. And, anyway, it's not myths that are dangerous, but the mentality that is inclined to prefer utopian dreams to bleak reality.

The universe of Russian literary mythology is endless. From this endlessness only a few myths that have become near to me and seem important are reflected here. This book was written over many years: the first pages were for myself in Moscow long before my emigration, then later on for *Samizdat*, and part after moving to America—in Texas, New York, California—and, finally, during my trips to the new Russia.

It's my conviction that none of these historical characters need to be passed over in silence and just allowed to win, if we discuss their actions openly and impartially, without taboo or sanctimoniousness. This especially concerns a writer's personality. It is important not only because it is reflected in what is written by him. The writer belongs entirely to his readers. More than that, at the end of the 20th century it has proved to be that—like it or not—the mistakes of writers of the past, their worries, goals, personal relations, illusions, problems, wiles, maneuvers, and secrets are no less interesting to the reader than the great truths discovered by them in their prose and poetry. Exactly in the same way, the personal qualities of historical figures are important. We want to understand the motivation behind their acts.

Some of the protagonists of this book by the will of fate were creators of myths about themselves and about the country in which they lived; others were active participants in the legends created by the former. And everyone, including their readers, at least sometimes became victims of these myths.

> Ah, it's not difficult to deceive me!..
> I'm glad to be deceived, myself!

—said Alexander Pushkin. But sobering-up time comes when finally you want to stop being glad, if we are being sincerely or by design led around by the nose. Pushkin, by the way, also preferred not to be deceived, and the ban on his telling the truth made him now furious, now depressed.

A Word to the Reader

Values are re-appraised in Russia only agonizingly, especially those that only yesterday seemed entirely respectable. The break with the customary, with illusions, is hard. At times, attempts to restore historical memory, to return to truth and justice, or at least to the patience to hear other opinions, are unavailing. But even the now-fashionable expression "the unmasking of myths" puts me on my guard, especially if the myths derive from sincere illusions. We shall endeavor to show how these myths have been created, to have a look at the essence of the dramatic events of the past, to try to separate their interpretation from what took place in life. Of course I foresee disagreement with the thoughts set out here. Before you is a historian of literature's subjective view of the literary process in which the author is a small particle: both creator, and victim. He attempts to explain phenomena the way he sees them, writes the truth the way he understands it, nothing less, and nothing more.

Y.D.
Davis, California

Pushkin, Stalin, and Other Poets

Alexander Pushkin is so popular in Russia that an educated person knows the poet, his wife, his friends, and his enemies almost better than his own wife, friends, and enemies, and probably himself. The family tragedy of the classic author long ago became our personal tragedy. The importance of Pushkin's figure for Russian culture has led to the fact that, for a century and a half already, the poet has been used not so much in the interests of the literary as the political. Pushkin has long been in heaven. But various authorities, parties, and movements, have all now and again usurped the right to be his interpreters on earth.

The historical tragedy of Pushkin, in my view, is that the poet has been turned into an idol to be worshiped, into an icon, into monuments, into names of cities, streets, libraries, and ships; moreover, the real Pushkin has been covered with thicker and thicker layers of theatrical make-up. In other words, the icon has been swiped and substituted time and again, retaining only the same glorious name.

Pushkin had to play various roles after his death. He was declared now an individualist, now a collectivist, now a Russian Schellingist, an Epicurean, or a representative of the *Natur-philosoph* school, now a genuine Christian or a militant atheist, now a Freemason, now a democrat, now a monarchist. And further—an idealist, a materialist, and even a historical materialist. This list (with reference to the corresponding works) could be extended. But one psalm has been sung in concert by all in authority: Pushkin is the personification of the omnipotent Russian spirit, the symbol of a great, united, and indivisible Russia, State Poet No.1. In the words of Apollon Grigoryev, "Pushkin is our everything." Or, as Gorky said of Pushkin, "he is the beginning of all beginnings for us."

Of course such a figure would be attractive to the comrades who came to power in 1917. Nihilistic slogans like "let's throw Pushkin overboard from the ship of modernity" worked against the new regime itself, which is why they started sorting out Russian classic authors according to the principle of their usefulness. Before being recruited into the service of Communism, the nobleman Pushkin had to undergo a clean-up. The People's Commissar for Education, Anatoly Lunacharsky, a "God-seeker," then a Marxist, bureaucrat, diplomat, and compulsive scribbler, declared that "Pushkin has unconditionally passed the test of the fiery portal separating the bourgeois world from the first period of the socialist world, and in our opinion, he will pass the final hurdle." And—"while we need assistants," the People's Commissar confessed, Pushkin would have to remain a "teacher of the proletariat and the peasantry."[1]

Even Lenin, as is known, constructed his model of the Russian Revolution as a ladder of three stages: the Decembrists crowding at the bottom (of whom, by the way, there was a total of 337, by the latest calculation), and, accomplishing mankind's progress at the top—the Bolsheviks, whose number during the Revolution was of course more than the number of Decembrists, but, for understandable reasons, has been concealed, exaggerated, and whose exact count we do not know to this day. After vacillations and purges, Pushkin was given a mandate to represent that liberation movement steadfastly leading to the shining future, that is, to the Soviet state. At some point Pushkin was less lucky than Belinsky, who was simply rated equal with the party apparatus. "In our times, Belinsky would be not the least member of the Politburo of the Central Committee of the All-Russian Communist Party (of Bolsheviks)," declared Lunacharsky.[2] Pushkin was never vouchsafed such an honor.

But Pushkin's biography and works were adjusted to fit political doctrine. In St. Petersburg and Kishinev, the young poet had become acquainted with the Decembrists, and wrote several poems about freedom. He never took part in their activities, and in his maturity, his views changed: he called revolution riotous and related to it negatively. This Pushkin was made into a singer and agitator for the Decembrist movement, was pronounced a friend of the Decembrists, then a Decembrist, and in some extreme articles, even a revolutionary. It is interesting, for example, to re-read the work of the famous critic Valery Kirpotin about the connections between the notions of "Pushkin" and "Communism"; different parts of this work could easily be taken as parody.[3] Kirpotin was the head of the Fiction Section of the Central Committee in those years, and, in this way, took part in the evaluation of the usefulness of authors.

It is known that official recognition of Mayakovsky came with a few words of Stalin's that were quoted in an editorial in *Pravda*.[4] The words about Mayakovsky had been taken from a letter of Stalin's in answer to one from Lilya Brik about Mayakovsky's usefulness for the business of the revolution and to the Soviet regime. Meanwhile, a newspaper editorial was devoted to a resolution of the Central Executive Committee about setting up a Pushkin committee. It said in it that Pushkin was the creator of the Russian literary language, and that that language had become the property of the millions of workers, and through love for Pushkin Soviet youth would be correctly educated. Further on it said:

> The vanguard of youth knows and loves Pushkin. Our best poets trace their pedigree to Pushkin. And of the significance of the best poet of our Soviet epoch, of the significance of Mayakovsky, Comrade Stalin recently said, 'Mayakovsky was and remains the best, the most talented poet of our Soviet epoch.'

And a little further on,

> the resolution of the Central Executive Committee of the U.S.S.R. on the Pushkin committee continues the line demonstrated in the words of Comrade Stalin.

This is all screwy. Pushkin's language had become the property of millions of workers, but Pushkin's death centennial celebration was due to Stalin's phrase canonizing Mayakovsky. Nonetheless, as we can see, the Writers' Best Friend had personally taken an interest in Pushkin. From 1935 the entire country was preparing for its "historic celebration of Soviet culture," that is, the centennial of the poet's death. The Pushkin committee, with Voroshilov and Gorky in charge, was working, it seems, under Stalin's personal leadership. Specialized works appeared about how to understand and interpret the poet properly. "Pushkin was searching for what Communism has found," wrote Kirpotin, "conditions for the equilibrium and harmony of the personal with the societal principle." And further: "The enlightened humanism of Pushkin flows into the socialist humanism of the renewed world like a mighty river flows into the eternal ocean."[5]

By 1937, the centennial of Pushkin's death, to which entire newspapers were being devoted at the very height of the mass repression, when the groans of millions were being drowned out by the loud reading of Pushkin's poems, newspapers were connecting the poet directly with the October Revolution. *Pravda* wrote:

> Pushkin is entirely ours, a Soviet . . . since the Soviet regime has inherited everything that is best in the people, and itself is the realization of the best aspirations of the people . . . In the final analysis, Pushkin's works flow together with the October Socialist Revolution like a river flows into the sea.[6]

Who was borrowing these images from whom?—or maybe Kirpotin himself wrote both of these pieces. We can't answer that.

"Only in the Stalin epoch," wrote Aleksandr Yegolin, a critic who worked at the Central Committee, "of unprecedented rise in the material and cultural level of Soviet society is it possible to have such a happy and deeply joyful phenomenon as the transformation of the poet's centennial into a holiday for all the people."[7] Never before had the death of the poet been turned into a rejoicing by the whole people.

Pushkin was being used for the Russification of the people inhabiting this multi-national country. "Pushkin came to the Uzbeks, to the Tadzhiks... to all nationalities joined to the culture of the Great Russian people by the Revolution."[8] The year 1941 was the next step towards Pushkin's canonization to Soviet sainthood. Among the multitudinous myths about this war that are now more openly discussed even by former Soviet historians, the Pushkin Myth remains by itself, and not everything about it is clear.

Usually official myths well up in stages, their signs becoming distinctly visible before any government announcements. However, for the Stalinist Pushkin Myth (let's name it that for the nonce), not only the year and the place of its first appearance can be indicated precisely, but even the day and the hour: the myth was born the evening of November 6, 1941.

We're talking, of course, about the plenary session that took place underground at the Mayakovskaya metro station in Moscow. Who came up with the idea of having a session between the subway platforms?—after all, quite a few bomb- and gas-shelters had already been built. Maybe Stalin was strengthening the connection between Pushkin and Mayakovsky? This happened on the eve of the 24th anniversary of the October Revolution. By the way, there remained this historical absurdity: the October Revolution was in November. Stalin's speech was made at this session. It would be interesting to know who wrote the General Secretary's masterpiece, wouldn't it?

The Leader mentioned Pushkin only once, but his reference determined the basic task of Pushkin scholarship, Soviet literature, and the entire culture of the Soviet Union in general for at least a decade and a half ahead. In order to appreciate this reference, we had to analyze its context in the General Secretary's speech. Rolling the tape, I listened to his Caucasian accent, the gurgling of water when he drank, and I could envision the glass shaking in his hand: the Leader was pretty nervous.

In his speech, Stalin is meditating on nationalism. "While the Hitlerites were busy gathering the German lands together ... they could have been considered nationalists by that well-known criterion." Can you feel that? Nationalism in prewar Germany was perceived as something rational—after all, they had to justify their good relations with the Nazis somehow. The Leader would need it for justifying nationalism in Russia. Further, the whipping-up of hate towards the leaders of Germany preceded the appeal to the patriotic feelings of the Soviet people in his speech.

Stalin quoted (none of the sources were available to his listeners) Hitler, Goering, and the orders of the German high command, which all reduced to one thing: kill the Russians. A soldier needs neither conscience, heart, or nerves. Destroy all compassion and sympathy in yourselves. "Here is the program and directives of the Hitlerite party and the Hitlerite command for you, the program and directives of people who have lost any human aspect and have fallen to the level of wild beasts."

He liked to repeat the very same words a number of times, like an incantation, having picked this up from Trotsky, probably. And how did he get from people who have lost any human aspect to Pushkin? Very simply:

> And these people, stripped of conscience and honor, people with the morality of animals, have the impudence to call for the annihilation of the Great Russian nation, the nation of Plekhanov and Lenin, Pushkin and Tolstoy, Glinka and Tchaikovsky,

Gorky and Chekhov, Sechenov and Pavlov, Repin and Surikov, Suvorov and Kutuzov...

Let's mention a subtext here that will come in handy later: the Leader of the great nation is also automatically enlisted among the great. From this follows his conclusion "to destroy every single German who invades our country's territory."[9]

If you re-read Stalin's appeal today, it seems justified for something from wartime. But we know that by the beginning of the war, Stalin and his circle, in their entirely peaceful situation, had destroyed the best part not only of the Russian nation but of all the nationalities inhabiting Russia in millions not yet counted, including, it looks like, Maxim Gorky, who was on Stalin's list of national heroes.

Stalin was addressing all the nationalities of the Soviet Union, but nevertheless spoke of greatness of only one nation, the Russian. Stalin's Nazism was more refined than Hitler's. Stalin's military mistakes would bring the Soviet populace to a destruction ten times greater than the waste of human resources that was people executed by the Reich during the war.[10] But the reality was that it was Stalin who found himself at the head of Russia's struggle with fascism, and at that time he was desperately looking for the support both inside the country and abroad.

It may seem that the list of great Russian names mentioned in the speech on November 6 was accidental, just sampling. But all the people mentioned in it are famous in the West. The names of these representatives of Russian culture are all connected with "holy places" in Russia: Pushkin's Mikhaylovskoye, Tolstoy's Yasnaya Polyana, Glinka's Smolensk, Tchaikovsky's Klin, Chekhov's Yalta, and Repin's Penaty. All these places had already either been occupied or were doomed to be captured and looted by the enemy. Surikov was a Siberian, but he was a painter of the people's tribulations, a patriot.

Anyway, it's very strange that, without any special necessity, Lenin's enemy, the apostate Menshevik Plekhanov, and even the outspoken anti-Soviet academic, Pavlov, got named in the same breath. Evidently, this wasn't accidental, either: this wasn't a time for internal political games in the face of the enemy—unity was what was most important at that moment. And this was all accepted at the time as liberalization, humanization of the regime. It was also logical that more than any other (four) on the list were "engineers of the human soul," writers, inspirers of the people to heroic deeds in the name of the fatherland.

All the people named were thereupon used as symbols of the nation, its spiritual icons, that needed to be defended from the enemy, saved. Moreover, Pushkin, next after Lenin, was being exalted above all the rest.

In the same issue of the newspaper *Izvestiya* that printed Stalin's subway speech, as it was done at the time, some verses were printed—on this occasion by Maksim Rylsky, illustrating the thesis of Stalin's speech. In circumstances like these, the poet, a rank-and-file member of the editorial retinue, would be telephoned at any time of the day and half an hour later would dictate his text over the phone or would personally hand it over to the editor.

> Where everything grows relentlessly,
> Where the mind blazes like a bonfire,
> Where with Pushkin's dear shade
> Mayakovsky carried on conversation,
> Where every monument is without price,
> Where every stone is the track of glory,
> Where to all the peoples of the earth Lenin
> Showed the unfading dawn ... [*etc.—Y.D.*]
> The Host of the People goes to battle
> For the light, for happiness, for Moscow![11]

Thus the ideological myth took its artistic, poetic form straightaway.

Now, half a century later, the question still remains why the Great Leader needed, as Rylsky put it, "the shade" of the great poet. In a newsreel reflecting that day's work, troops being sent off to the front right the next day were marching past the bronze statue standing pensively in Pushkin Square. Military honors were rendered to the poet: everyone goose-stepping, eyes right at the monument. In between falsified operational reports of losses and abandoned cities rang out the classical love *romansy* with Pushkin's lyrics, performed by the greatest soloists of the Bolshoy Theater. Stalin was suggesting that Pushkin be saved, not himself, and that was a clever move. But the reasons for Pushkin's involvement in the war lay deeper still, it seems to me.

The Pushkin Myth as it can be seen now represents in itself part of another, more general myth, one that I would call a supermyth. This supermyth is rooted in the distant Russian past: it is about the superiority of the Russians over other nations (elder-brotherly) and their messianic role in history that flows from it, the supermyth of Russia as a Third Rome (and there will never be a fourth one). This particular messianic idea, transformed into the Communist mania for the liberation of all mankind by the so-called premier country of victorious socialism, existed until the ninth decade of this century, and there is a hope that it has perished.

At the beginning of the war with Germany it became obvious that the official ideology was not effecting what was needed. Danger was spurring a rapid reassessment of its attributes. Until only recently, out of inertia, Moscow had been sticking to the 19th-century Marxist version of a nationless proletariat, that is, the ideal of brotherly solidarity of the workers of the world. It was considered that the idea served our Soviet Third Rome: the *Internationale* was sung in Moscow, but was heard in America and Africa as well. The war showed that, even if it could be heard in Africa, closer to home its words were ineffective. Brotherly solidarity with the German proletariat had proved fictitious. They had donned their helmets and marched off to enslave their class-brothers in neighboring countries. The war returned Red Russia to the myth of the Great Power, Great Russian, traditional "Moscow—the Third Rome." It was no accident that during the war the government changed to a different anthem from the *Internationale* and broke up the Comintern.

Let us recall: the situation was desperate. The capital had been evacuated, there was a huge panic, the regime was hanging by a thread. In this catastrophic situation, the panicky potentates were ready to hitch themselves to whatever would serve, and so they appealed to the icons of nationhood that from time immemorial have been considered the true treasures of Russia. The Orthodox church underwent rehabilitation. In the cultural sphere, there was a headlong return to the classics. The radio began broadcasting more classical music than Soviet (with the exception perhaps of military marches and songs); the best orators read out warlike passages from the Russian classics.

The great Russian poet could demonstrate something that Stalin needed like air, something that was reality: the natural love of people for their homeland at its hour of need, on the verge of perdition, a human love for the historic motherland, as distinct from love for the party and the socialist Soviet land that *Agitprop* (Agitation and Propaganda—the Department of Central Committee of the Communist Party) had been trying to instill. Nationalism similar to that in Nazi Germany began to be used as the basic theme of propaganda at home. True, this nationalism was termed patriotism, but its essence (the great, older brother—the Russian people) did not change because of it.

The quotation from Stalin's speech began to be included in the foreword of all publications of Pushkin's works, in his biographies, and in articles by Pushkin scholars. The works of the last-mentioned (articles, speeches, books, especially for the mass readership), becoming in this way an effective tool for victory, were consequently published in huge editions at a time when culture was being reduced to a utilitarian minimum. The famous Pushkin scholar Boris Tomashevsky wrote an important propaganda booklet called *Pushkin and the Motherland*. Staffers from the Academy of Sciences' Pushkin House were sent into factories and military units to give lectures on Pushkin's love for his homeland.

One elderly critic told me that in his lectures at the front he always paid special attention to D'Anthes. Pushkin's murderer had returned to Paris, where he fell out of favor because his French had a slight German accent. It turned out that D'Anthes was of German origin. That's who killed our Pushkin! Then the lecturer would add that the murderer of Pushkin became a spy in France. These discoveries of Pushkin scholars worked to the advantage of the war effort, and how: a German in disguise killed our greatest poet, then hied himself off to Paris and became a spy there, too. D'Anthes, by the way, was an informer for the Russian government. But this detail got in the way of instilling hatred for the enemy and was dropped from lectures at the front.

Pushkin the Decembrist and revolutionary became unnecessary for the while. Now he was appointed to the ranks of the battle-portraitists, in order to sing of the military gallantry of the Russian army. The Soviet Pushkin scholar Boris Meylakh noted later on that "old Pushkin studies had gotten it completely wrong."[12] The importance of the victory marches of the youthful Pushkin had been underestimated. The beginning of the poet's literary activities coincided with the victory of the Russian army over Napoleon. Now this fact was found to be of use for creating an image of a singer who hymns the glory of Russian arms and a strong and invincible Russia.

Literary criticism set the significance of the theme "Pushkin and the Year 1812" as one of the most topical tasks of Pushkin studies. Leaf through the pages of Pushkin studies for that period and you will see that in his Lyceum period, let's say, the only thing that the boy ever did was admire Russian heroism in the war against the French, and after reaching his adulthood, inspire the Russian army to victory in the war with Turkey, and hymn the heroic deeds of Peter in the war with the Swedes.

Special stress was being laid on the heroism of the Russian nation. Here is a typical article from the newspaper *Izvestiya*, entitled "We Are Russians!" Its author, Arkady Perventsev, was a war correspondent and eventually a Stalin-Prize laureate. His books, as the *Literary Encyclopedia* put it, "carry the imprint of the cult of personality." Perventsev wrote from the front:

> Now, in these years of severe trial and nationwide ardor, we can face our ancestors with pride ... The noble quality of the Russian character, the leading role of the Russian people ... has helped the unification and cohesion of all the peoples of our Soviet state ... We must remember the words of our Leader about our enemies, about the Hitlerites ...

And here follows the above-mentioned quote from Stalin's speech.[13]

Soon the same newspaper published an editorial article about Gorky entitled "The Great Russian Writer," using military terminology for literature: "A Russian writer is the conscience of the people, the vanguard scout of the people."[14]

Pushkin's shade came alive to take part in the war. His name was inscribed on tanks, ships, and aircraft. At a Pushkin conference after the war, it was said that Baltic artillerymen in autumn of 1941 sent off their lethal projectiles shouting "This is for Pushkin!"[15] The famous writer and Pushkin scholar Ivan Novikov, who was 65 in that year, lived in evacuation in Kamensk-Uralsky. On Pushkin's jubilee dates, the party organs arranged a series of entry-fee parties at which Novikov read chapters from his novels and lectures on Pushkin. The collected fees, amounting to more than 100 thousand rubles, went for the construction of an airplane. In July, 1943, a telegram arrived in town: "The *Alexander Pushkin* fighter warplane, constructed from funds raised by you, was sent on June 28 to Pilot-Captain Gorokhov of the Red Army Air Force." Later they were informed that "The *Alexander Pushkin* has destroyed nine fascist airplanes." After the war, the elderly writer composed a poem entitled "The Airplane *Alexander Pushkin*." It closes, stylistically not very successfully, but proudly:

> So, Russians, we and our Russian poet,
> Whose muse's captivating light fades not,
> Foreseeing its free, victorious flight,
> Have jointly hammered out a plane for him.[16]

So there the poet was, jointly hammering out an airplane with us. But Pushkin really did get into the fight. In their lessons, teachers had to tie his patriotism to the heroism of the soldiers at the front. Bullet-riddled volumes of Pushkin were put on display at exhibitions. Dispatches from war correspondents told of how soldiers died with his poems on their lips.

It goes without saying that anniversaries of Pushkin's birth and death were used for organizing rallies, where vengeance upon the foe who dared encroach on the sacred places was the topic. There were stories in many newspapers about soldiers at the Kalinin front, risking their lives to make a raid in winter on Mikhaylovskoye village, deep in the German rear, in order to spruce up the poet's grave. The liberation of sacred Pushkin places was always celebrated solemnly, with military honors.

The press kept people informed about atrocities and ruination in these districts. A special government commission under the writer Aleksey Tolstoy was set up. Commission members did on-site tallies of the destruction of cultural treasures, and newspapers were filled with calls for vengeance on the fascists for these outrages on our great poet. In reality these places were suffering a second destruction: the first time was when the fatherland's laboring masses looted, ravaged, and set everything on fire under the leadership of Red commissars during the Revolution and the civil war.

Now all the sites where Pushkin had ever been or lived were being turned into sacred places of the nation. In Mikhaylovskoye, Pushkin's ancestral estate, next to the ruined grave of the poet in Svyatogorsk monastery, there were stuck-on messages that read: "To the great Pushkin, from the tankers of the *nth* brigade," "To Pushkin from Stalin's Falcons," "Pushkin, you will reach Berlin in our company's ranks," and so on.

Material about Pushkin in the national newspapers was printed in conspicuous places, but now they were in connection with successes at the front, alongside doxologies to Comrade Stalin, and lists as well of NKVD workers getting awards for opening up the Far East (read: for constructing new labor camps—especially for German and Russian prisoners of war—and for organizing labor for them). There in the camps they too honored Pushkin, and the Cultural-Educational Units of the prisons organized rallies where the camp commanders sat in the front rows and the *zeks* read the poems of the great poet-patriot from the stage.

The newspapers kept everyone informed of successes in the restoration of the town of Pushkin (the former Tsarskoye Selo, or Tsar's Village). "The monument to Pushkin is in its former place," a headline said proudly. When the Red Army had to retreat, the "Soviet patriots removed and buried deep in the earth" the statue of Pushkin. In January, 1944, when soldiers broke into the town, they found only its smashed-up pedestal. The monument was dug up and put back onto its former spot.[17] In their retreat, the Hitlerites had destroyed the town and with it the Lyceum and the *dacha* where the poet had lived with his young wife. Now, on Pushkin's behalf, the authorities demanded compensation for the damage: "Our greatest treasures have been ruined. Germany must pay this bill in full."[18] The robbery of Germany in reply began.

Soviet troops were liberating Eastern Europe, occupying it at the same time, naturally. A new theme now appeared in Pushkin studies. The scholars of the Institute of Russian Literature of the Academy of Sciences held discussions and lectures on Pushkin in units of the Red Army and aboard the ships of the Red Banner Baltic Fleet. Rallies dedicated to the 145th anniversary of Pushkin's birth were held in Leningrad and Pushkin town. The House of Culture was restored overnight, and filled up with town-dwellers, Red Army officers, etc. The critic Victor Manuylov spoke of Pushkin's world-wide significance (at that time this was the most important thing of all). The newspapers were all harping on this topical task. Vera Inber, the then-famous poet, finished a speech with these verses:

> We say the word "Pushkin"
> And see before us the poet
> Loved in his homeland

Pushkin, Stalin, and Other Poets

> Like the sun, like the source of light.
> We say the word "Pushkin"
> And see his town before us;
> It is ours once again; over it again
> Blue skies shine.
> We say the word "Pushkin,"
> Not knowing whether town or poet.
> We hold the first and second dear,
> We join them together into one.
> Both the town and the man are ours—
> For us they are equal in strength,
> Fused together in victory forever
> In a single image of Russia.[19]

Of course this run-of-the-mill lyric, so to speak, was written for the event. But Vera Inber with political precision unites three different factors in her poem: the great Pushkin, the forthcoming great victory, and the great country—Russia. Inber was Leon Trotsky's niece, and lived her life in fear of the consequences of that relation, which left its imprint on the pathos of her poetry.

The war was moving still further westwards. In Stalin's secret plans the design for the liberation of the whole of Europe was ripening. It was a necessity to prove that Russian culture was loftier and better than the western European. That meant that God Himself, as it is said, was willing it to dominate other cultures. Naturally, a further elevation of Pushkin had to happen: he had to work for today, for the party, for Communism.

Ahead lay the campaign of Russification—gigantic in its sweep—of the Baltic states, the western Ukraine, western Belorus, Moldova, and the countries of Eastern Europe. Pushkin with his works for all ages, with his ties to Europe and its authors, was seen by the competent organs as the ideal salesman, so to speak, for the marketing of Russian culture, books, and, above all, the imposition of the Russian language in those countries. Awhile later, on every continent except Antarctica, they began setting branches of the Pushkin Moscow Institute of the Russian Language, which were used by the KGB for roping in agents in the various countries. If you love our glorious poet and our grand Russian language, why wouldn't you help these kindly fellows who are attached to Pushkin, too?

But that came later. Now, in 1944, a conference about the role of Russian scientists in the development of world science was being held in Moscow. And two men, of course, were declared the highest achievement of civilization, geniuses of the whole world. Moscow State University Head I. S. Galkin announced: "The majestic edifice of Russian science is crowned by the names of those geniuses of mankind, Lenin and Stalin."[20]

On Victory Day, May 9, 1945, the newspapers published an article by a famous official playwright, the heroizer of Party history, Nikolay Pogodin. Pogodin recalled the beginning of the war and Stalin's speech on November 6, 1941. "And in those hours the name of Pushkin sounded on the lips of Joseph Vissarionovich... what a lofty, shining idea from a proud, blazing soul that was!"[21] Pogodin quoted the greater part of one of the most shameful and chauvinistic of Pushkin's poems, the invective "To the Slanderers of Russia," written in 1831 on the occasion of reaction in the West to repression by the Russians of a rebellion in Poland, and published straightaway.

> ... Is it anything new for us to argue with Europe?
> Or has the Russian lost the habit of victory?

This poem reflected the animosity of the Russian government to Western attempts to interfere in Russo-Polish affairs. This story is as old as the world, but once again highly appropriate to post-war reconstruction of Europe. Stalin wanted to decide for himself what to do with newly-captured Poland. The Western Allies had played their role and could now shown what for. Pushkin turned out *a propos* here as well.

At the end of the article, Pogodin again quoted two lines from that very same poem, where it says that Russia is ready to annihilate any adversary, and worse.

> There is a place for them in Russia's fields
> Among coffins unalien to them.

After the war, I studied at a Moscow school, and my teacher demanded that we learn that long poem by heart. I remember how ringingly I recited it. Meanwhile, in Pushkin's day, his friends sharply criticized the poet for the extreme right-wing stance taken in it. That poem deepened the spiritual crisis of the poet. Many people turned away from him, accusing him of being a political apostate and lickspittle, and even of collaboration with the secret police. Now that shameful poem, by the logic of its ideology, went to work again, this time for a new imperial system.

There was a feeling, now already forgotten, as if Russia was preparing for war all over again, this time with the whole world. The cold war was flaring up, Soviet soldiers were coming home from Europe, and the authorities did not want the striking contrast between life in Russia and life in the West to stir up discontent the way it had after 1812.

The essence of what the newspapers were publishing was that Pushkin together with the Soviet people had been victorious, and manifestation of love for Pushkin was "proof of Soviet patriotism," "awareness and social activism of the citizen." The poet's biography in those years was frequently re-written, made to accommodate current events. Pushkin taught pride, confirmation of the idea that the Russians were better than anyone else.

The past was needed for confirmation that victory was a regular phenomenon of Russian history, meaning that the great Party that had brought the Soviet people to their great victory, and its great Leader, were all regular phenomena as well. The Academician Vladimir Potemkin, a historian, diplomat, and, at the time, People's Commissar for Education, declared without any proof or any appeal to specifics that "the first steps of the Russian nation already presaged the future greatness of Russia."[22]

Further on in the same article Potemkin contrasts Western cultural values with Russian ones. "The spiritual potentates of the West—Leibnitz, Voltaire, Grimm, Diderot [*a strange crew—Y.D.*] will be amazed to see with what kind of monster steps the Russian giant marches down the road of progress. Russian literature will shine with constellations of such names as Radishchev, Derzhavin, Pushkin, Lermontov, Griboyedov, Krylov, Turgenev, Dostoyevsky ... The luminaries of Marxist science—Lenin and Stalin, the Bolshevik party, have raised up Russia to unprecedented heights."

Academician Potemkin declared Lenin and Stalin to be the luminaries of Marxist science rather than the foreigners Marx and Engels. Let's leave without any comment the assertion that Russia, thanks to these luminaries and their party, found itself raised up to unprecedented heights. The most amusing thing is the assertion that Leibnitz, Voltaire, and Diderot, who died in the 18th century, would admire Russian writers who lived in the 19th. In June, 1945, Pushkin's foremost biographer, Vikenty Veresayev, died, and even his obituary was used for an exegesis of Pushkin's life, in order to get out propaganda clichés useful at the moment.[23]

In 1949 a new jubilee came around: the 150th anniversary of the poet's birthday. The report on it announced that 300 Pushkin scholars had participated in commemorating the poet. On May 24, Stalin gave an order to hold a fireworks display in Pushkin's honor. All sense of proportion had gone by the board: "The 150th anniversary of the birth of A. S. Pushkin was celebrated in the memorable setting of the mighty union of progressive forces of the vanguard of mankind around the first socialist state in the world."[24] Soviet criticism was once again bringing its work to a head, to create a new image for the poet who now worked for socialism—after all, "Pushkin is near and dear to the people of Stalin's epoch."[25]

The leaders of the Soviet writers' union who gave speeches at the ceremony at the Bolshoy Theater were all suddenly Pushkin scholars. "Now," reported Aleksandr Fadeyev, "approximately every family in our country has Pushkin's works ... all the new Soviet industrial and collective-farm Russia, all the peoples of the Soviet Union, have picked up and carry in their hands Pushkin's great heritage."[26] Konstantin Simonov disclosed in a speech the essence of the class struggle around Pushkin (cutting down the long passages): reactionaries, supported by Russian capitalism: Annenkov, Druzhinin, Fet, Minsky, Rozanov, Sologub, Solovyev, and many others—these were who were trying to take Pushkin away from the people and appropriate him for themselves.[27]

What was happening could be called a new purge of the poet. The Party had placed before Pushkin scholars the task of sweeping aside "pseudoscientific-bourgeois, idealistic and cosmopolitan conceptions in the interpretation of Pushkin's works," of showing "the connection between the great poet and the revolutionary movement contemporary with him, to emphasize the great brotherhood of the peoples of our socialist Motherland."[28] Hadn't they swept aside, shown, and emphasized already? Obviously, not enough.

Now the unmasking of the rotting West was one of the immediate angles for propaganda, and Pushkin the *avant-gardiste* was participating in the process.

Pushkin, Stalin, and Other Poets

> The radiant face of the greatest humanist and lover of life, Pushkin, who has unmasked all kinds of greediness, is in opposition to the Anglo-American imperialists' corrupt culture and its representatives, their masters' lackeys.[29]

Once again Pushkin's biography was being amended from childhood. No longer was the war at the center of the poet's life at the Lyceum, but something else. In Pushkin's education, the French language disappeared completely, and only Russian fairy tales were left. Authors who wrote that there were foreign influences at the Lyceum were being censured. "No," wrote Boris Meylakh, "the Lyceum system was a Russian system of advanced national pedagogy based on the highest principle and patriotism ... Pushkin at the Lyceum was the leader of the most avant-garde group of youngsters." So now he was one of the leaders of Russian enlightenment. And, again, "Pushkin devoted his whole life to patriotic service to his homeland and his people."[30]

And then within the year, in June of 1950, Stalin suddenly remembered Pushkin again, that is, nine years later, and there was hardly a phrase without an outstanding revelation in it. Judge for yourselves.

> More than a hundred years have passed since Pushkin's death. During that time the feudal system and the capitalist system have been liquidated in Russia. That is, the two bases with their superstructures have been liquidated, and a new socialist basis with its new superstructure has appeared. However, if we take, for example, the Russian language—during that huge stretch of time, it has undergone no kind of breakdown, and the contemporary Russian language is structurally little different from the language of Pushkin.[31]

The essence of Stalin's conclusion (if he wrote it himself) is that Russians speak Russian. And then the critics came to their own conclusions: "Joseph Stalin's brilliant instructions on the historical and everlasting significance of the language of Pushkin open up a new page in Pushkin studies."[32] In one of these works we read prolix proofs of how, in accordance with Comrade Stalin's instructions, Pushkin supports the thesis of the indissolubility of language and thought."[33]

In a program notice collectively signed by the whole Institute of Russian Literature (Pushkin House), it says:

> The study of the language of Pushkin in the light of the brilliant works on Marxist linguistics by Comrade Stalin is of paramount significance ... It is absolutely obvious that the study of Stalin's works on Marxist linguistics has a decisive significance not

only for research into the language of Pushkin, but also for the raising of all Pushkin studies to a higher stage.[34]

In one critical work we discovered that not just Lenin but Lavrenty Beria, the head of NKVD, too had engaged in Pushkin studies: "Thus, the phrase colorfully passed on to us by Pushkin,'...unto flaming Colchis,' so wonderfully employed by Lenin [Lavrenty Beria, *On the Issue of the History of Bolshevik Organizations in the Transcaucasus*, Moscow, 1948, p.123], who called the great Stalin 'the flaming Colchian,' was connected in the poet's work with that most entertaining myth, that of the Argonauts' voyage..."[35] But, indubitably, Comrade Stalin had now personally become Pushkin-Scholar-in-Chief.

The historical function of the poet Pushkin got elaborated. He "was paving the way for the greatness of our epoch." And therefore "our Leninist, Stalinist time accepts Pushkin with all its open heart." On issues of history and political science, Pushkin began to think in unison with the Chief Pushkin Scholar and became a critic of hateful capitalism: "Pushkin felt very deeply the flimsiness of the edifice of aging capitalism, and that edifice was loathsome to him."[36]

The cult of Pushkin was becoming part of the cult of Stalin. As expressed by the then-famous critic Nikolay Belchikov, who had just joined the Party, after which he was accepted as a member of the Academy of Sciences, only our Soviet epoch under the leader of the party of Lenin and Stalin is capable of saying a new, historically truthful word about Pushkin.[37] The Pushkin Myth was now transforming into something needed by the campaign against cosmopolitanism.

Now the chief merit of Pushkin lay not only in the fact that he was a great Russian poet, that he hymned the victories of Russian arms, that he created "an image of Russia as the savior of Europe, confirmed by history."[38] The most important thing of all was that Pushkin was a Russian, and even, as it had been said of him in the previous century, "the most Russian of Russians."

The famous half-joking tale of a conversation between Pushkin and Aleksandr Turgenev and Pyotr Vyazemsky, where Pushkin started knocking foreign parts and Turgenev advised him "Well, go on and take a trip, dear boy, even if it's only to Lübeck," was now termed "Pushkin's struggle with Aleksandr Turgenev and Poytr Vyazemsky for our advanced national culture." Meanwhile, that advice to get himself to Lübeck (that is, anywhere abroad) was cleverly excised from the dialogue.[39]

"Pushkin's criticism of Byron," explained Nikolay Belchikov, "was criticism from a political friend who saw the weaknesses and backwardness of the foremost man of the West. Pushkin saw this as the foremost man of Russia, and condemned Byron."[40] Boris Meylakh went even further, declaring now that Pushkin carried on a struggle with Byron, and even "that all Pushkin's activities were pervaded by ... the struggle against imitation of foreign literature." So now it turned out that Kondraty Ryleyev, in his ode "On the Death of Byron," wrote:

> Only tyrants and slaves
> Joy in his sudden death—

not knowing that Pushkin was glad about his death.[41] And moreover: "The greatness of Pushkin symbolizes and reflects the greatness of the distinguished Russian nation."[42] During the war, Pushkin had been fighting against external enemies; now he was fighting against internal ones. It was called "the ideo-creative evolution of Pushkin," and it was "the struggle for the Russian advanced national culture." The connection was being emphasized "between his patriotism and the progressive tendencies of historical development."[43] Oh, the great and mighty Russian tongue!

He again became a Decembrist, a revolutionary; he somehow acquired Party spirit. Particular parts of Pushkin's biography prevented him from participating in the struggle against cosmopolitanism, which is why they got adjusted, and a sub-myth gets created, so to speak.

Foremost of all was Pushkin's ethnic origin. He considered himself a descendant of black Africans, since the ancestor of his mother, *née* Hannibal, as every Russian knows from his or her schooldays, was abstracted from Africa and given as a present to Peter the Great. Besides, Pushkin's father's genealogical line derives from a Swedish emigrant, Radshe. Now the poet's marvellous multinational roots got hushed up; Pushkin's pure-blooded Russianness was accentuated, his patrilineal Russian ancestors are without any Swedes, and his mother's line gets no mention. By the way, later in the 1960s, Pushkin would again become a descendant of Africans, when the Soviet Union's political interest demanded it.

Pushkin would help the Soviet secret organs in their penetration of Africa, Cuba, and the countries of South America.

Then came the language and literary school of Pushkin. He grew up in a noble family where everyone spoke French. Pushkin was taught Russian by his granny, a poor speaker of the language, when the boy was five years of age. The Lyceum, the institution of learning from which he graduated, was of the French type. His first literary works were written in French.

And, later on, Pushkin would eagerly borrow forms, thoughts, and sometimes even content from works of European literature. Of course the great Russian poet wrote chiefly in Russian, but even at the end of his life he informed the philosopher Pyotr Chaadayev: "I will speak to you in the language of Europe, it is more familiar to me than our own ..." The poet would at times even write his signature in French: *Pouchkine*.

In the new Soviet myth, these aspects of his biography receded and got replaced by texts showing the abstract influence of the Russian people and Russian folklore on the poet. The influence on Pushkin of peasants, coachmen, postmasters, servants, and foremost of all, his Russian nurse Arina Yakovleva—whom he really loved, having cool relations with his mother and father, but who was illiterate, a great lover of drinking, and a deliverer of serf girls into his bed whenever the poet came back to Mikhaylovskoye—was exaggerated.

The evident influence of foreign literature on Pushkin was minimized in serious Pushkin studies; while in popular books and in textbooks it was completely negated. On the contrary: they emphasized the world-wide delight in Pushkin's works and his influence over various literatures—especially over the writers of eastern European countries, of course. Pushkin was turned into a fighter for friendship between the peoples of the Soviet lands as well as the whole of so-called progressive mankind—it goes without saying, under the leadership of the Big Brother. To reinforce speeches over the radio on the friendship of the peoples, lines from his poem "I have raised to myself a monument not of stone (*Exegi monumentum*)," about how the poet would be known by all the nations of the country and "the steppes' friend, the Kalmyk." The minor peoples of the south were subjected to repression to the rhythm of this poem.

Thus the great Russian writer-patriot, the national idol, the living monument, the one-man reservation, creator of the modern Russian literature and language, became a symbol of the great Soviet land and the personification of all that is best in the Soviet people. After victory in World War II, this people, according to the Kremlin's imperial myth, became the messiah, acquiring the right to lead other nations and countries into the shining future. This right was brought into practice by the Great Helmsman, standing at the wheel. In this fashion, the head of the country, Stalin, was united by the shortest of lines with its chief poet, since, like Stalin himself, Pushkin was now being called a "great leader."[44]

More than that—Pushkin was appointed Stalin's son: "The giant Pushkin equals in stature only our epoch, and Pushkin, with his ingenuous sage's smile, would surely join the circle of friends such as Chkalov and other *bogatyrs* [*heroes—Y.D.*], the sons of Stalin ..."[45] According to a joke, three prizes for the best Pushkin-monument project were awarded. Third prize was given for a project called "Stalin reads Pushkin."

"This is correct historically," says Stalin in his thick Georgian accent, "but not politically. Where is its Party line?"

The second prize was given to a project called "Pushkin reads Stalin."

"This is correct politically," says Stalin, "but not historically. Comrade Stalin had not yet written any books in Pushkin's time."

First prize was awarded to a project entitled "Stalin reads Stalin."

It was said that the Leader liked to tell Pushkin jokes. Maybe. But the case is, however, that Stalin himself in his youth wrote poems and evidently dreamed of becoming a poet (as Hitler did an artist), and tried his hand at translating *The Knight in Tiger-skin*. They say that the classic Georgian author Ilya Chavchavadze gave his approval to the young Stalin's poem and even published it in the newspaper *Iveriya*.

The poet and translator Aleksandr Oyslender told me how he was summoned one day to the Party's Central Committee secretary for propaganda and was handed a sheaf of poems to translate from Georgian into Russian. Oyslender had seen these poems in an old Georgian primary-school textbook called *The Native Word*, and realized at once that they belonged to Stalin. In Georgian these poems are on exhibit in the Stalin museum in Gori.

When Oyslender, limp with fright, brought back the translations, he was handed a briefcase. Once home, he opened it—the briefcase was full of money. The poems were never even published in Russian. We can only guess at the reasons.

But in the anecdotal stream of those years, Stalin's love of poetry was illuminated somewhat differently. Pushkin went to the Leader to complain:

"Comrade Stalin, I am not being published."

Stalin picks up the telephone:

"Comrade Fadeyev, publish the works of Comrade Pushkin."

Pushkin goes on:

"I haven't got an apartment."

Stalin calls the Moscow council:

"Give Comrade Pushkin an apartment."

"Thank you, Comrade Stalin," the happy Pushkin says, and leaves.

Stalin picks up the phone:

"Comrade D'Anthes, take care of Comrade Pushkin."

I met a mathematician who once told this joke while in a camp. His sentence was doubled.

Soviet patriotism meant that Stalin and the motherland were fused into one. The individual had to put this in his pipe and smoke it: life in the Soviet Union was better than in any other country in the world, and it was Stalin who had given us happiness. It was necessary to affirm your love for him at every step. And of course to the motherland—the very best and foremost socialist country in the world.

Pushkin worked, as Pushkin scholarship formulated it, in the capacity of "a teacher of whole-hearted devotion to the Motherland." The censors tidily carried out the demands of this selfless patriotism. Vladimir Tendryakov made a note in his memoirs, published many years afterwards, that after the war he read an edition of Pushkin's fairy-tales for children, *Tsar Saltan*. In the text there were ellipses in place of one line. The expunged Pushkin line was:

Life overseas is not bad.[46]

And here we stealthily tiptoe right up to one of the most curious gaps in the *Agitprop* myth of Pushkin as state poet and orthodox patriot. But this topic, however strange, has been avoided in Pushkin scholarship in the course of its entire history, with a few measly exceptions.

The live Pushkin never went abroad, for which he intended to set off in 1817 right after his Lyceum graduation. Pushkin told Pavel Katenin, who met the young poet at the theater, that "he soon would set off for foreign parts"; from his Kishinev exile he planned to run off to Greece; in Odessa he received two refusals to his official applications to the tsar and arranged with smugglers to be hidden in the hold of a ship. "... Or maybe just quietly get my cane and hat and take off to have a look at Constantinople?" the poet wrote his brother. "I cannot stand our Holy *Rus* any longer. *Ubi bene ibi patria* (Where you're all right, there's your homeland), and for me, *bene* is where the *tryn-trava* grows [*i.e., where I have no cares*], brothers."

He day-dreamed of getting to Italy, saw France in real dreams, he wanted to get to Africa, thought about America. From Mikhaylovskoye, after ordering a wig, Pushkin planned escaping to Germany via Poland in the guise of a servant of a friend who had permission to go abroad. He faked being ill, supporting his complaint with a certificate from a veterinary, in order to visit a doctor in Riga, since it would not be far from there to Europe by ship.

> Of course I loathe my country down to my boots—but I am vexed when a foreigner shares this feeling of mine. You who aren't on a leash, how can you stay in Russia? If the tsar gave me my freedom, I wouldn't be here longer than a month.

He escaped to the Caucasus in order to have a look and see if it were conceivable to cross over into Turkey; he was ready to go off to China. He unsuccessfully asked the Third Section chief, Benckendorff, to let him go to Paris. Beyond that, he wrote hymns to the tsar and patriotic verses (including military themes) in the hopes of getting into favor and possibly a trip abroad as a reward. "Wherever it comes into your head to go," he appealed to some friends who were going abroad, "I am prepared to follow you ..."

Russian turned him into a refusenik, and the poet died on his leash. A year before his death, the great patriot Pushkin complained in a letter to his wife: "It was the Devil's jest to have me born in Russia with a soul and talent!" And he used an exclamation mark, something that isn't often met with in his letters.

Let's ask a simple question, one that Pushkin scholars have never asked before: did the poet want to leave and come back—or did he want to emigrate?

At first Pushkin had intended to serve abroad in a diplomatic capacity, such was his education and the plans of his youth. Then he tried simply to leave with the purpose of traveling and gaining impressions. He wasn't permitted to do that, so then he tried to find ways of getting abroad in secret. It is clear to everyone who understands the traditional Russian situation that for an escapee or a voluntary exile (he called himself by both titles) to return meant to finish out his days in penal servitude. Pushkin more than once measured himself against such a fate, without any sort of enthusiasm.

Escape from Russia to the West automatically cut off any way home for the deserter. That means that we have to accept that, in thinking of escape, the premier poet of Russia was trying on the status of a political émigré: "... surely I shall never set foot in my home again." Did Pushkin love his country? He did. And wanted to die in his homeland. But no one has yet proven that émigrés love their homeland less than those who stay behind.

Such is the behind-the-scenes side to the poet's biography, which, for understandable reasons, always gets retouched, since it is difficult to connect up the official image of the state poet/patriot with it. In this sense, generally speaking, Soviet criticism could find true official patriots in the history of literature, like Bulgarin, Grech, Lobanov—with whom, by the way, literary bonzes connected with secret state organs had a greater kinship of spirit.

Has all this mythification become a matter of history today?

The two-hundredth anniversary of Pushkin's birth in 1999 is the best example of a fairly traditional wind-up to the jubilee. In a state that has lost its orientation in space and is sailing God-knows-where without tiller or sail, it seems that only he, Pushkin, remains the firm root of the culture, the only one that can be relied upon.

Pushkin's significance for Russia is indubitable, but his situation seems to remain ambiguous. History, literature, and art continue to be involved in politics, and it is very difficult to make one's way to shore. We live in an age of the overcoming of illusions, but the truth about Pushkin is still concealed. Exaggerating the international significance of Pushkin, official Pushkin scholars attached to this state religion have become the monopoly interpreters of the sacred poet's thoughts, priests in charge of Pushkin, his manuscripts, and even his relatives.

It is more difficult to do this in a democratic society, but in the meantime any non-traditional word concerning Pushkin's sanctity still meets with hostility. Even ordinary readers, schooled in filtered information about the poet, are at times intolerant. Instead of him, alive and bottomless in his contradictions, we are still offered up some kind of poster illustrating the leadership's instructions. In accordance with the demands of the time, at the Pushkin conference at the Institute of Russian Literature (St. Petersburg, June, 1995), the majority of the speakers concentrated on religious views of the poet, to create an image of Pushkin as a genuine Christian in place of the old image of Pushkin the Atheist. Obviously we haven't yet grown up to the real Pushkin.

"Hitting It Off With Pushkin"

When you read it, every now and again you stumble over phrases like "the friendship of the two writers," "the story of a friendship," "a literary friendship," "friendly ties," "friendly intimacy" ... These phrases are taken as examples from a most capacious (350 pages) monograph by Georgy Makogonenko, *Gogol and Pushkin*, about the relations between the two greatest Russian writers.[1] There is no doubt about the importance of a friendship between Alexander Pushkin and Nikolay Gogol for the assertion of a hierarchical order in classical Russian literature, for the ladder of so-called progressive traditions of realism. "Gogol, the Heir of Pushkin," is the title of a paper by Dmitry Blagoy.[2]

In addition to that friendship, the canonical approach to the subject was formulated in this way: Pushkin and Gogol were "comrades in arms on the basic issues of the socio-literary struggle of the 1830s."[3] The less said the better about college and high-school textbooks and literature for the mass readership. As an American Slavic scholar observed, "The present state of Gogolian studies in the Soviet Union is comparable to the state of Soviet genetics when it was controlled by Lysenko."[4]

Gogol had to be Pushkin's friend and comrade-in-arms in the struggle. But does such a point of view, appearing ubiquitously in recent decades, correspond to the real ties between the two classic authors?

Careful study of major literature on this topic, piling up over a century and a half and numbering several dozen serious works, reveals to the unprejudiced eye an entire spectrum of appraisals—all the way up to enmity between the two writers. As for the real relationship between them, it appears to us to be ambiguous, undeciphered, and, in any case, not so primitive as it was proving to be in ideologized Soviet literary studies. The truth is still cloaked in mystery, whose existence had its own reasons.

Different opinions on the issue have always existed. "In the words of Nashchokin, Gogol had never been a man close to Pushkin," Poytr Bartenev wrote as well.[5] "For a long time the study of Pushkin and Gogol's relations was not a subject of criticism," considered Vasily Gippius. "The close-friendship-of-two-great-writers version has never been revised, never elaborated."[6] The attitude of Western Slavic experts to their friendship can be called restrained, skeptical, and sometimes, as we'll see later, ironic. "But there was never any real intimacy between either Pushkin or Zhukovsky and Gogol," noted Dmitry Mirsky.[7]

And ultimate rejection of Gogol entirely, not just Pushkin's friendship with him, can be met with among a number of émigré critics. "Pushkin had no sooner died than Russia betrayed him and followed after Gogol," wrote A. Pozov. "This was a relapse into Russian non-civilization, 'unenlightenment.'"[8] V. Ilyin said that the light of Russia is reflected in Pushkin, and the gloom is concentrated in Gogol.[9]

At the source of the myth of their friendship stood Belinsky, who conceived an outline for the development of literature and placed Gogol in first place "together with Pushkin, at the head of Russian literature."[10] Then Belinsky considered Pushkin's prose weak, and that his creativity ended at the beginning of the 1830s, and came up with an alternative in the form of Gogol. Pushkin was still alive, but Vissarion Belinsky had already declared that "at the present time, he [*Gogol—Y.D.*] is chief among writers, the chief of poets; he takes the place abandoned by Pushkin." And as well, "… we see in Gogol a more important significance for Russian society than in Pushkin: for Gogol is a more social poet, consequently, more a poet in the spirit of the times…"[11]

Harping on his usefulness became important for Marxist critics: Gogol "unmasked" things in a way that intensified the more neutral position of Pushkin.

Nikolay Chernyshevsky exaggerated the political significance of Gogol as a critic of autocracy. For him, the satirist Gogol was more important than the lyricist Pushkin.[12] Repeating and simplifying him, Vladimir Lenin wrote that new literature was "steeped utterly in … the ideas of Belinsky and Gogol."[13] The aggrandizement of Gogol's role as a founder of the naturalist school passed into Soviet criticism; his friendship with Pushkin, who had been made into a semi-Decembrist, became an important factor in the re-adjustment of Russian political history under the Bolsheviks.

It is convenient to trace this re-estimation in the example of the already-cited Vasily Gippius. "The personal intimacy of Gogol to Pushkin in Gogol scholarship is suspicious, and the former idealization of their personal relations has been shaken up"—these are the words of Gippius, spoken at the beginning of the 1920s.[14] After becoming the deputy chief editor of the complete academic collection of Gogol's works, Gippius stopped rocking the boat of the relations—idealized by others—between the two classic authors. It turned out that "in Gogol's latest stories about his literary intimacy with Pushkin (he never spoke of personal intimacy), there is no kind of basis for seeing insincerity." In his commentary to the complete collection of Gogol's works (the volume was issued in 1940), Gippius lost his sense of proportion: "Pushkin was the literary adviser of Gogol, who had already won himself a name in literature."[15] As we can see, Pushkin is now allowed to be a consultant to the famous writer Gogol.

The reasons for Gippius's making this compromise are understandable. Soviet Gogol scholarship, elbowing aside extraneous points of view, gradually ensconced itself in the bed of the official myth: Pushkin is the founder of modern literature; Gogol is the leader of critical realism and the friend of the greatest poet, "the immediate successor and heir of Pushkin."[16] Tomashevsky noted, "... almost all the main works of Gogol were written in the period of his relations with Pushkin, and under the immediate supervision of Pushkin."[17]

Makogonenko makes this relationship even deeper, harnessing both writers in the same traces: "The connection between the two writers, as is known, had a dual nature—friendship and creativity."[18] The duties of "literary mentor, adviser, tutor of the young Gogol" were conferred on Pushkin, and even the title of "brother-in-pens."[19] Even the critic Igor Zolotussky, among the more restrained towards this brotherhood, wrote: "And at the same time there were no other people in Russia closer at that time than Pushkin and Gogol."[20]

Attempts to utter a critical word about this friendship were called "hair-splitting humbug."[21] Let's risk disagreement. We will look at relations between our two favorite writers from childhood, from several points of view: (1) How

Gogol envisaged this friendship; (2) how Pushkin envisaged this friendship; (3) how their contemporaries saw it; (4) how their relations were interpreted by literary historians; and, finally, (5) how it looks to us today. These categories are so intermixed that it's not always possible to separate them.

We'll start with an initial long quotation, with apologies for giving it to you in its entirety. Annenkov wrote down, in the words of Gogol himself:

> Right away upon arrival in St. Petersburg, Gogol, moved by a need to see the poet who had occupied his entire imagination since he was at school, set out from his home straightaway to meet him. The closer he got to Pushkin's apartment, the more timidity overcame him, and, finally, at the very door of his apartment, it reached such an intensity that he ran off to a brasserie and demand a shot of liqueur ... Fortified by it, he went back on the assault, bravely rang the bell, and to his question, 'Is the master home?' heard the servant's answer: 'Asleep!' It was late in the day already. Gogol asked with great concern, 'Truly, has he been working all night?' 'What, working?' the servant replied. 'He's been playing cards.'
>
> Gogol confessed that it was the first blow to his schoolboy idealism. He never imagined Pushkin to himself in any other guise but constantly surrounded by clouds of inspiration.[22]

That blow did not subsequently change Gogol. Becoming a great prose realist, he remained unceremonious in his contacts with Pushkin and an idealist in what he wrote about the poet. In December of 1830, Gogol finished an article about Pushkin's drama *Boris Godunov*, which was unpublished: "As if riveted, everything around me obliterated, unhearing, unheeding, remembering nothing, I devour your pages, marvellous poet!" It seems more like an incantation.

In 1832 Gogol wrote an article called "Several Words about Pushkin" (published in *Arabeski* in 1834). It was precisely here that the famous Gogolian saying is to be found: "Pushkin is an extraordinary phenomenon, and, maybe, the only phenomenon of the Russian spirit: this is Russian man at his final stage of development, in which he, perhaps, will appear in two hundred years." What does this mean—the final stage of development? What is this estimate based on, and why would the development have reached its end? These speculations represent a remarkable example of a utopian mentality.

There is no analysis of Pushkin's work or his craftsmanship in Gogol's article. It is full of intemperate praise for the living poet. One word gets repeated many times—"dazzling": minor works by Pushkin are "dazzling," pictures drawn by him are "dazzling," shoulders depicted by him are "dazzling," and, finally, "everything is filled with an internal brilliance." Pushkin is opposed to all other poets, whom Gogol calls "leisure-time scribblers." As A. Dubovikov restrainedly noted, "Gogol expressed a rapturous worship for Pushkin."[23] Calling things by their real name, we see simply a shameless toadying.

The most interesting thing is the conclusion that Gogol came to, and that conclusion leaves no doubt that this article was written for just one reader, that is, for Pushkin. Offering up his oft-repeated praise to the genius of all time, telling off his critics, and declaring that only the chosen can appreciate the greatness of this poet, Gogol concludes, "The more he depicts feelings familiar only to poets, the more noticeably the circle of the crowd surrounding him shrinks, finally becoming so close that he can count all of his genuine appreciators on his fingers." Herein lies the essence: he would have done anything to squeeze himself into that close circle, so that the great teacher would notice him, Gogol, among his genuine appreciators.

Flattery is the best way to turn not just women's heads. After reading a publication of Vasily Zhukovsky's, Gogol wrote to him in September, 1831 that the beginning of his tale "nearly made me lose my mind." In this very same letter, he calls Pushkin a "holy angel," and himself a "true devotee" of both poets. If there is such a thing as "oriental flattery," then it is in an oriental style that Gogol flatters shamelessly.

Pushkin and Gogol met for the first time in 1831, and parted ways in 1836. After 1834, Pushkin never answered Gogol's letters. According to contradictory recollections, Gogol, in order to get in with Pushkin, became acquainted with his good-natured friend Anton Delvig, bringing to *Literaturnaya gazeta* a praise-filled review of Pushkin. Via Delvig, he was introduced to Zhukovsky, and by Zhukovsky to the publisher Pyotr Pletnev. Pletnev found private classes for the money-strapped Gogol to give, and sent Gogol's first prose pieces to Pushkin.

Publishing Gogol's book *Evenings on a Farm outside Dikanka*—whose title Pletnev himself, by the way, thought up—and starting to sell it, Pletnev wanted to place the new author, as he phrased it, under Pushkin's blessing. Pushkin learned of Gogol's existence from Pletnev's letter of February 22, 1831. Pletnev (most likely at the request of Gogol himself) sent Pushkin Gogol's book, with the fledgling author's real name unrevealed, concealed under a pseudonym.

Pushkin answered Pletnev only after a second reminder, almost two months later, and very indifferently. Between his remarks about De la Rue and a request to rent an inexpensive *dacha* for them, Pushkin noted: "I won't say anything about Gogol, because I still haven't read him for lack of time." Pushkin had just got married in Moscow, and was busy looking for a summer home in Tsarskoye Selo, into which in his straitened circumstances he had to move his young wife, himself, and six or seven servants.

Gogol, so persistently seeking a meeting with Pushkin, met him on May 20, 1831, at a party in St. Petersburg that Pletnev gave. A couple of days before, Pushkin and his wife had arrived in St. Petersburg from Moscow and stayed as always at Demutov's tavern, and then shifted to their *dacha*.

Is it possible to overestimate the importance of this meeting for Gogol, and the reason Gogol had strived for it? Gogol's ambition is a singular topic; it seems that it is generally impossible to be a writer without any ambition. But Gogol had, in addition, according to Annenkov, a "congenital reticence, an adroitly-calculated cunning, and, remarkable in one his age, an ability to use others' will to his own ends."[24] For the fledgling poet-romantic from the provinces, a word from the *Maître* was important, but most important of all was patronage. With all his might, Gogol tried to get close to Pushkin in life, in order to be closer to him in literature—a thoroughly widespread mode of behavior. Let's see how both writers represented themselves at the beginning of their so-called friendship.

Pushkin was 32. He was the mightiest poet in Russia, an accepted genius. His every step, word, and gesture became famous, written down in diaries, retold in letters of contemporaries. The circle of his friends had formed long before, they were his age or older. They all were living classics, aristocrats, the elite, who had contacts with the tsar's family. In addition, Pushkin was busy with the arrangement of his own family life.

Gogol was 22. That is yesterday's schoolboy. Having just finished his studies at a gymnasium in the distant provinces, he had arrived at the capital burning with plans to prove to his mommy and relatives that they weren't sending him money in vain. He was poor, looking for his wherewithal. He was a fledgling writer, publishing under the pseudonyms P. Glechik, G. Yanov, Rudy Panko the Beekeeper, and Oooo (most likely he was writing the four "o"s of his name and double surname, Nikolay Gogol-Yanovsky), as well as without any by-line at all. In a word, he still had no name, but he, as Annenkov noticed, was seeking out "earthly glory with all the power of his soul."[25]

After trying various professions, Gogol, in whom it was difficult at the beginning to distinguish talent from graphomania, was breaking into literature and beginning to feel his own worth. He was seeking the favor of his idol. That's what was important for Gogol, who, as Andrei Sinyavsky put it, "himself placed [*Pushkin's*] hand in benediction on himself ... he needed to be on good terms with Pushkin, so that from him, from the greatest poet in Russia, he could start his own reckoning, his own genealogy—of prose."[26]

Mstislav Tsyavlovsky, in his *Guide to Pushkin*, noted: "Between July 17 and August 15. P.'s meetings with Gogol and Zhukovsky" (1831).[27] It is customary to consider this to be the period of the rise of their friendly relations. And even, according to Vladimir Shenrok, Gogol's biographer, that "Pushkin made him his favorite."[28] It is necessary to get to the bottom of the credibility of such statements.

At first, Pushkin was in Moscow, Gogol in St. Petersburg. Then Pushkin was in Tsarskoye Selo at his huge *dacha*, and Gogol was in Pavlovsk, in a tiny room next to the servants'. To make a living he had found a job as a tutor to the idiot son of Aleksandra Vasilchikova. Pushkin would stroll with his beautiful wife in the park, chatting with the empress. Gogol would walk from Pavlovsk to Tsarskoye Selo on foot—it's more than an hour's walk through the woods—and return home the same way. As A. Pypin wrote, "Gogol's higher understanding of his predestination had already contributed at this time to an extreme self-importance."[29] Thanks to Gogol's incredible effort, he managed to see Pushkin.

Here's a popular quotation: "Hitting it off with Pushkin. It so happens that I often say to him: 'Well, what's up, brother Pushkin?'" This is Gogol's character Khlestakov speaking, but it sounds autobiographical. Gogol called himself Khlestakov in a letter to Zhukovsky of February 22, 1847. Incidentally, A. Dolinin noted a particular detail: "Slapping Pushkin on the back was inserted into the comedy's text only after Pushkin's death."[30] Gogol was completely aware of his Khlestakovisms.

He wrote to his mother: "Address your letters to me in care of Pushkin at Tsarskoye Selo, thus: 'To His Honor Alexander Sergeyevich Pushkin. And I ask you to pass it on to N. V. Gogol.' "In his next letter, Gogol reminded her: "Do you remember that address? In care of Pushkin, at Tsarskoye Selo."

For Gogol's relatives in the country this was sensational. The trick with the mail was jauntily conceived. But to call such a prank tactless is putting it too mildly. Pushkin was indignant. Gogol had to take evasive action, to apologize, to lie. "I plead guilty ... Here I learned of the great stupidity of my correspondent ... [*although he himself thought up this chess move—Y.D.*] Perhaps you will upbraid me with harsh words, but where there is ire, there is mercy."

Pushkin often dedicated his poems to his friends, and even to accidental acquaintances, but there is not a single line of his poetry that mentions Gogol. It is usually asserted that there are nine letters from Gogol to Pushkin, and four from Pushkin to Gogol. Pushkin's letters to his friends—he liked to write them, and knew how—are rich in content, in ideas.

In his first letter (August 25, 1831), consisting of fifteen lines, Pushkin answered two long letters from Gogol. Gogol had gone to St. Petersburg, and Pushkin had entrusted him with passing on a letter and the manuscript of *The Tales of Belkin* to his publisher, Pletnev. Pushkin concealed his authorship, and the courier didn't know what he was carrying. Relating his accomplishment of the mission, Gogol told in detail about the delight of the type-setters reading his own book in the press room, which, we will note, looks little like the truth. Gogol "very likely had made it up," considers Vladimir Nabokov.[31] Then Gogol cursed Pushkin's enemies, demonstrating that he was his accomplice, that he shared all his views completely, that Pushkin's enemies were his enemies, that he was one of his own, or, as he himself signed off in letters to Pushkin "eternally your Gogol."

Pushkin in answer addressed Gogol as "My good Nikolay Vasilyevich" and in the polite second-person plural. It's well known that Pushkin had a broad set of salutations for his friends ("My dear one," "Friend of mine," "Priceless friend," and so on). For his elder to address the young man with that "My good Nikolay Vasilyevich" underscores the distance between them. Pushkin thanks him for the letter and for delivering the parcel. He refers ironically to Gogol's "project of scientific criticism" ("You are too lazy to bring that to pass") and congratulates him for the "typesetters' cracking up." Pushkin corrects Gogol's reference to his wife as Nadezhda Nikolayevna when her name is Natalya Nikolayevna. This last says more about the degree of closeness between the two authors than all the assurances of Gogol and his students.

In his letters in "A Literary Appendix to *Russky invalid*," Pushkin remarks on the jollity, poetry, and sensitivity of *Evenings on a Farm Near Dikanka* and wishes its author further successes. The poet straightaway rated Gogol's prose highly, but no friendship arose from it. A considerable part of his brief remark is dedicated to that very same apocryphal story about the typesetters' chuckling that had been related to him by Gogol. Pushkin's letter was never published independently but was included by the publisher in an edition of another writer—Lukyan Yakubovich.

On November 2, 1831, Gogol wrote a letter to his classmate A. S. Danilevsky, a fragment of which appears to be important evidence of his friendship with Pushkin: "I spent the whole summer in Pavlovsk and Tsarskoye Selo ... Practically every evening we got together: Zhukovsky, Pushkin, and I." Gogol's pronouncement of "practically every evening" gets passed off as the truth by many scholars. If it is so that Pushkin and Gogol saw a lot of each other during this period, then Gogol would have found out a wealth of details about Pushkin, but there are no such details of fact to be found in his texts, aside from those generally available.

Gogol was telling an untruth when he said that he was living at Tsarskoye Selo: he was only at Pavlovsk. And "the whole summer" is hyperbole. He calls one of Pushkin's tales "The Cook," that is, "The Little House in Kolomna," and makes reference to a Pushkin fairy-tale, but it's strange that he never mentions any of the more significant pieces that Zhukovsky was discussing frequently with Pushkin at that time. In a letter, Gogol made a ridiculously belated discovery of Zhukovsky, who was no less known than Pushkin to the whole of literate Russia: "It looks like a huge new poet has appeared ..."

The participants in those meetings wrote a great deal about one another later, but none of them mentions Gogol. The relation of equals between the great poet and the just-graduated grammar-school boy from the provinces is merely a product of Gogol's fantasies. And what would Gogol be writing letters to Pushkin for, if he was seeing him "practically every evening"? If Gogol had known a little bit more about Pushkin that summer, he would have been better off lying to the effect that they saw each other in Pavlovsk, to where Pushkin often went alone and on foot to see his parents who were staying at a *dacha* there, as the poet's mother said in a letter written to her daughter Olga in St. Petersburg. There is no proof that Gogol saw Pushkin more than once or twice that summer.

Gogol's assertion testifies to his urgent desire to be among the circle of literary celebrities. This fact acquires a doubly curious character, if we are to trust a publication by Faddey Bulgarin to the effect that, from 1829, Gogol was secretly collaborating with the Third Section of the Imperial chancellery and was getting payment from them.[32] He did need money, and his painful ambition could have been satisfied by that secret power over people wielded by an informer. However, that fact remains unproven. Mikhail Lemke undertook an attempt to locate materials in the Third Section archives, but they had been destroyed.[33]

The next time Gogol was to write to Pushkin was two and a half years later, in December of 1833, and then next in 1834 (which is to say that there exists no other correspondence than these). But, on the other hand, in Gogol's letters to various friends, the names of Pushkin, Zhukovsky, and Krylov can be glimpsed fleetingly every so often. Thus Gogol writes to the ethnographer M. A. Maksimovich on August 23, 1834: "Our people have almost all gone their separate ways: Pushkin to the countryside, Vyazemsky has gone abroad for the sake of his daughter's health." "Our people ..." In many of his letters, his friend Pushkin gets mentioned apropos or otherwise, as in: "Pushkin has already nearly finished his *History of Pugachev*." That is to say, as if Pushkin were constantly sharing his creative schemes with Gogol. But the information was usually the kind that everyone was aware of.

Pushkin's answer to Gogol followed around April 7, 1834. "You are right—I shall try. Goodbye." The note is six words long in Russian. Gogol had asked Pushkin to put in a word for him with the Minister of Education, Sergey Uvarov, to get him a post in the just-opening University of Kiev, but Pushkin never did. Incidentally, Gogol treated Pushkin's note without any sort of spiritual thrill, because he wrote a letter to M. Maksimovich directly on top of it, perpendicularly. But perhaps this was just a trick to impress Maksimovich.

In Pushkin's third answer, approximately a month later, on May 13, there were four lines, once again concerning patronage that Gogol was soliciting, this time on the pretext that serious illness was compelling his departure from St. Petersburg as quickly as possible. Gogol once again asked him to press his case. Pushkin answered: "I agree with you completely. I am going this very day to edify Uvarov about the death of *The Telegraph*, and I shall have a word at the same time about Yours. From this I shall move on in an imperceptible and artful fashion to the immortality that awaits him. Perhaps we shall get it settled." Pushkin was answering Gogol's letter on the spot, by return messenger. The poet obviously was in a hurry, for it happened that he did discuss Gogol's death with Sergey Uvarov. Pushkin and the Minister of Education did not speak of any service concerning him, though. At any rate, Gogol did not obtain any post.

Finally, the fourth and last note (three and a half lines, October, 1834) was in answer to Gogol's bringing him his story *Nevsky Prospekt*, from which the censor cut out the scene where Lieutenant Pirogov gets cut to pieces by the German artisans. "I read it with great satisfaction," wrote Pushkin; "it seems to me that the whole thing could be passed. It is a pity to cut out this section: in my opinion, it is necessary for the full effect of the evening mazurka. Perhaps God will decide." Gogol had asked, and Pushkin answered, without going into detail, in banal terms. After 1834, Pushkin did not answer Gogol's letters.

So then Pushkin did not in fact write Gogol four letters, as it has been maintained, but four notes. When burning his archives before his death, Gogol set aside and kept these notes of Pushkin's. Gogol sent not nine letters to Pushkin, but only four. The remaining five are also just notes of several lines with requests or complaints.

From the end of June through October 30, 1832, Gogol was away, and they could not have seen each other. On February 28, 1833, Gogol wrote to Danilevsky that "you won't see Pushkin anywhere except at balls." And again he was lying: no one ever invited Gogol to those balls. In 1833, Vladimir Odoyevsky and Gogol had a notion to publish jointly with Pushkin an almanac to be called *Troychatka* ("threebie"), the details of which are not known, but it is known that nothing was ever done about it.

"From the winter of 1833-34, relations between P. and G. became especially close," supposes Yulian Oksman.[34] This assertion is based in the main on the fact that on December 2, 1833, Gogol read to Pushkin "A story about some people falling out ..." and Pushkin wrote in his diary, calling Ivan Nikiforovich "Ivan

Timofeyevich," "very original and very funny." Gogol had gotten through to Pushkin, but there were no close relations.

In 1834 and 1835, via the good offices of Pletnev, Gogol got to give some lectures on general history; Zhukovsky and Pushkin attended one of them. The latter spoke politely and approvingly about the lectures.[35] But this is the way Ivan Turgenev recalls the lectures:

> In the first place, out of three lectures, Gogol certainly cut two; in the second place ... he didn't speak but whispered something entirely unconnected with it ... and was terribly mixed up the whole time. We were all certain (and we could scarcely be mistaken) that he hadn't got a clue about history.[36]

From May through September of 1835, Gogol was again absent. Here's yet another episode, one recounted by Tsyavlovsky: on April 4, 1836, "There was a reading by Gogol at Zhukovsky's Saturday night of his short story 'The Nose,' probably in the presence of Pushkin."[37] Gogol really did go to the gatherings at Zhukovsky's, and read from written works.

It's well known that Pushkin praised individual pieces of Gogol's, but a personal relationship never took shape; the one did not follow from the other. Simply put, Pushkin never sought to meet with Gogol. The latter would periodically ask him to read and improve his texts, to make efforts on his behalf, put in a good word for him. In a note from the end of December or the beginning of January of 1835, Gogol wrote: "It is a pity, though, that I haven't been able to meet up with you." Then, on October 7: "I've decided to write to you myself; I asked after Natalya Nikolayevna before, but to this day I have received no news." Gogol went to Pushkin's; the latter wasn't there; he asked to convey him his regards, but the *Maître* never responded, since his wife didn't consider it necessary to pass anything along to her husband. Pushkin's indifference and his dismissiveness were plain.

There is a widely known assertion that in 1835, Gogol, in Annenkov's words, "got the theme of *Dead Souls* from Pushkin."[38] There are many sources regarding this gift. In some of them it is stipulated that this is the presumption. Others, admitting to the fact of its origin, consider that "the concrete circumstances of this 'transfer' have not been finally elucidated."[39] Still others, including Yuri Lotman, assert categorically in exactly the same words: "The theme of *Dead Souls* was given to Gogol by Pushkin."[40] But the primary source of this information is once again Gogol himself. And if that's the case, it is especially important to establish when he began making this assertion.

Gogol informed Pushkin that he had "begun writing *Dead Souls*." It is curious, though: there is never a hint of any gift in the form of a theme, not a word of thanks. In a letter to Zhukovsky from abroad in 1836, describing in detail the idea for *Dead Souls*, Gogol doesn't utter a word about it being a gift from Pushkin. Gogol began talking about it only in March of 1837, after he found out about Pushkin's death. Consequently the latter could no longer either corroborate or refute it.

In a letter to Pletnev from Rome, Gogol wrote vaguely at first about his relations with Pushkin. "Not a single line was written without my having first imagined him in front me ... My God! My present labors, inspired by him, his works ... "Does "inspired by him" mean that Pushkin (a) told Gogol the theme for *Dead Souls*, and (b) gave it to him as a gift, that is, permitted him to use it?

Ten years after Pushkin's death, in "An Author's Confession," this very topic gets developed into a whole story by Gogol, full of praise for himself. He expansively describes how Pushkin delighted in his talents and his work, calling him the equal of Cervantes Saavedra, and how he gave him, Gogol, "his own theme, with which he had hoped to make something along the lines of a poem." Further on, Gogol, concisely passing on the fable from his already-written book, tells of how Pushkin discussed the theme with him, explaining how good a subject it was specifically for him, Gogol. Pushkin supposedly said that "he would not have given [*the theme*] away to anyone else." That's the sort of superiority over other writers that Gogol wanted to demonstrate, slyly placing the notion in the mouth of the poet.

In 1835, Gogol wrote to Pushkin: "I want to show all of *Rus* in this book, albeit from one side." But then, twelve years later, this notion migrates into Pushkin's mouth. It seems that Pushkin had advised him "to travel all over Russia with his hero." Pushkin's impressions from his reading of *Dead Souls* ("Lord, how sad our Russia is!" Pushkin supposedly exclaimed) we know about only from Gogol, as well. Apropos of this Vladimir Nabokov remarks reasonably: "also it seems of Gogol's making..."[41]

It is a glaring contradiction: if Pushkin himself gave Gogol the theme as a present and explained that he could show all of Russia through it, then why was Pushkin so surprised when Gogol read him the first chapters of Dead Souls, and even exclaimed "Lord!" in delight at his own theme?

In Pavel Annenkov's memoirs there is an assertion that Gogol unauthorizedly used an idea that Pushkin had related to him: "It's well known that Gogol took the ideas for *The Inspector General* and *Dead Souls* from Pushkin, but less well known that Pushkin not altogether willingly ceded his property to him. However, Pushkin did laughingly say among his family circle: 'You've got be careful around this Little Russian; he fleeces me so fast I can scarcely cry out.'" Annenkov possibly took that last bit down from something that Pushkin's wife said.[42] Pay close heed to the fact that neither Pushkin nor Annenkov says anything about a "gift": "took," "fleeced." Gogol's indecency in appropriating the theme, in the opinion of Pushkin's nephew Lev Pavlishchev, was the reason for Pushkin's cooling towards him. There isn't any corroboration of this opinion, however.

The history of the theme of *The Inspector General* is even more murky. Gogol brought Pushkin his comedy *The Marriage* to read "for remarks," and the latter evidently didn't even leaf through it. "Be so kind as to give me some sort of theme, no matter if it's a funny or unfunny one as long as it's a purely Russian story," begged Gogol. On October 7, 1835, he wrote Pushkin a letter asking for the return of his comedy. Gogol's desire to receive what would be in modern parlance an "order" (meaning, along with his blessing) from Pushkin himself is understandable. At the end of October, according to legend, Pushkin gave Gogol the theme of *The Inspector General*. A gift like that is possible, but unfortunately the prime witness to this event was Gogol alone, yet again.

One version has the source of *The Inspector General*'s theme as various apocryphal stories about the Bessarabian adventures of the diplomat and writer Pavel Svinyin, supposedly related to Gogol by Pushkin.[43] In support of another variant of Pushkin's gift, some cite his unfinished fragment that goes "At the beginning of the year 1812 ..." It is about a group of young officers, quartered in a provincial city, who spend their time with women at parties, and, in particular, visit the home of the town governor, who is a bribe-taker, and who has a wife and daughter. There is nothing in it of the theme of *The Inspector General*. Besides, this fragment of Pushkin's was published in 1831—Gogol simply read it. All this seems to indicate not a gift, but a simple influence, or, more strictly speaking, a borrowing.

Yet another argument is considered to be a Pushkin rough draft that goes "Krispin shows up at a provincial town fair —he is taken for ... The Governor is an upright fool ... The Governor's wife flirts with him—Krispin woos their daughter." The date of the writing is unknown. Krispin in French and Italian comedies is a constantly-encountered servant-swindler. "Taken for" is the typical *qui pro quo*, on which comedy of all eras is founded. Relying on these three lines, some people have proved that Pushkin gave Gogol the theme of *The Inspector General* as a gift.[44]

What is still more evident is that there existed the well-known comedy *The Man From the Capital, or, Chaos in a Country Town*, by the Ukrainian writer Grigory Kvitka, where the exact same story is played out. And a year before *The Inspector General*, in the *Biblioteka dlya chteniya* (*Reading Library*) magazine, there appeared a story by Aleksandr Veltman called "Provincial Actors," where the familiar theme gets played out. In America of the present day Gogol would have to face legal proceedings for that kind of plagiarization, and not even Pushkin as a live witness would be able to help him, if the gift wasn't his own.

In connection with the weakness of his evidence, Gippius proposed a compromise explanation: the "concession" by Pushkin of the theme of *Dead Souls* to Gogol and the beginning of Gogol's work on *The Inspector General* as well came about "as a result of anecdotes related by Pushkin."[45] Georgy Makogonenko rescues the legend with the following exegesis: "Gogol asked Pushkin for a theme, and Pushkin gave him the idea!"[46] Igor Zolotussky still further widens the possibility of a borrowing outside of Pushkin: the theme "wafted about in the air; it was already nearly folklore."[47] It is difficult not to agree with this.

Pushkin wrote to Odoyevsky about Gogol's previous comedy *Order of Vladimir of the 3d Degree*, "There's a hook in it," which evidently can be interpreted as praise. When he was arranging a theatrical performance for his new comedy, Gogol nowhere mentions in his letters that Pushkin had given him the theme, although that could have helped the success of the play, and Gogol was an inveterate dropper of Pushkin's name anyway. Pushkin mentioned *The Inspector General* in a letter to his wife, but even here there was no hint of his own personal contribution. Panayev later wrote that Pushkin "rocked with laughter" at a reading of the comedy at Zhukovsky's, but this typical Gogolian hyperbole migrated into Panayev's recollections from those of Gogol.[48] Thus the legend of Pushkin's gift of the two themes was made up by Gogol himself.

The later Pushkin related more critically to Gogol. Speaking of *Evenings on a Farm Near Dikanka* in *Sovremennik* (*The Contemporary*) in 1836, he noted the lively manner of Gogol's epistle—and the "unevenness and inaccuracy of his style, the incoherence and improbability of several stories." As Andrei Sinyavsky noted, "His innocent—to all appearances—distinctions of taste had far-reaching consequences and testified in the final analysis to the gulf separating Gogol from Pushkin."[49]

Pushkin suggested to Gogol that he take up criticism, noting in his diary: "Gogol on my advice has begun a history of Russian criticism." It was evidently Gogol's caustic comments about Pushkin's enemies and his flattery towards the poet that served as grounds for this. In the opinion of A. Zholkovsky, Gogol "slavishly accommodated himself to the tastes of his superiors (among them Pushkin)."[50]

Let's look again at Gogol's article "Pushkin's Poem *Boris Godunov*," that the young author wrote in search of closer relations: "As if riveted, everything around me obliterated, unhearing, unheeding, remembering nothing, I devour your pages, marvellous poet! ... Great One! I swear upon this eternal creation of yours!" This servile piece contains whatever you like except for anything about the drama itself that Pushkin had written.

Gogol the critic turned out to be wordy, devoid of any gift for critical analysis, and, as it turned out, unable to orient himself in the social life of literary people. Pushkin's advice to Gogol to try his hand at criticism testifies to Pushkin's ignorance of his admirer's point of view—a point that has already been expressed.[51]

Pushkin needed an editor in order to publish his magazine, *Sovremennik*. It wasn't easy finding such a man, and the young Gogol, if we recall his feeble attempt at a lecturing job, courageously got down to whatever business he could. Gogol's competence at editorial work was nil—a fact to which no significance was attached by Pushkin. Yulian Oksman wrote that Gogol undertook "all of the editorial/technical work" on *Sovremennik*.[52] His editing of the first issue of the magazine *Sovremennik* for the year 1836 proved that he was not just incompetent, but dangerous, too.

Upon getting the opportunity to decide what to publish in the magazine, Gogol, instead of seeking out different authors, put his own "The Carriage" and "A Businessman's Morning," which Pushkin had approved, into the first issue, along with eight of his own reviews on a wide variety of books, and still another notice—eleven pieces altogether. A scandal flared up because of his (unsigned) article on "The progress of magazine literature in 1834 and 1835."

Gogol described everything that had been published in both capitals in negative and sometimes in just plain abusive terms: "The greater part of periodical publishing manifested as colorlessness," "the poverty and glum appearance of our magazines," "nothing fresh," "the absence of taste," "ignorance," "benumbed coldness." Gogol blew every magazine, publisher, and author to smithereens, severally and singly.

It remains a mystery how this across-the-board massacre could have happened. Probably, it came to pass unknown to the publisher himself, that is to say, Pushkin. The widespread scandal placed the existence of the new-born *Sovremennik* in danger. Its publisher decided to dissociate himself sharply from Gogol, who had stirred up all this ugliness. In order to extricate himself, Pushkin had to resort to guile.

He composed a "Letter to the Publisher" and signed it "A.B." (*Sovremennik*, No.3), in which he condemns Gogol's haughty opinions. It is possible that "A.B." is just the first two letters of the alphabet. The published article, wrote Pushkin, "did not correspond to what we were expecting." Gogol was accused of praising some people for the same thing he was indignant with others for, that is, of being unprincipled, and even sometimes of an absence of that sense of humor for which Pushkin had praised him.

The article's imaginary author, A.B., calls upon the publisher to "sincerely repent of the weaknesses inseparable from the nature of people in general and journalists in particular . . . before the flock of his subscribers." The piece ends on a sarcastic note, with the hope that the critic will avoid in his own criticism the inadequacies so severely and justly condemned in his own article.

Then follows a commentary "From the Editor," in which Pushkin justifies himself: "Circumstances did not permit the publisher to engage personally in the printing of the first two issues of his magazine; certain errors crept in ..." Pushkin was forced to dissociate himself publicly from the evil critic, to promise not to criticize books that Gogol had noted with asterisks for an analogous harrowing in a subsequent column. The second issue of *Sovremennik* carried a review of Gogol's comedy *The Inspector General* by Poytr Vyazemsky. Gogol's "The Nose" was published in the third issue. As a footnote to the title of that tale, Pushkin wrote four lines about the pleasure that the manuscript had given to the publisher, which was why he had decided to share that pleasure with the readers. Not a single article or piece of criticism by Gogol appeared in the magazine from the second issue onwards. Gogol's activities as editor, columnist, and literary critic were terminated by the publisher. Yulian Oksman wrote that Gogol was "painfully wounded."[53] With this, their practical relations came to an end.

On June 6, 1836, Gogol went abroad. Nabokov noted that

> It is said that on the eve of his departure, Pushkin, whom he was never to see again, visited him and spent all night rummaging together with him among his manuscripts and reading the beginning of *Dead Souls* ... The picture is pleasing—too pleasing perhaps to be true.[54]

We would add that it was yet another fairy-tale foisted on the public by Gogol, of course.

Gogol never wrote Pushkin a single line from abroad, while complaining to Zhukovsky, "I never even managed to say goodbye to Pushkin; that was his fault, however." From this it follows that perhaps Gogol had undertaken some attempt to see him, but Pushkin had refused the meeting. But he loved saying goodbyes and seeing off people going abroad. Offense, a quarrel, or, even more, say, a duel would have been too high an honor for Gogol. Pushkin had expunged Gogol from his milieu and didn't care to know him any longer.

When Pushkin was no longer around to write a refutation, Gogol began to view his own role in Pushkin's *Sovremennik* in an altogether different light. It seemed that it hadn't been Pushkin who had given Gogol the opportunity to be published in his magazine, but he, Gogol, who had "entreated" Pushkin to publish *Sovremennik*. Moreover, as it now began to appear to Gogol, he turned out to be a more gifted journalist than Pushkin: "In my articles he found a lot that could impart a periodical's liveliness to the publication, of the sort that he did not acknowledge in himself." And not a word about their conflict. In "Selected passages from correspondence between friends," Pushkin's name is entirely arbitrarily used by him, and the poet's views distorted to reinforce the author's own authority.

Gogol was not merely a talented prose writer, but a brilliant fantasist as well. Vyazemsky wrote to Aleksandr Turgenev: " From a surfeit of gaiety Gogol often gets tangled up in his own lies ..."[55] In letters he confided that he was writing a "History of the Ukraine" in six volumes, a general history and geography of "The Earth and Its People" in three or two volumes, the "History of the Middle Ages" in eight volumes—in all, that is, sixteen or seventeen tomes. But what he wrote in that time was *Taras Bulba*. "Gogol lied to himself the same as he lied to others. Mendacity was his way of life, the essence of his genius," wrote Helen Muchnik.[56]

Gogol's fantasies extended not just to literary themes, but to dates as well. Similarly, N. Tikhonravov established that Gogol arbitrarily changed the year that he wrote his articles in the anthology *Arabeski* (*Arabesques*), in order to represent them as having been written much earlier and by that means avoid the reproof of critics. It was Gogol who made up the legend about Pushkin's "With Homer long you conversed alone" that asserted that Pushkin dedicated it not to Nikolay Gnedich, but to Nicholas I.

Gogol was always mistaking his wishes for the achieved reality, his own inventions for the really existing. A dreamer and a fantasist, he made up human relationships not just in his fiction but in his life as well. He told tales about his intimate contacts with women with whom he had no such relations. Similarly he was always fantasizing Pushkin's friendship into more than it ever was.

In Russian studies of the theme we are discussing here, one circumstance has been completely ignored. True, Veresayev could perhaps have had it in view when he wrote: "Pushkin kept his distance in his relations with Gogol."[57] Meanwhile, this question has been painstakingly studied in the West. From his youth Gogol devised strange costumes for himself to wear. He wore his hair long, fluffing it into a quiff, accentuated his waist, and stuck shoulder-pads in his coats. "Pushkin was a frivolous, Frenchified card player," John Bayley wrote severely. "Gogol: a deviant, a homosexual, a complete outsider."[58]

Using psychoanalytical methods, some studies of Gogol's homosexual tendencies as well as of his life and works have been undertaken.[59] We will note only that Pushkin related to homosexuals with irony or otherwise inimically or mockingly (for example, his attitude towards Philipp Vigel, to say nothing of Baron Hekkeren). But did he develop an attitude like that towards Gogol? It would be naive to bundle the whole complex of human relations into a single cause, but it would be a mistake to ignore it.

The Russian word *druzhba* is inadequately rendered by the English *friendship* or the French *amitié*. There is a huge distance between the meanings of the two Russian words for "friend," *drug* and *priyatel*. The latter is closer in meaning to "acquaintance," and Pushkin's acquaintances of one degree or another are numbered at 2700. Friendship for Pushkin was a relationship of many years of deep spiritual proximity, mutual openness, trust, understanding, shared feelings, unselfishness.

What Pushkin and Gogol had, putting it into contemporary terms, was a business contact, one that Gogol strove to stimulate with all his might. Pushkin played a decisive role in Gogol's life. For Pushkin, Gogol was just one among many young writers. For many years the assumption was that it was Gogol that Pushkin had in mind when he called an unknown author "one of my friends (*priyatel'*), a great melancholic, who sometimes has his brilliant moments of gaiety." Earlier, Gippius had his doubts, but not long ago Vadim Vatsuro quite cogently proved that the passage in no way relates to Gogol.[60] However, having become ever gloomier himself over the years, Pushkin took Gogol's humor and strangeness both as author and personality as an amusement and a distraction. He saw what Gogol had written as a joke in which "there is a lot of the unexpected, the fantastic, the cheerful, the unexpected." Having thus garnered the poet's attention, Gogol worked all the harder at being a joker.

In the 1840s, Pletnev, who had brought Gogol and Pushkin together, agitatedly wrote to Gogol: "So what are you? As a man, you're a secretive creature, egotistical, arrogant, sacrificing everything for glory. As a friend, what are you? And can you even have any friends?"[61] Fate went on to order the two classic authors in its own way, making them distantly related. Nearly half a century further on, the poet's granddaughter Maria Pushkina married a lieutenant in a hussar regiment, Nikolay Bykov, the grand-nephew of Gogol.[62] But this curiosity has no relation to literature.

We said earlier that Belinsky was among the sources of the myth of the two authors' friendship, but now let's clarify the fact that the myth's very first originator was of course Gogol in his own right. Pushkin's life, the basic events of it, were unknown to Gogol. "Gogol writes about Pushkin in a way that is not acceptable to write about real people, living today or living at any time," noted Boris Bursov. What Gogol had to say about Pushkin, in Bursov's words, was "properly typical for a legend, but not for literary-critical description."[63]

In a fit of daydreaming, Gogol in a letter to Zhukovsky tried to pass on that his friendship with Pushkin had come to him in a dream: "Oh, Pushkin, Pushkin! What a wonderful dream I was lucky enough to have in this life, and how sad was my awakening from it!" Deeply significant phrases like "Gogol acquainted Pushkin with his literary plans, himself read him his newest works or sent him manuscripts for preliminary inspection" are often encountered in the literature.[64] They are generalizing something that took place at most two or three times, creating a false picture of personal and creative relations on a permanent level.

Gogol himself spread among his associates the legend of the friendship that he desired. Thus the recollections of Gogol's close friend Danilevsky have carried down to us the tale of Yakim, Gogol's servant: "Himself [*i.e., Pushkin—Y.D.*] really loved the master. Let it be snow, rain, slush—himself would be running here in his little overcoat. [*It happens that both Pushkin and the Gogol's character Akaky Akakiyevich democratically ran around in the same little overcoat—Y.D.*] Himself would be sitting whole nights at a stretch with the master, listening as our fellow read himself his compositions, or read him his poems." In Yakim's words, Pushkin, dropping in on Gogol and not finding him in, would root around in his papers in vexation, burning with impatience to find out whatever new thing the other had written. "He kept a loving eye on Gogol's development and would repeat over and over to him 'write, write,' and laugh over his stories, and would always leave Gogol happy and in good spirits."[65]

This illiterate servant, all unknowing, laid the foundation of the Soviet approach to Gogol. Yakim was evidently more than just a valet. Gogol, grown angry once, threatened to beat him, but Yakim, improbably, answered his master back, and Gogol tenderly took care of him and even provided for his future.[66]

Every writer writes his own biography for himself, making it more interesting, full of conflict, brighter, sewn into literature. Leo Tolstoy in his article "About

Shakespeare and About Drama" noted that it was Shakespeare that made Goethe great, and in general, writers make a big deal out of other writers for mercenary reasons, and then climb onto their shoulders. Anyway, the majority of writers do this on the basis of realia.

The uniqueness of the situation described lies in the fact that the great prose author Gogol himself, from the beginning of his literary career to its end, made his fundamental work the myth of his friendship with Russia's great poet. He set this myth at the head of his biography. This truly splendid fiction of Gogol's became an important stage in literary history, but, at the same time, did not become historical reality.

A curious question arises: how would Gogol's literary fate have unfolded if he had not from the very start made it his task to obtain the blessing of Pushkin, but had merely written and made his way in literature without a patron?

We will never get an answer to that question. It is possible only to suppose that in a country so intolerant of deviance as Russia, Gogol, with his undoubted genius, but with his strange behavior, his provinciality, his suspiciousness, and his peculiar literacy, for which critics would now and again take him to task, would have remained in obscurity for a long time. It is possible that he would not have kept pace even with other writers of the second or the third rank.

This is why we firmly recommend to young writers that they first find themselves a worthy master, then spread a viable myth about their close friendship with him, and then begin publishing under the real or imagined blessing of that great writer. Only be sure to get his wife's name down correctly beforehand.

The Poet's 113th Love

> "Petty-bourgeois tragedy
> attained the greatness of myth."
> *Marina Tsvetayeva*[1]

The number of writers' wives considerably exceeds the number of writers—a phenomenon that requires some special reflection. Beyond that, none of them in the Russian patrimony, as well as probably in the whole of world literature, obtained such significance and achieved such popularity as Natalya Nikolayevna Goncharova-Pushkina-Lanskaya.

Neither tsars' wives nor the wives of Soviet leaders were ever that popular. A vast literature and iconography is devoted to Mrs. Pushkina. She was the only writer's wife ever to be honored by a postage stamp. And so many contradictory opinions were never expressed about anyone else's wife.

As it is known, in spring or fall of 1829, Pushkin was busy with his love accountancy. First, as a joke, he wrote down in Ushakov's album his so-called Don Juan list of 16 women, ending with Natalya, and then continued it, including 21 more lovers; the two lists sum up to 37 names.

Pavel Kiselev, Yelizaveta Ushakova's son, was the first to call the enumeration the "Don Juan" list.[2] Modest Gofman considered the first list to be Platonic, and the second to be carnal.[3] In Poytr Guber's opinion, the second list "mentions heroines of lighter and more superficial attractions."[4]

It goes without saying that compiling the list in the presence of two splendid creatures, one of whom, Yekaterina, he was measuring up in terms of a bride, was a sort of flirtation. "To consider that Pushkin was in this way pouring out the secrets of his soul (which he had, like any other person, of course) before the aristocratic young ladies"— Yuri Lotman persuasively considered—"means to gravely underestimate his culture of feeling."[5] Probably that accounting made by Pushkin, although done as a joke, made it easier for him to fling himself into the search for a bride.

In reckoning his lovers at home, not while a guest somewhere else, whether on his fingers, on an abacus, or on paper, Pushkin increased this number by over three times, and we have no grounds on which to dispute him. He informed his old friend Vera Vyazemskaya about it in a letter about half a year later, around April 28, 1830. "My marriage to Nathalie (who, I note in brackets, is my 113th love)—is settled," he wrote. There was a Vera in the Don Juan list, and most likely it is that selfsame Vera Vyazemskaya. But she was the wife of one of his closest friends, and it would be better not to mention this old Odessa tale.

It is curious that Pushkin liked to boast about his affairs in front of women. And generally, as well, in front of his friends, too. But there were many names that he didn't include in his list. Perhaps ones that he forgot? Or ones that could be easily guessed at? Or names that were "active" a that moment? But if so, why did he include Goncharova?

One hundred and thirteen is not that many for someone with Pushkin's lifestyle. Of course Pushkin scholars would have considerably more work if Pushkin had left behind him a complete list, instead of just a third of one. If you divide 113 over 17 years, from the first love of the 14-year-old adolescent for the serf actress Natalya in 1813 to Natalya Goncharova, it turns out to be that, on average, Pushkin had six and a half women per year—an improbably low number for his circumstances. One would think that the real figure was significantly higher, if you compare it with one of Pushkin's closest friends, Sergey Sobolevsky, who maintained that he had had 500. In addition, the easily-accessed women, who were innumerable, were left off his list.

In Nashchokin's words, Pushkin even had a sensual attraction towards the empress.[6] However, the poet himself in other notes of his widens the scope of his love: "I was more or less in love with every pretty woman I knew." Pushkin's words were elaborated by Modest Gofman: "As a poet he considered it to be his duty to be in love with every pretty woman and young girl that he met."[7] The defector Gofman's work, "Pushkin—A Don Juan," published in 1937 in Paris, is in opposition to the sanctimonious Soviet jubilee books. In Moscow of that time, Pushkin had been made into an exemplary family man, but in Paris—he was a Don Juan.

According to Pushkin's amorous doctrine, there is nothing more important in life than love. The poet's purposefulness and energy and generosity in the sexual sphere were equal to his genius. "Among Pushkin's passions," wrote Koenig, "the first was his sensual and jealous love."[8]

It is difficult to find another writer for whom Woman played such an important everyday, or, we would rather say, absolute role—day and night, at his leisure or at his desk. His heroines are chaste and modest: Tatyana Larina and Masha Mironova—but as for himself, all his life he liked dissolute women of easy access, both before his marriage and afterwards, although before his marriage he had been looking for something closer to his literary ideal.

His theoretical conception of the woman as keeper of the hearth is quite conservative, and at the same time idealized. For the poet, love was not just above all other passions, it was sacred. At least until it was over. Which meant that Woman was sacred, too, since only she concentrated that love in herself, and under favorable circumstances, rewarded a man with it. She was purer, less self-seeking, than men. She could change the path of a man's life while he was in love. If he were attracted, Pushkin would find heavenly features, holiness, godliness, in any woman, even in completely ordinary ones. Even the professional intriguer and informer Carolina Sobanskaya turns into a angel in his poems.

Many of the women who belonged to the poet at different times were lucky: they occupy an honored place in the history of Russian literature, although the majority of them did not deserve that honor, deriving from nothing but amorous contact with Pushkin. A long line of dainty young Lauras, frivolous Laïsas, whom he loved for their "open desire," young nun-Cytheras, accompanied him from his early years. He loved the Parisienne prostitute Olga Masson, who had come to work in St. Petersburg, Dorida, in whose embraces he "drank voluptuousness with his soul," Fanny, whose touch he promised to remember "at death's door," but whom he had forgotten by the next day. They were followed by Natasha, with whom he spent some time in a meadow, the prostitute Nadenka, and the Polish Anzhelika, a ticket-salesgirl at a traveling zoo.

Another passion of his was women who were 15 to 20 years older than he. These latter comprise a special list, including Yevdokiya Golitsyna, Yekaterina Karamzina, Praskovya Osipova, Yelizaveta Khitrovo, and the very same Sobanskaya. The poet's passion for adult women is a special topic, and we will say only that their experience, wisdom, taste, and sensitivity affected his disposition. Then came several brides who never became his wife. Many of his paramours in one way or another shared the poet's joys and vicissitudes of fate until the end of his days. Some of them entered their second or third go-around with the by-now-married poet.

There is still a lot that is mysterious, despite a century and a half of careful attempts to investigate the poet's every amorous gust. All the more important, then, is the completely unquestionable fact contradicting the thesis that began our discussion: that, in comparison with every other Russian writer, the Pushkin of so many loves on such a broad scale had only one wife.

1. A Polarization of Opinion

The myth of Pushkin as Official State Poet No.1 diminishes the real significance of the greatest Russian poet. This is a special theme that has just begun to be worked over, at first, mainly in the West, and later by Russian Pushkin scholars. Writer Yuri Nagibin in *Literaturnaya gazeta*—and you can read this with irony—named Pushkin "the General Secretary of Russian literature."[9] Let's focus here on a part of that myth, on the "submyth" of the State Poet's wife. The poet became an icon, and an official portrait of his wife was created to match it. The poet was turned into an idol, and his wife was, too. The poet's wife, then his widow, remains the First Lady of Russian literature.

The polarization of public opinion that took place while Pushkina-Lanskaya was still alive was reflected in the various approaches towards her in literary scholarship. Different Natalya Pushkinas have been divined in the literature about Pushkin in the succeeding century and a half. In fact, the woman who was seen by and left her stamp on contemporaries was gradually crowded out of the literature.

Pushkin was alive when the first critical comments on his wife appeared; the criticism increased after his death. A new surge of negativism occurred in 1878, when an heiress of his handed over Pushkin's letters to Ivan Turgenev. Then the first decades of this century afforded a lot of material for a quiet, balanced analysis of Natalya. Then, from the end of the 1930s, the politicization—or, more precisely, the Stalinization—of Pushkin studies began. Literature about Pushkin's wife was exposed to revision in the later Soviet period as well; moreover, any disputable facts that did not fit the official conception did not get republished, and disappeared from museum expositions; and a hypocritical puritanism left its mark on every study.

A vulgar one-party mentality was reflected in this appraisal of Pushkin's wife; moreover, the grand achievements of several preceding generations of Pushkin scholars were ignored. In a book devoted to her, we read that everything was much simpler than we thought:

> In the light of a Marxist understanding of socio-political relations, it is quite clear that if there had been no episode of D'Anthes's making advances towards Natalya Nikolayevna, the drama would have had to burst out at any minute, anyway, because all its social preconditions were present.[10]

The politicization of Pushkin's wife's biography became obvious in the 1940s, when the terminology and methods of the NKVD began to be used in Pushkin scholarship. Vladimir Yermilov wrote:

> Secret agents of the government had penetrated everywhere," "they had penetrated the Goncharov family. Taking advantage of Natalya's high-society frivolousness, the Court clique made a weapon out of the poet's wife ... Creating in this way the groundwork for its further activities, the Court clique sent its agent to Natalya Nikolayevna, a cosmopolitan rogue without kith or kin, a Frenchman by birth who had become a Dutchman by citizenship ...[11]

This Soviet mythology reached its height during the last two decades before the collapse of the regime. To this day, despite the ruination of official dogmas, the mythological tendencies remain, and partisans of the various points of view are in a state of permanent conflict. Different Natalya co-exist in Pushkin scholarship, but it's not clear who the real, historical one is. Reconciling their positions is extremely difficult, so far have they diverged from one another. What is at hand is an excess of facts and an insufficiency of scientific ones that are independent of external interpretation.

2. Paradoxes of Courtship

Pyotr Vyazemsky could not believe the rumors of Pushkin's courtship for a long time, and indignantly wrote to his wife:

> You mystify me as much as Pushkin, telling me about his outbursts of lawful love. Surely he couldn't really be thinking of marrying, if he's fooling around the way he is now. You can tease a woman that you're running around after, pretending that you're in love with somebody else, and base your hopes for victory on her vexation, but how could you expect that she'll come to be your bride, that her mother would hand over her daughter to an airhead or a fop on the rebound?[12]

Anna Akhmatova retells Poytr Vyazemsky's words more simply: "How it is that, while loving one woman, you can court another." And she adds: "Princess Vera, probably, could understand whom her husband had in mind when he mentioned the other woman. We are a long way from that understanding."[13] However, that first woman could hardly be any other than Carolina Sobanskaya, and why Akhmatova could not guess it is the mystery.

Pushkin was hunting around the bridal markets of St. Petersburg and Moscow, meeting especially frequently with the Ushakov sisters. At their house, a literary and musical one that he visited three times a day in 1830, the poet was an object of worship. He amused himself there, composed impromptu verses, fell in love with the elder daughter, Yekaterina, who reciprocated his feelings. Moreover, Pushkin was stopping by the famous brothel of Sofya Astafyevna, and not just after his Lyceum period, but during his courtship and after his marriage.

Natalya Goncharova attracted Pushkin's attention instantly, appearing to him to be absolute perfection. The poet forgot that not long before he had written of his namesake Sofya Pushkina, whom he had decided to marry all of a sudden, "there can be no fairer."

The Goncharov girl was radiant at her first balls. The bud had just begun to bloom. Vikenty Veresayev said that "she hasn't read Pushkin yet," but we have too little evidence that she read him even afterwards. We know that once she wrote to her brother about how she'd heard about deficiencies in the structure of the head from the magazine *Inostrannoye obozreniye*. From Veresayev's point of view, in general she "was all her life absolutely indifferent to poetry. And what kind of communication could there have been between Pushkin and the undereducated 16-year-old girl, instructed only in the dance and how to chatter in French?"[14] The level of aristocratic young ladies with whom the poet kept company in both capitals averaged considerably higher.

The poet's courting of Natalya Goncharova took place against the background of his stormy relations with Carolina Sobanskaya. Pushkin called Sobanskaya a demon, but it seems he loved no one so passionately as he loved her. Certain of Pushkin's friends knew that she was writing secret denunciations. For instance, Philipp Vigel said that she hid a vileness beneath her ultra-fashionable form. But Pushkin did not have the slightest idea of her secret life, and wrote that his soul was the timorous slave of hers.

On March 4, 1830, the poet unexpectedly said goodbye to Sobanskaya in St. Petersburg and left for Moscow. On April 6, he proposed to Goncharova. The gesture is psychologically understandable: marriage to an alternative out of disappointment in love, a way of taking revenge on a lover who did not want a continuation of their relationship or a more serious relationship. Sobanskaya had her General Witt and many passing admirers.

On the day of Pushkin's betrothal to Natalya Goncharova, his poem "What is in my name for you?" addressed to Sobanskaya, was published in *Literaturnaya gazeta*.

> But on the day of sorrow, in the stillness,
> Pronounce it longingly;
> Say: there's a memory of me,
> In this world is a heart where I live.

If the bride and her circle had read the verses and had known to whom they were addressed, the betrothal would never have happened. Two months after the engagement, Pushkin, leaving his fiancée behind, rushed off to St. Petersburg again, as if on business, but in reality to see Sobanskaya. We do not know what this woman looked like; no portrait of her has been preserved, though she died at the age of 91. Neither do we know her attitude toward the poet, but we can guess: in the diary that she carefully kept from 1822 to 1843, the name of Pushkin is never even mentioned.[15]

The whole process of the poet's transformation to the married state is well enough known from a lot of different sources. To read over these texts again today is both sad and funny. It is obvious how difficult and absurd it was for Pushkin to overcome his situation: his fiancée's indifference, her mother's enmity, his own internal resistance and that of his own family and friends, and finally the irony of his former and present lovers. Despite logic and common sense, life experience and the advice of relatives, the smartest man in Russia was bursting to make a pretty doll into his bride.

So what did his last fiancée, the one who became Pushkin's wife, actually look like? There is a range of drawings of her, but only one portrait, made by Aleksandr Bryullov, the brother of the famous painter, is from the time of their marriage. The first daguerrotypes and photographs were made only after Pushkin's death, in her second marriage, when she was about 40.

The insightful Dolly Ficquelmont mentioned in her diary that "it is not possible either to be more beautiful or to have a more poetic appearance, but at the same time she has very little intellect and even, it seems, little imagination."[16] And in the same place, bitter words about Pushkin: "As for him, he ceases to be a poet in her presence." Jealousy? Maybe. But years later Sergey Bulgakov made the comment: "Her beauty was just prettiness, form without content, a deceptive radiance."[17]

And, anyway, the expression "the genius of pure beauty" that Pushkin borrowed from Vasily Zhukovsky and presented to another woman, would probably have suited his wife even more. However, Pushkin said to Pavel Vyazemsky, the poet's son, that it looked like even his famous "Madonna" had been written at first for another woman.[18]

He wrote a few verses for his wife. If Goncharova had been a little older and had been kept in less strict circumstances, affording Pushkin an opportunity to relate to her at closer range, it is possible that she would have bored him faster than many of his previous women. Ignorance lent an aureole of mysteriousness to her beauty. The experienced Pushkin was hooked and behaving like an adolescent who had fallen in love for the first time. Surely he was just pretending to be that naive.

The Poet's 113th Love 61

Three years before, itching to get married, he very soberly evaluated himself and another of his brides-that-never-were as something incompatible. "My life, until now such a nomadic one, such a stormy one, my character—uneven, jealous, suspicious, sharp and weak at the one time—that's what sometimes leads me to a distressing meditation," he wrote in French, just after crawling out from under an overturned sleigh, lying all crushed in a strange bed and breathing heavily, to his friend Vasily Zubkov on December 1, 1826. "Should I bind the fate of a creature so tender, so wonderful, to a fate as sad and with such an unlucky character as mine?" At that time the person under discussion was Sofya Pushkina.

One way or another, a hundred and twelve lessons from other women could not help him. It appeared as if he was trying to get the girl just because she had appeared so inaccessible at first.

> I please youthful beauty
> With the shameless rage of my desires.

And he didn't even succeed in getting left one on one with his fiancée, to stun her with that mighty and irresistible weapon of his. Forbidden fruit seems a hundred times sweeter from a distance. But as soon as he received consent, we see how he began to shrink back, vacillating between his pledged word and doubts about the reasonableness of the undertaking as a whole. He was enraptured with heavenly beauty, but married a gray provincial. He called her a Madonna, but wanted to obtain a woman, a wife, and a housemistress. But, as the old joke has it, polygamy is against the law.

At times he hoped for circumstances that could prevent the marriage, and furiously tried to leave the country. But he got turned down yet again. It was so stupid: Russian literature—and not just that—the whole cultural history of Russia became hostage to the querulous and dull-witted woman who became the mother-in-law of the great poet. But you can't change history.

A year and a half later, having obtained the consent of his future mother-in-law, he became distinctly conscious of the fact that his bride did not like him. "I can hope to bind her to me in time, but there is nothing in me for her to like." He realized that she was not a match for him; nothing that he lived for was of the slightest interest to her.

Beyond that, his own ardor for her cooled, perhaps even passed: "I have coldbloodedly weighed up the profits and losses of the condition that I choose," he wrote to Nikolay Krivtsov on February 10, 1831.

> ... I am marrying without any thrill, without childish fascination. I can see my future not in roses but in its severe barrenness. Troubles will not surprise me, I will simply reckon them in my domestic accounts.

It is easy to consider his actions stupid now, but he never lost the sobriety of mind to understand the impending step.

Marina Tsvetayeva, as partial herself as if Pushkin could have belonged to her, declared that the name of Natalya Goncharova was an "ill-fated assonance."[19] But at the same time she believed that Natalya was not guilty for what happened. Pushkin wanted to get married, and, an experienced man, knew what he was getting into: eternal indifference, apathy, dull-wittedness, and selfishness. "He wanted a nothing, because he himself was everything."[20] Beautifully put, but he could hardly have "wanted a nothing"; at first, blinded by his infatuation, multiplied by his longtime desire to get married despite everything, he did not know to quite what an extent she was "a nothing."

"A nothing" is unjust, offensive, but you cannot help agree with Tsvetayeva that Goncharova also suffered a defeat, and won nothing at all after Pushkin's onslaught. Her life showed that she quite suited other men, fit together with them, and was happier with them than with her first husband.

However, with his mystical premonition of something bad, Pushkin painted himself into a corner of his own free will. And, once his victory had been gained, he started thinking of how to get out of his marriage. He needed the support of his friends—"and now he's not altogether happy." "Judging by his physiognomy, you would think that he was vexed by the fact that she hadn't turned him down, as he had expected," wrote Nadezhda Ozerova, after meeting Pushkin and Natalya Nikolayevna at a Noblemen's Assembly presentation.[21]

In his poem "Let's go, I'm ready," he calls her "haughty," "proud," and "wrathful." But could he have married someone haughty? Aleksandr Bulgakov told his brother that Pushkin was asked "... they say that you're getting married?" "Of course," he answered. "And don't think that it will be the last stupid thing I do in my life."[22] And the poet himself in a letter to Pyotr Pletnev seemed to bemoan the fact the he had plighted his troth: "The Devil made me rave about happiness as if I had been created for it. I would rather be content with my independence."

The poet's friend Sergey Sobolevsky recalled that from his bride-to-be's house on Bolshaya Nikitskaya Street Pushkin could look down at an undertaker's premises, and wrote his "Gravedigger" because of it.[23] The poet itches to get married, but he enjoys being alone, without his fiancée: "You cannot imagine how nice it is to sneak away from the bride-to-be, and then sit down to writing verse," he wrote to Pletnev from Boldino.

"Pushkin is marrying Goncharova—to tell you something just between the two of us, a heartless beauty—and I believe that he would conclude a bill of retraction with pleasure."[24] The poet's friend Sergey Kiselev tells us this below the text of a letter from Pushkin that was sent to a mutual friend of theirs, Alekseyev, so it is almost without a doubt that Pushkin read the text of their joint friendly letter before it was posted and, as we can see, did not contradict anything. At Boldino Pushkin had an affair with Fevroniya Vilyanova, the daughter of a prosperous peasant, while he could not get to his fiancée; it wasn't serious, of course, and therefore never made his list.

Pyotr Bartenev wrote down this story from Pavel Nashchokin: "... he wanted to avoid the married state entirely and go to Poland for the single reason that the marriage, for financial reasons, could not take place soon. Nashchokin had a heated conversation with him on this subject at the home of Prince Vyazemsky." I think that the word "single" here should not be understood literally: there were other reasons, and the situation was more intricate.

"Intending to go to Poland," wrote Bartenev, " Pushkin would sing to his friend Nashchokin: 'Don't marry, my fine fellow, and with the money buy yourself a horse.'"[25] "They have again taken to saying in town that Pushkin's wedding is never coming off," Aleksandr Bulgakov wrote his brother. "It seems that nothing good can be expected out of it, and I think that not only for her alone but for him as well it would be better if the wedding never did come off."[26] Leonid Grossman believed, however, that Pushkin's unwillingness to get married was exaggerated, although he introduced no evidence of this.

Before his wedding, Pushkin had to ask a man who was secretly spying on him to confirm his loyalty to the state, at the demand of his mother-in-law. One could imagine Benckendorff's grin when he handed over that "certificate," so that the poet could show it to his mother-in-law. "I'm coming to see you," Pushkin informed Vyazemsky, "but I am on duty today and tomorrow at my fiancée's in Moscow." "On duty" is a joke, of course, but you can catch a glimpse of his onerous obligation, anyway.

It was clear to him already that his marriage would not add happiness to his life. Not long before, he had written to his neighbor Praskovya Osipova: "On the issue of happiness, I am an atheist; I don't believe in it ..." Or: "I have never taken any pains about happiness: I could manage without it. Now I need it for two, but where can I get it from?" But, having married, three months later he reported to Pletnev otherwise: "I am married and happy ... This is such a new state for me that it seems I have been born again."

If it was really so, it seems he was happy both for himself and for her. And did the loving for the both of them. From the very beginning, he understood that, since even earlier he had written to his future mother-in-law: "... if she agrees to give me her hand, I will see in it merely proof of the quiet indifference of her heart." And—making up her love for him, Pushkin, invented this fateful, alternativeless moment: "My angel, your love is the only thing in the world that prevents me from hanging myself ..."

In his letter to his future mother-in-law on the eve of their engagement, he clairvoyantly mentioned the possibility of a brilliant widowhood for Natalya. And on the same occasion he described in three pages the entire history of his unhappy marriage ("My fate is sealed. I am to be wed ..."). "Marriage was his misfortune, and all his close friends regretted that he had gotten married," recalled Nikolay Smirnov.[27]

Before the wedding, the poet Nikolay Yazykov recalled: "Pushkin had a hen party, so to speak, or better say a farewell drinking bout for his bachelor's life." Pushkin recited poems about parting with his youth and repentance for his sins. The poems got lost in the booze-up.

3. A first experiment with a matchmaking bureau

In our speculations about Pushkin's fiancée, we have to make one reservation. Whether we want to or not, we have reckoned Natalya Goncharova by the standards of the 20th century, laying our notions, manners, and morals on her and Pushkin and their environment. Other generations will probably look at it differently.

In search of an independent judgement, we decided to help Pushkin in his choice of bride, or, in other words, to check the correctness of his choice by modern means, for which purpose contact was made with a matchmaking bureau in San Francisco, one of the most reputable, with experience of successful work over the course of seventeen years.

The work of the matchmaking bureau, with the exception of the data entry, is completely programmed: subjective factors are minimized, which determined our choice of that particular institution. We won't bore you by recounting the breadth of the data base that the bureau requires. Some of the questions were important for the computer: for instance, a person's height (Natalya Goncharova and Sofya Pushkina were both considerably taller than Alexander Pushkin), outward appearance, temperament, etc.

We'll also make the reservation that, like the reader, we realize perfectly well the conventional nature of the experiment. As an example, we will give you part of the data entered. To avoid possible mistakes, even numbers at the matchmaking bureau are for women, odd numbers are for men.

Search for registered number 0809457

Surname: Pushkin
Name: Alexander
Age: 31
Nationality: Russian
Racial origin: mix of white and African
Appearance: (determined by the taste and experience of the matchmaking-bureau employee from a photograph: A—handsome, B—ugly, C—ordinary): B—ugly.
Education: Tsarskoye Selo Lyceum.
Profession: author, poet
Position: (instead of the given "10th-rank official, discharged from service," we had to enter something the computer could understand) clerk, translator, presently unemployed.
Material means: (sufficiency—insufficiency) insufficiency of money.

Hobbies: playing cards, billiards, drawing, traveling, going for long walks, sauna, shooting pistols.

As it is known, over the course of four years, Pushkin focused his attention on four wifely candidates: Sofya Pushkina, Anna Olenina, Yekaterina Ushakova, and Natalya Goncharova. Age indicated is as of the date of his proposal.

Candidate 0809460

Surname: Pushkina
Name: Sofya
Age: 20
Nationality: Russian
Racial origin: white
Appearance: A (beautiful)
Education: at home
Profession: none
Position: not working
Material means: sufficiency
Hobbies: handicrafts, embroidery

Candidate 0809458

Surname: Olenina
Name: Anna
Age: 20
Nationality: Russian
Racial origin: white
Appearance: A (beautiful)
Education: at home; the humanities, including languages
Profession: none
Position: maid of honor
Material means: sufficiency
Hobbies: reading French novels, poetry, the theater, socializing

Candidate 0809462

Surname: Ushakova
Name: Yekaterina
Age: 17
Nationality: Russian
Racial origin: white
Appearance: A (beautiful)
Education: at home; the humanities
Profession: none
Position: not working
Material means: sufficiency
Hobbies: the theater, literary pursuits, poetry, drawing, correspondence and socializing with friends.

Candidate 0809456

Surname: Goncharova
Name: Natalya
Age: 17
Nationality: Russian
Racial origin: white
Appearance: A (beautiful)
Education: at home (French, dancing)
Profession: none
Position: not working
Material means: insufficiency
Hobbies: horse-riding, cross-stitching

The computer interrupted its analysis of the data and demanded an elaboration on the point of whether Sofya Pushkina was his relation, in order to warn against the possibility of consanguinity. She was not, and this was entered into the program.

Let's not talk about the method for matching up couples and the preparation and processing of information by the computer, since that will divert us away from the topic. We will inform you only of the final answer given by the computer. The program considered Yekaterina Ushakova the most suitable for Pushkin. An alternative was Anna Olenina. The computer declared Number 0809460, that is, Sofya Pushkina, as well as Number 0809456, that is, Natalya Goncharova, to be unsuitable candidates.

It is interesting that the computer choice of a wife for Pushkin turned out to be similar to Vikenty Veresayev's opinion of Yekaterina Ushakova, to the effect that

> ... I want to know as much as possible about this girl, who not only loved Pushkin but could appreciate him. If the shallow beauty Goncharova hadn't stolen a march on her, pulling Pushkin into court captivity, corrupting his entire life and bringing him to D'Anthes's pistol—Pushkin's lifelong friend could possibly have been Ushakova, and she would have saved Pushkin for us for yet long years more.[28]

Incidentally, the computer got an opportunity to elaborate on its conclusions even further, but we'll get back to that a little later.

4. "Marriage castrates the soul"

That was what the poet wrote five years before his own marriage, on the subject of the wedding of Boratynsky. Later, Pushkin wrote to Nikolay Krivtsov: "You are missing a leg, and I am married!" But the poet saw marriage in even gloomier tones: "The unhappiness of the married state is the distinguishing feature of the ways of the Russian people ... Wedding songs are as doleful as a funeral wailing."

The Russian publisher and literary critic Pyotr Pertsov called Pushkin's marriage a typical marriage of an older man with a young girl, but it wasn't true. Weddings with such age differences were typical and normal. Pushkin was 31, Natalya was almost 19. The trouble lay elsewhere.

> Oh, how agonizingly happy I am with you,
> When, giving in to my lengthy prayers,
> You give yourself up to me, tender without rapture,
> Bashful-cold, my delight
> Barely answering, heeding nothing,
> And your passion rising more and more—
> Till finally you share my flame against your will.

In his works this poem is traditionally said to have been published around 1830. But Sobolevsky placed a date on the manuscript, evidently, from memory, and Bartenev added: "19 January." However, beneath this poem, that was not published during her lifetime and was found in Natalya's papers after her death by her second husband, Pyotr Lanskoy, there is a date of 1831, and, in certain manuscript copies, even 1832.

Vikenty Veresayev, without any proof, considered the time of the poem's creation to be the beginning of the Pushkins' marital relations, and we feel that to be logical; Sobolevsky's and Bartenev's dates are hypothetical. In Pushkin's ten volume works (1977), the poem is placed in the section headed "1827—1836," that is, without any dates. If it really relates to Natalya, then, according to its contents, it was written in 1831, no earlier than February 18, that is, after, and not before, their first conjugal evenings.

At first this coldness of his wife delighted him. Did this last for long? And what can be sadder in a marriage than bedding someone against their will? Today they call it sexual harassment. A sexual life "heeding nothing"—that is the husband's first poetic testimony. Evidently, even further on, their temperaments on a sexual level remained different, which could scarcely have drawn Pushkin to his wife.

Marriage radically changed the status of the young Miss Goncharova. And what of the poet's lifestyle? Pushkin was inspired to believe that he was starting a new, different style of life, but continued his old one. He left his wife alone on the morning of their first day in a rented house in the Arbat in order to spend the day with his friends.

But even she impressed the poet's friends. Colwell Frankland, an Englishman who met Pushkin not long before this, recalled how he had been invited to dinner at his house. Ivan Kireyevsky and Pyotp Vyazemsky were among the guests as well. Frankland noted: "The beautiful newlywed failed to appear."[29] It seems as if Vyazemsky understood the situation best of all at the time: "He must not try to keep up with everyone else now, but I am certain that in his love for his wife there will be a lot of vanity. Being now married, he should leave for foreign parts—with his wife, of course—and I am sure that in this case he would be allowed to leave the country."[30]

A detailed note by Pushkin's old friend Vasily Tumansky, who visited their apartment shortly after their marriage, is seldom cited.

> Don't imagine, however, that it was something extraordinary. Pushkin's wife is a pretty, clean girl with direct black and cunning eyes, like any *grisette*. You can see that she is still awkward and not unduly brash, but, anyway, Muscovite manners show quite noticeably in her. The fact that she has no taste was evident in her shocking manner of dress; the stained napkins and tablecloth and the confusion of furniture and dishes all testified that she was neither tidy nor orderly.[31]

Let's imagine the six years of the Pushkins' family life as a curve on a graph, the peak of which represents their happiness, or, better, their prosperity. Knowing the facts, we discover that the peak after their marriage was not a lengthy one; it now and again clouded over with material and psychological problems. Then for quite a while the situation stabilized. Children appeared.

Archpriest Sergey Bulgakov refers to the opinion of Foydor Dostoyevsky that there was a seductive mixture of Madonna and Venus in his Pushkin's wife. She is the Madonna-maid-of-honor, the Madonna-housemistress, the Madonna who bore one child after another.[32] The poet wanted to throw off the chains that he, impassioned, had put upon himself. In the expression of Father Bulgakov, he sought shelter in Dionysianism, in spiritual philistinism. His life split into two.

Pushkin loved his children, but there is no evidence that he played, went for walks, or spent any time with them. There were servants for that. Pavel Nashchokin recalled that Pushkin "wept at the birth of his first child and said that he would run away from the second." And really did start running. In the spring of 1835, when Natalya was nearing her time, the poet, without any obvious need to do so, left for the country and returned only after his wife had already given birth. A year later, when his wife was at full term with their next child, Pushkin was living at Nashchokin's in Moscow, and, returning home, learned at his doorstep that Natalya had successfully borne him a daughter. After a ball, Natalya had a miscarriage, and Pushkin wrote in his diary: "She danced herself into it."

The poet did his connubial duty, although in his own way. He still loved his wife, at least according to his letters. In letters to his brother that have come down to us, there is a practicality, a provincial banality, endless requests to send more money. His letters are testimony to the fact that he is trying to adapt to his wife's level and tastes.

Did he try to raise her up, to get her interested, to make her educated and closer to his spirit? Did he satisfy himself that it was impossible, or did he from the very beginning separate his working and spiritual lives from his family one, and live that life with others, not letting his wife very far into his holiest of holies? After all, in his letters to her, if he speaks about literature, it is only from the point of view of attracting more income. And if he talks of life, it is only about trivial rumors, coquetries, and jealousy.

Jealousy was surely the strongest feeling in Natalya's spectrum, and we think it was not her fault. She was jealous of Pushkin's friends, of all his old girlfriends. And of course of his new ones. She had good cause, concerning the latter. Catching sight of a new pretty woman, the poet would catch fire on the spot, and his marriage did not prevent him from doing so. "Pushkin's wife often and very sincerely suffers from the torments of jealousy," testified Sofya Karamzina, the historian's daughter, "because the mediocre beauty and mediocre minds of other women do not stop turning her husband's poetic head." However, he himself did not consider other women mediocre.

In the poet's footsteps, we can continue the Don Juan list of his lovers who appeared in parallel with Natalya. Number 114 is Countess Nadezhda Sollogub, number 115 is Aleksandra Smirnova, number 116 is Countess Darya Ficquelmont, number 117—the fair-haired beauty Amalia Kruedener, whom Pushkin energetically pursued in front of his wife at Ficquelmont's ball. Taking note of it, Natalya left, and at home slapped her husband's face. The poet informed Vyazemsky laughingly that "his Madonna has a heavy little hand."

Pushkin's wife was beautiful, but scarcely beyond all competition, as the myth would have it. Or—by that time she had stopped being the most beautiful in the poet's eyes, since a serious rival, the delightful Baroness Amalia Kruedener, had appeared. Fyodor Tyutchev dedicated his "I remember a golden time" to her. Incidentally, Nicholas I was busy with her in 1838, and later gave Baroness to General Aleksandr Benckendorff.

After Kruedener on the poet's list comes number 118, the Countess Elena Zavadovskaya, of whom the Persian prince, Khozrev Mirza, said that the beauty's every eyelash stabbed him to the heart.

> She has no rivals, nor friends;
> The pale circle of our beauties
> Washes out in her radiance.

It was thought for a long time that Pushkin's poem "The Beauty" was dedicated to Natalya, but it turns out that it was written by the poet himself into the album of Countess Elena Zavadovskaya. Thus, just a year after his marriage, in comparison with number 118, Zavadovskaya, his own Madonna number 113 is left in the shade, in "the pale circle of our beauties." His new women seemed superior, not least because they were new.

Two and a half years after his marriage, in "The Bronze Horseman" and in "The Queen of Spades," which were being written in Boldino in October and the beginning of November of 1833, the tragic theme of the separation of man and woman by supernatural forces appeared—not something new in literature, but new in Pushkin's works. This variant itself was carefully investigated by Rostislav Schultz in America.[33] We, for our part, mention the arresting subconscious connection of that literary theme with Pushkin's family problem. A crack had appeared in the edifice of the poet's family.

The end of 1833 was crucial to the poet's fate. Pavel Shchegolev wrote:

> With the poverty of her spiritual nature, aristocratic-love romanticism gave Natalya the principal content of her internal life. A most beautiful woman, she made her husband the object of an aristocratic whirl that he himself enjoyed, but where he could not control himself. The universal pursuit of his beauty-wife made him suspicious, jealous, an Othello ... Pushkin continually reproached and cautioned his wife against coquetry, while the whole time she would share with him her successes in that craft, continually suspecting Pushkin of betrayals and being jealous of him.[34]

Many people behaved towards his wife in no way as to a Madonna: theirs was ordinary philandering. In a letter Pushkin tried to frighten his wife: "If upon my return I find that your nice, simple, aristocratic tone has changed, I'll divorce you, by Christ, and I'll go become a soldier from grief." The words about a divorce were said as a joke, but the essence is serious: in 1834 the curve of their relations continued to sink lower. The poet was getting bored; the burden of a family was weighing down on him. The first crisis of their six-year marital union was ripening at its half-way point.

"I shall think 'we'," he had planned beforehand. Now it was clear to him that it wasn't working that way. He remained alone, his wife not becoming part of that 'we'. Four years earlier, during his engagement, he wrote in the already-cited letter to Pyotr Pletnev that "A wife is not the same thing as a fiancée. No way! A wife is your brother. You can write as much as you like around her, but a fiancée is a worse censor than Shcheglov, tying your tongue and your hands." In reality, quite the contrary was happening. It had turned out to be difficult to write around his wife; moreover, he was constantly was bound hand and foot by their inordinate expenses: "Let me make money, not for myself, but for you." And he took to playing cards and losing heavily. Was his passion for cards aggravated by his disappointment with family life?

Natalya continued to exist off on her own, in another dimension. But now a lack of faith in her was aroused in him. From someone (we don't know whom) Pushkin found out something (we don't know what) that gave the husband grounds to think that his wife was talking too much.

Look here, dear wife: I hope that you aren't giving my letters out to someone to copy; if the post office opens a letter from a husband to his wife, that's their business, but ... if you are guilty, that would be very painful for me ... Nobody should be allowed into our bedroom. There is no family life without secrets. I don't write to you for publication; and you shouldn't take the public into your confidence. I know that this could not be so; but people's swinishness has long since ceased to surprise me.

If "this could not be so," why, then, did the poet scare his wife about the leaking of confidential information that was going on? Yanina Levkovich, interpreting this notion of Pushkin's, believes that "he does not exclude the possibility of the interest of a readership (a readership and not a domestic interest) in his letters."[35] But why, we ask, would there not be domestic interest? And not a police interest? And not the personal interest of Benckendorff, and especially, of the tsar, the more so since he is being mentioned in the letters?

Then his distrust becomes something even sharper, more ultimatum-like, almost like a decision to dismiss his wife from the circle of his dearest friends. "There is no news, but even if there were any, I wouldn't tell you." He could have used "wouldn't write it," bearing in mind the censorship of the mails, but here it's "wouldn't *tell* you." The split between the spouses was widening, and his wife's conversations with unnamed friends more and more turned up in the interests of his literary and political enemies. He realized that other people had more influence over his wife than he did.

Even in small things Natalya acted in defiance of him, as she felt like it. He asked her not to go to Kaluga, not to attend some sort of ball; she ignored him. She described her admirers, teasing and insulting him: "Wife, dear wife! If even in such trifling matters you don't obey to me, how can I stop myself from thinking ..."

The poet was look for peace, support, and the main thing, happiness, in his marriage: "I had to marry you, because I would have been unhappy my whole life without you," he wrote. And it's like he's trying to convince himself most of all. He was burdened with the work that his endless family debts had harnessed him into. "Now they look at me as if at a lackey who can be treated any way they like ... But you are not to blame for any of this; it is my fault because of my good nature, that I am filled with to stupidity, despite all the experience of my life."

The fact that he addressed her in his letters as "My dear angel," "My soul," "My dear soul," "Dear friend," "My Empress," calls her "clever and dear thing," does not change anything. His attempts to bring her closer to him ("and I love your soul even more than your face"), to explain to her the role of a writer's wife, were unsuccessful. Anyway, in 1834 his addresses to her in letters sound more often otherwise: "What, wife!" "Well, wife!" "It's not worth scolding about!" "You, my slatternly wife!" "chamber-pagette," "All you ladies are cut from the same pattern," "For shame, wife," "What an idiot you are, my angel!"

The string of their family relations stretched tighter and tighter, the curve dropped lower. She was busy with her successes. He could no longer live as he had lived before. His family and his creative work—or, more precisely, his wife and his creative work—were turning out to be incompatible.

Pushkin is idealized as a family man in literature, and that creates the illusion of a kind of lightness to Natalya's life with him. He loved her, which his letters now and again spoke about. At first, the universal attention toward his wife flattered his ambition, made him more popular not for his own sake, but as a focus of rumors and gossip. But what prevailed in him was the selfishness of a man who lived by his professional dealings, and who had strong habits and features of character that he would not get rid of in his married state.

After the demanding work of their union he was looking for some relief. This consisted of plentiful relations with friends, looking for a place to move to, playing cards, and women. "Pushkin would get home only at dawn, after spending the night now at cards, now at merry binges in the company of women of the obvious category ... and often, laughing, would let her know of his amorous escapades," wrote Natalya's daughter from her second marriage, evidently in her mother's words.[36]

His wife bore it, but we don't know what was going on in her soul. It is possible that resentment built up drop by drop; her husband's lack of any desire to consider important the things that interested her was reflected in her behavior, in her relation toward him. Her dissatisfaction found no exit. Deprived of her fair share of his attention, she looked for sympathy elsewhere.

In 1835 the changes in his family life were more distinctly apparent to Pushkin. He was proceeding down the list of his old Don Juan conquests. He drove to Trigorskoye and Golubevo estates "to collect some arrears," which is to say, in order to carry on his love affairs with some old girl-friends.

In September of 1835, within a couple of months after requesting retirement, thinking of moving to the countryside, came his tenderest-ever letter to Osipova's step-daughter, Aleksandra Bekleshova, with whom he had had an affair ten years earlier. She shows up on his Don Juan list at position number 20. "Come," he prays, "please God... I have three baskets full of confessions, explanations, and odds and ends for You. It might be that we'll even fall in love at our leisure." She was already married, but ... Boris Bursov was the first to surmise: "...reflecting on his getaway 'to the far abode of labors and pure abundance,' wasn't he thinking that his girl-friend would be someone else, too?"[37] In January of 1837 he was seeing Bekleshova again.

Romance number 119 arose with his wife's sister, Aleksandrina, with whom the poet stepped out when his wife was yet again about to have a baby. Veresayev wrote: "It can be considered established that in his last years, Pushkin was having a secret affair with Aleksandrina."[38] "Alexander introduced me to his wives," wrote Olga, Pushkin's sister; "now they are a three."[39] According to legend, a lost crucifix of Aleksandrina's was found when the valet was making Pushkin's bed. But it was a fact that the poet had a greater closeness of spirit with her than with his wife. Dying, Pushkin gave Vera Vyazemskaya the chain and crucifix from around his neck, asking her to pass it on to Aleksandrina, and she was delighted when she received it. This all had to be repudiated by chaste Soviet Pushkin scholars, which never helped very much in red-blooded studies of the poet's life.

In May of 1836, Pushkin wrote his wife from Moscow that he wanted to stay there for around six months, understanding that she would not feel like coming to him. Amazingly, his letter of May 18, 1836, begins like this: "Wife, my angel, even though I thank you for your kind letter, I have to scold you anyway: what did you write me for? This is my final letter, you won't be getting any more."

Of course, it should be borne in mind that it was his last letter in connection with that trip to Moscow. But the shock comes anyway from the coincidence with what happened in reality: although Pushkin lived for another eight months, this was indeed his last letter to his wife. A second crisis approached, which in train brought his duel.

5. Mutual unhappiness

From abroad, Sobolevsky was surprised that Pushkin had begun to write "colorlessly and cloyingly. Whatever has happened to him, to our Pushkin? From what has he become so weak? Is it because of his wife, or because of some other all-excluding, all-supplanting great work?"[40]

Karl Bryullov, with whom Pushkin had become very close towards the end of his life, saw "a view of a tightly-stretched family happiness." Bryullov could not restrain himself and asked: "What the devil did you get married for?" Pushkin answered: "I wanted to go abroad—they wouldn't let me, and I got into such a state that I didn't know what to do next—and got married." This tale of Bryullov's was recalled by his pupil Mikhail Zheleznov.[41] We should note here the contradiction in the poet's various explanations: after all, earlier he had maintained that he wanted to go abroad because he couldn't get permission to marry.

A Russian philosopher, living in the West, saw her like this: "… an azure, wasp-waisted beauty, light and ethereal only at flirting and dancing, but rock-heavy as a life-companion."[42] "He loved his wife," Natalya Goncharova's childhood friend Princess Yekaterina Dolgorukova considered, "and found his happiness in her; but nevertheless he didn't suit her," and Pushkin "was an unfortunate fellow."[43]

Natalya could not stand her husband's closest friend, Sergey Sobolevsky, and took a dislike to Adam Mickiewicz, but failed to conceal it the way an intelligent woman would. Karamzina noted: "It is painful to say it, but it's true: the great and good Pushkin should have had a wife better able to understand him and more suited to his station."[44]

Aleksandra Smirnova regretted the fact that Natalya was so uneducated. Pushkin asked his wife to bring him an essay by Montaigne from his library, explaining: "4 light-blue books on my long shelves. Find them." Natalya's ill-wishers consider that the fact that she was unaware of the disposition of his books on their shelves, or had never read Montaigne, was in no way the most important thing. It was much sadder that her activities away from him and even in front of him were sometimes in defiance of his wishes: she associated with people she shouldn't have, received those whom he didn't want to see in his home, and so on.

Her husband's interests in the same way failed to become her interests. The recollection of her exclamation still survives: "Good Lord, how you bore me with your verses, Pushkin!" Yevgeny Boratynsky asked if he could read some new verses of his to Pushkin, hoping that it wouldn't distract her from her affairs. "Read on, please!" she said. "I'm not listening."

But, for all that, Pushkin was among her interests. Visits to the tailors', fashionable shops, banquets, pleasure-strolls, festivities, flowed past in an endless stream, balls from which she (or they together) would get home at four or five in the morning. There was no time to occupy herself with home or children. In her first marriage she bore four children. In her youth, that is, with Pushkin, she was so attracted to high-society life that she could not have been a caring mother or dutiful housemistress.

She was forced to delegate caring for her husband and children to servants, nurses, sisters. There is a considerable amount of eyewitness testimony to this effect. Like any society lady, she got up late. She would take her dinner at eight in the evening, after which followed the lengthy ritual of dressing, primping, and the usual stepping-out.

A wife, under the rules of the etiquette of the day, could not show up at a ball on her own. Pyotr Pletnev wrote Vasily Zhukovsky:

> You are right to have contempt for those lazybones like Pushkin who don't do anything—as soon as morning comes he looks through old letters to himself in his vile case, while in the evening he takes his wife around to balls, not so much for her amusement as for his own.[45]

The end of the quote doesn't convince us that that was the case.

In others' recollections, the poet would stand at the wall or sit in a corner, wanly gazing at the revelers, seldom speaking, eating ice cream, brooding. At home he was lonely, and, unkempt, would go for walks by himself, frequently eating dinner elsewhere, even though dinner was always prepared at home. Even in summer, Natalya resisted going to Boldino, Mikhaylovskoye, or Polotnyany Zavod—she would only go to the *dacha* outside St. Petersburg, where the *beau monde* was.

Life in high society required money for elegant clothes, going out, a good apartment, innumerable servants, and a *dacha* in a fashionable place. "Worrying about life keeps me from getting bored. But I don't have the spare time of the free bachelor life necessary for writing. The social whirl, wherein my wife is very fashionable, requires money; work affords me money, and work requires solitude..."

He was borrowing money from his friends and acquaintances; he went to creditors, pawned things, including ones belonging to his friends (Sergey Sobolevsky, Aleksandra Goncharova), but his debts kept growing. Sixty thousand rubles for the first four years of their life together, and sixty thousand more in debt for the following two years. Natalya asked her brother for additional money, not stinting herself in anything.

Natalya belonged to the cream of Russian society, and Pushkin and Nicholas I had introduced her into that society. If not for the poet and the tsar, even the narrow circle of period specialists would never have known about her. In order to understand better what kind of person the poet's wife was, let's pay attention to the following.

She lived in this world for more than half a century; out of that, six years were with Pushkin, and 26 years came after him. She lived in a time when the culture of writing was flourishing; there was no noble family where the girls did not keep albums with poetry and drawings. There is a lot said and written about Pushkin's wife. Friends and acquaintances, enemies and strangers, left behind their impressions in their memoirs, diaries, letters, filling out our conception of Pushkin and of her.

And what did the poet's wife leave behind about others, even people close to him and her? What did she say about Yekaterina Karamzina, Dolly Ficquelmont, Vera Vyazemskaya, and ultimately about Pushkin himself? About him—insignificance, a patina of jealousy, complaints about the poverty of the family budget. Pushkin wrote about his fiancée that she was "without a temperament." Maturing, becoming the writer's wife, to whom did she ever write a letter from among her girlfriends, from among the huge multitude of his friends and acquaintances—one of them at least during the whole of their life together?

Nobody has preserved or remembers a single one of her lines or thoughts. In the letters written by Natalya after Pushkin's death that have survived, there is very little of interest. She could see the external aspects of things and primitively describe them: what she was doing, whom she visited, who was beautiful and who was not: "Today I didn't find his wife ugly, even quite the opposite," she wrote about Pletnev's family. "As for his daughter, to the contrary, she is a regular plain Jane."[46] In her letters about guests and receptions, she would count how many times she had been complimented in an evening.

At the beginning, Pushkin sang Natalya the very same inspired song that he sang to his other sweethearts (he did not sing any other kind of song to women), but his poetry fell on deaf ears. On the other hand, vulgarities uttered by chance-met philanderers could rouse her. Goncharova never plumbed his soul, and he never became part of hers. Even the gypsy Tanya, his accidental acquaintance, was warmer-hearted.

None the less, his wife remained sacred to him, and she could only be reproved in some mentor-like fashion, and finally forgiven, before his death, with his claiming her innocence, that she had been slandered. With surprising foresight, he at first called his favorite character, Tatyana Larina, Natalya. Ten years before he wed, he crossed out that name as unsuitable for the persona of his favorite heroine.

The poet's widow realized who Pushkin was after his death, and preserved and handed over the poet's letters to her daughter (the Countess Merenburg). The fate of his wife's letters to him—so important for an understanding of their relationship—is mysterious. These letters were handed over to the Rumyantsevsky Museum by Pushkin's grandson. In 1920 they were being prepared for publishing—three printed pages in all—and suddenly disappeared. Not a trace of them was ever found. In the 1960s an article appeared called "Where are the letters of Natalya Nikolayevna Pushkina?" by S. Engel. Discussion on this topic came to naught, and only a weak hope remains that the letters will ever be found.[47]

It is unlikely, nevertheless, that these letters would reveal anything new to us. Judging by her husband's replies, her letters irritated him, provoking objections, the ramming into her of elementary rules for the behavior of a married woman, that she either failed to understand or just ignored. However, if we could read Natalya's letters to her husband, we might get some additional brush-strokes explaining how she was becoming estranged from him, and how the curve of their family relations and his creative life was coming to its inexorable nadir.

To be the wife of a great man is a heavy burden: it's not within everyone's grasp. She became neither a homemaker, busy all the while with her balls, nor a Muse, since she was indifferent to her husband's creative endeavors. And her beauty became a source of slavery for him. He had fallen in love with her physical endowments, and had no knowledge of any spiritual ones, being confident that his spirit would do for them both. When Natalya matured and fell in love, it became clear that her idol was not Pushkin.

She suffered in the marriage, too—from the intellectual gap that separated her from the poet, from his binges, from the fact that he didn't want to understand her. The absence of any complaint, a quiet persistence in the realization of her own interests, as opposed to his concerns, her private life in contradistinction to his life, and, finally, her patience—that was her achievement.

6. D'Anthes as her ideal and the problem of divorce

In the tale leading up to Pushkin's duel we will touch only upon aspects which have been given insufficient attention, to our mind. Having become the lover—probably for variety's sake, for his career, or riches—of the homosexual Hekkeren, who adopted him, D'Anthes never felt any love for him.

In the summer of 1834, Pushkin met Georges D'Anthes in a restaurant while he was staying in St. Petersburg without his wife. They made friends very quickly. Witty, resourceful, a lover of women and binging like Pushkin himself, D'Anthes hit it off with him and became welcome at his home. D'Anthes was well received by Natalya and her sisters.

This cliché situation with D'Anthes remains unclarified by virtue of the most important details of the conflict having been ignored, it seems to us. Paying court to the fair sex, in secret or out in the open, was an indispensable, important, and quite acceptable element of society life: a woman would suffer from an inferiority complex if there were no sexual claims made on her. As Gogol wrote, "every woman would expose her charms to the point where she could feel to her own conviction that they would be able to ruin a man."

And family members were no exceptions in these games. Lucky womanizers and temptresses were society's real heroes, legends about their escapades spread, and the luckless were eager to imitate them. The Pushkins, both husband and wife, behaved like the rest. The poet reproved his wife in his letters, warning against inordinate coquetry: "You're happy that the dogs run around after you with their tails in the air, sniffing at you like a bitch ..." At the same time, he made no limitations for himself, any more than any of his friends. Vyazemsky, for instance, as Nashchokin recalled, also ran after Pushkin's wife: "however, he was running after her just out of his man-of-the-world's habit of paying beauty its due."[48]

D'Anthes considered her a silly little thing, and chased after her totally without ceremony, until falling seriously in love. They corresponded, and, as D'Anthes admitted in court, his letters "by their phrases could arouse Pushkin's husbandly sensibilities." They would dance together at balls, now and again lingering together. Soon the whole of St. Petersburg was talking about the triangle.

The Frenchman excited Natalya like no other man before him. "He confused her," Pushkin himself noted, and then realized that D'Anthes's passion was not a joke. The mental equilibrium of the poet's wife collapsed, her coldness replaced by heat. D'Anthes seemed to be the man who had been created for her: the same age, handsome, understandable and close in his tastes, his temperament, his interests. "I have fun around him. I simply like him," she told Vera Vyazemskaya. And what does it mean, when a woman says "simply like him"?

She has fun around him, and not her husband! He became more interesting to her than Pushkin was. She lost control of the situation. Their encounters took place almost openly, and their love was mutual.[49] "Pushkin's wife, entirely innocent, had the imprudence to tell her husband everything, and just infuriated him," Aleksandra Vasilchikova told Pyotr Bartenev.[50] Aleksandrina poured oil on the fire. Having drawn close to Pushkin, she naturally found herself in conflict with her sister, which was quite humanly understandable, drawing Pushkin to her and willingly or unwillingly fanning the flames of passion with regard to D'Anthes and Natalya's affair.

The poet's wife voluntarily set off for a meeting with her lover at someone else's apartment. It would be fruitless to speculate what in reality happened in that bedroom. It remained the couple's secret. To trust the story told by Natalya herself, as her apologists do, is simply ridiculous. But whatever happened there in the room, activity in bed or an emotional dialogue—the crash of Pushkin's family life had not yet come.

Let's allow ourselves now to express a long-ago expounded point of view on the essence of this scandal, an essence that earlier was beyond the attention of any analysts. It wasn't the running after his wife that tore up Pushkin, it was the fact that D'Anthes's intentions grew from flirtation to something more serious. Now D'Anthes was in love with Pushkin's wife. And since she returned his affection, her husband was in both their ways. From the point of view of both lovers, Pushkin was superfluous. It is difficult to believe, but the fact is that the poet complained to Benckendorff about it in writing.

The moment that represents the sore point in their marriage had arrived. Pavel Vyazemsky, the poet's son, found his attention attracted to this turnaround in their relationship: the poet's rage overflowed its banks not because of D'Anthes's philanderings after his wife, but because of the baron's attempts to persuade Natalya to leave her husband completely, that is, we elaborate here, to become Natalya D'Anthes-Hekkeren.[51]

The high-society flirtation had come to an end. She did not come to a breakup with her husband, but she undoubtedly was being led to it. D'Anthes proposed marriage to the already-married Natalya. We know that such a rearrangement of figures can happen on life's chess-board.

Hekkeren senior, begging Pushkin's wife to take pity on his son, proposed a plan of escape abroad to her, under his diplomatic protection. Moreover, he spoke to her on this topic more than once. Ignoring Pushkin, they proposed to his wife that she follow Baron D'Anthes, with whom she had fallen in love and to whom she confessed that love. Before her opened a real opportunity to go with her beloved to Paris or to his parents' estate, Sultz, in Alsace, and there be officially wed.

Thus a threat of divorce, the very thing that he had earlier threatened his wife with in jest, overhung Pushkin. Divorce and his wife's departure abroad. With her children or without them, we don't know; but the question could not but have arisen both with the two who were proposing it to her, and with their mother, herself. If with the children, then this would have meant that the exit-denied Pushkin was never going to see his children again. Divorces were not that frequent in those days, but precedents existed in St. Petersburg society, and the Pushkins, both of them, knew about them.

Not long before this, the poet had described Onegin's proposal to Tatyana. The producer of a Prague Opera performance of *Eugene Onegin* that we managed to see caught the ironic tone in relation to the elderly general. The general enters the scene in a wheelchair, turning the wheels with his hands. But if we ignore this modernized approach, Pushkin had placed his favorite hero in D'Anthes's position. That is, that Onegin wants Tatyana to leave her unloved husband for him, he attempts to get them to divorce.

And here the status not just of a betrayed husband but of an abandoned one hung over Pushkin himself. Fortunately or unfortunately for Pushkin, Natalya never divorced him, but, nevertheless, the situation had already gone way too far.

In the summer of 1836, Natalya's other sister, Yekaterina Goncharova, who was in love with D'Anthes, pandered to Natalya's rendezvousing with D'Anthes, in order to see him more often. The situation became even more entangled, as D'Anthes, according to certain sources, was seeing Yekaterina Goncharova in order to meet with Pushkin's wife more often. As a result, Yekaterina Goncharova married D'Anthes. Nor was the issue resolved by D'Anthes's marriage to Yekaterina, undertaken, it is normally considered, in order to settle the conflict.

"But it was unlikely that Natalya Pushkina had any power to change anything in those days. Her more 'careful' behavior could only delay the outcome," considered Stella Abramovich.[52] It is difficult to agree with this statement. Surely it was important to delay the poet's death not just for months or weeks, but at least a few days? Even if there had been a infinitesimal chance of changing the course of events, surely his wife was obliged to try it? She either did not understand or did not want to change that course—and in that lay her indubitable tragedy.

Natalya Pushkina really did not know (she could scarcely have pretended not to know) either about the anonymous letter or even less about the forthcoming duel, which confirms how distant she was from him and from his friends. Otherwise she would have butted in, talked him out of it, raised a racket, thrown herself athwart her husband's path. She would have appealed to the emperor, and they would have sent policemen, and she would have saved both her husband and her admirer. What a terrible irony of fate: she hadn't been at home when was getting ready to go to the Chernaya brook, and she then tore past him in her carriage and from her nearsightedness failed to notice him heading off to his death.

Pushkin was dying, but Natalya called attention to herself with her strange behavior, having hysterics in the neighboring room. Ignorant of the upcoming duel, she was also now unaware of his real state after his wounding. Aleksandr Turgenev noted with amazement (in his diary): "He was in his death throes, and his wife found him to be in better condition than yesterday!" Before his cold body, in front of everyone, she begged his forgiveness, swearing that she had been faithful to him, cursing herself for ever letting D'Anthes chase after her.

Shchegolev and Veresayev, who collected vast amounts of material, place the blame for Pushkin's death squarely on his wife, and their arguments are very weighty. It is not the task of a historian to reproach, but, putting it mildly, Natalya Pushkina inadequately comprehended the full situation, and the poet himself over the course of years had never done anything in order somehow to graft this alien branch onto the tree of his life, his spirit, although he was twice her age and possessed no small experience in life.

It is nonsense to speculate how Pushkin's life would have gone if he hadn't met Natalya, or had met her earlier or later. It is also unclear how much longer his life would have been prolonged if he had managed to escape the duel with D'Anthes. The fact is that it wasn't death that was looking for him, but Pushkin who in his later years was persistently looking for death, and could have finished his life without any help from D'Anthes. Father Sergey Bulgakov was right: neither the miniscule D'Anthes nor the perfidious Hekkeren was guilty of Pushkin's death, but that path that he had set out upon in getting married. Catastrophe had shattered the Pushkin home long before the fateful duel. If he had thirsted for his enemy's blood ... But he wanted his friend's blood. He could have perished with equal success at an earlier time, when in his search for death he had challenged his friend Vladimir Sollogub to a duel, as well as Nikolay Repnin, and Semyon Khlyustin.

> I spied the enemy in a passionless judge,
> My betrayer—in a comrade, shaking
> My hand at the feast—all before me
> Seemed to me a traitor or a foe.

The shocking misanthropy of these words remained in the rough drafts of the peaceful and enlightened poem "Anew I visited," in fact, alongside the famous address "Hail, young tribe unknown!" Was Pushkin's death not the price he had to pay for getting married without achieving mutual love?

7. Natalya plus Nicholas

The poet's friend Pavel Nashchokin recalled that the tsar was chasing after Natalya "like he was a young subaltern." But this was all considerably more serious than the poet supposed. The hand shrinks from writing that even his friend Vasily Zhukovsky fulfilled the role of pimp. This is Zhukovsky's note to Natalya: "It seems to me that I clearly wrote to him [*to Pushkin—Y.D.*] about this evening's ball, about why he is not invited and you absolutely [*Zhukovsky's underlining—Y.D.*] have to come ... You absolutely must come."[53] "Absolutely," even more so, twice repeated, because the tsar obviously charged the teacher of his children, Zhukovsky, with securing Natalya's presence, and Pushkin would have been in their way, which is why he "is not invited."

Nicholas would sit next to her at dinner. In fact, for the sake of getting close to Natalya and for a better chance of chasing after her, the tsar made Pushkin a Gentleman of the Bedchamber, which gave the poet and his spouse entree to intimate imperial soirees in the Anichkov palace. In Pushkin's letters to his wife, we find discontented hints at the tsar's maneuverings: "Don't be a coquette with the tsar."

In reality, the "Natalya plus Nicholas" alliance was much simpler than it appears now. The situation was explained by the French writer Ach Gallet de Kultur, who lived in Russia and served as secretary to a rich grandee. "The tsar is an autocrat in his love affairs as well as in the rest of his deeds; if he picks out a woman on a stroll, at the theater, or in society, he says just one word to his duty adjutant. The spouses, if they are married, or the parents, if they are maidens, are given warning of the honor that has befallen them. There are no examples of this distinction being accepted otherwise but with an expression of the most respectful acknowledgement. In equal measure, there are no extant examples of dishonored husbands or fathers not profiting from their disgrace. 'Surely the tsar has encountered resistance on the part of the victim of his fancy?' I asked an obliging lady, clever and virtuous, who had informed me of these details. 'Never!' she answered, with an expression of extreme amazement. 'How would that be possible?' 'But, watch out, your answer gives me the right to ask you the same question.' 'The explanation embarrasses me a lot less than you think; I would comply, like everyone. More than that, my husband would never forgive me if I refused.'[54] It is curious testimony, even if it was being laid on thick.

Pushkin was probably the only exception. Natalya, flirting with the tsar, tried to keep her distance. However, Nicholas wasn't in a hurry. And if he had been, what could the poet have done? As a literary exercise, one could propose a composition for students on the topic of "Alexander Pushkin Challenges Nicholas I to a Duel." Mikhail Lunin challenged Grand Duke Constantine to a duel, but he wasn't exactly the tsar. In real life, Pushkin would have had to shut his eyes to what was happening or have a duel all by himself. We'll say here what has long been on our mind: should we, perhaps, consider Pushkin's duel as the equivalent of suicide?

Nicholas, busy with other women, realized perfectly well that the bird was never going to fly very far from its cage. There is yet another proof of the lack of any affair with the tsar during Pushkin's lifetime: Natalya would scarcely have given in to D'Anthes and secretly been meeting him if she was already the emperor's lover at that moment.

The emperor took care of Pushkin's enormous debts and provided financially for his widow and children after the poet's death. When she returned to St. Petersburg two years later, Nicholas came by Natalya's to see the children. It seems unlikely that her love affair with the tsar started at that very time.

However, sometime after the young widow's return to St. Petersburg, suddenly her triumph, so to speak, was sanctioned from above, and society's negative attitude toward her changed immediately. On Christmas Eve, Pushkin's widow and his majesty were buying children's gifts together in a store. The earlier society life full of temptation, fun, flirtation, and conquest had turned her head. A court artist sent by the tsar painted her portrait in biblical costume. That was, most likely, the beginning of her intimacy with his majesty.

Modest Gofman, for instance, considered these two people's affair to have been gossip. But Natalya's daughter Aleksandra Arapova felt that she was

Nicholas I's daughter. This is considered to be her own conjecture, but, in principle, such a hypothesis could be checked today by genetic means.

The mythological conception, based on a range of literary works that we'll name later, superimposes Natalya's second marriage on her first one, one more important to Pushkin studies. In these works, Pushkin's shade is constantly beside Natalya in her second marriage: she confides in the poet, preserves his manuscripts, publishes his works, now and again repeats by heart his old letters to her, and their children read only Pushkin's fairy tales. General Pyotr Lanskoy, in this model, is some kind of appendage to his wife and her dead husband; for us, she remains the widow of the great poet, in her second marriage. However, at the heart of Pushkin's widow's re-marriage lies an intrigue, the understanding of which will throw light on the romance of Nicholas and Natalya Pushkina.

Pyotr Pletnev half-jokingly asked the young widow on her return from the countryside if she were going to be remarried soon—after all, Pushkin had told her to do it in two years. Her answer was that she, first of all, was not going to get married, and, secondly, no-one would have her. Pletnev gave Natalya some advice: to answer either the one thing or the other, but better the second, so that she could say that it was simply the wish of fate, in case she had to deviate from it.

Despite her numerous admirers, the widow remained unmarried for her two years' residence in the country, and another five years after returning to St. Petersburg. In 1844, a contemporary of Pushkin's, a horse-guardsman, Major-General Pyotr Lanskoy, had in store an appointment as commander of a regiment in a dim and distant province, when all of a sudden he was appointed commander of a Life Guards Cavalry regiment, whose colonel-in-chief was the emperor himself.

Lanskoy proposed to Natalya, and she accepted right away. They were afforded a luxurious apartment at state expense. Nicholas wanted to stand in for her father at their wedding, but Natalya insisted that the wedding should proceed modestly, without attracting any attention. The tsar sent a precious necklace as a bridal present, and informed them that he would baptize their first child. For the baptism, the emperor arrived at their home in Strelno. Now and again he would lavish favors on Lanskoy and his wife.

In high society, relationships like this were understood immediately. Under these circumstances, public opinion, that—as we mentioned before—had been set

against Natalya, changed. Those who had disapproved of Natalya started seeking her friendship. Pushkina-Lanskaya was putting on a party for the regiment's officers. When General Lanskoy reported to the tsar on business, the latter asked: "I heard that there's going to be a dance at your house?
I hope you won't avoid inviting your colonel-in-chief!" At the ball, the emperor went to the children's room and put the little girl on his lap, kissing and petting her. When they were getting ready an album for the tsar on the occasion of the 50th anniversary of the regiment, Nicholas gave an order that a portrait of Lanskoy's wife be given pride of place next to the commander's. In his marginal comment on this story of the regiment's album, Veresayev puts two exclamation points, and asks, "!!What does his wife have to do with this?"[55]

But a still more important detail was revealed after Nicholas's death. His valet opened the inside lid of his gold watch and saw a miniature portrait of Natalya there. "So there would be no awkwardness in the family, the valet took away the watch. Even if this is just a legend, there is nothing unlikely in the fact that marriage to Lanskoy covered up the intimate relations of the lonely, widowed beauty with the emperor, and probably the fact of their child.

Her second marriage was successful and seems to have been happy. In contrast with life with her first, exit-denied husband, the general's wife began going abroad, taking the cure in Nice. The advantages of marriage continued to benefit her second husband: soon Lanskoy was promoted to adjutant-general, and afterwards appointed chief of the 1st Cavalry Division, and then as Petersburg governor-general and chairman of the commission on trials and hearings in all political cases.

But the first time Lanskoy saw her, according to Natalya's daughter's version, was when, in 1836, Idalya Poletika instructed him to walk up and down the street in front of the apartment where she had arranged a secret rendezvous between D'Anthes and Pushkin's wife. Poletika's lover at that time, Lanskoy was keeping an eye out to make sure that D'Anthes wasn't disturbed. D'Anthes begged Natalya to surrender to him, he pulled out his pistol and declared that he would shoot himself. In Natalya's own words, a girl, their hostess's daughter, entered the room, and Natalya supposedly threw herself on her. Here's Veresayev's commentary on this episode in Lanskoy's life: "Of course, he realized that those sorts of secret rendezvous were arranged not for Platonic conversations on elevated themes, and he must have gotten an unambiguous impression of the woman who would agree to such meetings."[56]

According to another argument advanced by Soviet Pushkin scholars, Lanskoy could not have been observing Natalya's rendezvous with D'Anthes, because he was not in St. Petersburg at that moment.[57] From other memoirs it appears that Lanskoy was a good-hearted person and a stern commander. An obliging husband, quite the man of the world and a good family man as well, he was a placid alternative to Pushkin.

8. A second matchmaking-bureau experiment

We did a second experiment at the same matchmaking bureau in San Francisco. It was a search for the most acceptable marriage partner for Natalya in the circumstances of the year 1836, that is, the year of the Pushkins' conflict and potential divorce. We filled out forms for one woman and three men.

There were four main men in the life of Natalya Goncharova: Pushkin, D'Anthes, Romanov, and Lanskoy. We entered three of them into the computer of the matchmaking bureau, because Lanskoy showed up in Natalya's life seven years after Pushkin's death. The question then is about a romantic rectangle. Let's stipulate that it's laughable even to think about the tsar getting divorced and marrying Natalya Pushkina; however, it is impossible to dismiss Nicholas artificially from the situation that arose, and our competition, as we have already said, is utterly hypothetical.

There is a whole range of data that is not included here, for instance, the height of Nicholas I and D'Anthes—both were considerably taller than Pushkin. To save space, we won't go into all the hitches that developed. For instance, for Nicholas, we indicated "the Winter Palace" in answer to the question "place of residence and living conditions." The computer demanded clarification of the meaning of Winter Palace, and then asked where number 0809461 (Nicholas) lived during the summer.

Search for Registration Number 0809456
Surname: Goncharova
Name: Natalya

Age: 24
Nationality: Russian
Racial origin: white
Appearance: A (beautiful)
Education: at home (French, dancing)
Profession: housewife, mother of four
Position: not serving
Material means: insufficiency of money
Hobbies: fashion, dancing, a little horseback riding

Candidate 0809457

Surname: Pushkin
Name: Alexander
Age: 37
Nationality: Russian
Racial origin: white and African mix
Appearance: B (ugly)
Education: Tsarskoye Selo Lyceum
Profession: poet, magazine editor
Position: gentleman of the bedchamber (compulsory explication for computer: in receipt of a research grant, that is, a government subsidy as a State historiographer)
Material means: insufficiency of means
Hobbies: playing cards, billiards, drawing, traveling, long walks, sauna, shooting pistols.

Candidate 0809459

Surname: D'Anthes-Hekkeren
Name: Georges-Charles
Age: 24
Nationality: French
Racial origin: white
Appearance: A (handsome)
Education: Paris military academy
Profession: soldier
Position: lieutenant in a Guards Cavalry regiment (officer)
Material means: sufficiency of means
Hobbies: high society life, dancing

Candidate 0809461

Surname: Romanov
Name: Nicholas
Age: 40
Nationality: Russian
Racial origin: white
Appearance: C (ordinary)
Education: at home, with specially selected Russian and foreign teachers
Profession: soldier, supreme officer, politician
Position: emperor
Material means: rich

Hobbies: horseback riding, dancing, literary criticism

The most acceptable partner for number 0809456, that is, Natalya, was named by the computer as number 0809459—Baron D'Anthes. A reserved candidate for Natalya was number 0809461—Nicholas. As for number 0809457 (Pushkin), for the given woman (Natalya), he was rejected by the computer as an unacceptable candidate for her in general.

For an additional fee, we arranged with the matchmaking bureau to continue the search for number 0809457 (Pushkin). Goncharova and Sofya Pushkina had already fallen by the wayside. To the remaining Ushakova and Olenina they added in the entire data base of the matchmaking bureau.

Now, casting aside numbers 0809462 (that is Yekaterina Ushakova) and 0809458 (Anna Olenina), the computer proposed as Pushkin's bride number 0803172, as more suitable than the previous two. As it turned out, this number was that of a graduate student at the Slavic languages department of the University of California at Berkeley. It appeared that this grad student was of Russian origin (Jewish, from Odessa). The matchmaking bureau refused to reveal the name of the lucky girl.

9. The creation of the myth

Boris Pasternak once noted that from the point of view of common sense, of course Pushkin would have been better off marrying someone from among the ranks of Pushkin scholars.[58] The Soviet myth of the exemplary wife of the national poet, as we said before, received a new twist in the 1970s and 1980s. It was not truth that Pushkin scholars were busy with at that time, but something else. "The correct understanding of what Natalya Nikolayevna, Pushkin's wife, represents has principal significance."[59] We won't pay any attention to why Natalya Pushkina in that sentence was a *what* and not a *who*. The question is to the point: what does "correct" understanding mean?

Today, Pushkin's wife occupies first place among his friends. For example, in the two-volume edition of *Pushkin's Friends*, 73 pages are devoted to her, Pyotr Vyazemsky and Vasily Zhukovsky 60 each, Anton Delvig 49, Aleksandr Turgenev and Sergey Sobolevsky 43 each, and the rest even less than that.[60] In the opinion of I. M. Obodovskaya and M. A. Dementyev, who found Pushkina-Lanskaya's letters to her brother in the 1970s (an indubitable service by them), that correspondence gives the impression that Natalya was a great figure. In our opinion, these new-found letters confirm her narrow outlook, practicality, and lack of spirituality.

The leitmotif of the letters and the stimulus for their composition was mostly a lack of money. Only once did Natalya mention her husband's creative work: "... I can see how sad and dispirited he is, how he doesn't sleep at night and consequently is unable, in such a state, to work to obtain for us our means of existence: in order for him to create, his mind has to be free." This reason, doubtless, is a mechanical repetition of her husband's words, repeated daily. That is her entire understanding of the goals of the labor of the greatest poet of Russia, whom fate had joined with Natalya: "to obtain for us our means."

Obodovskaya and Dementyev, indiscriminately reproaching the multitude of eyewitnesses—Pushkin's friends and acquaintances, Pushkin scholars from Annenkov and Bartenev to Shchegolev and Veresayev, as well as, in passing, Tsvetayeva and Akhmatova—for bias, are censoring history, throwing out all opinions that don't fit their iconography. If they mention them at all, it is just to inform that these are "slanderous fabrications, dominant until now in Pushkin scholarship."[61] Having labored over their work, the authors shamelessly come to the conclusion that "Pushkin and his wife were unusually close, spiritually."[62]

If it is agreed that Goncharova was a significant personality even outside the six years of her marriage to Pushkin, then her biography would not end with the poet's death. However, in the already-mentioned work by Obodovskaya and Dementyev, *N. N. Pushkina*, 288 pages are devoted to the heroine's youth and the seven years from her first marriage, and 57 pages to the 26 years of her subsequent life, including her second marriage, which lasted for 19 years; which, in fact, proves that Pushkina-Lanskaya was not interesting as an autonomous personality.

Pushkin easily rededicated certain poems or parts of poems written for other women; for instance, first to Anna Olenina, and then to another fiancée, Yekaterina Ushakova. The first redaction of "On the hills of Georgia lies the night gloom" was written by the poet for his old love Maria Rayevskaya. Noting the "indubitable" readdress of Pushkin's second redaction of the poem "to the one who two years later would become his wife, the mother of his children", Dmitry Blagoy elegantly wrote, "The succession of the two versions was the peculiar baton-relay of his heart."[63]

It appears that this myth reaches its zenith in the apocryphal papers by Agniya Kuznetsova, the wife of a formerly well-known head of the Writers' Union of the Soviet Union, Georgy Markov. These were entitled "Under the Storms of Cruel Fate," "But I Love Your Soul," and "Dolly," later joined together into the monograph *My Madonna*, and published in massive press runs with glossy white paper in classy bindings.

In the first of these papers, Kuznetsova makes up a link between her own relatives and Goncharova: it appears that Kuznetsova's serf ancestor Pyotr had been in love with Natalya, and the only thing Pushkin's wife did was talk with affection about this *muzhik*, a representative of the simple folk, so to speak a more-correct alternative to D'Anthes.

In the guise of historical discoveries, whole fairy-tales get contrived out of comments made in passing by the poet or his wife, out of the life of the poet's wife, and, even wider afield—the activities of the whole Goncharov family. It appears, for instance, that the fate of the British empire depended entirely on the business of Natalya's relatives. "The whole British fleet sailed using Goncharov sails."[64]

This juggling of history lies in the fact that, for the construction of a positive personality for the great poet's wife in the years 1831-1837, materials from 1844 - 1863 in connection with her second marriage were mostly used. The experience, knowledge, and quality of character of the mature woman of that second marriage, one who had lived through tragedy, of a mother who had borne seven children, is mechanically transferred onto the young Natalya. The things that she understood, the way she behaved *afterwards*, having already gotten older, get postulated as the things that she understood and did *before*. For instance, in 1854, when she and her husband came to Vyatka, they took an active part in getting Mikhail Saltykov-Shchedrin out of his exile. It is difficult to imagine that Natalya would have engaged in a similar socially significant affair in her youth.

Not all the evidence in the aggregate, but principally Pushkin's opinion, was considered to be objective in appraisal of Natalya Pushkina. But since Pushkin's canonization, everything that he said or wrote about his wife is honored as historically exact. It happens that Pushkin's letters are the "truth about the poet's wife," as proposed by V. V. Kunin, and everything else, as he puts it, is "putdown and pompous triviality."[65] Let's suppose that historians could effect their biographies of historical personalities like, say, Peter the Great, Stalin, Hitler, or their wives, depending exclusively on their own words.

We'd like to underscore our point of view here: that nobody else but Pushkin himself idealized Natalya (which is characteristic of anyone in love), and that means that it was he who gave birth to and, as we now say, put into circulation the myth of Tasha, as he called her:

> ... the Creator
> Sent you down to me, my Madonna,
> The purest form of the purest charm.

Without acknowledgement of Pushkin's brilliant mythmaking, there can be no objective attitude towards his evaluation of his wife, which means an objective evaluation of her, too. Mythology was a part of his courtship pattern; it assisted in him in achieving his victories. As applied to himself, Pushkin rarely gave cause for myth; he was realistic. But the women, including his wife, throughout all the changes in their lives he continued mythologizing to the very end.

However, it seems to us that Pushkin's mythologizing, taken seriously by certain Pushkin scholars, was ironic. The poet wrote: "Woman, says Galliani, *est un animal naturellement faible et malade* [*is an animal by nature weak and sickly*]. What kind of helpmeets and workers are you? You work only with your legs at balls and help your husbands' squandering." You have to read the "you" as singular instead of plural, that is, relating personally to his spouse, because Pushkin had no such opinion of other women. In his letters he talks to his wife the way you would to stubborn children.

The competitive element in any description of her appearance was also introduced by Pushkin himself, who called her "the premiere European beauty," as if she had participated in some European beauty contest.[66] Mrs. Pushkin's priority in beauty on an all-European level was the beginning. A century and a half later that competitive element was used for glorification of her achievements in various fields.

She and her sisters in childhood rode horses through the village of Polotnyany Zavod. In one of her letters to her husband, she informs him that they were out horse-riding and everyone was looking at them in admiration. In the Soviet mythology of the 1980s, it comes out like this: "All of them from youth were perfect equestrians" and "now the best of all in St. Petersburg."[67]

In a letter from the end of September, 1832, Pushkin wrote to his wife: "Thank you, my soul, for learning to play chess." We don't know if the poet himself played chess well, but his heroes played like this:

> Above the chessboard
> Leaning elbows on the table, sometimes
> They sit, thinking deeply,
> And Lensky, in distraction,
> Takes his own rook with his pawn.

Baron Boris Vrevsky wrote Aleksey Vulf in 1835: "In Trigorskoye and Golubevo we play chess, and since I play very badly, he [*Pushkin—Y.D.*] gives up one of his bishops to me beforehand." It means that Pushkin played better than the poor player Vrevsky. However, Aleksey Vulf played better than the poet. "Once playing chess with me, putting my king and queen in check with his knight," Pushkin wrote, "he told me, '*Cholera morbus* has approached our borders and within 5 years will be among us.'"

Natalya learned all the moves of the chess pieces with her sisters, which is what Pushkin praised her for, as you would praise an adolescent. In the 1980s, we read: "Pushkin's advice to his wife to learn chess fell on fertile soil: according to the testimony of a contemporary, Natalya became the best chess player in St. Petersburg."[68] Then she enters the world chess level, playing "with a foreigner, who was the recipient of glory on the scale of a grand master, and defeated him." Neither the name of the foreign champion nor the contemporary are supplied.[69]

She achieves even greater success now in literature and journalism, although nothing was known about it in her own lifetime. Once, it is clear from a letter to her from Pushkin, she composed some verse that she sent to her husband. He answered simply "I don't read your verse," and asked her to write to him in prose. She ordered paper from her brother for her husband. He sent her on an errand to hand over some manuscripts, but she confused Koltsov with Gogol. He set her to writing out the French text of the notes of Catherine II. She wrote out nine pages, but made so many mistakes that Pushkin refused any further services from her.[70] Her written Russian, judging by a letter that has come down to us, was even worse. That, it appears, is all that we know about her contribution to Russian letters.

> She knew Russian poorly,
> Didn't read our magazines,
> And expressed herself with difficulty
> In her native tongue.

Although this had been written before meeting Natalya, it makes you think of the kind of young lady she was.

In the myth she is not only a poetess, but becomes a journalist and an editor, her husband-publisher's right hand. When Pushkin started publishing his magazine, wrote Nikolay Rayevsky, "she practically filled the job of editorial secretary for *Sovremennik*."[71] Here is a typical Soviet formulation ("editorial secretary," that is, an experienced journalist-administrator in charge of all preparation for publishing the magazine) applied by a Pushkin scholar to the magazine edited by Pushkin.

In the myth, we discover her "considerable talent for mathematics." Even that Natalya could have become (in the subjunctive mood, if she had been a teacher) "a good pedagogue," and, doubtless, she was an ideal mother.

Finally, on the basis of the title of "Premiere Beauty of Europe" given to her by Pushkin, endless repetitions in Pushkin scholarly papers about her fantastic beauty turned from composition to composition to ideas about her holiness, her unearthly essence: she is "godlike," and even "there is a heavenly radiance around her."[72] On the threshhold of the two-hundredth anniversary of the poet's birthday, his wife's icon has taken on a finished appearance in mass publications.

Skeptical voices in the matter of this lacquering of this woman's image have periodically rung out, but they have been drowned out by the chorus of official guardians of the poet's image. Thus, the inordinate elevation of the personality of the poet's wife did get mentioned; it was said that the study of her affords little towards our understanding of Pushkin. Boris Bursov wrote: "... in recent years they have almost made Natalya Nikolayevna into Pushkin's guardian angel around here." And he proposed a new approach to Natalya Pushkina:

> ... we have no basis (the most important would be necessity) either to extol or, so to speak, to stomp on her. We should be busy not with her, not with her personal qualities in general, but with how Pushkin and his wife's life together is reflected in the poet's verse and fate.[73]

That kind of formulation of the problem had been necessary for preceding stages of Pushkin scholarship. But the fact is that the poet's wife already occupied the shelves alongside him; a huge literature on her exists, both extolling her and, more modestly, stomping on her. Besides, the problem is not only with Natalya. Number 113, the poet's wife, did not by herself replace all the other women who set the tone of Pushkin's life.

The difference is not even in the fact that she bore his children—after all, he had an unknown number of children from other women, children that he himself called whoresons. The role of women who ignited the incandescence of the poet's passion, pouring out into magnificent lines, the impetus that each of them in her turn gave to the poet, as it has already been said, is impossible to overestimate—all of them together, and each of them separately.

From here it follows that Pushkin without the women that he loved, including his wife, of course, is not complete enough for study. She is supposed to interest us more than the others, since it was she who became an icon, a symbol, a myth parallel to his. Pushkin gave her number 113, but Russian literary criticism corrected the poet by making her number one. The role of other women is artificially diminished, so that his wife would stand out in higher relief. Except that no memorial has ever been set up to her. However, suggestions to place her somewhere at the poet's feet in a monument have been made.

The folk-culture ritual of swearing eternal love and fidelity on the wedding day at poetically-significant spots is evidenced not at Natalya's grave, however, but in Putna, at the grave of a passing girlfriend of Pushkin and many of his friends, Anna Kern. There we were witnesses to a parody ritual many times.[74] Natalya's headstone has her name as Lanskaya, which is logical. But at Anna's her name isn't Markova-Vinogradskaya, after her second marriage, but Kern, and the famous Pushkin poem is chiseled onto her marble plaque.

In textbooks, in digests and mass literature, as well as in part of Pushkin studies, the myth about the ideal Pushkin—the happy family man—continues to get elaborated. And the myth about his wife, his faithful comrade-in-arms, the caring mother and guardian of hearth fires of the premier poet of Russia, his co-author, and even a poetess—after all she once scribbled something in rhyme in an unpreserved letter—and the myth of her innocence in Pushkin's death, and the myth of the platonic relationship between her and Nicholas. A little bit more restrained, but unfortunately far from being objective and therefore mythological in essence, is the appraisal of the poet's wife remaining in the anthology *Legends and Myths About Pushkin*, put out by the research fellows at the Pushkin House, without any censorship or ideological pressure.[75]

The following, as well, seems humanly curious. All my live, willingly or unwillingly, observing the numerous wives of Russian writers, I gradually came to the conclusion that they can be divided (although, of course, the division is hypothetical) into three categories.

First category: the muse-wife. Such a spouse is a confederate, a co-author, the first reader, adviser, stenographer, typist, editor, proofreader, etc. Examples: Sofya Tolstaya, Anna Dostoyevskaya, Nadezhda Mandelshtam, Vera Nabokova ... If you added today's extant writers, you would find a good few of this sort of wife.

Second category: the neutral wife. She isn't a bother, but doesn't help, either, nor impedes, but is little interested or out of politeness accepts the writing process like a disability. Evidently, this is the most widespread category.

Third category: the bothersome wife, distracting from literature, pulling down, demanding engagement in something more practical that affords more money. Finally, if it is impossible to sell it, she throws her husband's archive onto the trash-heap and quickly marries an upstanding soldier or bureaucrat. It seems that such an extreme is a rarity.

Doubtless, there could be in-between variants—life is richer than any schematic.

And, anyway, appraisals of the poet's wife made by anyone who has ever written about her also fall into these categories. But what does the reader, free of anthologized dogmas, think? Which one should we put Natalya Pushkina in?

A Divorce for Pushkin's Tatyana, *née* Larina

It is predictable that the reader will protest on principle, since we're going to be talking about what is acknowledged *not* to exist in the novel *Eugene Onegin*. Therefore, as a compromise, let's elaborate on our title: this is a meditation on why there is no divorce in Pushkin's novel, and if there *could* have been one.

The stimulus to take on this question was afforded us by Pushkin himself. For the epigraph to his eighth chapter, he took two lines from Byron's cycle *Poems of Separations*:

> Fare thee well, and if for ever
> Still for ever fare thee well.

The argument over what the epigraph is hinting at has gone on for many years, and various conclusions have been drawn. Let's emphasize just one fact by itself: in describing Onegin and Tatyana's final conversation, Pushkin had *Poems of Separations* in mind.

1. A Drama of Misunderstanding or a Parody?

Fyodor Dostoyevsky has already noted in a lecture on Pushkin in 1880 that "the question of why Tatyana did not go off with Onegin has for us, at least in our literature, its own utterly distinct kind of history ..."[1] The succeeding century substantially increased the volume of discussion on this topic.

Two approaches to *Eugene Onegin* as a romantic novel have been taken in the past, and, from our point of view, they sound like some banal joke about pessimists and optimists: it is either a novel about *happiness that doesn't come to pass* or it is a novel about *love that does*.[2] The theme of construction and destruction of the family is afloat throughout the novel. It is what the main characters are engaged in. Pushkin mentions marital problems between Tatyana Larina's parents, and with Olga Larina after Vladimir Lensky's death, when she leaves the novel on a cavalryman's arm. Onegin's parents had their own difficulties: his father "held three balls annually and finally squandered his fortune," but his mother was absent, for some reason. Complaints about family life are heard even from the nanny and Vanya.

Marital relations almost never interested the young Pushkin: free love was more important. His initial idea was a plan for a novel to be "something like *Don Juan*" (in a letter to Vyazemsky of November 4, 1823), and the Russian Don Onegin, judging from his literary heredity, was simply obliged to chase after every passing skirt, like Pushkin himself. Even the Goettingen romantic

> . . . Lensky, of course without
> A wish to tie the wedding bonds,
> Warmly wanted to be bosom
> Buddies with Onegin.

The "of course" here, written in Odessa in 1823, conforms entirely to Pushkin's state at that time, and reflects not Lensky's attitude to marriage but that of the poet himself. It never happened this way, but let's ask ourselves how it might have been if Onegin had reciprocated Tatyana's feelings at the beginning of the novel. Most likely, an early marriage to Tatyana wouldn't have lasted long—the hero himself said that to her. They would have split up because of Eugene's restlessness and ennui, and Tatyana would have gone back to her parents—where else could she have gone? What is more important is that at the end of the novel there is a sort of collision of heredities in operation, one mentioned by Pushkin at the very beginning: Tatyana's mother, primed with tales of romantic adulteries by Princess Alina,

> . . . pining for another,
> Who, heart and soul,

> Pleased her much, much more:
> This Grandison was renowned: a dandy,
> Gambler, and a sergeant in the Guards.

And her mother, having wed against her will,

> Broke down at first and wept,
> Near divorced her spouse; then
> Grew accustomed and content.
> Habit, from above, is given to us
> As substitute for happiness.

This last thought, from the second chapter of *Onegin*, was borrowed by Pushkin from Chateaubriand's novel *René*, and amounts to—secondarily, as if closing the circle in chapter eight—the culmination of Tatyana Larina's life. However, Onegin is not a lazy stay-at-home like Dmitry Larin. Pushkin stressed Onegin's "antifamilialness" on several occasions.[3] The young bachelor cannot wait for the death of his uncle, in order to inherit his fortune and start throwing it around. He wants to sound utterly cynical at the beginning about the married state, which "would be torture." The seriousness of other people's love, on the whole, little bothers this egocentric. If he hadn't been lazy, he wouldn't have refrained from taking Olga away from Lensky out of sheer boredom, something that he did start to do in passing. His alternative to marriage was a stereotypical circle: falling in love, achieving his goal, cooling off, replacement of the object of his affection, and everything "without purpose, without effort."

Onegin, in Dostoyevsky's words, himself represents a type of "unhappy wanderer in his native land." Dostoyevsky was contradicted on the grounds that he, in calling for moral perfection, was avoiding the political reasons for the existence of that sort of person in Russia. Arguing with Dostoyevsky, Gleb Uspensky rated Aleko and Onegin as wanderers cut off from their people, rootless, strangers in their own land.[4]

Pushkin scholars' energy is commendable in proving that Onegin was a model of the shining ideal of a fighter for just causes: "The formula of Onegin's country life was that 'freedom and peace are the substitute for happiness.' The content of this formula (in its higher, spiritual manifestation) is a working-out, an elaboration of an advanced social world-view..."[5] But the very next thing that Onegin does is to call freedom "hateful" and say: "What a mistake I've made." A mistake in what, we scoff: that he didn't marry Tatyana, or ... that he didn't work out his advanced world view?

Vladimir Nabokov notes the duality of Pushkin's nature reflected in his two characters, Onegin and Lensky. But the both of them also unite Pushkin, the bifurcation flows together, fire and ice.[6] Nikolay Dobrolyubov in his famous article "What is Oblomovism?" turned his attention to the change in Onegin. By killing Lensky, he killed the romantic in himself, the part that was closest to Lensky; that is, he parted with the remnants of romanticism and enthusiasm in himself, his own youth. When at the end Onegin meets Tatyana again, the issue is not just that she occupies a different status and is unreachable, but that he himself is in a different status. The Onegin that she loved is also unreachable. He has thrown something away, possibly his own youth.

Let's take still another step: the young Pushkin is also unreachable by the end of the novel: he occupies another status, too. Dostoyevsky ascribes Aleko to Pushkin's first period, while *Onegin*'s beginning belongs to his first period, but the end to his second period. From this, chapter eight of *Onegin* can be considered to have been written by a different or, more precisely, a changed Pushkin. Now, marriage for both of them—the hero and his creator—is the way to get across into another circle of life.

It has been mentioned more than once that Tatyana's progression from unsuccessful love to a marriage of convenience may be looked upon as the central line of the novel. What with the lack of suitors in the countryside, Lensky, suited to her in essence, chooses (in breach of the tradition of marriage of elders before juniors) her younger, more cheerful, sister. Onegin also flirts with Olga. The one that Tatyana falls in love with becomes the murderer of her sister's fiancé. In Tatyana's dream, a bear helps her get across a brook to unite with Onegin. Onegin declares "It is mine!" to the monsters. In psychoanalyzing Tatyana's dream, the neuter gender "it" used by Pushkin (*moye*) instead of the logically appropriate feminine gender "she" (*moya*) is explainable simply as referent of the neuter-gender word "body" (*tyelo*).[7] In Tatyana's dream, Eugene sets her down on a bench, and now *it* is about to happen, but at this inappropriate moment, uninvited, Lensky and Olga appear.

Aleksandr Potebnya views Tatyana's fateful history from the point of view of traditional wedding symbols. Tatyana doubtlessly is looking for an opportunity to join with Onegin. The unfreezing brook is a complex of impeding circumstances. And, according to ritualistic Russian tradition, it would have been possible to predict Tatyana's unloved betrothed-to-be, the general, even before Pushkin wrote the ending.[8] Turbin noted that both sisters' marrying soldiers in particular was also foretold in the novel:

> Serving-girls from all the estate
> Told their young ladies' fortunes,
> And every year promised them
> Husbands soldierly and a-march.

"And it all came out as it had been predicted by some Akulka or other: both Tatyana and Olga obtained their soldierly husbands—the nameless Uhlan and the nameless general."[9]

The unpersuasiveness of the image of Tatyana, in Gleb Uspensky's opinion, was that she "commits herself to the mercy of the old-man-general," even though she is in love with the wanderer. Uspensky accused Dostoyevsky, who extolled Tatyana's deed, of "advocacy of an stupid, forced, crude sacrifice." Yevgeny Boratynsky wrote to Pushkin about the novel that "old and new Russia pass before your eyes."[10]

A paradox is visible in the fact that Tatyana is probably a representative of the new Russia, but her behavior is in the course of the old Russia. Dmitry Pisarev sarcastically removes Tatyana from her pedestal of a positive heroine and ideal for the fact that (1) she falls in love with Onegin without having even spoken to him, (2) she marries for convenience, and (3) loving a man who loved her, rejected him. As the Pushkin scholar Douglas Clayton noted, "Pisarev's function [is] to educate the Russian reading public, to raise its consciousness.[11]

Why did Tatyana reject Onegin? That's a naive question, but the answers to it are very serious, and they help to analyze the potential possibility of her divorce.

According to Vissarion Belinsky, who was one of the first to advance the ideological point of view of the novel and its ending, "vexation and futility played their part in Onegin's passion." The critic, who changed his opinions about Pushkin several times, noted that Tatyana had "a fear for her virtue," "a trepidation for her good name in society."[12] Belinsky wrote:

> ...*Was given*, but did not *give herself!* Eternal loyalty—*to whom and in what way*? Loyalty to those kinds of relations that are a profanation of the sense and purity of femininity—because certain relations, unsanctified by love, are immoral to a high degree.

Tatyana is created by nature for love, "but society transformed her into something else."

How much better is Pushkin's Maria Kochubey—Belinsky values her higher than Tatyana Larina. What a society! Why did it affect Tatyana and not Maria? "What, beside her, is the over-glorified and so-admired by everyone and still much-admired Tatyana—that mixture of country dreaminess and city prudence?" In a letter to Vasily Botkin, Belinsky again wrote, "From the time that she [*Tatyana—Y.D.*] hopes to be eternally faithful to her general, her wonderful image turns dark." And yet again: "her brain was asleep," "she did not have those regular occupations and diversions characteristic of an educated life," she was "a passionate, deeply feeling, and at the same time underdeveloped creation, hermetically sealed up in the dark emptiness of her intellectual existence," "the poor girl didn't know what she was doing," etc. In a word, Tatyana is a "moral embryo."

Dostoyevsky built his own ideological model: this heroine was a symbol of virtuous Russia, a type of "Russian beauty, coming straight out of the Russian spirit, abiding in folk truth." Tatyana rejects Onegin, a type

> unbelieving in its [*Russia's—Y.D.*] native soil and native strength, in the end negating both Russia and himself (that is, society, his own intellectual stratum that had arisen on our native soil), unwilling to do anything with others and suffering sincerely.

In other words, according to Dostoyevsky, Eugene Onegin had happiness neither in himself, in his people, or in Christ, but Tatyana did. Tatyana stands firmly on her soil, but Onegin is a spiritual pauper. Do you get it? Slightly modernizing it, Onegin is a stranger, an enemy of the people, and the patriot Tatyana must not love him. "Pushkin would have done even better if he had called the poem by Tatyana's name and not Onegin's..." Only after his political verdict does Dostoyevsky turn to the moral essence of the rejection by the general's wife:

"Can a man base his happiness on the unhappiness of another?" Apollon Grigoryev also thought that Pushkin as a "highly moral poet creates an ideal image of Tatyana," who lives "holding on to the moral ideals of her ancestors in her heart of hearts, like a cherished treasure." Tatyana is close to "earthy morality," while Onegin has been uprooted from that soil.[13]

Yuri Tynyanov turns his attention to Tatyana's folksy-simple name and her idealistic world (Clarisse, Julie, Delphina). She should have fallen in love with Lensky, Tynyanov thought, but then the whole novel would have been gutted. Dmitry Blagoy has no doubt about Onegin's "sincere passion," but declares that Tatyana, rejecting Eugene, "is, basically, essentially right."[14] Such speculations of "right" versus "not right" represent a Soviet approach. Grigory Gukovsky and Georgy Makogonenko, to the contrary, considered Tatyana to be in the wrong. She never discerned Onegin's love, revealing her misunderstanding of whom she loved.[15] M. Umanskaya appealed to Belinsky to show that Tatyana is in the right, since "a petty sense of genteel pride and vanity" is what underlies Onegin's proposal, basically.[16] And absolutely without any sense of proportion, Turbin speculates about some sort of higher rightness of this heroine: "Tatyana is the founder, the initiator of some new kind of morality, invisible to those around her, that is, a miracle unrecognized by them."[17]

The variety of points of view is truly broad—from tragedy all the way to parody. Thus Nabokov saw a drama of misunderstanding in the finale of *Eugene Onegin*. Victor Shklovsky, on the other hand, considered that Pushkin simply parodied Tatyana, that the poet was joking.[18] "The irony can be easily tracked throughout all the levels of the novel," the modern critic Gumennaya continued this train of thought, considering that whenever Tatyana comes under analysis, that irony is forgotten. The poet parodies genteel love relations; Tatyana's lifestyle is depicted with scorn. In the novel, there is no idealization of her of the type found in Pushkin studies.[19]

Clayton has another view. "The sentimental scheme which Dostoyevsky imposes on *Onegin* reaches its apogee in his interpretation of Tatyana's rejection of Onegin." In Clayton's opinion, Dostoyevsky, sentimentalizing Pushkin's heroine and turning her into an ideal, is simply liberating Tatyana's family relations with her husband from any kind of sexual context.

But it was not Dostoyevsky after all but Pushkin himself—that eternally sexually obsessed person—who virtuously eliminates the topic of sex from all the relations of his heroes, not foreseeing that in our day the non-sexual relationship between Onegin and Tatyana would seem suspicious to a Japanese Pushkin scholar. "One would think that the two protagonists Onegin and Lensky do not engage in merely friendly relations," writes K. Kasama. "Especially with regard to Onegin ... And here one cannot but feel a psychological drama of abnormal homosexual love and hatred ... Pushkin probably hints at Onegin's homosexual inclinations and says that Tatyana understood everything."[20] So that is why Tatyana rejected Onegin: he was in a sexual bond with Lensky! And Pushkin scholars have been wracking their brains for a hundred and fifty years ...

Long before Flaubert, who announced "*Emma—c'est moi*," Wilhelm Küchelbecker wrote that "Pushkin is like Tatyana."[21] Tatyana's rejection, according to Andrei Sinyavsky, comes from the fact that Pushkin's Muse is closely associated with sweet young ladies of the type that always aroused the poet. "Onegin's luckless partner," "the general's cold-blooded wife," Tatyana Larina was Pushkin's greatest Muse. Sinyavsky comes to a conclusion from this:

> I even think this is the reason she never got together with Onegin and preserved her fidelity to her unloved husband, in order to have more free time to read and re-read Pushkin and pine for him. Pushkin, so to speak, was keeping her for himself." Pushkin was keeping "her a virgin, his chosen one, who, like a nun, is given to neither the one nor the other, but only to a third, only to Pushkin.[22]

Pushkin's "I" can be found in all the protagonists of the novel. Lev Pushkin recalled about his brother: "he liked giving his own tastes and habits to his characters." An epigraph by Pushkin's friend Vyazemsky, "Both in a rush to live/And in a hurry to feel," describes Pushkin no less than his hero. "In Onegin's fourth song I have depicted my own life" (from a letter of May 27, 1826). His contemporaries' voices, saying "that I have sketched my own portrait," worried the author, and he of course refused to acknowledge them. But this literary veil is transparent, easily penetrated. Nikolay Karamzin observed, "But what is more interesting (just between us) to a man than himself?"[23]

2. The anti-Tatyana

The Boldino autumn of 1830 saw two processes brought to an end simultaneously: the poet's bachelor life, and his work of many years on *Eugene Onegin*, a long and rich creative period and a bachelor life. Both of them were accomplished by a different Pushkin, the one who belonged to the beginning of the 1830s. He had now already been engaged for half a year. The forced stay in Boldino, in quarantine, afforded him the opportunity to re-examine his views, his passions, his desires. The reckless playboy had to transform himself into a settled househusband, a landlord, a bureaucrat.

There was one surprising premonition: at first he named Tatyana Larina, his favorite character, Natalya, ten years before his marriage, but crossed that name out as unsuitable for his favorite heroine's image. Now that name was coming to him, so to speak, in a living form. Creating the novel during the whole fundamental part of his mature life, Pushkin fashioned in it his earthly ideal of a woman, one that would eventually turn into the ideal model of his own future wife. His own, and not Onegin's.

In the year of Pushkin's marriage, an article called "Tverskoy Boulevard," by M. Makarov, appeared in *Moskovsky kaleydoskop*, and in it was a poem about people strolling down the boulevard:

> Here too is the half-drunk romantic;
> And the graying chief of classicism
> Cursed by Tatyana's singer,
> And the singer himself with his wife.

Whoever the classicist was who was catching abuse from Pushkin, the poet was here with two of his girlfriends: Tatyana and his wife. Pushkin's marriage was necessary to Russian literature—that is what was thought at the time, and that is what the poet's friend Yakov Saburov wrote:

> ... Here no one can come to their senses about Pushkin's wedding; will he bend under the conjugal yoke, which is nothing other than *pool pure* (a gamble) and often not a very sure thing. How will he cope with the destruction of his life's habitual rhythms? However, we won't be losing anything. In any case, if worse comes to worst, there will be more beautiful lines of poetry; the writer's sum total is his book, and the way he approaches it is his own business. Let his marriage, his family be-

come an extra volume in his library of materials—I am agreed: it will only be richer and more fruitful.[24]

If only it had been so!

Two years before his engagement, in 1828, after finishing chapter six of *Eugene Onegin*, Pushkin wrote "End of part one." A complete plot outline still did not exist; the "distant prospect of the free novel" stretched away, unclear even to its author himself. However, it is entirely possible to suggest that he intended the gradual creation of a part two that was as big as the first, that is, five or six chapters more, for the symmetry. Three months after beginning the eighth chapter, the bachelor poet got engaged. The greater part of this chapter was written by Pushkin in the half-year period when he was thinking about family life and was getting ready for his wedding.

It is natural to suggest that the poet wanted to have accomplished his chief work by this event. The novel's ending was compressed. Two chapters were cut out. He wanted to tie up loose ends as quickly as possible, and the easiest way out was the chapter called "High Society," where the hero and heroine meet. On December 19, 1830, Vyazemsky wrote in his diary that Pushkin had whipped chapters eight and nine into shape, and "was even finishing with it."[25] "Pushkin was in a hurry to 'finish' the novel, and left it unfinished," a critic noted.[26] The denouement turned out to be "untraditional for the genre of the novel."[27]

There is no other writer in Russian literature who could have had the personal and the literary so close to each other as it happened with Pushkin. In *Onegin*, the personal and the novelistic were unified by its creator as it had never been done before. Modern attempts to explain the unity sound like this: "The unity of the novel *Eugene Onegin* is the unity of its author; that is, we can say, *a novel about its author*, inside of which is contained *a novel about its characters*, Onegin and Tatyana."[28] The contrary would be this point of view: "it would be truer to say quite the opposite, that *a novel about its author* is contained in *a novel about its characters*."[29] It seems to us, anyway, that the transposition of the words doesn't essentially change anything.

In creative work, there is such a unity of an author and his material, the presence of the author in all his characters, and, so to speak, an "I am Tatyana." But in life, his wife Natalya turned out to be the complete antithesis of Tatyana. Why, out of all 113 women that he loved, did he chose an *anti-Tatyana*?

> O people! you all resemble
> Our ancestor Eve:
> What you're granted fails to stir you,
> Ceaselessly the serpent calls you
> To it, to the tree of mystery:
> You want forbidden fruit,
> For without it paradise is not a paradise for you.

And he was himself no exception: he wanted forbidden fruit. However, even the union of Olga not with Onegin, whom she obviously suits better, but with Lensky, reflects the contradictions of Pushkin's life. Both plot-lines, the Onegin-Tatyana one and the Lensky-Olga one, anticipate the life-conflict of their creator. The paradox of this conflict is that the poet was on friendly terms with clever women, and depicted modest ones, but loved the empty-headed. His change of orientation came with his decision to wed; moreover, not a single one of the more suitable brides had caught his fancy.

Anna Akhmatova called Pushkin a moralist who thirsted for "the highest and only truth."[30] We can add: at every given moment. Five years before his work on chapter eight, in *Count Nulin* the poet looked at infidelity of wife to husband entirely playfully. The hostess openly flirts with her guest, and, although she gives the count a peck on the cheek, finding him in her bedroom, all the rest testifies to the utterly free morals both of the husband and, especially, the wife, throwing hints to her young bachelor neighbor. Dmitry Mirsky wrote:

> At the beginning Tatyana is closely linked to the spring of the progressive gentry, whose bard Pushkin was in those years . . . The Tatyana of Chapter Eight is on the one hand the apotheosis of the grand lady, the highest expression of that aristocracy to which Pushkin had to adapt himself, and on the other *a moral exemplar of the faithful wife for Natalya Nikolayevna* [*our emphasis—Y.D.*] who, being 'given' to Pushkin, related with the same lack of passion to him as Tatyana did to her general, but whose future marital behavior was an essential element in Pushkin's adjustments to the 'highest circles'.[31]

This sudden change in Pushkin's views can be noticed. This is obviously a superstitious playing-it-safe on the part of the poet, who had earlier strived to cuckold others, and not to give his fiancées moral lectures. As it is known, maxims in Pushkin's texts sometimes differed from his everyday practice. The poet himself had formulated and on one occasion experimented with the content of chapter eight of *Onegin* five years before:

> In my soul there came a wakening
> And once again you appeared ...

And it was Anna Kern, a general's wife, who appeared, not saying, however, that she would be eternally faithful to the unloved general to whom she'd been given. Quite the contrary, everything happened lightly and simply, and Pushkin later called her stupid, and boasted to a friend that he—if we translate it from the not-widely-used to a more appropriate form—had *scored* with her. In his poem "To Rodzyanka," written for a friend at that same time, betrayal of husbands is proclaimed with humor to be something obligatory for family life:

> Decent husbands
> Are necessary for clever women:
> Around them family friends
> Are either slightly noticeable or invisible.
> Believe it, my dears:
> One helps the other,
> And the bashful star of love
> Fades in marriage's sun.

It's fun to give advice to others; however, it's not funny when it happens to you. Pushkin died because he himself had no desire to be that kind of decent husband.

In the opinion of Mstislav Tsyavlovsky, the late and sad finale between Onegin and Tatyana reflects Pushkin's affair with Carolina Sobanskaya in the summer of 1830, paralleling his engagement. According to a letter written to his fiancée's grandfather, he was leaving her in Moscow "in order to sort out his affairs"; according to a letter to Vera Vyazemskaya, "I confess to my shame that I am having fun in St. Petersburg, and I don't know how and when I'll return." His passionate verses and letters failed to impress Sobanskaya, a sudden infatuation, notes Mstislav Tsyavlovsky, that "was several years late." And one more: "For his letters from Onegin to Tatyana, the poet in large measure draws on ideas, turns of phrase, and vitality from his letters to Sobanskaya."[32]

Another interpretation existed. On January 25, 1828, Olga Pushkina, the poet's sister, was wed at night, in secret from her parents. The poet supported his sister, but his mother never ever forgave her daughter for taking this step. "You have ruined my Onegin: he was supposed to take Tatyana away, but now ... he won't do it." That is what Pushkin told his sister, as Pavlishchev recollects it.[33]

In the last chapter, the author does palpable violence to his material. What should have been the most important part of the novel turned into an epilogue, and the author had to deal with his characters in short order. In making up Tatyana, Pushkin made her an admirer and follower of Delphina, the eponymous heroine of the novel by Madame de Staël. Delphina was rebelling in the name of freedom of love, protesting against fixed norms of behavior at the will of Mme. de Staël. The result of this Staëlization of Tatyana was her too-open declaration of love to Onegin.

Tatyana's behavior at the end of the novel is the direct opposite. Pushkin himself agreed with Pavel Katenin's observation that the transformation from Tatyana the provincial girl to the exalted lady is too unexpected and inexplicable. What happened was that Pushkin thrust onto his heroine the free manner of relating to men that had been realized by Mme. de Staël, and then himself took that manner away from her, as soon as he decided that Tatyana was supposed to become the bearer of conformist morality.

The novel's denouement took all his contemporaries by surprise. It would surprise us too, if we hadn't been steeped in it from childhood as a reality. What had been made up by Pushkin became *as if it were history* for us.

3. The shade of the general and his ideal wife

For some unclear reason, not excluding the possibility of haste, we almost do not see a very important character in the novel, one who isn't even named in it. He stayed unclearly drawn. Why is he "*some* important general," when he is the husband of the heroine and an old friend of the main hero? Even Tatyana loses her name: she isn't Larina anymore, and readers are left unacquainted with the new name of their favorite heroine, now married. In fact, she is now *some important general's wife.*

Moreover, the nameless general is supposedly a significant personage. He is entirely competition-capable, if not more interesting than Onegin. And Tatyana is evidently happy with him. Tatyana respects her husband more than she does her first passion. At any rate, it is unlikely that she would dare to tell him off the way she lets herself do with Onegin. At the same time, the general's shade in some sense parodies the knight commander from *The Stone Guest*. A living monument, a war hero, he wards off the hand of the potential seducer from his wife, manages her conduct.

"This geezer-general," is the carelessly-tossed-off phrase used by Fyodor Dostoyevsky in Pushkin's train. The ambiguity of the prince's image gives rise to interpretations far beyond Pushkin's schemes. Pushkin's lack of plot-material was felt by the opera's librettist, Modest Tchaikovsky. Here the name Gremin appears—in the Russian (gremit), the name roars; with the dominant notes re and mi, it could even be a name like Do-re-min. In the original version of the libretto, the third act begins this way: "The general appears. He falls in love with Tatyana. She tells him her story and agrees to marry him."[34] Tchaikovsky did not sense love from Tatyana either. Her romance is packed away in a trunk:

>...for poor Tanya
>All lots were the same...

And she sort of coldly prefers to live without love. Amending Pushkin, Tchaikovsky at first had Tatyana falling into Onegin's arms at the finale, whereupon the grizzled general enters.

A note of irony in relation to the old general was added by the producer of the Prague Opera's Eugene Onegin, that we went to in 1995. The general rolls out onto the stage in a wheelchair, turning the wheels with his hands. But if we discount this modernized approach, the general remains a shadow, anyway, and no liking for him is aroused in the reader, quite the contrary. Anyway, Lerner justifiably noted that, after the Napoleonic wars, men became generals at an early age.[35] Pushkin's friend Nikolay Rayevsky, Jr., for example, received his general's rank at the age of 29, and Mikhail Orlov at 26. Tatyana's husband recalled together with Onegin "the pranks, jokes, of former years," meaning that they were the same age, and Onegin was 28 at the time. So it had to be that the prince was young, and moreover loved Tatyana no less than Onegin did, all unknowing that it was only calculation on her part.

The fragmentary nature of the plot has called for a conjectural ending for the novel for over a century and a half. Discussions of Onegin's ending are unending, and perhaps the most complete viewpoint is offered up by Tynyanov: his notion is that the ending could be anything you like.[36]

The unfinished chapter entitled "Onegin's Journey" remains indeterminate, for the author never decides where and how his hero travels, anyway. The poet never managed to get abroad; to describe the beauty of Europe without personal impression would come out somewhat second-hand. As a result, as Nabokov further proved, Onegin traveled a cheerlessly long time from his estate in the middle of Russia to the south, to the Odessa of Pushkin's experience. Onegin shows up at Tatyana's, straight from his journey, like Griboyedov's Chatsky, only there was neither ship nor trip to distant lands. And that is probably how it came into Pushkin's mind in Boldino to throw away the "Onegin's Journey" chapter entirely, in order to finish the novel as quickly as possible. All that remained was to tie the final knot.

Finishing his labor of many years before his wedding (would he have time to continue it?), the poet once again tried different versions of the marriage relation for his characters, and as it often happened with him, wittingly or unwittingly related them to his personal situation. Biographical parallels can be seen on many planes.

Onegin's experience in "the tender art of passion" does not help him in his relations with Tatyana, as a Pushkin scholar noted.[37] But surely the living poet had the very same problem? Onegin "like a child, is in love" with Tatyana at the same time and in the same way that Pushkin was with Natalya. Surely the experienced lady-killer Pushkin could turn the head of a little girl? But that was the kind of state the poet was in, stupefied by his latest fiancée, feeling himself a callow youth. This was the sequence of Onegin's (and Pushkin's) mental states: infatuation—seeming inaccessibility ("forbidden fruit")—dismay—lack of self-confidence—a shift from habitual flirtation to seriousness of intent.

An old hand at it, Pushkin could not but have understood that his real intended was far outside, if not diametrically opposed to, the parameters he had worked out. But he was in love, and shut his eyes; he tried to persuade himself along with everyone else in the world that it was not important, that contradictions between the model he'd created and the real candidate did not exist at all.

For the poet himself, husbands had never been an obstacle, and he had never been sanctimonious about it. In the novel, the appearance of a spouse for Tatyana was no obstacle to Onegin, either. But, at that moment, the durability of a marriage, conjugal fidelity, seemed to Pushkin-the-fiancé to be scarcely less important than love itself, which he perhaps wouldn't have expressed seriously either before his own wedding, or a certain while after it.

Anyway, as soon Pushkin had married off Tatyana, in fact, the author was faced by not just any ending, but only two ways of resolving the plot: either Tatyana leaves the general for Onegin (the victory of love over duty and public opinion), or Tatyana says "No" (the victory of morality over feelings, the stability and solemnity of marriage, the strength of family bonds). True, there is one more in reserve, a third denouement through death, but we'll talk about that a little later. For now, though, let's just make clear once again that it is not for Pushkin but for us that two denouements exist for the plot of Eugene Onegin.

For the affianced author, who was seeking the refuge of a family, and who had just wrung agreement to give her daughter in marriage from his future mother-in-law, his favorite heroine's leaving her husband for her lover was hardly appropriate. It would have been the tiniest bit strange to make his chief heroine become an unfaithful spouse. To take pleasure in infidelity to a husband and happiness in a divorce on the eve of his own wedding and at the beginning of his family life would be illogical, you'd have to agree. The unacceptability of divorce at the end of Eugene Onegin was defined not so much by the credibility of the plot as by Pushkin's mood in his particular circumstances; he personally had no need for such an alternative at the time. That is why Onegin, the encroacher upon the stability of the marriage, gets punished. Now Pushkin almost mocks his good friend: "Onegin pines away ..." etc.

Pushkin shared his secret: "Can you imagine what sort of trick Tatyana played on me: she got married." Leo Tolstoy re-tells the tale: "'My Tatyana has shocked me,' said Pushkin. 'She rejected Onegin. I never expected that at all...'"[38] Of course, this is a game, but what is important is the degree to which the author takes his whims. He twists Tatyana's character; it isn't she, but he, the author, who plays the trick. Tatyana suppresses her love for Onegin.

Of course one should write, as the poet himself declared, "in accordance with laws that they [*the artists—Y.D.*] themselves admit to". But we should add that we the readers are not forbidden from having our own laws of perception. Her sharp, final rejection does not say less about Tatyana than the whole long depiction of her life. Merezhkovsky, for instance, quite severely defines her feelings: yes, Tatyana loves Onegin, but it's a sterile love, it's essentially dead.[39] If that is so, then her decision is entirely pragmatic:

> And today!—what has brought you
> to my feet? what a trifle!
> How can you, with your heart and mind,
> Be petty feeling's slave?

So then love is some kind of trifle, unneeded by the heart or the mind. Tatyana is shaming Onegin, being ironic, mocking him. Sergey Bulgakov recalled:

> Leo Tolstoy told me (at one of our few encounters) from the words of some female contemporary of Pushkin's, how he had bragged about his Tatyana's great dressing-down of Onegin. In this tale of one great master about another, all the ingenuousness of creative genius is on display.[40]

Translating this into the contemporary lexicon, Clayton wrote: "Tatyana is the instrument of his [*Onegin's—Y.D.*] punishment." And further, "The psychological level is coordinated with a deeper plot structure, in which she is the instrument of fate." Let's add ourselves, continuing this thought in a feminist key, that Tatyana is punishing Eugene for not marrying her when he could. She is settling with Onegin in the name of the many women whom he'd walked out on. This includes paying him back for his murder of Lensky, for her sister Olga's sake—vengeance, if you like. This vengeful Tatyana is not at all the ideal kind of woman written about in the literature on the subject.

But if Tatyana's "No" is as hard as stone, then her morality is questionable. To pretend that you love someone and then live with him unloving, adoring your old passion, or not pretending, but nevertheless, living with the one and loving the other—it's the same in both cases: where is the aura of saintliness? The one and the other are often met with in life, but they are deeply immoral. In such a context the ideal proclaimed by Fyodor Dostoyevsky looks a bit peculiar. It gets echoed in Apollon Grigoryev's formulation: Pushkin's Tatyana "stands for our Russian measure of feelings ..."[41]

Certain more contemporary "patriotic" interpretations of Pushkin's chief heroine are even more idealized: Tatyana is a myth in which a sense of proportion in appraisal of her completely disappears: "Tatyana is the founder, the initiator of some new kind of morality, invisible to those around her, that is, a miracle unrecognized by them," wrote Vladimir Turbin. And, a little further on: "Using an expression that has become widespread today, Tatyana is an everyday miracle."[42]

Voices skeptical in appraisal of Tatyana were traditionally absent in Soviet Russian literature, and even few and far between in the West. In Nabokov's train, Michael Katz calls the traditional approach "standard Soviet commentary to the novel, reiterates the basic theme." He thinks that there is no special saintliness about Tatyana: the model for her didactic behavior is taken from French literature, specifically from the novels by Samuel Richardson.[43] Y. Khayev noted Tatyana's unreality: "At the finale of the novel, Tatyana appears as a bearer of the higher morality characteristic of an idyllic person."[44] Carol Emerson wrote that her article "was summoned up by the surprise and even irritation that was provoked in me by the cult of Pushkin's Tatyana."[45] By the end of the novel, in fact, there does resound a feminist consciousness of victory over a man, a celebration of the fact that he is no longer needed. She gets pleasure from her rejection of him. Tatyana's "No" is considered by an American Freudian to be masochism.[46]

Why then did a quite average, poorly-bred girl become the model of a positive heroine for generations of Russian girls, for a century and a half? This mythological ideal of a wife, personifying half the population of Russia, filled a corresponding niche in ideological doctrine. But since real Russian women, before and now, are considerably more clever and charming than Tatyana and are capable of a keener appeal to men, and are, moreover, independent, then we have to accept that they have achieved their art despite this model that has been drummed into them from childhood.

4. Divorce as a step towards happiness

The problem of the triangle is resolved quite simply in a poem written simultaneously with the finishing of Eugene Onegin, one that remained unpublished during Pushkin's lifetime. In it, there is a Spanish beauty, and before her stand two knights in love with her. Both propose that she choose her favorite democratically, without conflict:

> Who—decide!—is loved by you?
> Both tell the maiden
> And with their youthful hope
> Look straight into her eyes.

The subtext of the novel's chapter eight, in contrast to this poem, appears to be quite significant. A sizable distance stretched between this artless—and for that reason extremely sincere—provincial maiden, declaring her love for Onegin, and the utterly pragmatic princess, splendid in high society ("I am rich and exalted") who is described in chapter eight. What kinds of variations went through Tatyana's head secretly of an evening, and maybe in sleepless nights, a mature and wiser woman lying in bed next to her repellent husband, suffering before her decisive dialogue with Onegin? Evidently there weren't a lot versions for her to choose from, but there were some.

Tatyana was agitated. And how: finally a bond with her loved one was achievable in reality. The victory of her love. Onegin was at her feet, and tomorrow might become her lover. Real happiness, of a kind she had never had even in her dreams, had arrived. For Pushkin-the-author, that would also be important: not boring lectures on marriage, of the kind he had always laughed at, but specifically a betrayal, a secret love affair, to make the work European, reader-friendly. Eugene Onegin, however, remained not even Platonic, but a novel childishly chaste.

Thirty-five years later, Vsevolod Krestovsky dramatized Onegin's plot in Peterburgskie trushchoby, making (if we keep their real names) Onegin married to a woman whom he does not love and Tatyana pregnant by Onegin. All the conflicts lose their romantic patina: a sexuality completely absent in the Pushkin novel (in contrast to his real-life practice) occupies a large place in Krestovsky's version.

Leo Tolstoy said that the idea for Anna Karenina arose "thanks to the divine Pushkin."[47] Even Dostoyevsky perceived it as the true source of Anna Karenina: "We could of course point Europe directly to the source, that is, to Pushkin himself..." Asking ourselves the natural question: but what if Tatyana had given herself up to Onegin? the novelist concentrates specifically on the betrayal and the divorce, the place where Pushkin halted. Inspired by several verses in chapter eight, Tolstoy answers this question over 375 pages. Pushkin, so to speak, was co-author of the work of Tolstoy, who reconstructed the ending of Eugene Onegin, turning the romantic Tatyana into the realistic Anna.

The general is transformed into an important official and depicted in detail, Vronsky, like Onegin, lives by the Golden Rules. "These rules," Tolstoy says a bit ironically, "undoubtedly define how you have to pay the card-sharp but not your tailor, that you shouldn't lie to men but you can to women, that you should never cheat on anyone, but you can cheat on a husband, that you should never forgive an insult, but you can insult others, etc. All these rules might have been foolish, bad, but they were not doubted, and, in carrying them out, Vronsky felt himself at ease and able to carry his head high." Reading this catechism of the genteel male, we discover that not only Onegin but Pushkin also in his practical life, in his relations with women, stuck entirely to all these rules, as did Tolstoy as well, until such time as he had to repent of his sins—we don't have to look very far for examples.

Tatyana became different when she turned into Anna, although in the original drafts Tolstoy even called his heroine Tatyana. Pushkin's daughter Maria became the prototype of Anna Karenina (seemingly only in appearance). Tatyana, wrote Vissarion Belinsky, "was out of touch," fell "into the category of the ideal maiden," and was not "ripened" to modern ideas—that is why she had "a fear of public opinion." Tolstoy did not agree with Belinsky, who thought that Onegin was interested in "the poetry of passion," but "the poetry of marriage did not merely not interest him, it revolted him." Tolstoy objected that the matter was a different one: it lay in the mysterious union of love, loyalty, and duty, but he constructed his plot taking into consideration this particular point of view of Belinsky's, after reading him with care at that very time. Beginning his writing, Tolstoy called his novel, just as Pushkin had done, "free." Finishing the work, Tolstoy called it "forced." The moralist in him had cast his vote, and that moralist sympathized more with Tatyana, which is why she (that is, Anna, now) had to be punished, that is, killed.

Anna goes further than Tatyana in self-realization, and says what Tatyana never said: "What kind of slave can be a slave to the degree that I am now, in my position." Quite a few women can be found in any epoch who would dream of such slavery: a super-prosperous life of luxury, a strong family, and, in addition, for her entertainment or compensation, a love on the side. But Anna suffers. In the canonical Soviet literature, it is asserted that she is justified for betraying her husband because he personifies bureaucratic officialdom in the tsar's empire. But nothing is said about the fact that the general, Tatyana's husband, personifies the very same thing. Moral values? "Everything is a lie, everything is a cheat, everything is evil," says Anna. But what is evil? It is only what Tatyana prefers: an unloved husband. The cuckolded Karenin punctiliously warns her of the "abyss," but Anna and Vronsky head off to have fun in Italy. Hypothetically, in Eugene Onegin, if Tatyana's husband did not agree to let her go in peace, she and Eugene could have eloped and set off abroad. By the way, Pushkin had read that ending to the story of two lovers in Yevgeny Boratynsky's The Ball, and perhaps did not want to repeat it.

Anna is separated from Tatyana by almost a half-century of development of this theme both in Russian life and in literature. It was already a different Russia, a more open society: less-sturdy authoritarian family structures, but the same old family dramas. "Karenin is a person of the old order. For him, the family is 'an indestructible fortress,' a closed world with its own immutable principles," as a modern critic explains it to us.[48] But surely this characteristic in its essence fits Pushkin, plucking up his courage before his own wedding and setting his bride on the right path "via Tatyana"? As Dostoyevsky's hero says in The Possessed, it is not you, but myself, that I want to persuade.

"In *Anna Karenina*," said Tolstoy, "I like the idea of the family..."[49] But in Tolstoy's condition, having written that, something more complex, a certain protest, came into being. "Something happened to me that made life in our circle—rich and erudite people—become not just repulsive to me, but lose all sense." And in his *Confession* he is even more precise: "The idea of suicide came into my head as naturally as ideas for improving life had come into my head before." Thus the consciousness of the author and his heroine merged. What happened was something that we would call Tolstoy's imposition of his own condition on his heroine, as Pushkin had done earlier. Only now in the opposite direction.

Levin, the happy family man, hid his bootlaces so that he wouldn't hang himself with them, and was afraid to carry a shotgun lest he shoot himself. Vronsky tried to shoot himself. Anna threw herself under a train. Isn't that a bit too many suicides for one novel? This somewhat vulgar overdoing of it is explainable, of course, by Tolstoy's own state. Thank God he decided to commit his characters' suicide rather than his own. The pseudo-will of the protagonists of *Anna Karenina* is explained by its author the way Pushkin does: Tolstoy had already finished the chapter in which Vronsky confronts Karenin, then started correcting his text and "absolutely unexpectedly for me, but without a doubt [*sic—Y.D.*] Vronsky was going to shoot himself." And it turned out that "this was organically necessary for later developments."

That kind of declaration is not unique at all and takes place in the creative process of any major writer: the author pulls his own subjective state like wool over the readers' eyes, like some kind of social necessity. "Gradually, unnoticeably, the strength of life returned to me," Tolstoy recounts in *Confession*. So if he had been putting finishing touches to *Karenina* one or two years later and his state of mind were improved, he might have reduced the number of attempts at suicide in his novel. It was no accident that Afanasy Fet, waxing ironic on the banality of the theme, proposed another more edifying name for the novel: "*Karenina, or the Adventures of a Prodigal Ewe.*"

Now it is time to return to our non-existent divorce in *Onegin*. Lying in bed with her repulsive husband in the quiet of the night, Tatyana, not for the first time in her life, thinks intently about the variants of her relations with Onegin, and that means remarriage, as well. And, consequently, glancing at the sleeping general, about divorcing him. The problem with divorce in the society of that time was always difficult to resolve. In Orthodox Christianity, marriage is sanctified by the Church, it is a sacrament, for marriage is made in heaven. It is eternal, indissoluble, passing understanding, "this mystery is great." Marriage somehow takes the form of religious relations between husband and wife. Divorce is heresy, and heresy is punished by God, or on his behalf.

In the real life surrounding him, the poet had encountered collapsing marriages every so often from his youth. The poet's grandma Maria Hannibal was separated from his grandfather; his uncle Vasily Pushkin conveyed the boy to the Lyceum in the company of his mistress; Pushkin's early infatuation, Princess Yevdokiya Golitsyna, was separated from her husband; his wife Natalya's grandfather was a bigamist; his mother strove to get his father put away in a lunatic asylum, and herself cohabited with servants, etc.

A Church marriage was extremely difficult to dissolve. At the beginning of the 19th century, a divorce needed permission from the consistory, which had to be confirmed by the archpriest of the eparchy, and needed the approval of the Synod after 1806. Valid reasons to accept the necessity for a divorce were the husband's or the wife's absence in a place unknown, a calling to a cloistered religious order, the spouse's banishment or attempted suicide, adultery proved by personal confession or by witnesses, as well as bigamy or a disease that impedes married life.[50]

In this list is nothing of any use to Tatyana. In practice, true, the issue could also have been resolved by large, judicious bribes. An instance is well known where a wife was lost in a card game, and the tsar intervened, personally allowing the divorce, but that was a scandalous story. What was practicably real and appropriate was the *razyezd*, a separation, but a long life in separation could become the basis for a divorce.

Or—Tatyana might think, "My husband is gentleman enough to let me leave in peace. We'll *separate*." And Tatyana and Onegin might then live without official registration of their marriage, with all the complexities for a genteel life that would stem from this. Or—there might be a conflict, and in its train the grave judicial procedure of a divorce *a la* Karenin. Pushkin-the-romantic created "Tatyana's sweet Ideal," the foundation for the mythological Russian heroine. In the framework of an ideal novel, a prosaic divorce with lawyers, witnesses, and a trial would be a breach of harmony. Divorce was beyond the bounds of the novel, it would have been a crude realism, and Pushkin with his absolute taste sensed that.

Finally—Tatyana might be quite capable of thinking about this on the eve of her decisive conversation with Onegin—a duel between her lover and the general.

A second duel in the novel doesn't seem so improbable. Pushkin's hero is not just a superfluous man from a string of people like him—he's twice over the odd man out. Pushkin-the-man had a fantastic ability to foresee things: twice he placed his favorite hero in D'Anthes's position. That is, Onegin, like D'Anthes later, wants Tatyana to leave her unloved husband and go away with him, like the D'Anthes-infatuated Natalya Pushkina. Adultery, and again a duel, seem quite in the mainstream of *Eugene Onegin*'s theme.

A new single combat would be right in character for Eugene. And it would be quite logical if he again played the role of Terminator, but this time of the general, his more successful rival. Despite the circularity of the novel, Pushkin never brings his protagonists to a second duel—probably thinking that a repetition would resemble farce. However, let's suppose that such a duel between Eugene and Tatyana's husband does take place. The readers are offered a psychological text with several unknowns. A model for comparison would be Natalya marrying D'Anthes. Would Tatyana have a happy life with a double murderer? Or, this time, what if the experienced warrior-general puts away his wife's admirer? The writing of another ending for a classic author (what they called a *re-make* in English) is a stylish hobby for literary amateurs, but it seems that such a plot has never appeared in any of the multitudinous literary piss-takes of *Eugene Onegin*.

Dostoyevsky was completely categorical about it in a similar reflection: "Even if Tatyana had become free, if her elderly husband had died and she had become a widow, even then she would not have gone off with Onegin." Here not the author but a completely incidental writer imposes his will on the characters of someone else's work! Let us suggest that Onegin married Tatyana, many of us argue with the famous writer. Would the marriage be a happy one, or would it break up from their differing sympathies and jealousy? Potentially, such versions of the development of the plot of *Onegin* can be traced out in their entirety. It's a pity that we cannot check up on all these speculations. Onegin never proposed marriage to Tatyana. And he didn't ask her to accompany him abroad (the favorite dream of the poet himself).

Yes, marriages are made in heaven. But Tatyana's fate was decided by Pushkin all on his own. Let us say what we have been thinking about for a long time, all the years of being on blacklists both in the homeland and in emigration. In a subtext of the steadfast faithfulness of Tatyana as a national heroine can be seen still another indissoluble marriage. Pushkin said to Bryullov that he had gotten married himself because he wasn't allowed to go abroad. For centuries, the divorce of an individual from Russia has been something strictly punished. Against his will, moreover, the separation of the poet from his homeland never happened. Before his marriage, he again asked several times to go to Europe, but he was refused. He found himself tied to his fatherland forever, and he remained until the end of his days in the position of the loyal subject. From here stems his combination in a single unit of hatred for his fatherland along with love for it, a phenomenon, we should add, so characteristic of hateful marriages between men and women.

"Yes, life here in the motherland is hard, bad," says the hypothetical Russian citizen, "but an individual must not divorce himself from Russia. From youth, I have adored Italy and France, but anyway I have to endure it. I am given to Russia, and I will be true to it forever." It seems to us impossible that Pushkin, with all his clairvoyance, could not see through such a transparent analogy. To this effect we can say that, in *Eugene Onegin,* the thread of Pushkin's life is subconsciously reflected: hedonism in combination with a single-mindedness of purpose in gaining freedom, love for Russia and the impossibility of divorce from his homeland.

5. Escape from the family to freedom

So then the denouement of the novel reflected the poet's views at the moment of finishing *Eugene Onegin*. Pushkin had firmly decided to get married, and it is understandable that the family had become more important in his hierarchy of moral values, higher than adultery. A clever and experienced man, he was doubtful of his wife Natalya's love in return, and, entering into marriage with this indescribable beauty, strove to forestall any misbehavior of hers with his incantation of "I will be true to him forever." The novel falters on such a didactic ending, but Pushkin saw it as important for his coming family life.

The poet returned to his novel in October, 1831, a year after completing it. An important inclusion, necessary for closing the circle, was made in chapter eight—Onegin's letter to Tatyana. And, two years later, in Boldino in October, 1833, there appeared a draft version of an Onegin verse, addressed to Pletnev, with the idea

> Again upon the stage to bring
> The long-forgotten hero,
> Once upon a time in favor.

The thing didn't go any further than a dozen-and-a-bit rough draft lines. That flash of an idea to write a continuation of *Eugene Onegin* was successfully forgotten.

Pushkin often and truly foresaw things, but couldn't always act in concert with his foreknowledge. In the Russian language, there are two different words for "marriage," each addressed to opposing genders: *zhenitba* (marriage, as in to take to wife) and *zamuzhestvo* (to take as husband), but only one noun, *razvod*, for divorce. In English it is quite the contrary: one word for marriage, but two for divorce: separation (the word that attracted Pushkin's attention when he read Byron) and divorce. If people split up themselves, it would be more precise to say in Russian *raskhod*, but the word doesn't carry that meaning. The word *razvod* comes from a root that means "to lead," that is, that there exists some third party to all this: a person, a boss, the church, the state, or—God, the devil, an unknown power, that *leads* two people *apart*. Indeed, if a marriage is made in heaven, then where does a divorce come from? Maybe from hell?

Two and a half years had passed since the poet's nuptials, and here in the poet's work appears the tragic theme of the sundering of a man and a woman by other-worldly forces. This first resounds in *The Queen of Spades*, and a year later the same force of separation is echoed again in *The Bronze Horseman*. This topic was quite new for Pushkin, but not at all new to world literature.[51] We, for our part, turned our attention to the subconscious connection of thoughts about the mystical uncoupling of a man and a woman in Pushkin's works from that period along with the growing tensions in relations in his own family.

This problem has traditionally been ignored by official Pushkin scholarship. Smouldering little by little, the crisis in the Pushkin family gradually reached a pre-divorce state. Earlier we observed the bachelor-poet, who had decided to put a full stop after number 113 in his Don Juan list, escaping into a family, and now, four years later, from family to his freedom. In 1835, Pushkin's debts had reached 60,000 rubles. He had pawned expensive clothing, pearls, silver. Leaving his family behind, the poet spent half of the month of May in Trigorskoye, returning only after Natalya had given birth to their son Grigory. Two weeks later, Pushkin asked the tsar's permission via Benckendorff to rusticate himself for three or four years. The poet was turned down, but was promised monetary help (10,000 rubles) and a six-month holiday.

That year, following the motif of John Bunyan's novel *The Pilgrim's Progress*, he created the genuinely confessional poem "The Wanderer," unpublished during his lifetime, about a man's anguish in his family and his striving to extricate himself from it. In essence, Bunyan was merely the setting-off point, but its thoughts were Pushkin's, and its form, and its realization, what he had suffered himself: loneliness and incomprehension.

> My gloom is understood by no one.

And the hero's plan to escape his family was ripening.

> Where can I run to? which path shall I choose?

Judging by the abundance of draft versions, the nuances of his state were causing the author huge effort; he carefully avoided speaking directly about his state, but the extant text is open and biographical enough anyway.

> My escape produced alarm among my family,
> Children and wife all cried out to me from the doorstep
> For me to come back quick. Their cries
> Drew my friends out onto the square:
> One scolded me, a second gave my spouse
> Advice, another felt sorry for a friend
> Who had reviled me, who made me a laughing-stock,
> Who proposed to my neighbors to bring me back by force,
> Others were already in pursuit of me...

It would be a mistake to tie up this creative fantasy directly with the chronology of the artist's life, but it would be stupid to ignore this source for an understanding of what was going on. The two letters put by Pushkin underneath this poem do not permit us to read the date: *26 Ju 835*—would that have been June, or

July? We are inclined to July, when Pushkin, in debt, was again trying to leave home. If that is so, then it works out that on that very day, on July 26, he wrote a most humble request to be given 30,000 rubles from the state treasury. Twenty days later, Nicholas I ordered that he be given the money. On September 7, Pushkin again left his wife and children and went off to Mikhaylovskoye and Trigorskoye for almost two months.

Within three days, on September 10 or 11, he was already in Mikhaylovskoye and Trigorskoye. And between September 11 and 18, he sent a letter to Alina in Pskov—Aleksandra Bekleshova (Osipova). He had had an affair with her when he was previously in exile in Mikhaylovskoye:

> I love you—though I rage,
> Though this is labor and shame in vain,
> And in this wretched stupidity
> I declare myself at your feet!
> This befits neither me nor my age...
> It's time, past time, for me to be the wiser!
> But by all the signs I recognize
> The disease of love in my soul...

This poem remained unpublished. However, Alina had been entered as number 20 in his Don Juan list. Now she was 27, and for two years the wife of a captain-lieutenant of police. According to a letter of Pushkin's, none of this meant anything to him: "Come, please God... I have three baskets full of confessions, explanations, and odds and ends for you. It might be that we'll even fall in love a bit at our leisure."

Bursov was the first to comment on the situation: "He (Pushkin) opposes this image of life with a life based on completely different spiritual aims, in contradiction to his nature as well as to everything that had already happened to him. Natalya Nikolayevna, as he was undoubtedly certain, was not a friend capable of coming with him on his planned exploits... He needed a friend who would walk hand in hand along with him in his creative pursuits."[52]

For reasons known already to the reader Pushkin's model of the family idyll was showing signs of cracking. Pechorin, Onegin's successor—whose creator was undoubtedly affected by Pushkin's death because of his wife—was to be promoted to the rank of the anti-marriage fanatic: "I am ready for any sacrifice except this one; twenty times I will risk my life and even my honor... but I will never sell my freedom." In his doggedness Pechorin is dismayed, anyway:

> Why do I prize it so dearly? What is in it for me... what am I readying myself for? what do I expect from the future?... Truly, nothing at all... When I was still a child, an old woman told my fortune to my mother; she foretold my *death from an evil wife* [*Lermontov's emphasis—Y.D.*]; this shocked me deeply then: an insurmountable revulsion to marriage was born in my soul.[53]

What is especially remarkable in this connection is not just that the thought of *Eugene Onegin*'s underdeveloped ending remained in Pushkin's consciousness, but that he returned to it precisely at the moment when a similar problem appeared in his own life. In the middle of September, 1835, all of a sudden the poet wrote three poems in a row continuing his dialogue on this subject with his friends, in particular Pletnev.

> You advise me, Pletnev dear,
> To continue /our/ left-off novel
> /And a strict/ age, an Iron Age of calculation,
> To treat with idle stories...
> You say: while Onegin lives,
> The novel is not ended—there is no reason
> To interrupt it... besides, the plan's a happy one—
> .... of his demise...

Pletnev really did propose several times that Pushkin continue the novel, considering it to have been "interrupted." And even Pushkin himself calls *Eugene Onegin* "left-off." He seems to have been in agreement with Pletnev at least enough to keep on writing things like "The novel is not ended" on this subject, and "there is no reason/To interrupt it..." We feel that previously there had been a personal reason to interrupt the novel, but now, perhaps by association, the desire arose to start thinking about it again. "Besides, the plan's a happy one," Pushkin wrote. Had he come up with some kind of happy new scheme? Happy for whom—for Onegin, for Tatyana—or for the author? Which one, in fact, we will never find out.

Two of three unfinished poems addressed to Pletnev on this subject are dated in the Academy collected works from the first half of September of 1835, and the third is dated September 16. It seems that they were all written in Mikhaylovskoye, where the poet had come from St. Petersburg, no earlier than September 10. It must have been that the first two sketches were done no earlier than the 10th, and no later than September 16 of 1835. In those very days the letter went to Alina Bekleshova with its summons to continue their love affair of ten years' antiquity, that is, to destroy his formula of 1830.

> But I am given to another;
> I will be true to him forever.

There was, so to speak, a technical difficulty for Pushkin if he decided to continue *Eugene Onegin*. How to extend the plot further if Tatyana had already said "No" in chapter eight? It looks to us as if Pushkin left himself such an opportunity. Tatyana pronounced openly that (a) she loved Onegin, and (b) *at the same time* would remain true to her husband.

This nuance is terribly important. It would be one thing if the author quietly elucidated his point of view to us, the readers, that *she* continues to love *him* after all. But no! Having made her decision to reject him, Tatyana herself declares to Onegin her love for him. For what, you ask. To our masculine understanding, it would be so that he could continue pursuing her with even more vigor, and she would have to give in, dumping the sin of betrayal of her husband on her invincible sweetheart. The "No" said by Tatyana under Eugene's pressure—and, let us add, with the assistance of the author—would gradually turn into a "Maybe," and the "Maybe" into "Yes." As in the decrepit joke, if a girl says "No," that means "Maybe."

Pushkin returned to his apparently exhausted theme. He seemed to be looking for a tonality. In his third sketch this variation repeats:

> You advise me, friends, in autumn leisure,
> To set to work again on Onegin.
> You tell me: he lives and is not wed.
> So the novel isn't over yet—it is treasure
> Perhaps I should—'t would be my pleasure—

Finally, in a fourth draft on this same subject, written on September 16, 1835, we can plainly see a return to the familiar Onegin-music of the verse, in essence, proof of the poet's train of thought in the direction of continuation of the novel or, maybe even, a straightforward continuation itself that we could call *a part of the introduction to a new chapter*:

> You advise me, friends,
> To continue the forgotten tale.
> You say fairly
> That it's strange, uncivil, even,
> To break the novel off unended,
> To've sent it to the publishers' already,
> That one way or another I should
> Marry off its hero,
> Or anyhow be the death of him.

Why did Pushkin stop without bringing the affair to divorce? There is no answer to this question. In Soviet Pushkin studies, it was explained without embroidery by the fact that the poet was distracted by the "topic of class warfare" (Nikolay Brodsky).[54] And maybe Pushkin, proceeding from his own experience, decided that his favorite hero would be better off not burdening himself with a family.

But... our readers' patience is running low. They demand that we cease these direct analogies between the poet's biography and his work. We shall obediently stop, noting, however, that it is incredibly interesting to ponder it. Let's for a moment imagine that Pushkin had lived longer and decided to continue *Eugene Onegin* ("to lead out of the labyrinth," as he himself said). Then the novel would get another ending. And, possibly, Leo Tolstoy wouldn't ever have created *Anna Karenina*: it would have already been written by his distant relative, Alexander Pushkin, in verse, moreover.

Pushkin's Hallowed Nurse

We Russians have known Alexander Pushkin's nurse since our own childhood, as if she had cared not just for the poet but for us as well. She has an honored place in every one of his biographies. Is taking up such a banal theme worthwhile? What could we manage to say that was new? Looking yet again at a thick folder with her name on it, documents collected over long years, we made up our mind to try to catch a glimpse of her as an historical-literary phenomenon, so to speak, and maybe as one of the unsolved riddles of Pushkin's biography.

Primary materials on his nurse are scant, but, to all appearances, the maximum possible has already been drawn from them and interpreted variously, sometimes at odds with historical fact—in turn, something with its own reasons. According to the unwritten law of Pushkin studies, the environment around the great poet has been staked out and divided up between friends and enemies, with a consequent hypertrophy of their virtues or deficiencies. His nurse has survived many a purge, with honor intact.

1. A nurse. But what kind?

First of all, the expression "Pushkin's nurse" itself, that has become an accepted traditional term in Pushkin studies, requires elaboration. In life she was called Arina. In her old age some called her Rodionovna, the way they do sometimes in the country. Pushkin himself never even once called her by name, and in his letters he wrote "nurse," once even with a capital letter. In scholarly Russian and Western literature she is more frequently referred to as Arina Rodionovna, without any family name, or, more rarely, with the surname Yakovleva.[1]

Arina was what they called her around the house, but she had two genuine names: Irina, and in other documents, Irinya. Her family name, according to the serf tax register, was Rodionova. She was buried under that name. In a recent publication it says: "There are no good grounds for the appearance of the family name Yakovleva in modern literature about Pushkin's nurse, as if it belonged to her. As a serf-woman, a nurse would have no family name. In documents (accounting ledgers, confessional inventories, parish birth registers) she was called after her father—Rodionova—and in an everyday context, Rodionovna (the normal patronymic). None of the poet's contemporaries referred to her as Yakovleva."[2]

This is a debatable issue, since children are named after their father, and her father's surname is Yakovlev. Meylakh called her Arina Matveyeva (after her husband).[3] Whichever way you look at it, Pushkin's and Gogol's serf-characters had names like Savelyich, Selifan, or Petrushka; and her respectful address by name and patronymic as Arina Rodionovna, without a family name, widely accepted in literature, puts the nurse straightaway on a definite level. After all, beginning with folkloric names (Mikula Selyaninovich, say), it has been the custom in print to dignify this way only heroes, tsars, grand dukes (for example, Nikolay Pavlovich, Konstantin Pavlovich for Nicholas I and his brother) and widely-known people (Alexander Sergeyevich, Joseph Vissarionovich for Pushkin and Stalin).

According to the parish register of the Voskresenskaya Suydinskaya church, she was born on April 10, 1758, in Suyda (the present village of Voskresenskoye), or more precisely, a quarter of a mile away, in the hamlet of Lampovo. This is the so-called Izhorsk land in the St. Petersburg *guberniya*, on the territory of Ingermanlandia, at one point belonging to Great Novgorod, then to Sweden, and then reconquered by Peter the Great. First Orthodox Christianity was propagated on this thinly-populated locality, then Lutheranism, then again Orthodoxy. Her mother, Lukerya Kirillova, and her father, Rodion Yakovlev, had seven children—among them two with the same name, Yevdokiya. While Arina was a child, she was reckoned the serf of Count Fyodor Apraksin. Suyda and its adjacent hamlets with their inhabitants were purchased from Count Apraksin by the poet's grandfather, Abram Hannibal. Arina (Irina, Irinya) Rodionova-Yakovleva-Matveyeva lived a long life, for those times—past her seventieth year.

In 1781 Arina got married and was allowed to move to her husband's in the village of Kobrino, not far from the present-day Gatchina. A year later, following Pushkin's birth, his grandmother, Maria Hannibal, sold Kobrino with all the people in it and bought Zakharovo, outside Moscow. She excluded Arina, along with her family and the house that they lived in, from the bill of sale. The situation isn't as clear as it has been represented. At one time, it was the custom to consider that Maria Hannibal either gave Arina and her family—her husband, Fyodor Matveyev, who died in 1801 or 1802 from drunkenness, and four children—their freedom, or wanted to.

Arina refused the offer of freedom. Pushkin's sister, Olga Pavlishcheva, alleges this in her memoirs. Arina remained a house-serf. Incidentally, a dictionary definition of the Russian word for house-serf, *dvorovoy*, gives the meaning as "a serf, one who has been brought into a lordly, seigniorial manor (used to signify peasant serfs who have been taken from the land into the service of a landlord and his house)."[4] Arina Rodionovna's daughter, Marya, married a serf and in this fashion remained a serf. Arina said, "I was a peasant myself, what do I need freedom for?"[5]

Arina's biographer A. I. Ulyansky claims that her children never received their freedom.[6] All her life, Arina considered herself a slave of her lords: "a loyal slave," Pushkin himself calls the nurse in *Dubrovsky*, although this is a fictional character, of course,. "To grant freedom to the nurse and her family," proposed Granovskaya, "was something that Maria Hannibal was evidently going to do ... but never got around to."[7] If this was so, then Arina's refusal of the offer of freedom makes no sense. At Mikhaylovskoye, according to the register, she and her children were again listed as serfs. "Arina Rodionovna was born a serf and died one."[8] "Thrice over" a serf, Nadezhda Braginskaya noted in retrospect: "of Apraksin, of Hannibal, and of the Pushkins."[9] And we should note that Pushkin was comfortable with this situation. He never touched upon this topic in regards to his nurse, not a word, although slavery in general stirred his civic indignation on more than one occasion.

What is important is that Arina and her children found themselves in a rather unusual position. Arina went back and forth between the Pushkins' and her village—and we don't know for sure which one that would have been. By necessity, she had been taken into service in the manor, but they evidently sent her back to Mikhaylovskoye, as well. She was something along the lines of a steward: she would watch over the estate, carrying out her lords' bidding; certain of her honesty, they would entrust her with various financial affairs. Vladimir Nabokov uses the English word *housekeeper* to try to explain her role to the Western reader.[10] In 1792, Arina was taken by Maria Hannibal to the house of the guardian of her daughter, that is, Pushkin's mother, to be a wet-nurse for the man's son. The poet's uncle, A. Y. Pushkin, wrote about the son that "Hannibal's wife gave the aformentioned Arina Rodionovna from Kobrino to him as a wet-nurse." She "was left with him as nurse until 1797."[11]

How does the birth of her own children correspond to the birth of the Pushkin children? This is not an idle question, for who nursed the poet at her breast? When Pushkin was born, Arina was 41; two years later she was widowed and had no more children. The ages of Arina Rodionovna's children by Fyodor Matveyev in the year of Pushkin's birth were: Yegor, 17; Nadezhda, 11; Marya (who left something like a primitive memoir), 10. Arina's last son, Stefan, was born most likely at the end of 1797, at the very time (December 20, 1797) as Pushkin's older sister Olga, and they took Arina from the village into the Pushkin's house because she was in milk. Pushkin was born a year and a half later, when she had already weaned his sister, or was about to. Most likely, Arina had already gone dry and had been sent back to the village. Arina's daughter Marya recalled, "She had just weaned Olga, and then she was taken to be Alexander's nurse."[12] The evidence isn't precise. A different wet-nurse was brought for Pushkin.

The expression "Pushkin's nurse" includes, at a minimum, two different women. In his sister Olga's testimony, the poet had two nurses. Both of them have been known as Yakovleva up to the present. Most likely his first nurse was taken from the village that belonged to Maria Hannibal. As is still normal to this day, a few family names would have sufficed for a whole village.

The poet's first nurse was Uliana (Ulyana) Yakovlevna or Yakovleva (born probably in 1767 or 1768, perhaps a widow, year of death unknown).[13] She breast-fed him from birth and, as a Soviet source euphemizes in order to avoid the issue of breast-feeding, Ulyana "for the first two years played a major role."[14] A year and ten months later after Pushkin, his brother Nikolay was born (who died six years later); and, four years further on, his brother Lev was born. Olga wrote that "Lev was born and Arina Rodionovna was entrusted with his care: that is how she became a general nurse."[15] Meanwhile, Ulyana remained with Pushkin until 1811.

After Olga, Arina was nurse to Alexander and Lev, but was wet-nurse only to Olga. Nabokov says that Arina Rodionovna is "more precisely, his sister's old nurse," and then says "formerly his sister's nurse."[16] She was not the only nurse, of course. There were lots of servants in the Pushkins' house; wet-nurses were easily found in the villages and returned to them, but this nurse was trusted with far more than the others. Pushkin's mother, when she needed her, allowed her to sleep not in the servants' hall, but in the manor itself. Later on, her daughter Nadezhda was also taken into service at their lordships'.

Arina's children were permitted to settle in the little village of Zakharovo. In 1811, Zakharovo was sold. The Pushkins had children who were born and died as infants: Sofya, Pavel, Mikhail, and Platon. It is not known if Arina nursed any of these children.[17] His parents, when Pushkin entered the Lyceum, left Moscow for Warsaw, where his father had procured a post. Arina was sent back to Mikhaylovskoye.

In Pushkin's autobiographical sketches, there is this line: "First impressions. The Yusupov garden, the earthquake, my nurse." His autobiography remained unrealized, and it is arguable which nurse Pushkin had in mind to describe during the earthquake of 1802. Let's take a look at his formal usage of the word "nurse." In Thomas Shaw's *Index of Pushkin's Poetry*, the word "nurse" is used 23 times in various grammatical cases in his poems, including 17 times in *Onegin*, with 6 left over.[18] In the *Dictionary of Pushkin's Language*, including letters and draft versions, the word "nurse" is mentioned 36 times; of these, 19 times in *Onegin*, and 17 others for the whole life of the poet.

Arina Rodionovna's significance to the history of Russian literature is based on several theses, whose most fundamental is sentimental: the poet loved his nurse and included her in his works. Did she really play an important part in his life?

2. In the master's service

Let's ponder the time of their relationship. The first summer of his life Pushkin spent at Mikhaylovskoye, to which he had been brought soon after his birth; only in the fall did his parents leave for St. Petersburg. When she started nursing him is not clear, but "in his seventh year," wrote Bartenev, "nurse and grandmother were replaced by tutors and teachers."[19] It is unlikely that they saw each other when, in November 1817, Arina was brought to the city to nurse the last-born Pushkin child, Platon. They went back with him to Mikhaylovskoye, where he soon died. In the summers of 1817 and 1819, Pushkin came to Mikhaylovskoye for his vacation, and she saw him during these visits, "*if* she was there at the time," as Nabokov stresses it.[20] His attachment to her, or, as has been written, his love for his nurse, meaning her role in his life, relates to his Mikhaylovskoye exile, which lasted for two years. He was living in the large, seigniorial manor, and his nurse lived either in the outbuilding where the bath was, or in the maids' hall. After his exile, the poet returned again to the village two months later, and still another time, in 1847.

His love for his nurse is confirmed by a range of sources. His sister, Olga, amplifies: he had loved her since childhood, but even more so when he was at Mikhaylovskoye. The tremendous precision of Pushkin's characterization (Arina Rodionovna was 68) leaves us in no doubt about it:

> Friend of my bleak days,
> My darling in her dotage . . .

As Nestor Kotlyarevsky noted, "Pushkin embellished his recollections."[21] Let's reread the poet's Mikhaylovskoye correspondence, often quoted in confirmation of his friendship with Arina Rodionovna. Mention of his nurse runs first from Pushkin's life into his letters, and then into his works, and it is difficult for the biographer to distinguish between facts of life and literary exaggerations. "Do you know what I'm doing?" he shared with his brother (November, 1824). "Before dinner I write up my notes, then dine late; after dinner I go riding, and in the evening I listen to Nurse's fairy-tales, making up for the deficiencies of my accursed upbringing."

Thirty years afterwards Pavel Annenkov wrote: "Arina Rodionovna was the go-between, as everyone knows, in his relations with the Russian fairy-tale world, his guide to finding out the beliefs, customs, and the very ways of the people ... " And more: "Alexander Sergeyevich spoke of his nurse as his ultimate preceptor, and that he was obliged to this teacher for correcting the deficiencies of his original French upbringing."[22] This was the Annenkov's fundamental observation. But Pushkin himself, in contrast to his biographer, never called his nurse either go-between or guide or ultimate preceptor or teacher. By the way, neither is there any phrase like "accursed French upbringing" in Pushkin; he has "my accursed upbringing." From these words of the poet, it follows that Arina, while his nurse, hadn't done a very good job of raising him, and neither had his parents ("the deficiencies of my accursed upbringing.") It's Pushkin who contradicts those Pushkin scholars who assert the huge positive role of Arina in the development of the child-poet.

In a letter to Dmitry Shvarts, a chancellery official in Odessa, Pushkin wrote (December 1824), "... in the evening I listen to the fairy tales of my nurse, the original of Tatyana's nurse; you, it seems to me, saw her once—she is my only friend—and only with her am I not bored." In a letter to his friend Pyotr Vyazemsky (January, 1825), on the same subject: "... I loll on the stove-bench and listen to old fairy-tales and songs." And in *Eugene Onegin*:

> But the fruits of my daydreams
> And ventures in harmony
> I read to my old nurse alone,
> That friend of my youth.

All these reminders of his nurse were after a fight with his father, when his parents had gone away and Pushkin was left alone. "I read to my old nurse alone"—only to her, because his constant contact with the inhabitants of Trigorskoye had not yet come to pass. Lines from his poem "Winter's Evening," in our minds from childhood, are brilliant. However, the poet's mood in the storm covering the sky with gloom, and even the text of a letter written on a frosty winter's day at the beginning of his Mikhaylovskoye exile, being boundless generalizations, distort the real picture of the poet's life in the country, narrow his pastimes to the constant spending of his time only with his nurse. However easy and comfortable he might have felt with her anyway, it was his *enforced* solitude that she was taking the edge off.

A letter to the younger Nikolay Rayevsky is important here: "For the time being I live in utter solitude: the only neighbor I could visit left for Riga, and I literally have no other society except for my old nurse and my tragedy; the latter is coming along, and I am satisfied with it." Judging from the letter, he had to while away his time with Arina Rodionovna *for the time being* because of the absence of Osipova and her company.

> Sad am I: with me no friend
> With whom to drown the long parting...
> I drink alone...

I have no friend; I drink alone. And several lines later he repeats: "I drink alone..." This is addressed to his Lyceum comrades after a year at Mikhaylovskoye. He wrote no more about his nurse. Aleksey Vulf recalled that Pushkin's desk was piled high with books by Montesquieu and other authors. There is a lot of eyewitness testimony that the poet would spend whole days, and of course evenings and sometimes nights as well, at Trigorskoye. Imagine yourself a passionate 25-year-old man: would you listen for a long time, and especially every day, to fairy-tales from your nurse, when there was a house within two miles full of cheery feminine laughter and flirtation?

"Every day about three in the afternoon, Pushkin would show up at our place from his Mikhaylovskoye," wrote Maria Osipova, the daughter of Praskovya Osipova.[23] Pushkin would go to the Osipov-Vulfs' at Trigorskoye sometimes on horseback, sometimes by wagon, sometimes on foot. There was company there, there he carried on affairs with everyone in turn, starting with the mistress of the estate. His nurse would come to Trigorskoye to carry out various tasks for her master. "She often visited us in Trigorskoye, and, consequently, it was at our place that she composed those letters that she sent to her nursling."[24] As for Mikhaylovskoye, the poet spent most of his time there alone, taking target-practice with a pistol in his cellar, and, as he confessed himself, frightening the ducks on the lake by reading his poems to them.

In his Mikhaylovskoye exile, Pushkin's nurse was his aide in practical affairs, in everyday life. Her kindness and caring for him and for visitors made her irreplaceable. Pushkin once even quoted her in a letter to Pyotr Vyazemsky: "Thou'rt such a game cock, as my Nurse puts it." At that same time, in December of 1824, he wrote to his sister Olga, whom he missed, that "nurse has carried out your commission: she went to Svyatye Gory and had a requiem mass said or whatever was necessary." On August 25, Pushkin appended the following in Russian to a letter in French to his sister: "Nurse sends to kiss your hand, Olga Sergeyevna, my little darling." Pushkin wasn't a good landlord; the bailiffs would cheat him, and he was able to eke only a miserable existence out of the estate. Arina would look into the estate's affairs, telling her master what was going on in the village.

Pushkin's love for Mikhaylovskoye was changing. On December 1, 1826, he wrote to his friend Vasily Zubkov that he had left "my accursed hamlet." And after his exile, he would sometimes, in his freedom, hide himself away in the country from the "vulgarity and stupidity" of Moscow and St. Petersburg "almost like Harlequin, who, to the question of whether he preferred being broken on the wheel or hanged, answered, 'I prefer milk soup.'" (a letter to Osipova, the summer of 1827). Pushkin told Vyazemsky: "You know, I'm not making myself out to be sensitive, but a meeting with my menials, louts, and my nurse—really and truly tickles my heart more pleasantly than glory, than taking pride in something, than distractions, and so on. My nurse is hilarious. Imagine, at 70 she has learned off by heart a new prayer *for the softening of her lord's heart and the curbing of his soul's ferocity*, a prayer probably composed during the reign of Tsar Ivan. Right now priests are bawling the service in her room and keeping me from going about my business." It's most likely that that's a joking exaggeration at the end of the letter, about the priest's pilgrimage to his nurse's room. The description of the company the poet met with is interesting as well: menials, louts, and nurse, who is *hilarious*.

"Among the letters to Pushkin from almost all the celebrities of Russian society there are notes from his old nurse, that he kept on an equal footing with the foremost." Thus Pavel Annenkov sings the praises of Arina Rodionovna. He came across with a brilliant euphemism: "The idea and the very form of the idea, evidently, belonged to Arina Rodionovna, although she did *borrow someone's hand* [*my italics—Y.D.*] for their exposition."[25] Two such notes exist. The first letter was apparently "composed" by Arina, as Maria Osipova put it; that is, she didn't ask someone in Trigorskoye to write it for her but found a peasant who could write. She sent off the letter with Arkhip the gardener, who was entrusted with bringing Pushkin's books from Mikhaylovskoye to St. Petersburg (1827). Both letters are here presented with their original style attempted in translation.

> Genuary—30th day. Dear Sir of Alexander, sergeyevich ive the honor to wish you a happy past new year in a new happiness, ani wish you my kined benefactor health and prosperity; ani notify you that iwasin petersburg: annabout you noboddy—cant know, where you are an your parents, Condole for you that youwont come see them; and Olga sergevnna have writ toyou infrontof me withone lady knowen to you But We, *batyushka*, were awaiting a letter from you When you order us to bring Books, but we failed to wait it out: thats why we conceived the idea in accordance with your old order to send: that's why I send big and small books in number—134 books igive arkhip money, nos. 85 rub. [*crossed out—Y. D.*] 90 rubles: meanwhile Kined friend ikiss your hands by your leave a hundred times anwish you whatyou wishyour self iremain sincerely yours *Arinna Rodivonovnna*.

The second letter was written for the nurse by the poet's girl-friend at Trigorskoye, Anna Nikolayevna Vulf, who missed the mischief-maker and ladies' man Pushkin no less than Arina Rodionovna.

> Alexander Sergeyevich, I received your letter and money that you had sent me. For all your favors I am thankful with all my heart—you are constantly in my heart and in my mind, and only when I fall asleep I forget you and your favors to me. Your kind sister does not forget me either. Your promise to visit us in summer makes me very happy. Come, my angel, to us at Mikhaylovskoye, I shall post all the horses along the road for you. Ours will not be in Petersbur. in summer, they are [*all*] going without fail to Reval. I will await you and pray to God that he will grant that we meet. Prask. Aleks. [*Praskovya Osipova, Pushkin's friend—Y.D.*] has arrived from Petersburg—the young ladies send their regards and are thankful that you do not forget them, but they say that you remember them in your prayers before time, since they are thank God alive and healthy. Farewell, my *batyushka* Alexander Sergeyevich. For your health I have taken the communion host and said a mass, live on nicely, my little friend, you will like it. I am well, thank God, I kiss your hands and remain your much-loving nurse, *Arina Rodivonovna*. Trigorskoye. March 6.

In the second letter, as we can see, Arina seems quite different, thanks to the intelligence of her ghost-writer. She sometimes uses the respectful second-person plural, sometimes the affectionate singular. He uses only the singular, it goes without saying, as was the custom. The tone of both letters is similar: her tenderness, love, and care for her master. Pushkin answered at least one of his nurse's letters.

He saw his nurse for the last time at Mikhaylovskoye on September 14, 1827, nine months before her death. There is no information about his ever seeing her in St. Petersburg. To one side of a draft version of his poem "Fatigued by Life's Emotion," dated June 25 (1828), we find: "Fanny *Nyanya* + Elisa e Claudio *nya*." "Fanny" is, in the opinion of Mstislav Tsyavlovsky, a prostitute whom he probably visited that day; "Elisa" is the name of the opera in the St. Petersburg Imperial Theater, which he attended, and in the middle there is a cross. Supposedly, Pushkin found out about the death of his nurse, who had been taken not long before from Mikhaylovskoye to St. Petersburg in the retinue of his sister Olga, who had just gotten married, and according to one version Arina caught a cold on her way. Pushkin didn't come to her funeral, nor did his sister. She was buried by Olga's husband, Nikolay Pavlishchev, alone, who buried her in an unmarked grave. It's normally accepted that "*nyanya* +" in Pushkin's manuscript signifies the death of his nurse.[26] Supposedly, it just happened that way, his feeling sad about his nurse's death in between a prostitute and the theater.

The date, however, still remains unclear. For over a hundred years it wasn't known in which cemetery she was buried. Ulyansky in his book *Pushkin's Nurse* proved that she died on July 31, 1828, of which there is a record in the church of The Icon of Our Lady of Vladimir: "Arina Rodionovna, serving woman of 5th-class Official Pushkin. Disease: old age." N.Granovskaya considers that she died on July 29, since, in that period, one was interred and the burial service read on the third day. But how can that be matched up with the date of June 25, marked with a cross by Pushkin? Even if we suppose that it's worth considering it to be not "June" but "July," they wouldn't have been able to delay a burial for six days in high summer anyway. Attempts to explain the June 25 date have led to nothing. Maybe Pushkin marked with a cross the onset of some irreversible illness of hers that he had found out about and understood that she would never recover from—something like a stroke, for instance. He doubtlessly and sincerely loved his nurse, but the place for this affection was Mikhaylovskoye; in St. Petersburg he had no need of her.

His nurse's grave vanished immediately. Several different versions of where the spot should be make their way around in the literature: that her grave is in the

Svyatogorsk monastery, near the poet's grave; that Arina was buried back in her home country of Suyda; and also at Bolsheokhtinskoye cemetery in St. Petersburg, where for some time there was even a headstone with "Pushkin's Nurse" inscribed instead of a name. Only towards the end of the 30s of this century did they find the registration of her funeral at the Smolensk cemetery in St. Petersburg.

3. The Prototype and the Poet's Friends

Pushkin's nurse became a literary model and found a second life in his imagination and in his texts. Apart from everything else, that was the style of those times and of Pushkin's circle—a humane attitude towards common people, or, in Pushkin's favorite word, towards the mob. It's acceptable to say that his nurse was the prototype for a whole range of his heroines. For instance, Filipyevna, Tatyana Larina's nurse, whom he called in his drafts Fadeyevna or Filatyevna as well. Then there was the nurse Kseniya in Boris Godunov, and Dubrovsky's nurse Orina Yegorovna (Pakhomovna), who even wrote a letter similar to the ones that Arina dictated.[27] The same type is the princess's wet-nurse (in "The Mermaid") and perhaps even the female dwarf Swallow in "The Blackamoor of Peter the Great." Always secondary characters, similar to one another.

Nabokov, too, searched for the roots of the prototypes of the nurse in Pushkin. "The story-telling old nurse is of course an ancient thematic device. In Maria Edgeworth's *Ennui* (1809), she is Irish, and her tales are of the Irish Black Beard and the ghost of King O'Donoghue."[28] The facts of Arina Rodionovna's own life, as a prototype for a heroine, were almost never used by Pushkin. For example, his nurse was married at the age of 22, but Filipyevna in Onegin at 13, and her story is more interesting. In other words, Pushkin used information that he obtained outside of his relations with his nurse. We're paying particular attention to this because the poet's literary characters subsequently enriched the legendary image of Arina Rodionovna.

The unfinished draft of the widely known poem "Friend of my bleak days…" had no name. The heading "To Nurse," put to it on its first publication by Annenkov, was indicated at first in brackets, and then subsequent editors began deleting the brackets as well as the half-finished line "Then you imagine..." Annenkov first published it in 1855, having connected the artistic image straightaway with Arina.

The real life, the tragedy of the existence of the slave Arina Rodionovna, although she was probably completely satisfied with her life, found almost no reflection in Pushkin. It was a serious topic, not a romantic one, because both "her youth and her love were taken from her by strangers, without asking her."[29] "Both character-types and pictures from the lives of common people are almost absent" in Pushkin, wrote Kotlyarevsky. And further: "The only filled-out portrait from this collection of sketches was the portrait of the friend of his incarceration, the nurse of his Tatyana. The kind friend of his wretched youth, this "darling in her dotage," can be glimpsed in his poems as some kind of vision from what is in reality a world that was foreign to him."[30] She remained in his works as a romanticized, happy character, without a private life, and outside of the social context so important to Russian literature.

The attitude of several of Pushkin's friends toward his nurse is also bound up with the Mikhaylovskoye solitude of the poet. His friends knew about her basically from his poems, and imitated him, their care for her exaggerated. Delvig wrote to Pushkin just after he had left Mikhaylovskoye: "My soul, your nurse's situation frightens me. How could she bear this altogether unexpected parting from you?" It's impossible not to mention this loss of a sense of proportion: after all, she is a servant, not his mother, wife, or lover.

Pushchin, however, recalled with vexation how Arina, during a visit by him to Mikhaylovskoye, closed the dampers of their heating-stoves too early and nearly poisoned the two friends with carbon-monoxide fumes. Naturally, the poet, returning to Moscow, had no more need of his nurse. He was in a state of euphoria: a meeting with the tsar, carousing in the capital, new plans for his life. In 1827, Praskovya Osipova sent Pushkin a letter with a poem in it that Yazykov had sent to Vulf. It was dedicated to Pushkin's nurse:

> Vasilyevna, my light, shall I forget thee?
> Those days when, in love with country freedom,
> Both glory I abandoned for it, and science,
> And Germans, and that city of professors and boredom—
> Thou, beneficial mistress of that shelter
> Where by bleak fate Pushkin is unwhelmed,

> Despising people, rumors, their caresses, betrayals,
> Performing rites at the altar of Camena—
> Ever in greetings heartfelt, kindly
> Wouldst thou meet me, and salute me ...

It is clear that Yazykov's love for Arina derives from his friendship for Pushkin; had she not been Pushkin's nurse, there would never have been any poems about her virtues. He addressed her as Vasilyevna, but of course she was Rodionovna. Somebody clued him in, and Yazykov changed the line to "My light, Rodionovna, shall I forget you?" Delvig published this poem in his Severnye Tsvety (*Northern Flowers*) in 1828. The name was not that important: she was a "nurse in general," a romanticized heroine of the people. She could never have read those poems, and most likely would never have had a notion of what they were writing about her.

Pyotr Vyazemsky told Pushkin on July 26, 1828, "Give Olga Sergeyevna my hand in greeting, and Rodionovna a bow from the waist." Pushkin evidently couldn't pass on the bow, because he wasn't to see his nurse, and she was to die in five days. Pushkin's friends wrote one another on the subject of her death; for instance, Orest Somov wrote to Nikolay Yazykov about the departed. Meanwhile, Pushkin's relatives, whom she had served faithfully and truly all her life, were more restrained in their expression of feeling or gratitude towards their servant.

Anna Kern, who visited Mikhaylovskoye for well-known reasons in 1825, left the following line in her memoirs of Pushkin: "I think he never loved anyone truly except his nurse, and then his sister."[31] Kern wrote about this more than a quarter of a century later, and to say that Pushkin loved nobody was for her to equate her fleeting affair with him to his serious passions, including the one for his wife. But we have to think that whomever Pushkin loved, he loved *truly*.

4. The "Generalized Nurse"

One of the laws of idealization seems to be the purging of bothersome information from the image, followed by its generalization, simplification, and then romanticization. That is why two nurses turned into one, and various characters from literature (typical of a family at that time) found a single prototype. "A kind of collective *my nurse*," said Nabokov, and, in another place, "the generalized nurse."[32] The menials in service to the young master at Mikhaylovskoye totaled 29 souls, including "the widow Irina Rodionovna," as she is called in the serf register. And everything "folkloric" that Pushkin absorbed during his exile (if he actually came into contact with common folk in any way at all) was written into the "composite" Arina Rodionovna.

In Pushkin's biographies, his nurse overshadows yet another servant, one devoted to Pushkin no less, and perhaps more, than she—her daughter's husband, Nikita Kozlov, who was originally a lamplighter to the poet's father. Kozlov was unlucky. Veresayev was the first to turn his attention to him: "How strange! He was a person evidently passionately devoted to Pushkin, loved him, took care of him, perhaps no less than Arina Rodionovna; accompanied him throughout the whole of his independent lifetime, but who is nowhere to be mentioned: neither in Pushkin's letters, nor in the letters of the people closest to him. Not one single word about him, either good or bad."[33] Nikita rescued Pushkin from utterly serious and risky situations; saved him from search, carried the wounded poet home in his arms, and, along with Aleksandr Turgenev, lowered the coffin with Pushkin's body in it into his grave.

> Help me to dress, Nikita:
> The metropolis is abuzz...

If we overlook these two accidental lines, then the loyal Kozlov passes unnoticed through the poet's works.

Nadezhda Pushkina, in a letter to Kern, informs her: "From time to time Alexander writes two or three words to his sister; he's at Mikhaylovskoye now, close to his 'darling little nurse,' as you call her so lovingly."[34] There is some evidence that he called his nurse "mama," while she would say to him: "*Batyushka*, why do you always call me 'mama'? how could I be your mother?"[35] But the fact is that he called his mother *maman*, in French, while *mama*, *mamka*, or *mamushka*, as he called his nurse, is quite acceptable as an expression in Russian for "wet-nurse, a woman breast-feeding another's child; [*or*] a senior nurse, a kind of supervisor of young children," according to Vladimir Dal. Later on, the tendency among Pushkin's biographers to replace his mother with his nurse became more categorical:

"Let's recall Arina Rodionovna—the nurse who was dearer to Pushkin than his mother."[36]

Idealization always has a dark side, an antithesis. If someone gets idealized, somebody else has to get anathematized. This shows up especially clearly in the Soviet tradition. The class-based approach: aristocrat-mother versus the representative of the people, his nurse. In the process of idealization, his nurse got better and better and his mother worse and worse; the nurse gets more and more frequent mention, and his mother less and less. The poet's nurse became his sublimated mother.

A paltry number of Pushkin's letters to members of his family has survived; in fact, he hardly wrote to them at all. He wrote his father three letters, his father and mother one letter, his father, mother and sister one letter, his sister five letters—all basically just notes. And personally to his mother—none. However, when his mother died, Pushkin went to her funeral and bought the grave next to hers for himself. And since one's mother correlates to one's motherland, which must be loved, in official Pushkin studies the people's nurse is invested with parental functions, becomes a surrogate mother for the poet. However, you can find this in Pushkin himself: at the author's whim, Tatyana calls to mind not her mother's grave, but her nurse's—a fact that Anna Akhmatova drew attention to.

> Where now there is a cross and branches' shade
> Over my poor nurse.

The next tendency in Pushkin studies was the liquidation of the role of the poet's aristocrat-grandmothers, and the inclusion of his grandmothers' features in the image of his nurse. We'll just note that his grandmother Maria Hannibal is the one usually discussed, since Pushkin was just two and a half years old when his other grandmother died, his father's mother, Olga Chicherina. Her sister Varvara liked Pushkin, and gave him a whole hundred rubles to buy nuts when the boy set off for the Lyceum. There is almost no mention of the grandmothers in the poet's biographies. His grandmother Maria Hannibal served more than once as material for a model of the ideal nurse. For instance, his poem "The Dream" (a fragment beginning with the words "Allow the poet with a rented censer"), evidently part of an unfinished poem begun in 1816, includes these famous lines:

> Shall I fail my *mamushka* to mention,
> On mysterious nights a-wonder,
> When in mobcap and antique garb
> She'd fend away the ghosts with prayer,
> Bless me zealously
> And in a whisper start a tale for me
> Of men dead, and Bova's hero-deeds...
> And I in terror never stirring,
> Scarcely breathing, snug beneath my blanket,
> Feeling neither legs nor head.
> The simple lamp of clay beneath the icon
> Dimly limned the deep wrinkles,
> Great-grandmother's mobcap, costly antique,
> And wide mouth with two teeth gnashing—
> All instilled unwilling fear into my soul.

Traditionally, ever since Bartenev, this fragment has been considered to be describing his nurse. Boris Tomashevsky's interpretation in the ten-volume Academy edition of Pushkin is that "Here Pushkin describes either his grandmother M. A. Hannibal or his nurse, Arina Rodionovna."[37] However, the line "Great-grandmother's mobcap, costly antique, " affords us the opportunity to be more precise: in the poem, Pushkin combines the two of them together (on the one hand, *mamushka*, on the other, an object of worth).

Gradually, yet another generalization crystalized: it turned out that the poet's muse was none other than his nurse. Thus M. Shevlyakov writes further: "Pushkin embodies his muse in the person of his dear nurse."[38] This assertion is based upon the poet's lines:

> Confidante of olden, magic times,
> Friend through fancies playful, sad;
> I knew you in my springtime's days,
> Primal days of dream and of delight;
> I'd wait for you. In evening's quiet
> You'd appear a jolly beldame
> Looming over me in your jacket,
> Big eyeglasses, and your playful rattle.
> You rocked my infant cradle,
> Charmed my youthful ear with melody,
> And in my coverlet you left a whistle
> That you'd bewitched yourself.

This poem, about which much has been written, by tradition is ascribed to 1822 (when the poet was in Kishinev), and for a long time was considered to be dedicated to Arina Rodionovna, the "jolly beldame" seated before the poet in her jacket. However, the end of the poem was sometimes omitted in quotation:

> Whirled by th'unruly wave, your cloak
> Just ashroud your half-ethereal form;
> All in locks twined in a chaplet round
> Your sweet-scented head, my lovely;
> White bosom beneath yellowed pearls
> Flushed and trembled softly.

Half-ethereal form, ringlets, fragrance (that is, expensive French perfumes or lotions—they were all from France alone in those times), decolletage (the boy remembered for years seeing the half-undraped bosom), and finally, eyeglasses and pearls ornamenting a breast—could that have been a serf woman? That was Maria Hannibal, his aristocrat-grandmother, who played a major role in the education and upbringing of her little grandson Alexander. She was divorced (at that time termed "in departure") from her husband, Osip Hannibal, and, naturally, her life's interests were concentrated in her favorite grandchildren.

5. Nurse's tales and tales of a nurse

Undoubtedly Pushkin loved his nurse, but Pushkin scholars have loved her even more. The glorification of the "people's nurse" was not just the contribution of the Soviet school of Pushkin. Pushkin created a romantic, poetic myth, and the poet's notion was extended by his friends. Close on their heels, the first Pushkin scholars extolled Arina, expressing thoughts consonant with the official national ideology. According to Bartenev, "Arina Rodionovna skillfully told fairy tales, spewed out proverbs and sayings, knew folk beliefs, and indisputably had a great influence on her nursling, unextirpated either by later foreign tutors or by education in the Lyceum at Tsarskoye Selo.[39] Just imagine that: foreigners and the Lyceum trying to extirpate everything Russian and good in Pushkin, and his nurse saves him.

However, if we're to speak seriously, it's impossible to clarify what his nurse's real contribution was to the poet's upbringing. Contemporaries noted that she was loquacious, garrulous. Annenkov wrote:

> A union of geniality and querulousness, an affectionate disposition towards youth with a pretended sternness, left an indelible memory with Pushkin. He loved her with a kindred, unchanging love, and in the years of his maturity and glory would talk to her for whole hours."

Common sense gets lost in the hyperbola of Annenkov's esteem for Arina Rodionovna: "The whole of the Russian fairy-tale world was known to her intimately and she passed it on with extraordinary originality."[40]

It's known for sure that Pushkin wrote down seven fairy tales, ten songs, and several folk-expressions from her words, although he heard much more from her, of course. However, it's not clear if Pushkin copied down the plots of songs about Stenka Razin from his nurse's words or took them from Chulkov's collection, which he had read. Lotman turned his attention to this fact.[41] The argument about from where Pushkin had borrowed the plots of certain fairy tales—from Arina Rodionovna or from the Brothers Grimm—continues. But political victory during the Soviet regime was definitely not on the side of the Brothers Grimm.

That same Annenkov introduced into tradition unhistorical exaggerations like "the famous Arina Rodionovna." He went even further: "Rodionovna was one of the most typical and noble figures of the Russian world." And, it turns out, Pushkin "let the venerable old lady into all the mysteries of his genius." The contribution of genius is defined thus: he is the poet "who glorified her name to all *Rus*."[42]

Slavophiles picked up on Arina Rodionovna because she helped them bring the poet into their camp. Ivan Aksakov said, in 1880, at a Pushkin celebration, "So that's who was his first inspiration, the first Muse of the great artist and first truly Russian poet, that simple Russian country woman... From her stories as if at the breast of an earth mother he greedily drank in the clear stream of the people's speech and spirit." This was said before Freud had ever published a line. The sprouting of Russian populism—the guilt and misfortune of the Russian intelligentsia—was embodied in this 19th-century passion for her.

After the October *coup d'état*, the myth of his nurse was used for the political adjustment of Pushkin's image as a poet of the people. It is irrefutable that, from among all of the people of servile rank, the poet's nurse was closest to him. As far as mythologization goes, it's always characterized by an immoderate widening of spheres of influence. "The significance of Arina Rodionovna for Pushkin is exceptionally great and well known, but not yet completely apprehended, not summed up... " wrote Ulyansky in his Academy monograph, *Pushkin's Nurse*.

He called her "a worthy representative of our people," a typical formulation of the Soviet era. Boris Meylakh wrote of Mikhaylovskoye: "Here the poet's close acquaintance and intimacy with the people came to pass."[43] Pushkin donned a peasant shirt on one occasion and went to a fair, as Semevsky wrote.[44] This fact is presented now as if it were the poet's usual method for getting close to the common people. That same Meylakh later on substituted "direct relations" for the words "acquaintance and intimacy," at the same time widening its territory as well: we discover that the poet, while in exile at Mikhaylovskoye, "had direct relations with the Pskov peasantry."[45]

Down through the years, his nurse's role has been growing among Soviet Pushkin scholars. Arina Rodionovna is settled into all of Pushkin's biographies, has taken up residence in all the textbooks of Russian literature—from primary school to higher education. His nurse has become one of the pillars of the ideological adaptation of Pushkin himself. In an editorial in *Pravda* in 1937, following the postulate that Pushkin's Decembrist friends had made him into a revolutionary poet himself, his low-born nurse is placed in opposition to his aristocratic parents, bringing our poet closer to the people. Now, thanks to his nurse, Pushkin has been brought closer and made more understandable to the common Soviet people.[46] A year after the hundredth anniversary of Pushkin's death came two more solemn anniversaries: the 180th anniversary of Arina Rodionovna's birth and the 110th of her death.

The nurse is an example for other people; she is "a remarkable model of the beauty of soul, the wisdom and the spiritual qualities of our people." Finally, she became a genius herself: Arina Rodionovna—"the poet's good genius." When Stalin was called "the inspiration of the Soviet people," the nurse became "the inspiration and the source of certain of the poet's creative ideas."[47] In official Soviet mythology, Arina Rodionovna was ranked with other folk heroes such as Aleksey Stakhanov, Dzhambul, Pasha Angelina, and the like. The Soviet Army

Song and Dance Ensemble would sing, their mighty voices threatening their enemies with: "Why do you fall silent at the window, my old one?"

Either the myth simply marks time on the spot, repeating what was said by Annenkov, or it picks up torque, acquiring parodic overtones. In dozens of research papers, the woman undergoes apotheosis. It has even been said in complete seriousness that "under his nurse's influence, he loved the Russian language and the Russian people from childhood."[48] "The nurse, missing her 'beloved friend,' as she called Pushkin, would often go to the nearest post station in hopes of hearing of him from people passing on their way from St. Petersburg."[49]

All sense of proportion got lost: "The poet's original acquaintance with the people, with the folklore, along with his mastery of the Russian folk language, was through her."[50] And even this: "If Pushkin, as he once resolved to say, grew up 'without griefs or troubles' in his childhood, he owes it to his nurse, Arina ..." In her cult she acquires the idealized features of the heroine: "For the poet, his nurse was the embodiment of the soul of the people, a 'representative' of the people, as one would say now."[51] She appears as a preceptor, the bearer of higher wisdom, the poet's teacher, his guru.

Her literary talents have grown, too. She's "the talented teller of fairy-tales, absorbing into herself all the wisdom of folk poetry." Pushkin did the writing, but his nurse's glory keeps on growing: "From the second half of the 1820s the name of Arina Rodionovna herself became famous ... But her name obtained wide popularity after the third chapter of *Eugene Onegin* came to light in 1827."[52] It is especially interesting to read this since Pushkin, as is known, soon began to lose his popularity, and here it seems that his nurse was becoming popular in his place. That synthesized folk wisdom, so to speak, wasn't introduced into the literature by accident. Pushkin studies became a kind of hagiography, as it has remained to this day. The topics of "Pushkin and the People," and "Pushkin and the Motherland," along with his patriotism, were decreed to be fundamentals of literature, while his nurse became the initiating element for the construction of such models.[53] And here the name of Rodionovna becomes entirely apropos.

It goes without saying that etymology has nothing to do with it, since "Rodion" supposedly comes from the Greek *rodon*, a rose. But the unconsciously similar sound of one word in particular is superimposed on the other: Rodionovna – *rod* (kin) – *narod* (people) – *rodina* (motherland). "Figuratively speaking, the land nourishes the peasant like a mother nourishes her child. The land to a certain extent controls its inhabitants, almost like a mother does her child."[54] In this construction, Arina is exactly the right figure necessary for Pushkin's formulation as Russian national poet No.1, without whom he is incomplete.

Speculation about the folkloric element in his works became an integral part of scholarship on Pushkin. Certain Slavophile notions proved useful in this context. Included in the Soviet understanding of his folkloric element was: (1) the writer's origins, (2) the folklore bases of his works, and (3) his expression of interest in the same things as the mass of the people. In the first case, Pushkin was in trouble—he was an aristocrat; in the second, however much you juggle it around, his work is a long way from folklore (*The Queen of Spades*, say, is not derivable from Russian folklore); and the third was just made up, verbal trumpery necessary to the ideologues. It was about then that a literary joke appeared: the *iznarodovanie* of literature.

Arina, for that matter, helped Pushkin escape the Revolution, saved him, the nobleman, the class enemy, with her simple peasant background. She was the one who helped the poet to answer to all three points: his origins were corrected by intimacy with the common people, and she led his work in the proper direction, giving him her folklore, that is, a popular basis. Finally, in naming his nurse close to him in spirit, they came to a conclusion: he expressed her interests, symbolizing the interests of the whole of the Russian people. An envoy of the people, his nurse became the symbol of the whole of Russia, whose greatest son is Poet No.1.

Meanwhile, the voices of some Western Pushkin scholars long ago sounded a note of skepticism. Vladimir Nabokov wrote: "She is the tremendous favorite with demophile Pushkinists. The influence of her folk tales on Pushkin has been enthusiastically and ridiculously exaggerated. It is doubtful that Pushkin ever read *Eugene Onegin* to her, as some commentators and illustrators havebelieved."[55] Soviet critics, who had to exaggerate Pushkin's obligatory sympathy for the wide masses, according to D.J. Richards and C.R.S. Cockrell, naturally attached especial importance to Arina in her role in the making of the poet, sometimes to such an extent that she looked as if she was bearing almost the whole of Pushkin's patriotism on her feeble shoulders.[56] John Bayley formulated an even stricter role for his nurse: "The representative of the people, canonized in Pushkinian hagiography."[57]

Reading Soviet works one thinks that a similar approach could not be called otherwise but the misrepresentation of Pushkin and the essence of the literary process in general. One of the cleverest people in the history of Russia, who from childhood began his comprehension of the treasure of world literature, who studied in the best educational institution of the empire and his whole life was in intimate contact with outstanding writers, philosophers, and politicians—that brilliant intellectual came to know his language, folklore, and his very people through one old woman who couldn't remember the letters necessary to write the word *nurse*.

It is well known that, with Pushkin, the authorial "bio" and the lyric "I" of his heroes are often very close, almost merging. But these aren't the same thing, anyway. The literary myth of the ideal nurse, as in many other cases (the poet's wife, Madonna Natalya; the noble bandits Pugachev and Dubrovsky; Peter the Great, the idol on a bronze horse), set the tone. After him stretched the work of the first Pushkin scholars. The romanticized nurse of the First Poet of Russia entered into the literature. Then the literary heroine came to life, gradually pushing aside the poet's other nurses, his grandmother, his mother, and all the rest of the serfs in his biography, and, as a result, now represents the entire Russian race for Pushkin scholars.

As Apollon Grigoryev has it, Pushkin "is our everything"; similarly, the poet's nurse in his biographies became Pushkin's *everything*, replacing his family, and, periodically, his friends and society. In winter, as a Pushkin scholar informs us, his nurse even replaced his heating stove: "In the house at Mikhaylovskoye on a frosty winter evening ... only his nurse's love kept him warm."[58] Although the Soviet regime is in existence no longer, the nurse who is the proper one from the point of view of the official mythology fills up not only mass literature on Pushkin, but, with the rare exception, research articles too. The circle has closed: the literary image became biographical, the great nurse became an important part of the mythologization of the great people's poet—now they are national icons.

As evidence of his nurse's influence, role, and importance his later poem, "Once again I visited" (1835) is adduced:

> Here's the little house, disgraced,

> Where I lived with my poor nurse.
> The old one's here no longer—no more behind the wall
> Can I hear her heavy steps,
> Nor her painstaking patrol.

The continuation after these lines serves as the most important argument of the nurse's defenders:

> I shall not at evening 'neath the storm's noise
> Attend her stories rote-learned
> By me from childhood, but heart-pleasing still,
> Like ancient songs or pages
> In a favored old book, in which we know
> Where stands each word.
> Her simple speech and counsel
> And love-full reproaches
> Would cheer my weary heart
> With quiet delight...

"What other proofs and references to the role which the illiterate Arina Rodionovna played in the life of the great poet are necessary?" the scholar inquires emotionally. "And didn't Pushkin himself give the answer to those *memoiristes* who spoke of 'exaggerations'?"[59]

Pushkin really did give an answer to Pushkin scholars: he himself crossed out these lines.

Poetical evidence is used in the capacity of documentary evidence, while his nurse is just an image in the poems. He's the one who carried out the historical role played by the illiterate Arina Rodionovna. More simply put, Pushkin's nurse told him fairy tales, and his biographers themselves made up fairy stories about her. And the more they praised his nurse, the more vivid became the point that the authors did not want to make: they were misrepresenting Pushkin, the artistic level of whose works was ostensibly appreciated by kindly but illiterate servants. Besides, it became clear that the remaining "broad environment of the people" around the poet played no role, since only his nurse herself was a genius. The people kept silent.

6. A Visual Mythology

On February 17, 1918, Trigorskoye was looted and burned to the ground. On February 19, Mikhaylovskoye was robbed and then burned. Or, as it was written in Soviet guidebooks, "After the Great October Socialist Revolution, a genuine, caring master came to take over the Pushkin lands—the people."[60] A woman who witnessed it wrote:

> From a distance I could see how two peasants and a woman were carrying off bricks and ironwork from the charred ruins of the museum-home ... I found shards of a marble bust, pieces broken with axes from the marble base of a billiard table, in the snow. I took a piece of the long-suffering temple of his smashed-to-smithereens death mask as a souvenir.[61]

The outbuilding where Arina lived was supposedly restored in 1920 by Red Army soldiers, a difficult thing to believe. "I summoned the leader of the engineer company, Turchaninov," recalled the chief of staff of the Independent Bashkir Brigade of the Red Army, "and gave the order: the engineer company was to proceed to Mikhaylovskoye and restore the nurse's cabin."[62] The chief of staff was recalling this in the 1930s, when for well-known reasons they had begun the restoration of what the peasants had looted.

In 1949 the house was again "raised from the ashes." The design of the premises in which Arina had ostensibly lived was planned and executed by the best architects and decorators of the Soviet Union. The outbuilding was renamed "The Nurse's Cabin." In the place where at one time a "tumbledown shack" had stood was raised the literary studio of the Great Custodienne of Russian folk spirit, folklore, and language, the poet's Muse and the creator of his genius. In the noble house, reconstructed as a museum, the maid's room was renamed "The Nurse's Room." On the walls, as it says in the guidebook, hung "a literary exposition telling of Arina's friendship with Pushkin."

Let's note how the order of the names has changed, and now the nurse is the one with friends. Arina's cabin in Kobrino, as some sources have affirmed, was discovered to be genuine, its old framework of logs from the 18th century. It was said that the nurse's distant descendants lived there, but it wasn't said that they had abandoned it and managed to move to Leningrad. A village teacher-enthusiast had settled in the house, preserving it from ruin. A sign was hung on the cabin: "Here lived Pushkin's nurse, Arina Rodionovna."

For the 175th anniversary of Pushkin's birth in 1974, an ethnographic museum was founded, representing in a general way the house-furnishings of a poor peasant family. "Portraits" of Arina by various artists were hung on the walls. In an audio recording, a voice "reminiscent" of the nurse's recounted her fairy-tales. It goes without saying that all the furnishings of this "nurse's genuine house" were purest window-dressing: whatever and however it could or must have been, one would have to say what a museum of visual mythology it now was. By accident, we overheard some children who had entered the museum asking their elderly guide: "Are *you* Arina Rodionovna?"

Of late even the authenticity of the nurse's cabin has come under suspicion. A part of the showplace is "The Arina Rodionovna Reading-Cabin." That's an interesting idea, a reading-room named after someone who never read anything, because she couldn't. There were suggestions for a monument to Arina, and one was erected in Kobrino, and another one in Pskov, where Arina Rodionovna, apparently, had never been at all.

In Kobrino's neighboring museum at the noble estate of Suyda, the patrimony of the Hannibals, Arina is ranked one of Pushkin's relatives on a memorial sign, along with his father, mother, and sister, at the behest of the ideologically-inclined directorship.

It is understandable that a serious defect diminishing the role of Pushkin's irreplaceable preceptor remains the iconography—or, more precisely, the absence of any such. Arina's portrait had never been done in her life, but it was desirable to have such a thing. Attempts have been made to affirm that this or that depiction of a woman was a portrait of the nurse. In the Pushkin Museum in St. Petersburg, a portrait of an unknown woman by an unknown artist is passed off as Arina Rodionovna's portrait with a significant degree of possibility. A high-relief portrait in walrus ivory of a woman (which somebody had given as a present to Gorky, who passed it on to the museum) was made by a local carver something like twelve years after her death, and would also scarcely bear any relation to the real nurse.

There is no description of her appearance, if we don't take into account Maria Osipova's "extraordinarily venerable elderly lady, with a plump face, gone gray." If Pushkin's nurse was so intimate with him, why didn't he—a man who drew people even not very close to him in his manuscripts—draw her profile? There is a woman's profile sketched by Pushkin and much discussed in this context, in fact. The drawing is in a manuscript next to the poem "Foreboding" and a draft of "Fatigued by Life's Emotion." Perhaps "Pushkin Weeps for his Nurse in his Drawings" is what they should call it.[63] But then again, maybe not, we would add.

The myth required feeding. In newspapers and later in the Vremennik Pushkinskoy komissii (*The Journal of the Pushkin Commission*) articles appeared in which the assumption was made that Pushkin's drawing of an old and a young woman, next to the lines of the first song in *Poltava*, depict Arina Rodionovna at two different ages. Moreover, N.Granovskaya wrote: "In the first portrait she was drawn, probably, the way the poet saw her for the last time on her death-bed—in front of us is the face of an old woman with already stiffened features, with lowered eyelids. Next to it is rendered a portrait of the young Arina Rodionovna; it is more distinct: the expression on the young woman's face is lively and impassioned."[64] Nikolay Izmaylov contradicted Granovskaya: "Isn't the drawing of a girl in a headdress a portrait of Kochubey's daughter (who hadn't yet appeared in the manuscript of the poem), which was given some features resembling Maria Rayevskaya (Volkonskaya)?"[65] But then a decade and a half later Granovskaya published a book in which her assumptions are presented as reliable facts: "The poet immortalized her young image ... As if removing the wrinkles from his nurse's face, Pushkin imagined Arina Rodionovna as she would have looked in maidenhood."[66]

Illustrations in Pushkin's biography and selected works depicting his darling-in-her-dotage looking like a queen appear in profusion, but they are merely the imaginings of artists, and nothing more. The nurse becomes one of the main heroines of *Eugene Onegin*, since her portrayal appears so often among the illustrations of the various editions of the novel. Later there appeared oil paintings, bas reliefs, and sculptures of the nurse, but we don't know at all how the real woman who served the poet looked.

7. Obstacles to Idealization

Starting in the 30s of this century, differing views on Arina Rodionovna were silenced from the center, but critical voices rang out anyway at the dawn of Pushkin studies. Lev Pavlishchev, Pushkin's nephew, in his *Memoirs*, however muddled they may have been considered, was one of the first to declare that the poet's biographers and friends had unduly inflated the role of the illiterate peasant Arina in the development of Pushkin's childhood impressions.

Some of the poet's biographers who had immoderately praised her began to contradict themselves with the passage of time. Pavel Annenkov himself, after his eulogies, suddenly calls himself to order, commenting on the nurse's stories: "They are striking in general with their cunning and the intricacy of their plots, which are sometimes difficult to comprehend." Or: "It looks as if the kindly and limited old woman, Arina Rodionovna, played something like the role of a unconscious mystical agent in the life of her nursling." And further: "it was not her weak and enfeebled hand that showed the poet the road on which he found himself."[67] Valeryan Maykov wrote: "Let's be impartial and not exaggerate the influence of Arina Rodionovna on Pushkin ..."[68] Vikenty Veresayev, who likes details, although he called her "famous" in Annenkov's wake, only discusses her in passing in his book *Pushkin's Companions*, citing Pushkin's and Yazykov's lines.

Arina could hardly have understood exactly what her master was writing, and what significance these texts had. But any evidence of her role crosses over into immoderate generalization, and for that reason at times looks like parody. Ulyansky wrote: "Pushkin often would read her his works, and was interested in her opinion. It's a pity that her judgements of the poet's works have not been carried down to us."[69] However, this idea was merely borrowed from Annenkov. "Unfortunately, we know nothing about what his nurse thought about the poetry-writing pastime of her nursling."[70] So what then does her genius consist in? However, we should add that the ability to listen is also a talent, although one characteristic to a greater extent of dogs and cats rather than people.

At a critical moment of Pushkin's life, when the gendarmerie officer was taking him to Pskov, his nurse, according to the story, wept, and was comforted by her master. In the morning she appeared at Osipova's in a disheveled state, sobbing. "'What, did the officer take away any papers with him?' we asked the nurse. 'No, my dears, he took no papers, and left no mess anywhere in the house; a little later I myself did destroy something...' 'What, in fact?' 'That damned cheese, the one that Alexander Sergeyevich liked to eat, but as for me, I just can't stand it, and the odor from it, from that German cheese, is so foul...'" This quote is famous, but it testifies about Arina Rodionovna's level of understanding of what was going on with the poet.

Pushkin, as a Lyceum student, mentioned a woman in his humorous poems, one who is sometimes named as Arina Rodionovna in the literature.

> Leaving off book-study,
> In a leisure hour of mine
> At a sweet old woman's
> I drink a fragrant tea.

It goes without saying that this was not her, since further on it says that he kissed her hand and she read him the newspapers, fishing out rumors from them. And the main thing is that tea wasn't what his nurse liked to drink. Many of Pushkin's acquaintances, in recalling her, stress Arina Rodionovna's passion for strong drink. Pushchin's recollections are: "We never even noticed the second cork flying to the ceiling; we even treated his nurse to some bubbly..."[71] Nikolay Yazykov's "Epistle to Nurse" commemorates a drinking-bout:

> You whipped us up an intricate repast,
> Serving us yourself with vodka and home-brew
> And honeycomb, and fruit, and wine set
> On the dear antique table all a-groan.

Nikolay Yazykov's poem "On the Death of A. S. Pushkin's Nurse" isn't a grieving for a person's passing, either, but a recollection of three parting friends (Aleksey Vulf, Pushkin, and himself):

> The dinnertable was laid
> In richness of wines and country brews,
> And you, come to join us!
> We feasted. You did not shy
> From our lot—and betimes
> Were given back your springtime
> By your enspirited dream;
> You loved to hear our chorus,

> Living sounds of foreign lands,
> Speeches puffed-up and rebuffed
> And glasses ringing upon glasses.
> Already the night had snuffed its lights,
> Skyscape reddening with dawn;
> I recall some words about retiring
> That you told us long ago.
> In vain! The *tokay* had its way,
> The bold carousing grew still louder.
> Sit you down, sweet old one,
> And drink some brew with us! (1830)

The sweet old one has just died, and the poet invites her to a drinking bout. Towards the end, Nikolay Yazykov notes that the nurse was "eloquent as wine." Inspired by her strong liqueurs, Yazykov wrote more lines about Pushkin's nurse than Pushkin himself. "This was an extraordinarily venerable elderly lady," we have to repeat our quotation of Maria Osipova, "with a plump face, gone gray, who loved her nursling with a passion ..." The following part of the phrase is cut from some editions: "... but with one little sin—she loved to drink."[72] The nurse's Soviet biographer explains her inclination towards alcoholism in a Marxist-Leninist spirit: "That sin was an echo of the primordial feature of the entire village of Suyda and the harsh conditions of slave life."[73]

I discussed this issue with a Freudian colleague of mine, and his point of view is probably worthwhile bringing up. According to the psychoanalytical conception, oral gratification is given to the poet not by his mother but by his *mamushka*, that is, his theoretical wet-nurse, who, in the absence of a real wet-nurse, remained for him in his adult years synthesized in the image of Arina Rodionovna. The difference is that the expert liqueur-maker treated him now not to milk or tea, but to moonshine. Almost a classic case of the Oedipus complex, in which, however, the mother is replaced by the wet-nurse and the son gets his gratification not directly but aslant, correspondingly repaying not his mother, but his nurse, with his love.

During the Andropov-Gorbachev Soviet campaign against alcoholism, it was not just vineyards that got the axe in the country. An instruction came out to review the classics in secondary-school and third-level textbooks from the point of view of the temperance struggle. After the vineyards, they began axing lines of poetry. An instruction was issued by the Ministry of Education for the editors of *Rodnaya rech'* ("Native Language") textbooks and readers. From Pushkin the following was to be excised:

> Let's take a drink, dear friend
> Of my meager youth;
> Drink from sorrow; where there's a mug?
> My heart will be the lighter.[74]

But it was a fiasco: the Soviet Radio kept on playing the popular classic *romans* with those very words, performed by famous singers, and children at school would sing these four particular lines during recess. They soon stopped broadcasting the *romans* over the radio.

Another aspect of Arina's activities was also kept under wraps, even though it was important for Pushkin. When the poet reckoned Natalya on the list. It goes without saying that it isn't worth looking at this with modern eyes. For example, Pushkin's friend Aleksey Vulf practically openly maintained a harem, and Sergey Sobolevsky boasted that he had 500 women.

Ivan Pushchin, after visiting the Mikhaylovskoye hermit on January 11, 1825, recalled: "We went into the nurse's room, where the seamstresses had already gathered. I immediately noticed among them one little figure, acutely different from the others, without informing Pushkin, however, of my conclusion ... However, he instantly saw through my naughty thoughts, and grinned meaningfully. I needed nothing else: I in my turn winked at him, and everything was clear without a single word ... Amid her young crew the nurse pompously walked around with a stocking in her hand."[75]

These girls, when they got pregnant, would be sent off out of their master's way, and the poet himself simply explained: "I have no children, only bastards."[76] In February 1825, Pushkin sacked his housekeeper, Roza Grigoryevna. In a letter he explained: "Otherwise she would have been the death of Nurse, who has already begun to grow thin!" Pavel Shchegolev suggests that the reason for the conflict with his housekeeper was that Pushkin was having an affair with the serf-girl Olga Kalashnikova, and his nurse was helping him with it. Shchegolev exclaims:

> Oh, that Arina Rodionovna! Through the idealistic fog surrounding her image you can see other qualities. Loyal not from duty but out of love for her lords and masters,

the serf-slave, winking and nudging, indulging her masters' whims, made their satisfaction her rule. She couldn't refuse her irrepressible nursling in any matter.

A Don Juan complex—*erotomania*, putting it plainly—is usually explained by Freudians by the fact that the Don Juan is not satisfied with his mother and fails to find her in another. Pushkin's interest from his youth in women much older than he (Karamzina, Golitsyna, Osipova, Sobanskaya, Khitrovo, and others) from this point of view corresponds to his filial love for Arina Rodionovna. And she, as the go-between, carried out the whims of her master, selecting and supplying him with girls when the poet couldn't fall asleep.

Let's be fair: certain Pushkin scholars, even in the difficult Soviet years, stayed moderate on the subject. "He listened to Arina Rodionovna's fairy tales and wrote them down, he wrote down the songs and the fairy tales of other singers and storytellers," only once, in passing, does the distinguished folklorist Mark Azadovsky mention the nurse in his researches into Pushkin's folklore interests.[77] Others made the reservation that the poet gathered his folklore materials "of course, not from the words of Arina Rodionovna alone."[78]

In a commentary to the post-Soviet Russian publication of an edition of Pushkin's Lyceum verses—the so-called experimental first volume of a future collection of his works—a bit more is said about the French education of the poet, and about what "could have become the source of the boy's interest in the Russian literary language and—to a certain extent—in the folkloric tradition: Pushkin's grandmother Maria Hannibal and his nurse, eventually poeticized by him, Arina Rodionovna."[79] The hyperbole seems to be diminishing: *could have become* a source of interest in the Russian language, *to a certain extent*—not to folklore, but indefinitely—*to the folkloric tradition*. In first place, as we see, is his relatively intellectual grandmother, Maria Hannibal—similar formulations could never have escaped in the past from the Institute of Russian Literature. And even the *poeticized-by-Pushkin nurse* (if we don't indulge in wishful thinking) seems to sound a bit ironical.

Today the myth of Arina Rodionovna is still essential to many people; it is part of a person's upbringing in Russian culture and in a particular spirit. Our task was not to destroy that myth but to understand it. But anyway a question as simple as a swallow of water arises which the author directs at himself, but which can summon indignation in the nurse's partisans: is it necessary to waste fast-fleeting time considering her in such detail? It seems to me that if the nurse didn't play such an important role in the poet's life, it would be better to write less about her in his biographies—and that in modest tones.

The Dangerous Jests of Albert Robida

1. Humor Lenin Couldn't See

The very first phrase makes you shudder:

There has been an accident at the huge 'N' electricity reservoir ... As a consequence of an incident whose cause still remains unexplained, a horrible electrical storm has burst over the whole of western Europe... Causing deep perturbations in the course of public and private life, the storm has brought a lot of surprises along with it...[1]

Chernobyl...

Bursting from its electrical bounds, if one can say that, a free current of this terrible, mighty, elemental force—only indignantly subjugated by humans who dared to place their imperious hands on it—is now enveloping approximately a fifth of Europe, with its whirlwind jets relentlessly raging over the whole of the area.[2]

And further:

The engineers and lower ranks of Electrotechnical Post No.28 showed heroic courage ... Having captured the free current, they conducted it to its corresponding reservoir. The assistant senior engineer and 13 workers fell victim in carrying out their duties, but because of them the electrical storm came to a halt and new disasters were no longer in store, until the next accident happens.[3]

We have read even more colorful depictions of the disaster, but with this difference: they were all describing what had already happened. But this author was telling the story of what was yet to come. And published it in the last century.

165

Two and a half centuries after his compatriot Nostradamus, but more concretely, as if he himself had been in that gloomy future and returned.

A hundred years ago, in 1894, a book was published in St. Petersburg, a book that seems like a hoax now, but I hold the original in my hand. The text and drawings in the book *The Twentieth Century: An Electric Life*, are by Albert Robida, the translation into Russian is by V. Rantsov. The book had been passed by the censors and brought out in St. Petersburg, printed by the Panteleyev brothers.

The marks on it bear witness that the book was passed from hand to hand. I bought it by accident, a little over twenty years ago, in a Moscow writers' shop on Kuznetsky Most Street. And at that time it came to me that if I lived until the hundredth anniversary of the book (not an easy bet: the times reeked of prison camp), I would write something about it. Something of a funny jubilee: the translation a hundred years old, and the translation connected to the fate of Russia. When I bought it, Chernobyl hadn't been foreseen—and could such a turn of events have come into anyone's head?

Now I see: the author of the antique was out by almost 30 years in his dating of the explosion; and, besides, Chernobyl is not the most important event in the book. The seer did turn out to be right in a number of spheres. Albert Robida was prematurely and unjustly forgotten by history.

He was born in 1848 in a provincial French town. He was three years old when the first novel by Jules Verne appeared. In his youth he worked in his father's notarial office. The old man, Albert's father, wanted to make sure that his business would pass into trustworthy hands. However, Albert didn't at all behave in the way that a staid small-town notary public should, in a town where everybody knew everyone else.

A jokester, as we might say now, he would sit in his office at the open window, firing quips at passers-by, sometimes jokes not at all inoffensive. He would throw paper airplanes into the cafe across the street from his office, make spitballs from pieces of legal documents and shoot them from a slingshot into the plates and backs of the patrons' heads. When anyone turned their attention to him, he would pull a face or parody them. Or, to the indignation of his subjects, he would instantly draw caricatures of them and throw them out his window.

Albert didn't place any value on what he was doing, and wouldn't have thought that pieces of paper thrown out of his window would be highly valued at auctions in a later time. His father would also get outraged at his pranks. The staid citizens would get exasperated and send for the police. But the laughter of the people around the victims would usually bring these conflicts with the guardians of law and order to naught.

The older notary couldn't understand why Albert was being so deplorable. In fact, a decision was ripening in the younger man's brain to exchange his father's tiresome notary public for the risky career of a political cartoonist. Like many another young seeker after fortune, he set his steps for Paris. Did Robida know that he was following in Jules Verne's footsteps? The famous science-fiction writer had the same inheritance in a lawyer's office, the same chase after glory and escape to the capital.

But there was a difference between them. Jules Verne had a reputation for being a systematic man, and Robida a frivolous enthusiast—methodical labor wasn't his way. Fortunately, he didn't have to overcome any special handicaps. Robida became a popular political cartoonist comparatively easily. His drawings were published by many newspapers and magazines. At the very height of French painting and graphic arts, when geniuses were chockablock around him, among them such masters of the grotesque as Gustave Dore, Robida managed to perfect his own style, restrained and precise. He became recognizable to his readers.

But, with time, even drawing for newspapers began to bore him. He took to illustrating the books of venerable authors, and soon new editions of Cyrano de Bergerac, Swift, and Flammarion were released with Robida's graphics. And it seems to me that it must have been Camille Flammarion and his popular astronomical works that attracted the artist to the world of science, as well. But his irony never disappeared.

Moreover, fantasy had started adding itself to his sense of the grotesque. Robida even began to write half-humorous texts—commentaries accompanying his drawings. At first, he began with what I would call a light piety to do parodies of the novels of Jules Verne. He published them as excerpts in periodicals. He ended up with exactly a hundred pieces, all tied together with an artless plot, a kind of parody collection of drawings depicting what science-fiction writers foresaw in the next century. Jules Verne had made the topic popular, and a publisher was found for Robida's book. The hundred parts were grouped together into five small books, and they were published.[4]

A satirist at heart, Robida, as distinct from the great science-fiction author, was never very keen on utopian myths. Verne was always serious in his projects. Robida foresaw the future as a huge caricature of the present. I think I can see how much he enjoyed his work. In the eighties of the last century, he first published 50 small articles with his own illustrations, and then assembled them in a book called *The Twentieth Century (Le vingtième siècle)*. After that, in the same way, *The Electric Life (La vie électrique)*, and still another: two hundred excerpts in the magazine *La Caricature* under the title *War in the 20th Century (La guerre au vingtième siècle)*. The Russian translator Rantsov got ahold of the whole trilogy and squeezed them into one book, combining the names of the first two.

Meanwhile, Albert Robida was in the public eye, and he was invited to design the World's Fair for 1900. Out of the blue, instead of the science fiction that everyone had been expecting of him, the artist reconstructed a corner of an old Parisian quarter for the Fair, introducing the figure of Moliere and other writers of the past into it. What came about was an ironical look at the past, half in sadness, at an epoch that had gone forever.

Thus the author was a complete dilettante at science, a self-taught artist, and no kind of a writer at all. Prognosticating about the future was his hobby. The book can be considered science fiction, *belles-lettres a la* Jules Verne. Or a social and scientific forecast, one full to the brim with black humor. It depends on the point of view you adopt to understand the thing. There are a lot of formulas in it, as familiar as a toothache. We had to learn them by rote in our colleges, courtesy of the Scientific Communism departments.

"The old world is doomed to demolition," said Vladimir Lenin, in multitudinous variations. But this is a quote from Robida.[5] Revolution, the forced redistribution of wealth, post-revolutionary cataclysm—all this is depicted in Robida, in contrast to Karl Marx, vividly, drawn in detail, and even indicating when what would happen. Where could the slogan "Paradise is Soviet Power plus Electrification" have come from? And "Radio is Like a Newspaper without Post Offices or Distances"? Or "The Most Important of All Arts for Us is the Movie"? All this is used to good effect endlessly in *The Electric Life*.

Let us make the connection: at the end of August, 1893, a 23-year-old young man by the name of Vladimir Ulyanov (later Lenin) moved from Samara to St. Petersburg, finding a job as a barrister's assistant ("a legal cover for revolutionary activity," as it is written in the official biographies). He frequented bookstores and libraries, looking for literature useful to his circle of the like-minded.

On November 7 (Good Lord, again a coincidence with the date of revolution!) of 1893, the book *The Twentieth Century: The Electric Life* passed the censors in St. Petersburg without any problem, and came out after a bit more than a month. It was snazzily printed, sold everywhere, and sent free to subscribers of the then-popular magazine *Vestnik inostrannoy literatury* (News of Foreign Literature) as a bit of French spice. Everyone was talking about the book, young people most of all.

I have no direct evidence, but I'll wager that an inquisitive young man Vladimir Ulyanov stuck on utopias could not but have noticed this book about the future by Albert Robida. He wouldn't have understood Robida's irony any more than he understood the universality of Shchedrin's satire. He read *The Electric Life* carefully and remembered its useful concepts. The provincial dropout had none of his own, yet, and the shining future that so excited him would have looked much more jolly and vivid in Robida than in the sick scientific Marx. And what was it that drew all these apprentice legal types from their good profession to their dubious fantasies?

Robida predicted the Revolution, although he was out by five years: his took place in 1922. Chaos and disorder happen after his revolution, but its author was unable to conceive the number and fanaticism of the destroyers. In his book, how fast those coming to power get fat is clearly described.

> A famous revolutionary . . . having made himself a tidy little sum, returned to more sensible notions and lives now on the income from his own real estate and personal assets . . . looking around with a good-humored but slightly mocking smile upon the never-ending series of human delusions unfolding before his spiritual gaze.[6]

However, changes of regime take place periodically after his revolution. A gloomier prediction of Robida's also came true: the state seizes "the right to dispose of the lives of its citizens as they saw fit and pave the ground with their corpses."[7]

Albert Robida died in 1926, after managing to follow that very same revolution that he had predicted, and its first consequences, in the newspapers. Did he think that he had been right, when he read about it? Or perhaps he wasn't interested in how his prognostication had come out, at all? It is not within our destiny to find that one out. In France, never mind Russia, they quickly forgot the 70-year-old eccentric who had been a big noise in his day, an artist with the mind of an engineer, a pessimistic optimist.

2. Genes as a marketable product

However naive the fable of *The Electric Life* might seem to us, who have swallowed heaps of contemporary pulp, it is a 300-page novel, after all. As authors John Clute and Peter Nicholls wrote in an article about Albert Robida in the *Encyclopedia of Science Fiction,* "the texts to the above works, are generally undistinguished."[8] These two critics praised his drawings in pen and pastel.

True, the plot line developed by Albert Robida is banal, but that was not by accident, I would think. Connecting up passing events in a disjointed outline, the author was striving not to distract our attention from his warnings about the future. And the future looked like a parody. Of course all his great inventions, including the above-mentioned huge destructive-creative force, belong to the main hero, who, like the author himself, was French.

A kind of composite personality, an Edison-Einstein-Mamontov-Sakharov, is the dominant character throughout the book. Philoxene Lorrice is "a specialist in all branches of knowledge," who gets made a member of all academies and scientific institutes in the world as well as being the bearer of numerous honors from old Europe, mature America, and young Oceania.[9] He also bears the title of Prince of Tiflis in the Transcaucasus. Recently in Paris I tried to find Lorrice's splendid house in the Ste.-Oise district by its description, but failed. Evidently, Robida didn't have a real house in mind.

Lorrice is of course a genius, and not the banal aloof-from-life eccentric typical in science fiction but a prominent and masterful organizer, "the ace-of-aces of contemporary scientific industry," capable of making money and investing it in vast enterprises, a businessman.[10] Like a true Frenchman, he never misses a chance for a little worldly pleasure. The Russian translator made a good job of it, even overdoing it, translating francs into their equivalent Russian notes, so that the French millionaire in Paris, Lorrice, makes his payments in rubles. Maybe that was just a prophecy based on the visit of the Russian army to Paris at the beginning of the 19th century, and luckily still unrepeated.

The genius's son, George, established by his father as a subaltern in a unit of chemical artillery, remains a layabout and wastrel, even though he is a college graduate. The father wants to make his son the director of 200 of his factories, but the son accuses his father of already having invented and created everything, thus dooming the succeeding generation to laziness. These are typical enough problems with our children—yet another good guess by the French utopian.

In order to improve his bloodline, the wise and rational father wants to get his son married scientifically and get four grandsons—a chemist, a naturalist, a physician, and a mechanic—and considers the intermediate link (that is, George) worthless, "a market product without any value."

To start off the process, he selects a maiden "with a brain of a strictly scientific type," possessing "highest-level doctorates in science."[11] His son refuses to marry her. Then his father offers him another bride, a representative of three generations of mathematicians, 39 years of age, possessing doctorates in medicine and jurisprudence, who, in addition (for the complete happiness of the young man), is an "arch-doctor of socio-science" (and here's where Lenin must have gotten his favorite prefix, "arch-").

Inasmuch as the author is a Frenchman, *amours* play a big role in many of his scenes: love, jealous scandals. In the process of reading it becomes clear that Robida doesn't like women very much, and any psychoanalyst could pick up on the author's personal problems hidden in the text of *The Electric Life*. His heroines are vulgar, malicious; they nag their husbands, and either don't live with them at all or are there in a pre-divorce state. Family spats continue between two competing record players belonging to husband and wife when the spouses themselves aren't at home.

One of his heroes, Arsene Marette, composes a treatise called "The History of the Troubles Wrought by Women on Men From the Stone Age to the Present."[12] The composition reviews the whole of human history in a new light, as one influenced too much by women, in his opinion. In the course of all this, the great scientist Lorrice and his friend Marette make the discovery of the century: that conflicts with women are conducive to the scientific success of their husbands, not allowing them to fall into the somnolence of peace and quiet, and delivering stimulating impulses to the nervous system.

Robida thinks about how to perfect the process of marriage: "Every family possesses a definite spiritual capital that serves as a reservoir for heredity."[13] A lot depends on chance, the author says, but nature has to draw on the capital stored up by one's ancestors; that's why a great deal of circumspection is necessary for the conclusion of a marriage, in order to escape "atavistic influences."

Against the background of such a serious conjugal doctrine, Lorrice junior makes a call on his phonoscope (that is, a videophone). As soon the contacts connect, George can see on his screen everything that is going on at the other end of the line. Naturally, he checks out the girl, her little nose, eyes, her dainty leg under the table; and she, not aware that a stranger is looking her over, elegantly reads at the table in her room in Switzerland. Her mother has gone to Paris by subway (on the pneumatic train) to buy a new pink hat.

Of course, the girl (her name is Estelle Lacombe) is a budding young engineer, listening to lectures from Zurich University on her phonograph. To deepen her education, she is taking additional private phonograph lessons. Only one hangover from the past survives: examinations still have to be taken, and not over the phonoscope.

The daughter is embarrassed by their acquaintance, but her mommy (also a very unpleasant woman) quickly latches on to the fact that this is the kind of profitable contact that can help daddy on his way up to a better position. The mother had already met Philoxene Lorrice himself in a dream, where he gave her his latest electrical device, for increasing employees' salary. Not a bad invention, at all; wouldn't it be handy right now!

Gradually, emancipation in the novel reaches its maximum. "A woman now works alongside a man, like a man, as long as a man does—in the office, at the shop, in the factory, on the stock exchange"—Robida was the first to tell us.[14] A woman acts in the capacity and style of a man. She victoriously ousts man in the political sphere. Louise Miouche, the leader of the women's party, becomes Minister of Internal Affairs of France, and radical changes begin in the country.

Meanwhile, Robida shows, women lose their charm, softness, warmth, and sexual attractiveness.

As a result, a counterweight appears in the guise of "the chief of the men's party, who organized a menacing opposition to the women's party."[15] Members of the men's party are not against women, they are against the excessive claims made by women. To save the sex that is the opposite of the fair one, a "League for the Emancipation of Men" is formed, in the novel. But they fail to stop the process of women's emancipation. No, there is no denying that Robida has a sense of humor. In the end, emancipation is so successful that a separate women's stock exchange is set up, and, in this way, the economy of France is divided up into men's and women's.

Not without irony, Robida tells the story of a mediocre actress, Silvie, who all of a sudden feels a mediumistic force in her and starts a screen career healing people with her "mediumistic energy," a Kashpirovsky in skirts. At times she invites dead authors—Voltaire and Hugo—onto the stage, and they read their poems, "testifying that their genius continues to develop even in the life beyond the grave."[16]

A medical engineer, Sulphatene, who derives huge profits from his various schemes to rejuvenate the elderly, decides to marry the medium, Silvie, so that she can summon up the spirits of the brilliant minds of the preceding centuries in secret; then he can introduce them to modern technology, and they should be able to come up with new discoveries that he can use. What happens is something even worse than Nikolay Gogol's Chichikov—such a peculiar family business, based on dead souls. At the same time, jealous of Silvie, Sulphatene puts into place "miniature and completely unnoticeable photophonographic devices... to make easier the delicate task of secret surveillance."[17]

Meanwhile, the son of the great inventor is not as pragmatic as his father, and having fallen in love with Estelle in the old way, he proposes to her. The author of *The Electric Life* figures that, by the middle of the 20th century, honeymoons will be replaced by engagement trips, before marriage. During the time of this antenuptial trip, young people will get to know each other better. And for the peace of mind of their parents, the engagement trip is under the escort of an elderly, trustworthy person, who is always in the presence of the young ones. On their return, it is enough for one of the engaged couple to send a notarized statement for the projected wedding to be canceled. Thanks to these engagement trips, writes Robida, the number of divorces is considerably lessened. If only he had been right!

And when George sets off on his engagement trip with his fiancée, Robida takes a second step in his plot, something that has become hackneyed by present-day science-fiction writers, but was original back then. From a future made up by him he sends his heroes back in time to the present, to the everyday life surrounding the author. Here the author's satirical talent develops on the soil of realism, since his present is a special zone of the future into which progress has not penetrated.

These territories are protected by law from being tampered with. Scientific and industrial progress are restricted from them. The old life goes on in them—peace and plenty. There aren't even any newspapers. And "all the anemic intellectuals overtired from the electric life" seek salutary relaxation there, considering it the height of pleasure to go for a jaunt in a *diligence*.

In essence, there is no prediction in this sub-plot. The first national park in the U.S.A. had been founded two decades earlier than when Robida published his prophecies, and of course French newspapers had covered it. Something else is more important: that kind of contrast between technology and wild nature, between black smoke from chimneys and a dewdrop hanging from a lily-of-the-valley leaf, had never been before, and the pictures drawn by the author correspond more to our time than to the one in which he lived.

George and his fiancée are traveling around with no cares, but it turns out that the engagement *voyage* is also being recorded for his father, who is against his son's marriage. The father tricks his son into returning from his engagement trip. The son gets drafted into the army.

3. Benevolent war

Another of Robida's prognostications of extraordinary importance was about the wars of the following—that is, *our*—century.

When the book came out, war wasn't foreseen. The First World War began 20 years later, and the Second a half-century later. Robida tells how the world shudders. Chemical artillery and medical assault troops with weapons that suffocate are being readied, teams ready at the poison-gas pumps, and at the aerial torpedoes. Aren't these rockets? The brilliant inventor becomes an engineer-general of chemical artillery.

A little bit earlier I mentioned the division of the world into three parts, including Oceania. The idea of periodic wars between them, thought up by the French artist, gave impetus to another utopia, composed by George Orwell, who lived in Paris in his youth and believed in Communist ideals. *1984* was being written when the future, according to Albert Robida, had already come, and Orwell had to shift the time ahead still another 30 years. Much of it had become a reality by that time, judging by the first country in the world to realize a utopia; but the technical and—most importantly—the social devices of Robida came in handy for Orwell. A secret love affair, all-seeing screens in every home, denunciations.

Progress does not bring to perfection a person's moral qualities, concludes the author from the preceding century. "The good-natured daydreamers of the preceding centuries," Robida writes, "imagined that progress in its triumphal march around the arena of our civilization would improve both people and institutions and introduce eternal peace once and for all. In reality, however, it turns out that progress, bringing nations into close contact, arouses in consequence just more complicated collisions of interests, and correspondingly an increasing number of excuses and reasons for war."[18] Humanity, laughing in the faces of the anti-utopians, voluntarily sucks itself into the maelstrom, and there is nothing that can be done about it.

It sounds as if it was written today, but this is the way the political sage Robida reasoned it out:

> ...An old proverb 'if you want peace, prepare for war,' seems more just now than at some other time. To provide for external peace, it's necessary to maintain an army in constant armed readiness and zealously guard one's boundaries on land, on sea, and in the air. In order to keep the military machine in constant readiness every hour and every minute to expend all its energy at first call, or, putting it more precisely, at the signal made by pushing an electric button in the office of the military minister, a thoroughly detailed fixing of the whole military mechanism and the maintenance of all of its parts in complete working order is necessary.[19]

Military considerations are more important for a country than any other. War urges science on. "A whole city can be blown into the air by a miniature bomb the size of a pea from a distance of 20 kilometers away."[20] And endless re-armaments described in the book are accompanied by calculations of how much it is going to cost the taxpayers and how the standard of living of the populace will be reduced by it. Having described in detail the vilest means of mass annihilation of people a half a century before it came to pass, the author, in despair, exclaims: "Hurrah for progress!"

As it is known, the gas mask appeared during the First World War. But, in contrast with Rembrandt's goddess of war, Bellona, hanging in the Metropolitan Museum in New York, Albert Robida's Bellona is in a gas mask, holding a long list of explosive substances and asphyxiating and paralyzing gases in her hand. Robida put the then-nonexistent gas mask on every one of his soldiers. They were "helmets with sliding visors, that close up during the conduct of chemical operations with poisonous substances." And even "a reservoir of oxygen with an elastic tube."[21]

Robida guessed the date of the war (1941). When he originally published excerpts of his book in periodicals, he indicated that a world war would happen in the 1970s, but in his book he changed the date, carrying the war back to the 1940s. His descriptions of war are so up to date that it again makes you think it is a hoax, for instance when he talks about artillery reminiscent of the *Katyusha* rocket launcher.

One mistake lets us off the hook: it is not German Nazis who occupy Europe, but Chinese. The Chinese engineer-mandarin aims his weapons at Paris. The victory of the West is achieved under the leadership of

> the aged Field Marshal Zagowicz, the former generalissimo of the European armed forces that repulsed the great Chinese invasion in 1941 and annihilated, after 18 months of battle on the vast plains of Bessarabia and Rumania, two armies of the Mediterranean kingdom, in each of which were 700,000 people under arms, equipped with military devices vastly more effective that anything that was then at the disposal of people in Europe.[22]

A shiver runs down your spine. Robida was mistaken to ignore the aggressiveness of Russia. But it was Russia that had become a threat to humanity in the second half of the 20th century. God grant that the threat of the engineer-mandarins to fire upon Europe will drag out into the future, and perhaps won't happen at all. However, experts do assign a leading role in the political games of the 21st century to China. When the war comes to an end, energetic dark-faced people in military uniform, from South America, appear in the novel. They tell Lorrice: "In the interests of securing peace, we would like to obtain a consignment of your newly invented cannons."[23] And Europe, to its own perdition, arms both warring parties, earning gigantic profits.

The novel's hero announces: "Science, as you will be satisfied then, will succeed once again in transforming war radically, making it short and benevolent and not barbarously destructive."[24] Armies can be abolished, medical troops will do the attacking, using means that render enemy armies supine, after which it will just be necessary to dictate conditions of peace to the stricken enemy. And, if necessary, a government can secretly resort to "reprisals"—undetectable lethal substances. Or to "miasmas" that can cause epidemics. Miasmas that can cause slander and backbiting are also thought up. That would be for an enemy.

And, for their own citizens, they breed health microbes. Robida understands the price of verbal propaganda, and the populace is prescribed "salutary national medicine" in the form of injections. In another place, Robida calls this medicine "patriotic." The Senate decrees: "An inoculation of national and patriotic medicine is compulsorily prescribed once a month for every Frenchman, beginning from three years of age."[25] In short, "medical warfare" finally transforms the military art.

The brilliant inventor of the miasmas and patriotic medicine, Philoxene Lorrice, finds himself in an embarrassing situation when, at a ceremony in his house, his celebrated guests become infected with some sort of disease—fortunately, of course, not a lethal one—due to the absent-mindedness of his assistant, who improperly secures a faucet in the laboratory.

4. "Sticking out your tongue at progress"

Robida predicted that the population of Paris would rise to eleven million, and was only one million off; at the same time, he mentioned the growth in the number of Asians and Africans within it. He predicted the construction of skyscrapers out of steel and glass, with flashing beacons on their roofs. A decade before the first flight of the Wright brothers, the development of aviation is shown in his book, including aerial helicopter-taxis, and direct flights between the cities of the whole world.

Robida, who had never flown even three meters off the surface of the earth, describes, very precisely, one's physical condition during an intercontinental flight. The author gets a little carried away and transfers all transport from the ground to the air, causing incredible chaos and non-stop crashes over the cities. Even three-year-old children fly aeronautical machines. As for space, Robida is indifferent to it. Yes, they have reached other planets, and there is communication with them, but it doesn't interest him a lot: Albert Robida's interests are quite mundane.

Because of overpopulation on the five continents, a new continent is being constructed in the otherwise useless-till-now Pacific Ocean. A hundred years before *Jurassic Park*, he tells us about resurrecting primordial animals, birds, and fish. They discover how to make children in test tubes. Moreover, artificially-made people have an advantage in that they don't carry the burden of genetic defects, and their brains are entirely open to development along logical paths. Besides, a test-tube person has no fear of disease-producing infections.

It is easy to foresee the awful environmental pollution that Robida comes up with. It is harder to foresee how energy will become all encompassing. In his books he has "electrical communications over a world-wide network of cables," a video screen that he calls a "teleplate," a postal service that consists of phonographic printing—that is, putting it simply, a fax. Bibliophiles are transformed into bibliophonophiles, and collect phonobooks, and music is available at home "even in bed, without any orchestra." Robida's head was aching from the wild sounds of contemporary pop music, amplified over loudspeakers, a hundred years before the appearance of electronically produced stereophonic music. "Such a huge consumption of music to an insane degree... This music squeaks and squeals; separate notes stick one to the other."[26]

Robida was the first to think of the commercial advertising on television so popular in the modern world, and cable television for a fee. This author from the previous century just throws around details of our lives in the second half of the

20th century: "Even in those cases when the most successful and brilliant performances are given," he says, "modern theaters are very often almost completely empty, since, thanks to telephonoscope, the performance can be seen without leaving home, and even without getting up from the table."[27] Robida came up with the idea that the faded Moliere Theater would sell telesubscriptions, and had the theater selling them to 400,000 television viewers. In passing, the author proposed the modernization of classics for the stage, which directors in our century have successfully pursued.

Do you remember this passage from in Ilya Ilf's, Russian humorist, notebook? "The biggest thing in science fiction novels was the radio. With radio, the total happiness of mankind was to be expected. Here we have radio, but no happiness."[28] A half-century before that, having a presentiment that it would be that way, Robida clutched at life without changes with all his strength, but ultimately without success. However, socialist ideas had developed such popularity at the end of the century that they influenced our skeptical prognosticator, as well.

There wouldn't be any kitchens in the home, he promised his readers, since it isn't profitable from the point of view of a rational economic policy. People would have coupons for the Main Joint Stock Company for Provision Rationing, from which they would receive cooked breakfasts, lunches, and dinners by means of a special system of pipes and tubes. Or maybe this is a clairvoyant parody of Soviet Public Catering?

"Creamery butter from petroleum oil," Robida enumerates. "Nourishment elements from coal. The fabrication of chemical wines and milk. Mineral flour. Artificial margarine. The recycling of all wastes."[29] "Pharmaceutical restaurants" appear, where people get fed by pill. Several of the heroes of the novel actively protest against food preparation by culinary engineers, preferring the kind of old-fashioned cook from the back of beyond, of whom there were very few left.

Second-rate stars are easily forgotten; however, among them are writers who did stimulate others. Without doubt, Albert Robida is one of these. He's one of those who launched ideas that were picked up by later science-fiction writers. Garin-the-Engineer is the double of Lorrice-the-Engineer, with whom Aleksey Tolstoy must have become acquainted while an émigré in Paris.

It appears that Robida's book *The Century Clock*, published in 1902, was the earliest one about time-travel. This idea was used later by Philip K. Dick in his science-fiction novel *Back Into Time*, Brian Aldiss in his novel *Age*, or, shall we say, Martin Amis in his *Vector of Time*.

Robida makes a brief reference to the banker Ponto's arranging the construction of "a great electro-pneumatic trans-Atlantic communications pipe between France and America."[30] Out of these few lines, the Soviet writer Aleksandr Kazantsev, changing the French into Soviet Heroes of Labor, tricked out the thick novel *Arctic Bridge*. The poet Sven Birkerts borrowed the name *The Electric Life* for his book of essays about modern poetry.

The idea of an ancestor's influence upon his heredity, described by Albert Robida in detail, has frequently shown up in science fiction. Much gets said about the transfer of heat and cold between the poles and the equator. He mocked the gigantic building projects of Communism a half a century before their realization. I counted around a dozen of the satirist's ideas that are still awaiting their realization, so political madmen should study his book.

The artist Robida couldn't say anything original about the future of art, though.

> The place of what used to be painting—timid artistic attempts from various Rafaels, Titians, Rubenses, Davids, Delacroix, Durers and other pioneers of art—was taken first by photo-painting, which already represented a huge step forward with regard to them. Today's photo-painters will in their turn have to retire into the background behind tomorrow's photo-personless-mechanicals.[31]

An education in the humanities loses its practical value, and everyone is becoming an engineer. The engineering bent starts among 12-year-olds. Mind and knowledge will further the development of cynicism. Brilliant technical inventions will lead to maximum harm for mankind. History, says the business genius in Robida's work, will write about him thus: "This knight of the intelligentsia knew how to tax ordinary mortals to the benefit of his own more-developed mind."

Robida foresaw the growing mass of idlers hanging around the neck of the state. These consumers of public wealth do nothing; they "sit sticking their tongues out at progress."[32] But the author misses his mark a bit, deciding that these would be principally the descendants of the aristocracy.

Robida didn't end his time-travels, and later drew a series of pictures with his own stories for some French magazines, and also the book is entitled *Ages Ago With Us Today*. He wrote a jolly book about women, *A Lady's Past: A Century of Elegance*. His last fantasy, finished not long before his death, became the illustrated book *Castle in the Air* (1925). But he was repeating himself to a certain extent, and it was less interesting than any of his previous creations. His acme remained *The Twentieth Century*, *The Electric Life*, and *War in the 20th Century*. His Russian translator, Rantsov, guessed right, and got straight down to business. It wasn't difficult to translate a book like that. The translator could not have dreamed even in his worst nightmares what practical thoughts could be extracted from the book by one of his compatriots seriously committed to world revolution.

So who is he, after all? A mythmaker or a fighter against myths? A fantasist? A seer? Did he guess right by accident, or based on the latest achievements of science? It seems it was a synthesis of all of them.

Reading the novel, we can't shake the feeling that the young George Lorrice is the alter ego of Albert Robida himself, whose father forced him to work, demanding seriousness, the study of science, and was possibly against his son getting married. This son—and maybe here we come to the reason for this strange book's coming into being—was trying to break out of his accustomed circle, to change his life. But he couldn't find any other out except emigration. Not to America, as many Frenchmen—and not only them—did at the end of the last century, but into the future. His life didn't change; he became neither rich nor happy, but he got to express himself, he was listened to, and that means a great deal.

Once in the 1970s a Soviet newspaper ran a piece on Robida.[33] He was depicted as a frivolous jokester who, although he fantasized unbridledly, never—ha!—foresaw the huge successes of the Soviet land. But Robida foresaw its grandiose sunset as well. A writer and artist who never once visited Russia or even once mentioned it, Robida nevertheless penetrated into it in some mysterious fashion, and perhaps, however funny or strange it may be, had some kind of influence on the historical process.

Without any use of the Marxist lexicon he showed the finale: Communism is Soviet Power plus the Chernobylization of the whole country. Generally speaking, we know that not one of the forewarnings or anti-utopias of Nostradamus,

Shchedrin, Zamyatin, or Orwell had any effect on those who decide the fate of mankind.

By a strange twist of fate, the satirical drawings of a French cartoonist came to life in Russia. He prompted Ulyanov, the young barrister's assistant, with several Leninist slogans, contributing the little bit that was within his powers to the construction of a state that was built on myths. Is Robida responsible for this? No more than any other humorist whose jokes are taken seriously by people without any sense of humor.

But that is what is interesting: although many of his hellish propositions came true, the world as a whole during the last hundred years after his predictions has developed more reasonably than Albert Robida foresaw it.

Not all of us became Communists or neurasthenics, not everyone grew lazy or degenerate. And that means that you and I have learned something then, if not the powers that be. Laying it on thick, trying to scare us, the anti-utopian attempted to stave off something worse. Thank God that humankind sometimes manages to dodge to one side and not find itself squashed by the wheels of its own history.

The ironic-minded reader will ask: what is this, a book review a hundred years after its publication? And he will be right—however hard I might try to get out of it.

The Overt and Covert Lives of Konstantin Ventzel

> Never inquire of which
> Age we are an edition,
> But tell your own weighty word
> And be yourself in everything.
>   *K. N. Ventzel* [1]

I should have published this before now, but the circumstances of my life have resisted it. In the basement of an ancient mansion in Polyanka in Moscow, I found a pile of unpublished manuscripts by Konstantin Ventzel, and day after day I went there, to the archives of the Academy of Pedagogical Sciences, to read them. That was in the autumn of 1977, and one night in January of 1978 a pipe burst in the basement and part of the archive was flooded. Using my collected (transcribed or photographed on the sly) materials, I wrote an essay resurrecting the ideas of this unknown Russian philosopher, giving pride of place to his thoughts over my own commentaries.

There was no way even to think of publishing this work in the Soviet Union. And even if it had been possible, by that time I had already made it onto the blacklist. The manuscript made its way to Paris, to the *Pamyat* almanac of *tamizdat* materials (things published outside the Soviet Union), but the KGB gutted its Leningrad editorial staff, arresting its compilers, and the succeeding collection was never born.

In order to get some advice on where to publish it, I gave my essay to my colleague writer Georgy Vladimov to read, but on February 5, 1982, a search was made of his premises and my manuscript was confiscated. I thought that there were no copies left, and I resigned myself to the loss. Years later, a remarkable woman died in Vologda, the guardian of a part of my own archive, Tatyana Vasilevskaya. In her papers was a copy of my composition, that I have finished and offer up for the attention of the reader.

1. From anarchist to Tolstoyan

Most of his colleagues both in post-Revolutionary Russia and in emigration thought that he had disappeared, like many another in the years of the Terror. You will almost never find any reference to him in the works of the pillars of Soviet pedagogy (Nadezhda Krupskaya, Stanislav Shatsky, Pavel Blonsky, Anton Makarenko). Rarely can his name be glimpsed in the historical works of Soviet pedagogy, while his plagiarizers have been studied closely and called the original exponents of ideas belonging to him. The philosopher Ventzel does not exist on the Russian intellectual horizon.

The long list of books published by Ventzel—over thirty years of energetic labor in pedagogy and social and political journalism, in a period so important to their development—has its beginning in the last century and breaks off in 1923. After that he became a recluse. He quit the game, or more precisely, he was shut out. For a quarter of a century he lived like a Trappist, in voluntary confinement at home, living in poverty, by some miracle avoiding arrest, writing until the very end, even when he was ill. In 1947 he had nearly reached the age of 90. The main part of what he had done remained in the notebooks that he had secretly written during the Stalin years.

Konstantin Nikolayevich Ventzel was born in 1857 to a noble family in St. Petersburg. His father, an acting State Councilor, served as Desk head in the Governor-General's chancellery in St. Petersburg, after finishing university. His grandfather on his mother's side was a teacher who compiled a German-language reader. Because of his father's service transfers, the family lived in Odessa, Warsaw, and Vilnius. After gymnasium and modern school, Ventzel entered the St. Petersburg Technological Institute. But he was more interested in the humanities and therefore soon quit the Tech and entered the legal faculty of the University.

At the beginning of the 1880s he became enamored of revolutionary activity. "What have you taught and still teach to us from childhood?" he says indignantly in his diary. He was looking for something to buttress his youthful criticism. At the age of 20, looking for some action, he could find nothing better to do than join People's Will. Full of the naive ideals of brotherhood, the youth Ventzel was thinking of the role of the individual in such a brotherhood. "By way of logical reasoning, I came to a denial of man's responsibility," he reveals quick-temperedly, and he elaborates that people will behave "by their own bent, in the name of their own happiness, and not in the name of consciousness of any kind of responsibility."

Soon, having thought better of it, Ventzel moderated his anarchism: "I went a little bit too far ... every individual person is conscious of his responsibility for his deeds." He parted company with his recent confederates. "The general impression that I got from encounters with 'new people' is coldness, lack of any warm, good, vivacious feeling. Really and truly, they smell of carrion flesh ..."

He said that there was no organic connection between the new people, there was boredom, they had nothing to talk about except reading aloud from the requisite books. "Thus, my principle and keystone has always remained the individual, his internal mental world, and his happiness."[2]

He was no longer heading the same direction as those who wanted to perfect the world by means of force. He studied Herbert Spencer and other Western philosophers, wrote poems. And, suddenly, his arrest. It wasn't his naive arguments with himself in his diary about the future of mankind, not his abstracts on ancient philosophers, or his poetry, but an appeal to the workers that he had earlier composed, that had been found in a search of his former confederates—together with People's Will literature—that were grounds for jailing him. A month later his wife was arrested. Her correspondence with her husband, from which "her knowledge of his revolutionary activities was evident"—that is, the crime of non-denunciation—was grounds for her investigation.[3]

He was put in jail together with the People's Will members with whom he corresponded for many years afterwards, after they had been banished to Siberia. In his cell, he read and wrote a lot. The status of political prisoner secured him this right. His diary sparingly details prison life: the criminals had to empty the politicals' chamber-pots.

In his cell in 1885, Ventzel wrote his first thoughts about freedom in education. He re-read Rousseau and declared that the point of education was not to create a *virtuous* person, but an *active* one. The goal should lie in bringing up a person who can feel the fullness of life, understand life, and would like to increase the sum of life in himself and others, in mankind and in the world. People "are free from the dominion of every sort of authority and tradition, and, guided by strict criticism, can independently work out their own philosophy, and, constantly checking it out critically, make amendments to it."[4]

Here, in jail, the divergence of Ventzel's humanism from Marxism and its Russian enthusiasts was taking shape, and, moreover, it was essentially immediate. "As Jesus Christ said, 'The Sabbath is for man, not man for the Sabbath,' as we must say, 'Society is for the individual, and not an individual for society.'"[4] Ventzel amplifies:

> I am unconditionally against every kind of *enforced brotherhood* [*his emphasis—Y.D.*] and for that am against that Communism that denies the right of an individual to the product of his labor. This right has to be guaranteed above all else; as far as another, morally relatively higher, economic form is concerned, one founded upon the principle of 'Labor in accordance with one's strength, distribution in accordance with need,' that should in my opinion be the result of a free agreement of people among one another, a free public concord.[5]

Ventzel sat out his thirteen months, and his wife her six. Then both of them were sent into exile in Bobrov in the Voronezh *guberniya*, under the open supervision of the police "for habitation outside places declared to be in a state of increased security," putting it into the language of the police protocols. In his exile, Ventzel wrote articles on freedom of will and corresponded with Vladimir Korolenko, who had with pleasure read Ventzel's article, "The Morality of Life and the Free Ideal," in manuscript form. Proximity between both their viewpoints came to light. Korolenko noted: "... I have already rather long since been dissatisfied with so-called rational systems of morality."[6]

Trying to define his place under the moon, he called himself a writer on ethical and pedagogical issues. He energetically occupied himself with philosophy, discussing things by letter with philosophers. John Mill's utilitarianism in combination with altruism was dear to him at that time: the greatest happiness for the greatest number of people.

After his exile, Ventzel moved residence to Moscow. As politically unreliable, he was not allowed to engage in government work. He made a living with music lessons, and then by journalism, then as editorial head of the magazine *Izvestiya moskovskoy gorodskoy dumy*.

The end of the century found Ventzel concentrating on socio-pedagogical problems. In their sensible resolution, he saw a way out of the dead end that, in the opinion of a part of the intelligentsia, Russian society was getting deeper into. The existing system of education had been borrowed from the Austrian empire, and then refined in the Prussian style. The school as an institution through which government bosses strove to bottle up succeeding generations within the framework of what was allowed today did not excite any sympathy from Ventzel.

He saw a way out of this vicious circle in something Tolstoyan—in moral improvement. A more perfect society is impossible without freedom in education. "The principle of the absolute authority of our generation over the succeeding one has to be shaken up," he wrote. He was published in the magazines *Vestnik vospitaniya*, *Obrazovaniye*, and *Pedagogichesky listok*. In 1896 his work *The Basic Task of Moral Education* came out. He offered his program to the Moscow University Pedagogical Society, which was carrying on a polemic against the "bureaucratic school." From that moment he can be considered to be the leading theoretician of freedom in education.

A whole scientific school existed, whose throne was occupied, of course, by Leo Tolstoy. In Russia this theme was thrashed out by A. Zelenko, F. Rau, L. Shleger, I. Nikashidze, S. Durylin, M. Klechkovsky, A. Dauge, the husband and wife N. and M. Chekhov, and the husband and wife Y. and A. Fortunatov. These names were all thrown out of the history of Russian pedagogy, or until nowadays have been falsely interpreted. Ventzel agreed closely with the outstanding Tolstoyan Ivan Gorbunov-Posadov, the publisher and editor of the famous liberal magazine *Svobodnoye vospitaniye* ("Freedom of Upbringing").

2. Against slavery of the soul

Rousseau's ideas of natural influences on children found a re-birth (with changes suiting the new epoch) in the ideas of freedom in education that were floating around in the European air. They were being worked out by the Swedish writer Ellen Key, the anarchist theoretician Pyotr Kropotkin, the American philosopher John Dewey, the Frenchmen S. Faure and P. Robin, and the Italian lady Maria Montessori. In the West, and especially in the United States, kindergartens and schools that follow their methods still exist. In Russia this all got strangled at the end of the 1920s. But it was Ventzel who placed the foundation under the Russian version and built its future. He proposed the idea of the gradual spiritual and moral improvement of people in the society of the future, proceeding not from the demands of society but from the demands of the individual.

He was reproved for the fact that he was underestimating the role of the intellect, relying on will and feelings. He replied to his opponents that a rationally-constructed educational system would afford even less and become narrowly political. He could see that clear as a bell!

Separation of the school from the state was one of the main propositions of his theory of freedom in education, proposed in 1905 as a supporting principle by the Society of Philosophy and Psychology, of which Ventzel was a member, and who at that time wrote his article "On the Application of the Principle of Freedom in Upbringing and Education." Ventzel's theory applied to religion as well. Though no opponent of religion in education, he believed that there should be no goal set to inculcate one religion or another into the consciousness, in some orthodox form.

Practical steps then followed. He organized family schools that he called "schools of life," synonymous at that time with free schools. Ventzel believed that a child should receive knowledge in whatever amount it wished, and only when it felt the necessity. He was against regimentation (that is, coming down from above) of what a child was allowed to do and what it was prohibited from. At this time he wrote the book *The Struggle for the Natural School*. The word "struggle" in Ventzel's terminology is understood to mean polemicizing, striving, and persuasion, but under no circumstances in the modern sense.

He was against using force on a child's individuality, its will, against police supervision of pupils and their forms of thought, against formalism in school and ideological narrowness of subjects taught. The natural Family Kindergarten was in operation until the spring of 1906, when the House of the Free Child was founded. This was a community of children, parents, and teachers, in opposition to the ministerial school. The House with its freedom of upbringing lasted less than a year and was closed down. Not giving up, Ventzel founded a parents' club with a library, information bureau, a work-room, a toy museum, a laboratory, and a natural-history room.

Ventzel got his own magazine going, *Pravda*, a name that later got taken up by the Bolsheviks. The editor's goal was to strive for truth, to avoid the idealization of particular doctrines. In his magazine, the pluralist Ventzel eagerly published authors as various as Aleksandr Bogdanov, Anatoly Lunacharsky, Sergey Melgunov, Pyotr Maslov, Mikhail Olminsky, Mikhail Pokrovsky, and Ivan Skvortsov-Stepanov.

In 1905, Ventzel wrote the article "Revolution and the Requirements of Morality," which he failed to publish: "It is not revolution that is the supreme judge of morality, but it itself, its pace, its forms, that are liable to the supreme court of morality..."[7] His notion of the role of the individual in the cataclysms of history never left him. Pondering freedom, he singles out three of its stages: (1) the liberation of a child (a pedagogical task); (2) liberation of oneself (an ethical task); (3) liberation of society (a political task).[8]

He was among the first to discover a gap in Marxist theory: the absence of a psychological component, about which a lot has been written lately. Setting out from the Marxist idea of human liberation in economic terms (i.e., visible external slavery), Ventzel called for liberation from slavery of the soul. People are tools in other people's hands their whole lives; they think other people's thoughts, they feel other people's feelings, are obedient to someone else's will. He warned of the great moral responsibility of those persons who came up with slogans like "The authorities are terrible phantoms hovering in the dark night that modern mankind is plunged into."

Suddenly, in 1908, Ventzel sharply dissociated himself from Leo Tolstoy, whose sympathizer he had always been considered. He denied the "inculcation of goodness," considering it to be a delicate force, rather than a coarse one. The authority of the still-living Tolstoy was too great to be able to contradict him. Ivan Gorbunov-Posadov refused to publish his article.

Ventzel's position of principle—in particular, trust in the succeeding generation, the guarantee to that generation of the right to choose where and for what to strive—can be glimpsed in this argument. "For its moral progress," speculated Ventzel, "mankind needs as many free, individual creators of the new, independent, original morality as possible, and as few as possible of the representatives of 'herd morality.'"[9]

His skeptical attitude towards the machine of the state was not in connection with just the Russian system of government; his criticism was of a global nature. "The so-called state," Ventzel wrote, "is not the embodiment of the highest form of society, it is a great resistance to the development of that highest form, it is a great obstacle standing in the way of its achievement."[10]

"Do we need to teach children morality?" is what he called a lecture that he gave in 1912. Methods of education in morality should be methods that liberate a child's creative forces.

> For purposes of children's free questing for a higher personal morality, for their unrestricted working-out of an independent moral outlook, the people placed by circumstance in a position of supervising children must strive to supply the latter with material as wide and as complete as possible from the sphere of mankind's search for the highest forms of morality.

Otherwise, morality becomes an animal-style training operation. It was clear to Ventzel how far things could be distorted. "Thus this exaggeration turns rational love for the motherland into strutting national boastfulness, into pugnacious nationalism and vulgar chauvinism."[11] He is speaking here about French schools, which gave a graphic example of forms undesirable for Russia, in Ventzel's opinion.

Soon Ventzel's two-volume collected works were published: (1) *The Ethics of the Creative Individual*, and (2) *The Pedagogy of the Creative Individual*. At the All-Russian Congress for Family Upbringing in 1913, Ventzel gave a speech entitled "Freedom of Upbringing and the Family," on whose theses it will be necessary to linger awhile. The speech's author systematized his principles of an unfettered upbringing into ten points, offering them as the next step in the development of Russian education.

> First of all, the theory of freedom of upbringing stems from the principle of diversity in upbringing: there are as many systems of upbringing as there are children.
> Second, bringing children up is not the deliberate moulding of children in accord with an ideal, but the process of liberation of a child's creative forces.
> Third, the highest goal of upbringing is the development of creative individuality.
> Fourth, individuality does not exist in contradiction to community and culture but, on the contrary, a true community, a true culture, are tied to the development of individuality.
> Fifth, a child's initiative, its active nature, is important.
> Sixth, a child's contact with nature is indispensable.
> Seventh, the development of mental activity and the will is of primary importance, without which any upbringing would be inharmonious.
> Eighth, an upbringing should lead to the ability to set goals consciously for oneself and to strive to achieve them.
> Ninth, the basis of any upbringing is free, creative, productive labor.
> And, tenth, assistance is necessary for a child to work out a personal morality and personal religion. Any teaching of one moral codex or another should be rejected.

One can imagine how many adversaries Ventzel had. He was accused of complete unreality in the goals that he set. Nevertheless, his book *The Theory of Freedom of Upbringing and the Ideal Kindergarten* ran into three editions. The author's speech was sent off to America. The crisis in education became secondary, however: all countries were now drawn into the world war and its subsequent events later in Russia.

3. "Parents of the world, unite!"

With a journalistic passion equaled in strength and ardor perhaps only by Tolstoy, Ventzel expressed the essence of war in one word: *misanthropy*. He wrote and himself distributed a "An Open Letter to All the People and All Peoples," with the subtitle "A Strike Against War." His thinking is simple and straightforward. People plead the responsibility of the tsar and other heads of state, who have appropriated to themselves the right to declare and start wars at their own whim. But this just is not so: you yourself are the war-perpetrator.

The essence of the strike against war, he explains, is for people to reject any direct or indirect participation in the business called *war*. Those who are conscripted to serve out compulsory military service should refuse to comply with it. Soldiers should refuse to carry out soldierly service, refuse to fire or follow the commands of their leaders to spill blood and cause damage to their enemies. Engineers and workers at military factories should refuse to produce lethal weapons, explosive substances, and poison gases. Technician-inventors should refuse to improve the murderous means that afford an opportunity to send still more people to the other world. Railway workers should refuse to transport troops and munitions, freight-handlers to load the latter onto wagons and seagoing vessels. Journalists should refuse to write articles justifying the war and its horrors, clouding readers' consciousness with their untruthful illumination of events. Don Quixote Ventzel went forth all by himself to do utopian battle with the armies of the various countries.

Violence remained violence for Ventzel, whether war or revolution. He had no illusions, either in February of 1917, or later, in October. On April 14, 1917, simultaneously with Lenin's April theses, "Ventzel's April Theses" were made public. In contrast to the Bolsheviks, Ventzel appealed that "School should not serve as a tool for realization of one set of transient political tasks or another." He demonstrated the necessity for the independence of the school and its separation from the state.

The Bolshevik party called for the proletariat to unite. But he appealed: "Make way for the children and young people in general! Down with the tyranny of the adult generation! Liberation for young people from all sorts of pedagogical enslavement!"[12] He was always speaking up at the wrong time, butting in. And they weren't going to forget that.

Yes, there was a lot of the impractical dreamer in all this. In his pamphlet *The Abolition of Prisons*, (April, 1917) he called for the knocking down of all prisons and the construction of Palaces of Education in their place.[13] The fate of the intelligentsia alarmed him in the event the proletariat was to seize power (his article was entitled "On the Issue of the Intellectual Proletariat and Its Tasks"). In an attempt to save children, as if he knew in advance of the millions of homeless waifs who would appear in the following decade, he appealed to all the peoples of the planet in his "Declaration of Children's Rights." It represented something more significant than the one adopted a half-century later by the United Nation.

The natural school is a school for free children, independent of the political situation, a school for the development of individuals and not obedient carriers-out of the will of the group of people who at any given time are in power. Ventzel understood what the destroyers of the old school were deaf to. The payback for pedagogical ignorance was to come later, and would be reflected on everyone in succeeding generations, including the children and grandchildren of those who affirmed their correctness by force and silenced everyone else.

And, anyway, he still sympathized with socialism. He took seriously the myth of the creation in the near future of a classless society propounded by the Russian interpreters of Marxism. Capitalism, he believed, could only partially realize freedom in upbringing. But under socialism, that achievement would be "more or less total." Capitalist society had no need for creative individuals, but here the flowering was beginning. Ventzel was hoping that socialism would secure children's rights in train after securing the rights of adults.[14]

Criticism of tsarist schools by the partisans of freedom of upbringing looks ridiculous now. Rejecting the old form of schooling, they helped the coming of a new one—with an ideologized pedagogy—in its place. After the revolution the regime did not know what to do with Ventzel at first. The Bolsheviks had latched on to the theory that had made him famous in the preceding century, since they had none of their own ideas on education. But in place of their slogan "Proletarians of the world, unite!" he proposed his own slogan, "Parents of the world, unite for the good of your children!"[15]

This appeal, to put it mildly, went nowhere. But the slogan's creator would not give in. In 1918 he appealed for young people to organize a new party—*a party of pedagogical liberation.*[16] One person joined the party—he himself.

In the early period it was possible to experiment within the framework of school, since, before the revolution, the Bolsheviks had promised to create schools that would be a "free association of students."[17] In 1910 Krupskaya had written to Gorbunov-Posadov that, in the sphere of pedagogy, they were even of like minds. After the October Revolution, when the majority of teachers refused to cooperate with the new regime, the People's Commissar for Education invited specialists in the sphere of freedom of upbringing (and Ventzel first among them), promising "to create a free people's school."

For some time a group of officials from the People's Commissariat for Education (Lepeshinsky, Okunkov, Polyansky, Pozner, Shulgin, Terekhova) remained partisans of freedom of upbringing. In 1918, P. Lepeshinsky, who was in charge of the Department of reforms at the People's Commissariat for Education, even argued with Lenin that the new school should be a self-governing commune. Ventzel could still raise his voice in defense of apolitical education. In the 1920s you could still see some ambivalence in their appraisal of his activities.

At that time they even wrote that "Ventzel's ideas had considerable effect on Soviet pedagogy in 1917-21, but that influence could not be of long duration, because of the elements of idealism and individualism present in Ventzel's pedagogical system, on the one hand, and Ventzel's lack of understanding of the class nature of any pedagogy on the other."[18] However, they soon began talking about the penetration of petit-bourgeois Tolstoyan ideas into Soviet schools. And here not only did the magazine *Svobodnoye vospitaniye* cease to exist, but the innocent educational publishing house of Gorbunov-Posadov as well, and he and his wife, also a famous pedagogue, were advised to head for the Ukraine.

A part of the pedagogical intelligentsia managed to adapt rather quickly to the new requirements. The philosopher-idealist Konstantin Kornilov became a methodologist of the reconstruction of psychology on the basis of dialectical materialism. The psychologist-idealist Pavel Blonsky, who was also accused of anarchism and petit-bourgeoisness, left the Socialist Revolutionary Party and declared: "The spirit of the October Revolution has inspired me in my pedagogy."[19] For that, Blonsky was soon appointed a professor at Moscow University. I called Kornilov and Blonsky idealists only because they considered themselves such before the Revolution. One of Ventzel's confederates of yesterday, Stanislav Shatsky, who had called for the bringing up of individuals independent of the state, joined the Bolshevik party and became director of the Conservatory. He easily shucked freedom of upbringing for the trendy "*sotsvos*" (socialist education) and declared the necessity for inculcating the collectivist instincts required by the People's Commissariat for Education.

Ventzel's sympathy with the new regime did not last long; compromise was no longer acceptable. Soon he would no longer consider it either lawful or stable. He was offered a secondary job at the People's Commissariat for Education. He starved, he froze, but, in contrast with other more flexible colleagues, his pedagogic position was not going to change. A school was supposed to be autonomous, outside politics, and that was that!

Ventzel was certain that talking about proletarian school policy and the proletarian school was a mistake. School is an alien concept in narrow politics, both in proletarian and bourgeois politics. "A natural school in a socialist society should not and will not be characterized by social class."[20]

It can appear to be strange that, in Ventzel's autobiographical recollections, the fifteen-year period after the October coup is allotted a total of ten pages out of 467. It is difficult to believe that he had nothing to write about. Did he get lost? Not understand what was going on? Take everything indifferently?

The philosopher's last reflective thoughts are sad:

> I cannot fail to admit everything that I succeeded in doing is infinitesimal compared with what I could have and should have done if the circumstances of my life had come together more favorably, and if I hadn't had to waste so much effort to no effect in the fruitless struggle for existence.

He sparingly noted that he worked "despite the difficult conditions of life in both material and political terms."[21] Bringing his recollections to a close in 1932, he writes as if his life is ended. But we know otherwise: he had another fifteen years ahead of him, and he lived herded into a communal apartment, a persecuted but unyielding intellectual.

His attitude to what was happening in Russia did not soften. "Socialist militarism has changed guard with imperialist militarism," he wrote on a scrap of paper.

> From one world war, only now overcome by us, the Bolsheviks want to drag us into a new world war, even more terrible in its scale, even more shocking in its cruelty. Hasn't the world been saturated with blood enough already? Hasn't the human soul tired of the whole nightmare of malice and misanthropy that it has survived over the past years? Surely a revolutionary Germany and other countries will not let themselves be swept away in this whirlpool of new slaughter? I don't want to believe this. I want to think that the kind of elements who will manage to deflect the Bolsheviks from this course can be found among the Russian people, as well as that the majority of the populace in Germany and other countries that have raised the banner of revolution will not take this bloody path that the Bolsheviks are calling them to.

Ventzel was uninhibitedly engaging in polemics with the regime that had enmeshed the entire country.

4. The Religion of the Creative Individual

He wasn't allowed to work in Moscow, but he was promised a series of lectures at Voronezh University and a tiny post in the Regional Department of People's Education. It seemed to him that in the province he would be far from the center of authority. In 1919, he moved to Voronezh. One year before that, another prominent pedagogue, Pyotr Kapterev, had had to move there, to Voronezh, as well. In fact, the People's Commissariat for Education was rusticating the people who enjoyed huge authority among the teachers who were inclined against Red ideas and did not want to train their children to jump through Leninist hoops.

Ventzel had a dizzy career, one that calls up a smile. For three years he walked the path of a People's Commissariat for Education official, starting with the post of assistant head of a sub-department for teacher training and finishing in the post of head of the scientific-methodological section of the Regional Department of People's Education.

In the collapse of the civil war, when the districts of Voronezh *guberniya* passed from the hands of the Whites to the Reds many times, and each of the sides used schools for barracks and stables, and, in retreat, would set them afire to deny them to the enemy, *Pomzavpedotdelom* (Asst-head-ped-dept—the lexicon of the times!) Ventzel tried to collect the dispersed teachers together. His attitude toward the civil war was expressed without any ambiguity: "If a war of one nation against another deserves condemnation, then even greater condemnation is deserved by a civil war, and woe betide those who throw the burning brand."[22]

Ventzel was getting ready a series of lectures in memory of Leo Tolstoy at the Society for Genuine Freedom, then on its last legs. He was turned down: somebody in Moscow prohibited it. In Voronezh, he organized an Institute of People's Education that, a year later, was transformed into a faculty of Voronezh University, and started giving lectures on the philosophy of religion and the theory of freedom of upbringing.

Rumors of these topics flew around the local intelligenstia in a flash. Whenever he finished a lecture, they would give him a standing ovation. "In the overcrowded auditorium," wrote the Voronezh teachers, "not just students but scientific staff as well would usually be present." Let us add: and officers of the local VChK as well, the All-Union Extraordinary Committee, or Cheka, and simply minor proletarian-snitches.

The man was a marvellous orator; he could quote by heart philosophers, musicians, writers in their native languages. His lectures provoked many arguments and discussions. After his speech "Revolution and Morality," because of night coming on, the debate was carried over to the following evening. His lectures contained "propositions clearly mistaken and not in keeping with Marxist-Leninist theory."[23] Ventzel himself did not want to understand why his thoughts in Voronezh should be in keeping with Lenin's thoughts in Moscow and even with Marx's notions in the London of the past century.

The security organs could not make out which philosophy the lecturer was talking to his students about. A slashing article appeared in the local newspaper. It said: "We would advise him to set off for another shore to do his preaching."[24] But he didn't want to head for another shore. He concentrated on his new theory—of a person's constructive activity in an atmosphere of non-freedom and in defense of the individual from dictatorship—which he called "The Religion of the Creative Individual."

The bounds of party associations dispirited him. Whose reason and whose conscience is being offered to us? the thinker speculated. The mass murder of people during the Terror—was that in the name of revolutionary conscience? Both reason and conscience were so splashed with blood that it was better not to touch them. Ventzel filled up a whole notebook in Voronezh, discussing the topic with himself.

Russia and all of mankind was undergoing a great spiritual crisis. The task was to liberate the younger generation from the slavery that the adult generation was ensnaring them in. "All party-mindedness," he reasoned,

> any kind at all, is a chain of invisible slavery and should be thrown off if a person wants to be free in the genuine meaning of this word. All party-mindedness narrows a person, fetters and enslaves him . . . It is necessary to reject slavery under whatever slogan it might appear, and it is necessary to approach slogans freely, expose them to constant study and review. It is not concrete reality that should be sacrificed to slogans, but slogans that should be amended in every instance to conform to concrete reality.

Ventzel proposed founding a Union for the Struggle for Spiritual Liberation of Mankind—an alternative to the party that was leading to spiritual slavery. Then he crossed out the words "the struggle for . . ." and wrote "Reason and Conscience." He talked about an organization in which everyone would respect the freedom of others. Observing the civil war, Ventzel quoted Tolstoy: "War is a crime permitted by people."[25]

In Voronezh, Ventzel gathered all his articles written during the revolution of 1905 into a collection entitled *Revolution and the Requirements of Morality*. Evidently he read them to his audience in the course of his lectures. His thoughts on human rights amaze you with their non-transient values.

> I refuse to look at any person at all as a instrument of the historical process, as a means for social struggle to achieve some kind of social goal ... I defend the right of every individual to go their own way, down their own path, and not the one that is prescribed for me by anyone else, even if that other is the whole of society ... Slavish dependence upon society is as shameful as upon any individual person, and slavery does not stop being slavery just because of it. And no historical period, even if it is a period of revolution, can demand from the individual that he stop being an individual and become a unit of the herd . . .[26]

Now tougher inserts appear in these old articles:

> If former fanatics of religious faith were possessed by a mania for the salvation of people for the heavenly kingdom, then the history of recent times has shown us, in the sphere of political activity, a type possessed by a mania for the salvation of people for the earthly kingdom, and for achieving that goal—like those religious fanatics—not stopping at anything, not even at the commission of the most horrible crimes, that only to hypnotized people could seem not crimes but heroic deeds.

In the aforementioned manuscript collection compiled by Ventzel from his own articles, a composition entitled "Chains of Invisible Slavery" attracts attention by formulating the problem.

"If I found a path in life that, in my opinion, would bring all of mankind to its salvation, do I have a right to drag other people by force down this path?" the philosopher asked, and appealed "to provide the younger generation with the opportunity not to fall into a state of 'invisible slavery,' not to become a slave internally, in the region of the spirit, with the external appearance of a person completely free."

In the article there was not just this appeal, but also an analysis of the situation. "What makes people agree to such a slavery? Why don't they avoid it like the plague? Why do they sell with such ease and even give away gratis the thing that is the most valuable to anyone, and that is their free spirit, free will, free mind, and free feeling? Why do they value that highest blessing obviously less than anything and why can they so calmly and so easily reject it?

> At first sight, it seems strange, incomprehensible and inexplicable. But if we think deeper, then we can see that the reason for that phenomenon is quite simple. The reason is that people who reject their will and allow themselves to be enmeshed in the chains of invisible slavery do not understand and do not realize what a great blessing it is to possess a free spirit.

The issue of non-conformity is difficult one, however, and not acceptable to everyone.

Earlier, Ventzel had been looking for a path of peace through the conflict tearing the country apart. "Individualism and socialism do not represent two doctrines contradictory to each other," he thought. They complement each other. He saw the future Russia getting closer to some type of free public agreement. Right now that was not the case. He no longer believed in public common sense: "You must select, in your personal activity, the path of the greatest good and the least evil." Oh, how we needed this thesis in the 1960s!

Bolshevization was overwhelming the periphery. Oppression on the local authorities became unbearable. In 1922, Ventzel ran off from Voronezh back to Moscow.

5. A time unsuited for polemics

After his return, he was allowed to compile new programs for the People's Commissariat for Education. He tried to argue about the content of education in the new schools, demanding acceptance of the sovereign will of the individual personality. Morality was supposed to be personal, and not of the herd.

> Any authority," he explained, "is the negation of that will, and for that reason the cult of authority is indeed the real nihilism, in whatever form it may have manifested itself. And with that cult of authority, so widespread and rooting itself so deeply into

the consciousness of modern people, we should fight hardest to liberate the individual human will from any kind of submission.[27]

It can't be helped: the Russian, fighting with one myth, creates another.

The officials in the People's Commissariat for Education whom he talked to laughed openly at him. All his thoughts now diverged from the sanctioned ones. "School," in the words of Commissar for Education Anatoly Lunacharsky, "is a political institution that the state establishes for its own purposes."[28] And no exceptions will be made!

Ventzel's attitude toward the tsarist school was negative. In 1911, it took in 43 percent of all children. According to data from the People's Commissariat for Education for 1923, expenditure for education had decreased by two thirds in comparison with the pre-war period.[29] The number of homeless children in 1922 was two million; in 1923, four million.[30] But the official magazine of the People's Commissariat for Education reported boldly: "Public interests are growing at a quick pace; class-consciousness of proletarian solidarity among children is penetrating deeper and deeper."[31]

He withdrew into himself more and more. Long lists of books that he was reading, in four different languages, trail through his diary. Philosophy, religion, creativity, upbringing—these are his articles. He was keen on parapsychology, he thought about mankind's connections with the Cosmos—perhaps looking for a way out of the condition of slavery? Ink was cheap, almost water, it would freeze; you couldn't find an ordinary pencil, a sheet of paper was worth its weight in gold. Books and manuscripts fired people's stoves. But he wrote on in deep concentration.

Ventzel believed that for a long time to come the individual would have to be the scapegoat on the way of society's striving for greater orderliness. "The mechanization of public relations," he writes, and then suddenly (I can feel this) *shouts* in his diary,

> Free creative individuals, do not allow them to put you under the murderous press of the mechanization of public life! Fight against the machine-ness that, like a fatal brand, they strive to put on all aspects of life, on all of its young shoots![32]

A geezer, an eccentric, God's fool—a lone ranger against blind mechanism, a homely fighter against Soviet myths.

Ventzel was returning to the notes of his youth, once again seeing them confirmed: "It is asked why we need peace and order in society if, for the sake of that order, the individual is trampled on! That's a nice kind of order where, instead of free people who follow their own bent and inclinations, their own notions of truth and fairness, we have slaves of law, people who blindly and unquestioningly submit to the will of the majority." Has nothing really changed, even though yet another epoch has become the past? "Every person," he wrote almost half a century ago, "should be the measure of truth and right for himself; any other measure is false, immoral, and in disagreement with the freedom of the individual."[33]

He proposed to the new society to reform the family on a different basis—the equality of children and parents. He advised organizing an International Union for the Struggle for Children's Rights. He spoke of the necessity to condemn political upbringing as a form of violence upon future generations by people temporarily in power.

The semi-literate proletarianized officials of the People's Commissariat for Education unceremoniously cut out of his texts everything that wasn't in keeping with the new party line. Only Ventzel's understanding of work as a means for educating people was acceptable. And in the January issue of the Commissariat's magazine *Na putyakh k novoy shkole* (*On the Paths to the New School*) for 1923, they published Ventzel's report on work schools. The essence of his views was emasculated; even his innocent notions of respect for the individual were struck out.

An official attitude towards Ventzel was gradually being formulated. He was "a follower of the petit-bourgeois theory of 'freedom of upbringing'... by means of which ... he anarchically rejects [*the party line*] ..." And, further, everything continues in the same class-based spirit: "The helplessness of the petit-bourgeois intelligentsia ... proclaims itself in his views ... that found itself incapable of understanding, proposing, or grounding a correct, genuinely scientific system for bringing up children."[34] This genuinely scientific system was what we Russians experienced.

The philosophy of freedom of upbringing was reclassified, from "petit-bourgeois" to "bourgeois."[35] Then it became "so-called," which, in translation from the official lexicon, has to mean "false, unscientific."[36]

It has to be said that there was a weak link in the concept adduced by the theoreticians of freedom of upbringing. Before the Revolution their widely-interpreted ideas about freedom were advantageous for many parties, including the ones striving towards dictatorship. Behind some of Ventzel's ideas the utopianism shows through, the reckoning that, through schooling, it is possible to reform life. "The real key to a lasting, stable reorganization of the public system on new bases is the freedom of upbringing and education of all children, without exception," Ventzel was quoted as saying by the theoretician-pedagogue Vasily Zenkovsky. And he added: "In his passion for freedom, Ventzel goes beyond all bounds of pedagogy, replacing the school with life."[37]

According to the exegesis of the official Soviet pedagogical historian Fyodor Korolev, "failing to understand that, after the victory of ... the Revolution, new social conditions had appeared for the creation of a truly free school, Ventzel continued for a while to uphold the idea of a school's 'autonomy' from the state and preach apoliticality in upbringing."[38] "For a while," because they simply stopped publishing him.

He had no means of subsistence. On Tuesdays and Fridays from seven to nine o'clock in the evening, at the Lenin Rest Home for Veterans of the Revolution, they held "Evenings of Intimate Music with Pianist K. N. Ventzel." They let him play, wordlessly, giving the veterans their revolutionary pleasure. He had to ask the management for a free tramway ticket: the pianist didn't have any means to get himself to the place of his intimate musical sounds.

Without any special hope he once again asked to be allowed to lecture at the second campus of Moscow State University—and once again a refusal followed. He was not surprised: "We are still ruled by the spirit of autocracy and bureaucracy, and the spirit of feudalism and serfdom ... the spirit of cannibalism, the spirit of destruction, of vengeance, of insane torturing, of pleasure in the suffering of others."[39]

The Western philosopher and pedagogue with whom I would compare Ventzel in sweep and depth is John Dewey. They were contemporaries, and both lived for nearly a century (Ventzel 1857-1947, Dewey 1859-1952), but they never met. They both differed from their colleagues in that they seriously put their beliefs into practice. But the sowing of new philosophical ideas into education is a process that has to bear fruit. Pedagogical science does not exist without it, and it cannot be replaced by any ideology.

Ventzel had something to sow, but, in the period of his greatest maturity, he was deprived of a field to sow it in. The People's Commissariat for Education was disturbed by the freethinking philosopher. In 1928, Dewey, on whom was hung the same label of idealist, came to the U.S.S.R., and they concealed from the American that the like-minded Russian was still alive. Meanwhile, the ideas of both of them concerning work education were being widely employed—but ascribed to Lenin and his wife Nadezhda Krupskaya.

At that time, Ventzel wanted to go beyond the bounds of the *sotsvos*, the socialist education, that replaced pedagogy, and proposed an alternative—*cosmic* pedagogy, in which a person is part of the Universe. In his notebooks, alone with himself, he muses on the merging of the individual with the cosmos. This fruitless fantasy was the result of his repugnance for the reality that seemed a horrible thing to Ventzel. But his ideals did not fade.

Reading dozens of philosophical works over and over in four languages (he got them from the Rumyantsevsky Museum—at the time, they still gave them out to the public at large), he compiled a list of the qualities necessary for a creative individual. He composed the "March of Mankind." He looked for ways to keep safe the only valuable that still had not been expropriated from him—his mind. After all, already in 1884, a year before his arrest, the young truth-seeker Ventzel had written in his diary: "If there is so little truth outside us in reality, then let it at least exist inside of us."[40] After the October Revolution, when the only thing that remained of truth was the name of the newspaper *Pravda*, he tried not to betray that principle.

Among the diary notes in an old bookkeeping log that had been cut in half across the middle, we came upon: "At the present ... time we can only speak of maximum creativity, admissible in given conditions of life and in a given milieu."[41] How can one engage in philosophy, in science? "Now each of them seems to be as if in a cell apart."[42]

He prepared himself for the writing of pieces that, already ten years before, had appeared to him to be worthy of serious work. It would have been absurd to engage in polemics with court favorites. The harm to mankind was already so evident that they would have stood no chance of success. Yet there they were, standing their ground inside the regime.

"One thing without doubt," he wrote into a notebook under the heading "Personal,"

> is that Bolshevism is not the last word either of Russian or of world history; what's most important is that it's the latest lesson on what kinds of socialism shouldn't be constructed, what kinds of devices for the realization of a socialist system on this Earth are resorted to merely to the discredit of that system, delaying and slowing down its realization. Oh, how I would like now to be in the know about what is really now happening in the wide world, and not have to examine all the phenomena of public life only through strongly-colored Bolshevik glasses . . . In the study of history and social phenomena we should have gone far ahead in these 70 years, and many of Marx's propositions, when reviewed and verified, can be found to be mistaken . . . Such dogmas have done mankind a lot of harm, the pernicious influence of worship before them continues to proclaim itself even now, and, probably, will proclaim itself for a long time yet to come.

A bit further on, Ventzel defends the theoretician against the practitioners: "Probably Marx himself would dissociate himself from those forms that his doctrine has taken in Bolshevik theory and practice."[43]

In one of the notebooks of the 70-year-old Ventzel, we find excerpts from the tenth volume of the first edition of the *Great Soviet Encyclopedia* that speak of him, himself. Suddenly the old man found himself stung to the quick by accusations of idealism, in that he had never participated in the class struggle.

The time was not suitable for polemics, but they themselves had goaded him into replying. Of course, a reply of one single copy only, for himself and posterity. Nevertheless, Ventzel got down to an analysis of the basics, to the untouchable. Now, heaps have been written about it. But let's read Ventzel from a historical point of view, that is, as if we were with him in Moscow at the end of the 1920s—the beginning of the 1930s. Look how elegantly he tops and tails the carcass of Bolshevism.

6. "The theory of dialectical materialism is idealistic"

While a part of the intelligentsia was still stepping out with delight across Red Square under mythic banners, the philosopher was getting down to the unmasking of the main myth of the 20th century—Marxism and its Russian variant. "It is necessary to understand Bolshevism as a historical phenomenon, where its roots are, and where are the reasons for its success," wrote Ventzel, "and you have to follow it through its possible and probable evolution: what it will finally degenerate into, and what it will lead to."[44] Having asked himself this question, the philosopher examines the phenomenon of 1917. Now, in view of what it has all come to, we have an opportunity to appreciate Ventzel's musings.

> In Bolshevism we have socialism in its dogmatic form, socialism that stubbornly declines the names of Marx and Engels and their follower and interpreter Lenin through all the cases of the language. This is socialism deprived of the elements of development, socialism pickled, socialism adopting the nature of a church with its professional, patent priests and infallible prophets, with all the defects that every church preserves in itself. This is a socialism in which is absent great truth and the genuine criticism of thought that strives to discover that truth objectively, to whatever it should lead us. Here known, definite schemes and starting points in time, that later would never be subject to revision but considered unshakeable, are given already in advance ... Bolshevism for us is a socialism that has come to a dead end, repeating what was learned before, marching in place with its Old Testament—the works of Marx and Engels, and with its Gospel—the works of Lenin. Every word of these teachers is sacred and indisputable, is not subject to revocation, but only interpretation.

Ventzel made synopses of the works of dialectical materialism and analyzed the views of its founders. He wrote down his own comments on the theory of dialectical materialism. From his unpublished works, here is an example of Ventzel's thoughts, on the subject of the not-unknown fourth chapter of *A Short Course on the History of the All-Union Communist Party (Bolshevik)*, that was "studied" by several generations of Soviet people.

"I entirely agree with the theory of dialectical materialism," said Ventzel, "that, in the resolution of every issue, it is necessary to proceed from objective reality itself and to take all sides of the latter in their mutual connection and development. Really, only in this way, i.e., taking all aspects of life in development and in reciprocal connection with one another, will we be in a condition to discover those real, and not imaginary, laws that govern that development. But from here in no way, shape, or form does it follow that such an approach to things and phenomena of life will be the most consistent materialism."

In the philosopher's opinion, notions of living reality and materiality by no means jibe with each other. The notion of reality is wider.

> Not only material things and material processes can be considered reality; for such are also the processes of consciousness, thought, feeling, will, conscious activity directed toward the achievement of one or another goal that the individual sets for himself, and generally all facts of a psychological nature. To stand at the point of view of reality does not at all mean to be a materialist. Eugene Dühring—who called his philosophy 'a philosophy of reality' and was nevertheless the antipode of the founders of dialectical materialism, Marx and Engels—could serve as an example.

Ventzel considered the assertion that every science and philosophy expresses the interests of a definite class to be nonsense. In practice, of course, it is difficult to free oneself from the preconceived point of view of one or another nationality, class, or party, and the thinker has to make an effort towards the free reduction of distorting influences to a minimum.

> But when preconception is made into a principle and has to become a requirement for the scientist and the philosopher, it is necessary to be suspicious in the highest degree towards the products of their activity. You can be certain in advance that their science and philosophy is a justification . . . of the party that takes upon itself the monopoly of being the only real defender of their interests, and even justification of the leaders of that party.

> There was a time when science and philosophy were servants of theology.

> Now, apparently, we are living through a time when it is desirable to make them into the servants of a political party, when the slavery of science and philosophy is once again being made into a principle.

But Ventzel is certain that mankind

> needs not bourgeois or proletarian but free science and philosophy, renouncing all preconceived points of view and interested only in the search for objective truth alone, and not its distortion to please or to benefit one political party or another.

Why was dialectical materialism turning out to be so tiresome?

> Dialectical materialism is a philosophical system that is especially useful for those political parties whose activity has a contradictory nature. No other philosophy can to such a degree justify the activity of that kind of political dealers as the philosophy of dialectical materialism in particular. It explains as well why the party that got dominion in our country hangs on so tightly to that philosophy, bases itself on it, and strives to make it the basis of the political and moral instruction of youth.

A person's behavior, according to dialectical materialism, is also built on contradictions, Ventzel considered. A contradiction between means and goals can be the contradiction at the basis of moral activity. The more they contradict each other, the more morally a person will develop. Hence, for the achievement of a high moral aureole, it is necessary simply to use those means that would negate the goal. Politics in general, which is applied ethics, and which denies the tendencies to unification and harmony governing in the world, leads to discord and struggle. This is the politics of the armed military camp, in which "if the enemy does not surrender, he is destroyed."

Ventzel thought that dialectical materialists, instead of stressing the positive side of the process of life and evolution, affirmation and creation, give particular emphasis to negation, destruction, and struggle, leaving everything positive and creative in the shadows.

One of the basic errors of Marx and Engels, he believed, was their taking Hegel, although turned upside-down, for their foundation.

> Do you understand anything at all when you are told about the interpenetration of antitheses that Lenin, following Hegel, calls the identity of antitheses? George Henry Lewes, in his *History of Philosophy in Biographies*, speaking of Hegel's system, asks: 'Can one see in it anything but an example of to what extent philosophy is capable of being mistaken?' He is the one who says that Hegel's logic is like the logic of the insane.

Ventzel then came to his main conclusion: in essence, *the theory of dialectical materialism is idealistic*, having nothing to do with what is going on. Hence there is an inevitable split in consciousness. According to Ventzel, Marxists remind him of the readers of *A Thousand and One Nights*: to anyone submerged in the world of make-believe, it begins to seem that it is the genuine reality.

Who is right, then, or, putting it better, who more objectively evaluates the world—materialists or idealists? Ventzel considered that neither pure materialism, which maintains that only existence determines consciousness, that consciousness is the product of the external, material world, nor pure idealism, which maintains to the contrary that only consciousness determines existence, that the external world should be considered by us a product of the spirit, of our consciousness, is right.

Dialectical materialists maintain, Ventzel said, that the roots of idealism lie in the class-organization of society, that idealism expresses the interests of the exploitative classes. With equal if not even more foundation, this can be said regarding materialism. Materialistic philosophy of the 18th century was a wonderful ideology for bourgeois society. And only when Marx and Engels entered into unlawful cohabitation with the most extreme philosophy of absolute idealism, when the fruit of that cohabitation became dialectical materialism, only then did materialism become a philosophy, but even that proletarian philosophy, so far as it is materialistic, is penetrated throughout by the bourgeois spirit.

Ventzel considered that it would be more appropriate to speak about the activity or passivity of a philosophy rather than materialism and idealism. In this instance, that would better express the essence and the goals of those who followed a philosophy. That is why the time would come when dialectical materialism would die, a philosophy of slavery.

> The founders of dialectical materialism, Marx and Engels, could not devise anything better than to raise the banner of dictatorship of the proletariat. And what is the dictatorship of the proletariat if not a reiteration of the dictatorship of the bourgeoisie? Moreover, an imitation fraught with many disastrous consequences. Along with dictatorship, one has to adopt as well many other nasty institutions that the bourgeoisie invented. And, besides, the fatal course of things leads to the fact that the dictatorship of the proletariat degenerates, as the course of the revolution in Russia shows this to be, into a dictatorship over the proletariat, into a dictatorship of the party that has appropriated the patent to be the only real defender of the interests of the proletariat, and even into a dictatorship by the single person who is the leader of that party, i.e., into an autocracy.

Ventzel's verdict on Marxism-Leninism was final, without right of appeal. But . . . the verdict was never passed down, either. To publish it, he would have to have escaped to Europe ten years earlier, along with Nikolay Berdyayev. And what way out could there be for him in the mid-Thirties, when he was nearly 80 years old?

7. The cult of the Child instead of the cult of Stalin

The home-bound philosopher strove for a long time to find some way out of the situation that had arisen in Russia, and to understand in what direction to move. The result of his speculations was, first, a small manuscript of about fifty pages, entitled *Three Revolutions (Political, Social, and Spiritual)*.

In it, Ventzel quoted the German philosopher Max Schtirner, who had noted that the Great French Revolution turned a limited monarchy into an absolute, unlimited one. According to Schtirner, freedom after a revolution means that the state has freedom in its power over the individual, the power holding sway over me and oppressing me has its freedom. The liberation of the state is the transformation of me into a slave.

This is why, proceeding from reality and (blame him again for his naivety) hoping that not everything had been lost yet, Ventzel guessed that, after the political act, that is, the *coup d'état* itself, and the social events, there should come a third step. "I can already feel how skeptical Pilates surround me on all sides," he growled. He was calling for a spiritual revolution, since a "void" had formed in the wake of the other one.

Instead of the end-justifies-the-means principle of all previous revolutions, Ventzel proposed the principle of a spiritual revolution: the means justify the end. In his opinion, it is necessary to humanize "the many-headed monster called '*the mob*' in English." Spiritual revolution, he said, is for those who have realized themselves as individuals. The philosopher again becomes the enlightener of the nation whose son he is. He elaborates: "Spiritual reform or revolution could also be called cultural or pedagogical, since a vital role is played by transformation of the system of existing culture and the system of upbringing and education of the rising generation."[45]

We'll say this sardonically, now: his voice was heard. A cultural revolution occurred first in the Soviet Union, and then in China. Did either or both of these revolutions make for spiritual liberation?

In Ventzel's opinion, tyranny in the realm of the spirit creates the most awful forms of slavery. All modern culture is a culture "of the externally hoop-trained person" and concerns chiefly the material forms of existence.[46] He wrote this even before the Revolution. His experiences accumulated, now totalitarian and Soviet, and Ventzel returned to the search for a means to spiritual liberation. That was his philosophical treatise *On Internal Slavery*, written in 1925-34 and still sounding immediate to this day.

> Let's take political enslavement. The 'state' is the master here, personified in one or another 'ruling class,' whose will is expressed in a range of these or those laws and the directives based on them. This will is alien to the individual and extraneous to his own will, and the individual has to be subordinate to it under threat of some punishment or other, or material deprivation. We are dealing with slavery here, and there can be no doubt about it...

How does a person have to behave in the circumstances of state X? Is there any chance to remain an individual? It always depends on the person himself whether to be a slave or a free man, and if he prefers slavery, it means he wants to be a slave. Ventzel supposed that even in America there was a gap between the Declaration of Independence and the Constitution that the plutocrats were to blame for.

According to Ventzel, there are three types of people in a state of spiritual slavery: (1) people substituting one or another provocative feeling (ambition, lust for power, carnality, cowardice, fright) for their own will; (2) people acting under the influence of a thought or idea (obsessed); and (3) people who substitute the will of another person or group (a master) or the idea of their state, nationality, party, or class for their own will.

The mechanism of enslavement, the philosopher believed, affects people via institutions and social organizations: the family, the state, trade unions, the party. In any group of people, there are two kinds of psychological interrelations: automatism, leading to slavery, and creative activity, as a path to spiritual freedom. The stronger wins.

As soon as a philosopher put his ideas into practice, his advice (not just Ventzel's, either) sounds considerably less weighty. He offers a means of defense against spiritual enslavement: to cooperate in the strengthening, the reinforcement and development of the creative activity of the spirit in yourself and in the people around you.

The will is the instrument that can turn a slave into a free person. The will is the most commanding and outstripping of all the attributes of human existence. The will is like a decisive and all-conquering force. And, after having limited himself in this fashion, Ventzel straightaway lays himself open to the arrows of his opponents. "Let us imagine," he wrote, "that the idea of a state will lose its charm for all the people, and all the people will understand that in the person of the state, they have a master, and political slavery will collapse all by itself."[47]

The will works only as far as internal slavery goes. But is it enough when the problem of a society's freedom comes up? Ventzel himself suffered many times from the loss of his freedom, and also suffered from the collective will of others being foisted upon him. Those who had *dismissed* him from social activity declared that he had *withdrawn* from it—there is your "will" for you.

Ventzel considered that childhood is when the future open or secret slave or genuinely free person gets formed. In the 1930s, pedagogy in the Soviet Union became a discipline for the explication of the resolutions of the Central Committee. The task of education became not the bringing up of individuals, but turning out "fighters for" and "fighters against."

Tolstoy's and Ventzel's idea of teaching work in the natural school was realized by Krupskaya and Makarenko, in the form of a children's forced labor colony. A long period of establishing uniformity in Soviet schools began. Experimenters were accused of left and right deviation, some of them arrested; the remaining ones called for fanning the flames of the class struggle in school. The People's Commissariat for Education, under the leadership of Andrey Bubnov, turned into a branch of the NKVD, but Bubnov himself finished his life in the Lubyanka as well.

It was already entirely impossible to picture Ventzel as an armchair Commissariat scholar: "Education now has a fettered, unfree nature; it has taken on the air of hoop-training and the one-sided development of human individuality in keeping with some goals or other of practical life, or demands provoked by the modern condition of society."[48] It was necessary to save children from the regime, but how?

In this disintegrating society, the philosopher called for a cult of personality—not in the meaning that appeared a quarter-century later (the cult of the dictator), but *the cult of human personality*. Ventzel proposed starting with the Cult of the Child.

> The genuine savior of mankind, who will bring new life to it, liberation from all the pressing chains of visible and invisible slavery, will be not a person and not a worker, but a child, who will be given, finally, the opportunity to develop freely and thoroughly and become a creative individual, feeling his relatedness and unity with mankind and the world.[49]

Ventzel was always trying to educate mankind to mind its highest purpose in the Universe, and not to utilitarian service of the masters of one sixth of the earth's globe.

Following his convictions about freedom of upbringing, he started composing addenda that would be needed for the published project for the Stalin-era constitution. The sense of these addenda was to help children to escape everything having to do with an authoritarian nature, anything smacking of sectarianism. He proposed a plank on the separation of the school and the state. He wrote a letter to the editors of *Izvestiya*. For so called Stalin Constitution Day, he recommended abolishing the death penalty, opening prisons; he proved the necessity of amnesty for all who found themselves in places of confinement. And that was in 1936, when there was a huge risk of finding himself in the same place he was asking others' release from.

What was happening continued to confirm an idea he had expressed before: "the sin of spiritual degradation of a person lies to a considerable degree" with his schooling.[50] He was having a hard time.

> The reality surrounding me oppresses me just too much, seeming to be not life, but some kind of twilight of life; this is universal idolatry, a universal mental derangement; this is herd instinct, servility and a boundless, broad-flooding outpouring of lies and hypocrisy. In front of our eyes, some kind of farce is being played out, in order to blind, shock, and amaze, and even intelligent people fail to notice it and take it for something serious.

The real life did not give him a reason for optimism. The communal flat where he lived was overcrowded, in essence, a flophouse. He had nowhere to write; his mood was grim. There was no money for a typist for his manuscript. Yet, somehow, the old duffer in everyone's way lived an intense, spiritual life.

His notebook was filled with tiny inscriptions, and so smudged that I could manage to make out the words only letter by letter with the help of a magnifying glass. He carried these notes in his pocket, and slept with them, afraid to lose them in the chaos of the communal flat. Completely switching himself off from participation in social life, he advised others to do the same: by boycott, by refusal to buy their books, by non-attendance at their meetings, where the undoubted goal was spiritual slavery.

Ventzel was 79; his strength was fading. His own children were bringing up his grandchildren with force, and that fact, as he confessed in his diary, added to his suffering. There were frequent rows in the family. He felt that he was getting in his children's way. They had a different life, their own, concerns incomprehensible to him. His communal-flat neighbors thought he was a nutcase. His daughter Vera forbade her children to play with their grandfather, telling them that he was not a human being, but a loathsome thing. This was done right in front of him. It seemed to him that his grandchildren were avoiding him. The superfluous man of the Soviet epoch. Now he dreamed of getting away. But where, and how?

A year of complete silence ensued. Then he again took himself in hand: "But I shall not lose hope. That which is the main thing in my life, I must see to the end."[51]

8. A voice crying out in the wilderness

He conceived of writing *In Praise of Slavery*, on the model of Erasmus's *In Praise of Stupidity*, about slaves with honorable reputations, and about methods of liberation from the chains of invisible slavery. The links in this chain were any kinds of *–ism*.

Before the war, Ventzel lived near our family in a dacha at Bittsa, near Moscow. I was young and didn't know who the old man was who would play with me and give advice to my parents. I liked the heavy chain across his chest with its antique silver watch. In the only photo that I could find, he is wearing a striped jacket, reminiscent of a prisoner's robe, that he had sewn up himself.

A quarter of a century later, my father told me that Konstantin Ventzel had tried to convince him and my mother of the necessity of a free upbringing for my sister and me. Now I discovered that it was that summer that he was laboring intensively over his work *The Evolution of Moral Ideals*. He didn't finish it, but did begin to put his finger on Revolutionary mythology. Here are several excerpts from that manuscript.

> In the sphere of political relations, wrote Ventzel, idealization is one of those points of rest that a regime of political tutelage stands on. The idealization of governmental authority—faith in its strength, might, and infallibility—conditions the passivity, in the political sense, of its citizens, makes slaves of government out of them instead of free citizens. There is nothing more dangerous than the delusion due to which we rely entirely on the wisdom of government and expect from them all kinds of changes for the better.[52]

Ventzel turns to history for proof that government in general is never wise and far from always on guard against injustice.

> Not one single citizen should blindly believe in the authority to which he submits, or entrust it entirely with the care of his fate or the fate of his co-citizens. Only faith in one's own strengths, faith that can be instilled under a regime of political freedom requiring every citizen to participate in one way or another in the government of the state, only that faith can put the people on the right path of political development.

In the realm of politics, the philosopher believed, everyone should be afforded the greatest possible range of creative independence: everyone governed should also be one part or another of governmental authority. In order to provide political creativity for everyone, Ventzel proposed undertaking the widest possible decentralization, self-government by the smallest possible units. The cells of the future state should consist of small, self-governing communities, whose requirements should define the limits of the centralized authority.

In a normal society—and this has some immediacy for today—Ventzel could see the widest centralization hand in hand with the broadest possible decentralization. "An excess of centralization, the concentration of power in a few hands along with the removal of all the rest of the masses from any kind of political activity, will either lead to the inculcation of complete political passivity and humiliation, or will push the citizenry down the path of clandestine revolutionary work. The creative strengths of the individual, failing to find an outlet in open, free political activity, secured by laws, look for their outlet in underground activity. The stronger the political oppression, the more consistently the principle of political tutelage is followed, the sharper and more intensive the revolutionary ferment, the more activity of a certain part of society takes on a militant character, the more inevitable becomes the catastrophe threatening the state. Revolution, like a shadow, follows everywhere after a regime of political tutelage, and the more unbearable and stronger the tutelage becomes, the higher revolution raises its threatening hand. If the authority does not want to make concessions in any way, if it does not want to limit itself, then revolution becomes inevitable."

Ventzel projected a broad outline of how the kind of political mythology that holds back life's progressive development is created. Its types were (1) idealization of the state in general, (2) idealization of the government, the regime, (3) idealization of the regime of unlimited monarchy, and (4) idealization of the parliamentarian forms of governing. In the Soviet Union, all of these types dwelt together.

> It is necessary to note that the idealization of parliamentarianism can be as dangerous as the idealization of an unlimited monarchy. Both will lead us to political metaphysics. A true political science must reveal the secret of political relations, should show things the way they really exist, without any coloration. It should destroy political illusions and overturn false political gods from their pedestals. Politics should be subordinate to ethics, in a servile position.

In other words, he believes, politics should be surmounted by ethics.

> It may be that the most dangerous of all delusions is belief in the omnipotence of politics, belief that politics can accomplish everything. It is true that you can achieve a lot through politics, but far from everything, and without a firmly ethical foundation, politics does not lead to anything good. The only creative force building a new order of things is an ethical upbringing, and it has to have in view the creation of such social institutions, such a political system, that could ethically educate the greatest number of people possible.

As we can see, Ventzel subordinates political tasks to the educational. He looks at a political system, at a state, as a gigantic school, where all the people are being educated. "Only a point of view like that of political tasks," he elaborates, "affords the opportunity to plant politics in the right soil. In this regard, the extreme revolutionary parties sin badly against the truth: they think that it is enough to seize political power in their hands and decree the ideal order of things, so that the ideal state of mankind will come." The belief that everything can be built up by means of decree or by means of legislative acts, in Ventzel's opinion, should be abandoned.

In the country that was a prison, he wrote that state's political tasks should be subordinate to the tasks of education. This followed from Ventzel's whole conception: politics as much as pedagogy is a part of ethics. And if it is not, you can expect whatever you like to happen. The tragedy of Russia consisted in the lack of strong, argumentative critics of Bolshevism. The vacuum got filled by demagogy. Ventzel was one of the few philosophers who *criticized*. One of the most intellectual enlighteners that Russia had ever borne, he did not publish his works, but nevertheless today his place by right is among the greatest thinkers to have defeated the Communist myth.

The general volume of material secretly written by Ventzel for himself was huge. I managed to read about 2,000 pages. But if only one line of his had fallen into the hands of a snitch-neighbor of his in the communal flat, their author would have been ground to dust. I have in my keeping a green leaf from a strange tree, pressed by Ventzel in his diary in the 1870s. But his thoughts are an entire living tree; they have immediacy today as well.

In his *Evolution of Moral Ideals*, he quoted Vladimir Solovyov: "We know that there is no good in the world, for the whole world lies in evil; there is no good in man himself either, for every man is a lie ..."[53] It is amazing that Ventzel himself, living as a recluse for the best part of his life, never became a cynic. He wrote only with melancholy that morality in its true sense is a very tender and rare flower that blooms through happy coincidence: "Mankind in a moral sense is going through a period of childhood, or at most adolescence, and it still has a long time to go before it reaches its maturity."

I am re-reading these lines on my way back to San Francisco from Moscow. Could Ventzel be right?

Alexander Kuprin:
From Midden to Mantelpiece

Once upon a time, in a far-away land where anniversaries once were an inalienable (and at times the only) adornment to everyday life, one date was not celebrated in the transitional year 1988, when something could have been said about it. Did it just slip people's minds? That couldn't have been the case. At the time, a special institution existed to set out in advance whatever anniversaries were to be noted, with indicated gradations of political suitability: it was "The Calendar of Significant and Memorable Dates."

The date we're talking about was still memorable—but not significant, not of the moment. It signified what was not wanted recalled, so they pretended not to remember it. The wind had just changed direction again in Soviet literature. Individual writers formerly forbidden in the motherland had begun to cross over from blacklist to white. The classic author referred to in the title, the fiftieth anniversary of whose death was then coming around, presented a special case. The indecision about his suitability demonstrated the limits of what was allowable at that moment, a certain amount of dismay, and, it should be said, a feeling of guilt about him. Alexander Ivanovich Kuprin had been a sanctioned writer in the Soviet Union for some time, but the truth about him remained half-hearted, concealed.

I remember reading about a Russian craftsman's useful invention in an old handbook for householders. How do you stop cocks from crowing in the early morning, so as not to wake the master? For that purpose, you need only stretch a wire above the perch where the cocks are roosting. When a cock starts flapping his wings and stretching his neck to greet the rising sun at the crack of dawn, the wire now gets in his way. Once he hits the wire, he won't crow.

A complicated problem had arisen for Russian literary scholars. What could they write about and what could they not? The moment was important, since photographs come either in color or in black and white. They can't really be all white or all black. But as far as Russian national literary scholarship was concerned (to say nothing of all the rest), in that particular age things had to be all white or all black, or—best of all—bright red. It was a long way from polychrome.

Even the officially-sanctioned classic Russian authors were familiar to the Soviet reader via distorted biographies and totally arbitrary interpretations of their works—not always published or published only partially. For three-quarters of a century, entire areas of the Russian cultural heritage were banned. A lot of what was in the archives disappeared irretrievably.

Let's take a look back. Let's have a quick glance at the story of Soviet Kuprin scholarship, the works of the domestic biographers of Kuprin.

1. "One of us" or not?

Soviet critics never avoided paying attention to his life and works—but is that a good or a bad thing for authors? For whole decades they could keep silence about a lot of other authors—as if they had never lived on this earth—but about Kuprin, never. But the author's views and activities were brought to light in different ways and at different stages.

The first Soviet writer to weigh and appraise Kuprin was a traveling representative for the newspaper *Iskra* (*The Spark*), called one of the "greatest Bolshevik writers" by Lenin.[1] This was Vatslav Vorovsky, who was published under the exotic pseudonyms of "Zhozefina," "Favn," and "Profan." Later on, Vorovsky, an undereducated engineer, came to be called "one of the creators of Marxist artistic criticism in Russia."[2] There is every reason to call Zhozefina-Favn-Profan one of the first Soviet Kuprin scholars, whose scientific method was highly pragmatic and—I would say—tendentious.

Borrowed originally from Lenin, this method of evaluating literary phenomena subsequently became universal, providing down to the present day for an unsophisticated sort of X-ray of any work of art. It was written into the regulations of the creative unions as well, for example, in the regulations of the Writers' Union of the Soviet Union. The gist of it is whatever usefulness the piece might have for Party affairs at any given moment.

Kuprin the prose-writer depicted "bourgeois" reality around him in strict and impartial tones. In his "Single Combat" (*"Poyedinok"*) he stripped it bare, in *The Pit* (*Yama*) he exposed it, in "Moloch" he condemned it, and in "Anathema" he pinned it down. In addition, Kuprin had been published before the Revolution by the *Znaniye* (Knowledge) publishing house, whose director was Maxim Gorky. That gave Vorovsky a basis for approving of Kuprin from the point of view of his acceptability to the Proletarian Revolution. Although Vorovsky took Kuprin to task for the fact that a repulsive "mankind-wide humanism" resounds through his works, and he has no class-based approach to phenomena, nevertheless, according to *Iskra*'s traveling rep, you could see a progressive "struggle for the new social principles"[3] in Kuprin.

The benevolent attitude of the Bolshevik press to Kuprin in those years could be explained also by the fact that, after the Revolution, he had worked together with the *Vsemirnaya literatura* (World-wide Literature) publishing house, while in December, 1918, with Gorky's help, the writer had had an audience with Lenin, where he made a proposal to publish a newspaper for country people, under the title *Zemlya* (*The Land*). The proposal met with approval, but, as they wrote at the time, it didn't get realized "for technical reasons." In fact, the Bolsheviks simply couldn't get their hands on all of the press yet; there weren't enough printing presses or paper. Printers, the highest-qualified segment of the working class, and so necessary to the Party, were anti-Bolshevik.[4]

Anatoly Lunacharsky became the second Party critic crucial to Kuprin's reputation. The People's Commissar for Education demanded working-class themes from the artist, ties that were absent in Kuprin's work. According to his scheme, Kuprin needed to be re-forged, to develop an integral world-view. Lunacharsky's basic judgements were similar to Vorovsky's.

But when Kuprin became editor of the *Prinevsky kray* (*The Neva Reaches*) newspaper, published at the headquarters of Yudenich's White army, and then left for Helsinki, later moving to Paris, the attitude towards his works in Soviet literary criticism changed from "plus" to "minus."

It appeared that there never had been any such progressive element of the kind mentioned earlier in the writer's works, not even his pre-Revolutionary pieces. In all Kuprin's life, according to Soviet biographers of the late 1920s and early 30s, he had had two opportunities to authenticate himself—during the 1905 and the October revolutions—but he never had enough acumen "to join up." As a result, in his works, "the appearance of the social-democratic intelligentsia was distorted."

Kuprin, unaware of the games going on in Moscow, was writing prose and essays without any censorship, getting published, becoming a famous writer—and was as homesick as any normal person in the world for the place where he'd been born and to which, in comparison with Turgenev, for example, he had no access. He bore material difficulties with humor: "When I'm asked how I am, I answer, 'Bad, thank God.'"[5] He wasn't even thinking of going back: he always dealt ironically with the subject. "But what can I do or know?" he wrote to M. K. Kuprina-Iordanskaya. "True enough, if they put me in charge of the Soviet republic's forests, I might be in the right place."[6]

But in the Moscow of those times Kuprin (as if he were subordinate to *agitprop*) was accused of "social blindness," of "epigonism," of "shallowness," and "blind submission" (to quote only a small sample of critics' expressions). The master was reproached for the fact that, before the Revolution, "he never mentioned the growth of the proletariat anywhere," while after the Revolution, he "never responded in any way to the armed struggle of the masses." It came to pass that (in the very same works that had been recently so highly appreciated by Vorovsky and Lunacharsky) literary spies could now track the presence of "reactionary triviality ... the gospel according to Nietzsche."

The important Bolshevik critic and editor Aleksandr Voronsky wrote an article on Kuprin—who was always the most punctilious of renderer of detail— entitled "Outside of Life, Outside of Time." His criticism was not as malicious as with other critics, but I would say that it was as severe as it commonly could be at that time. Voronsky, not a simple figure of those years, was extremely moderate against the background of the others, but the verdict that he pronounced on

Kuprin was unambiguous. An ideological wall was being built between émigré and Soviet literature. Voronsky himself fell victim to the same torment, and even in the 1970s he continued to be accused of "denying the hegemony of the proletariat in the field of art."

In the magazine *Na literaturnom postu* (*On Literary Guard*, a nice semi-military name) from 1926, there is a programmatic article entitled "Kuprin the Politician." Its author was Boris Volin, a noteworthy and undeservedly forgotten figure. The boss of the printing department of the People's Commissariat for Foreign Affairs, Volin soon became the chief censor of the Soviet Union—the head of *Glavlit* (Central Censorship Department), as well as holding down the job of Director of the Institute of Red Professorship, after which he awarded himself the title of professor.

Indeed, the class war with the 60-year-old Kuprin, peacefully living in Paris, was elevated to the rank of the most important external task of the Soviet state. In a drubbing article on Kuprin, the critic Mikhail Morozov pronounced: "Kuprin's notions of virtue and beauty cannot withstand criticism." Elaborating, he said that in Kuprin's works there were no "women social activists," but there were "captivating females"; the writer had "unhealthy scepticism and an ideological fuddledness." Kuprin, "having become the foremost sworn enemy of Soviet Russia, by his malicious attacks on it lowers himself to the most unbridled of black-hundredisms."[7]

The Soviet reader had to take every word of this on trust. Kuprin's name in those years was placed on lists sent from the People's Commissariat of Education to libraries: they suggested burning his books. This centralized elimination of harmful publications, including the compositions of Dostoyevsky and Kuprin, was overseen by Deputy People's Commissar of Education for Library Affairs Nadezhda Krupskaya. Another deputy people's commissar was at one time the aforementioned Volin. Literary scholarship drew its inspiration not from classic compositions but from police lists.

2. From "Anti-" to "Soviet"

Unexpectedly for readers, the torrents of abuse directed at Kuprin disappeared from the pages of the Soviet press. For a certain while, he ceased to exist. Then, in the spring of 1937, Soviet literary criticism again switched signs, but this time from "minus" back to "plus." Kuprin was coming back to Moscow.

Yesterday's "unbridled black-hundredist," we learned from the press, was "warmly greeted by the Soviet public." His books, the same ones written before the Revolution, just recently forbidden and "full of ideological fuddledness," were now re-published at top speed by many publishing houses at once, both in the capitals and in the backwoods. They became, according to the claims of the press at the time, "the favorite reading matter of the Soviet people." Kuprin himself, according to a newspaper, declared to a correspondent that he was bursting with desire to enter the family circle of writers of the Soviet Union. Could this have been published without being earlier agreed upon and approved? He was put back on the censor's list of approved Soviet writers.

And more than that. It turned out that the former "sworn enemy of Soviet Russia," Kuprin, had been exposing "ugly bourgeois reality" the whole time, formerly. Evidently even when he was writing anti-Soviet articles in the Western press. And what was earlier termed "malicious attacks" on the Bolsheviks was now to be considered the "rapturous hymn of fighters for the Russian Revolution." His pre-Revolutionary works disclosed only one shortcoming: he was a follower of "traditional realism" instead of following socialist realism.

Instructions were sent out to write dissertations on his works, and they were successfully defended by the same lynch mobs who had just been attacking him. Kuprin was translated into the dozens of languages of the peoples of the U.S.S.R. Screenplays were written from his stories, and his plays (weak ones, that he didn't like himself) were hurriedly rehearsed in the theaters.

In truth, a *mystère-bouffe*! Hundreds of Soviet writers, devoted to the regime and its ideals, disappear behind prison walls, and a totally active hater of the system gets surrounded with an aureole of honor. And what is especially noteworthy is that the very same professional literary critics from the secret police were in charge of both of these procedures —of course, enlisting the services of dilettantes from the writers' shop when necessary. Kuprin was fated never to see his new publications, movies, and stage performances, though. He died without achieving membership in the Soviet Writers' Union: he hadn't yet passed his probationary period.

Since that time a lot has been written about him, but, even half a century later, the last two short periods of his life remain the most mendacious in Soviet biographies of this outstanding Russian writer. The first one was when, after long years in emigration, he hurried back to his homeland without telling his friends. And the second was when he showed up in Moscow.

3. Back to the Shining Future

Arithmetic plays an insignificant part in the work of the writer, but it's interesting to count the years of Alexander Kuprin's life, anyway. Of the same age as Vladimir Lenin, he was even born in 1870 not far from Simbirsk in the Penza *guberniya*. Two representatives of a single generation, contemporaries. Both of them ambitious, clever, energetic. But they went their separate ways: their notions of good and evil, morality, and conscience were unconjoinable. However, that's another subject.

Forty-nine years Kuprin spent in Russia, and then, in the second year of the Revolution, emigrated. He spent 17 years outside Russia, mostly in Paris. Out of the blue, in the remarkable year of 1937, he returned, and died 15 months later (less three days), one night before his birthday, when he would have been 68.

Alexander Ivanovich Kuprin and his wife, Yelizaveta Moritsevna (also called Yelizaveta Mavrikievna) showed up at the Belorussky station in Moscow on May 31, 1937. Before this, Kuprin had been homesick but hadn't wanted to go back. One Soviet critic (a specialist also in the field of Bunin's home-sickness) called Kuprin's lack of desire to return "an émigré's prejudice." And all of a sudden ...

Kuprin's daughter Kseniya had been going to come with them, but then backed out. She told Andrey Sedykh, the writer and Paris correspondent of *Novoye Russkoye Slovo (The New Russian Word*, New York): "We kept their departure a strict secret, and none of the writers knew about it."[8] The Soviets had been trying to entice a lot of them home, and not always successfully. But here they hit pay dirt. The story of their departure seemed strange to many people already at the time. In the West, readers knew so much more—and there had been a lot of rumors. In his homeland, that aspect of Kuprin studies was as confidential as any other secret-police activity.

In the final months before his departure, the state of Kuprin's health began to deteriorate sharply. A representative from the Soviet embassy took to visiting their Paris apartment. Admirers of his talent—secret agents of the NKVD—offered their friendship. Konstantin Simonov arrived on a special mission with his mistress Valentina Serova—since it was known that Kuprin was of an amorous disposition and Serova was an actress of great beauty. The guests from Moscow told the Kuprins how popular the great writer was in his homeland—his works were literally in great demand. Ivan Bilibin, the theatrical designer and book illustrator, who had returned to Leningrad a year earlier, was working energetically on Kuprin.

The Soviet plenipotentiary in France, Vladimir Potemkin, who was in personal charge of the operation *in situ*, drew Potemkin villages (what a coincidence!) for Kuprin. An unappreciated figure in Stalin's coterie, Potemkin after that was appointed to the post of Deputy People's Commissar for Foreign Affairs. He rose as far as membership in the Central Committee, and was buried "above his station" at the Kremlin wall. It was he who, in various years, was in charge of the People's Commissariat of Education as well, involved in the process of making fools of several generations of students passing through Soviet secondary schools.

Materially, Kuprin hadn't had a soft life in Paris. Ivan Bunin shared his Nobel prize-money with him, but it wasn't enough for long. But now total abundance had arrived in the U.S.S.R., as its representatives in the Soviet embassy and special guests assured them. They were promised a free apartment, a *dacha*, and servants. He had cancer of the esophagus, that had apparently begun to metastasize, and he was told that in Soviet hospitals and sanatoriums complete recovery from all disease was guaranteed. Ultimately the Kuprins were quietly taken to the Soviet consulate in an embassy car and handed ready-made hammer-and-sickled passports with one-way visas and tickets to Moscow. Quietly, because they were afraid of protests by the press and public and friends: not without foundation, they feared an international scandal. But everything turned out all right.

True, having already agreed to go, Kuprin asked the Soviet embassy staff, "And may I take my kitty Yu-yu with me?" He was allowed to take along his cat, but his library—no. Getting on the train at the Paris station, Kuprin was fussing over his cat most of all, as witnesses recalled. "Utterly sick, he couldn't see properly, couldn't properly understand what was being said to him."[9] A rumor spread in Paris that Kuprin had been slipped a Mickey Finn.

So the elderly writer returned to his "new" homeland, while his daughter stayed behind.

At Stalin's personal behest, the secretariat of the Writers' Union, in addition to the NKVD and People's Commissariat for Foreign Affairs, executed the task of bringing home the living classic. As it does happen, the practical concerns were left to a low-level female staffer. She was Serafima Fonskaya, the manager of the *dacha*-studio (eventually the House of Creativity) of the Writers' Union in the village of Golitsyno, which was then an hour and a half's drive from Moscow. Thirty years later a little booklet was published—her brief and well-polished memoirs.[10] I lived and worked for a long time on several occasions in one of the tiny rooms of this house, most frequently in the room where Anton Makarenko had lived at one time. It was from here that he left for the station to go to Moscow, and died in the rail-carriage.

If Serafima Fonskaya knew someone and trusted him, she would readily and frankly tell him considerably more, tidbit by tidbit, than had been published in the booklet. Especially on quiet winter evenings when the electricity had been cut off and you had to sit around a kerosene lamp in the living room. I was far from the only quick-witted person to write something down and hide it away. Some things have already been published. Certain things differ from what is written below, but I don't consider that I have any right to rehash anything now.

Fonskaya's own life hadn't been that simple. A girl from a rich noble family, she had gone to the front as a nurse in the Great War. After the Revolution, she was always fearful that her aristocratic origins would be discovered. In 1939 a ragged and hungry ex-convict, a man who'd been sentenced for no crime at all, came to the House of Creativity and asked for her. "You can't come in here!" she said severely—to her own brother. She ran around the various rooms collecting money from the writers, brought some food from the kitchen and ordered him to go away. She never saw her brother again. But Kuprin she welcomed as cordially as any relative.

It was in that very Golitsyno that Aleksandr Fadeyev and his assistants decided to settle their rare specimen of a writer-returnee, in order to start their task of making an example for emulation out of him. But first, right after the solemn welcoming ceremony with brass band, and before his departure for Golitsyno, the Kuprins were kept for several days in the center of Moscow, at the Hotel Metropole, suitable for them and the NKVD, where the less-than-top-echelon Party elite lived then as well, along with Communist Party leaders who had managed to skip out of their own countries. Rooms at the Metropole were often vacated, for obvious reasons, as their occupants disappeared in Siberian camps.

The Kuprins were taken all around Moscow. "Young writers," dogging his every step, every contact he made, accompanied the returned author on his strolls. He often wept, but mostly kept silent. He was stubborn and wouldn't agree to do what they asked, but would agree if he was promised a glass of wine. At the next holiday the Kuprins were taken to the reviewing tribunal alongside Lenin's tomb and shown the military parade on Red Square. The writer's rapture at what he was seeing was regularly featured in the newspapers, but it isn't known if he was the one who had expressed these raptures, or in what form.

For the arrival of the Kuprins at Golitsyno, as Fonskaya related it to me, she rented a *dacha* with birch trees at its windows at the expense of the Literary Fund. It was supplied with state-owned furniture complete with inventory numbers. Fonskaya had found a cook beforehand in Golitsyno who knew and could be obliged to sing Russian folksongs. The Kuprins were brought in by car.

The weather was wonderful. From morning there had been a rehearsal of the greeting ceremony in the courtyard next to the house-studio. A detachment from a nearby military unit was lined up on the volleyball court to work on three cheers. Curious passers-by were crowding up to the fence. Ordinary Soviet writers had to come in through the back door, but for this occasion they ripped the nails out of the veranda door facing onto the garden and opened it wide. A journalist from *Komsomolskaya pravda*, Aleksandr Chernov, sat on the steps, making up questions for his upcoming interview with the author. The beautiful and talented Young Communist League writer Anna Kalma, sunbathing in the bushes in a swimsuit, was driven away, to clear the horizon of frivolities. Thirty years later, she, the elderly writer, told me about it herself.

As soon as the skinny, hunched old man with screwed up, tear-filled eyes, supported from both sides, climbed trembling out of the car, to the surprise of the representatives of the regime, he suddenly shouted animatedly to the detachment commander, "I salute you, Sergeant, sir!" "He isn't 'sir,' he's 'comrade,'" Kuprin's authoritative escort prompted him. The three cheers was muffed. An armchair was brought out of the house and placed in the courtyard.

Before the event, the Red Army soldiers had been read excerpts from Kuprin at their political classes and ordered to learn by heart the questions that they were supposed to ask the writer. His wife instantly swept aside these questions, pleading the writer's fatigue after his journey. Then the detachment commander, following the script, invited Kuprin to give a speech to the unit, every man-jack of whom loved his works. Here again, Yelizaveta Kuprina answered that the writer was ill and wouldn't be able to do it.

In the sitting room of the house-studio, a table had been laid, with a samovar already smoking away. The guests were seated in the place of honor. "How do you like your new Soviet homeland?" was the first question from the representative of *Komsomolskaya pravda*. "Mmmmm, they serve buns for tea here," answered Kuprin, who had begun drinking his tea, paying no attention to the others.

Understanding that he couldn't get anything out of this strange author, the correspondent turned to the man's wife, and the complacent Yelizaveta Kuprina answered for her husband. Then the Red Army soldiers did Russian folk dances to the accordion in the courtyard to cheer their honored guest. But he started whimpering that he was tired and wanted to go to bed. Serafima Fonskaya hurriedly took the Kuprins to the *dacha* that had been rented for them.

The old couple were lonely there. It was a long jolt behind a sooty locomotive just to get to Moscow. Now and then Kuprin would shuffle along to the mailbox and check for a letter from his daughter in Paris. Her letters never got to him. The old man would get down on his knees among the trees and weep and kiss the birches. After midday Kuprin would do a spell of guard duty at the gate by the road, waiting for when classes would end in the neighboring school. He would ask the passing children for their geometry copybooks, then bring them home and copy out their squares and triangles. Maybe he was trying to remember the rudiments of the mathematics that he had crammed in his cadet-school days.

The writer had been seriously ill for a long time. A profound sclerosis (possibly what would now be called Alzheimer's disease) had showed up in addition to his cancer, and the organizers of his return had been waiting impatiently for the sick man to arrive at a more useful state. It was when his symptoms became even more obvious that officials at the Soviet embassy in Paris decided to take drastic action. Not just Western eyewitnesses to these events, but Soviets as well, like the aforementioned reporter Chernov, testified to this fact.

It is curious that the so-called interviews with Kuprin, those during which his wife Yelizaveta did the talking for him, or others just made up in their offices, were sometimes published as articles ostensibly written by the returnee himself. Kuprin declared: "I am perfectly happy." He thanked the Soviet government and repented of the fact that he had not sufficiently grasped the advantages of the new regime in time.

> ... I personally deprived myself of the opportunity to participate actively in the work of reviving my homeland. I should only say that I was aching to get to Soviet Russia, since living among the émigrés I felt nothing but longing and a distressing isolation.

"I sharply feel and admit my heavy guilt before the Russian people," the writer repents. What guilt? For what? All this had been written for him—for internal and foreign consumption.[11]

Kuprin, who was already being called "a patriot of the socialist fatherland" in the press everywhere, now and then would repeat his gratitude to the Soviet government, choking with praise for everything he could see in the U.S.S.R.: cities, factories, palaces, the Moscow metro, the avenues (like nothing that existed abroad), the high level of everyone's education, including housewives.

Passers-by, according to the article, would shout in concord, "Hurrah for Kuprin!" "They are all happy that I have finally returned to the U.S.S.R." Kuprin was in especial rapture at Soviet boys and girls. "I am amazed at their cheerfulness and serenity of spirit," wrote this Last of the Mohicans of critical realism about the Moscow of 1937. "They are congenital optimists. It even seems to me that, in comparison with boys of the pre-Revolutionary epoch, they have a freer, more confident gait. Evidently, this is a result of regular sports classes."[12]

Its barely literate style, Young Communist optimism, and quotidian political trash in the place of observation all bear witness to the fact that Kuprin could have neither written nor pronounced it. Read it and you think, "Maybe the authors of these interviews consciously made up parody texts for their descendants, having no opportunity to voice the truth?" But everything was being done seriously, unfortunately.

Kuprin wrote that the cat Yu-yu, brought by him from Paris, was having a great time in the Soviet Union, "provoking wild delight among the little kids." "Even the flowers smell different in the motherland," the author said. "Their aroma is stronger, headier than the smell of flowers abroad." If he had been homesick, this would have been understandable. But right after this the newspaper blows an agrarian-political raspberry: "They say that our soil is richer and more fertile."[13] There's nothing of Kuprin's thoughts in these essays; what is reflected are the basic theses of Comrade Stalin's speeches at the time on the topic "life gets better, life gets happier." Kuprin was homesick for Russia, but had come back to the U.S.S.R.

The money invested in the transfer of the writer from the terrible world of capitalism to the bright world of tomorrow began to accrue political interest. A film version was made of Kuprin's *Staff-Captain Rybnikov*, in which a Japanese spy in St. Petersburg during the Russo-Japanese War gets unmasked, and a newspaper published the author's statement that his story "has the ring of present times." As if they could make a movie without having thought of that.

The organizers of the operation code-named "Kuprin" could never consider their work concluded at all. Soon Kuprin was persuaded to send a letter to Ivan Bunin, telling him how nice it was to live in the Soviet land, to talk him, too, into returning from emigration. The appropriate letter was written and was signed by Kuprin. Bunin never wrote back.

This accrual of interest to propaganda assets continued for a long time, even after the death of the writer. A film of *The Garnet Bracelet* (*Granatovy braslet*) was made, exposing everything that was called for. In January 1986 *Literaturnaya gazeta* published Valentin Katayev's memoirs of his conversations with the returned Kuprin. Katayev, it should be noted, always managed to be in the company of classic authors just at the right time. Any Russian might remember his recollections of Ivan Bunin. They were put together at different times, in layers. The earliest layer was "Bunin and I," the middle layer was "Together with Bunin," and the last layer was "I and Bunin." His philosophical talks during walks around Moscow with Kuprin, whipped up a half-century later, are just as precise.

Kuprin's illness quickly grew progressively worse. The writer's behavior was, as psychiatrists put it, inadequate. He was transferred to a rented dacha in Gatchina, near Leningrad; they had promised to return him his old house. Kuprin's library in his old Gatchina house had been looted after the Revolution, and even to the present day, rare books with his signature or with dedicatory inscriptions to him show up on the black market.

The world-famous author, returned from abroad, was now firmly cut off from civilization. Even if he had been capable of it, he wouldn't have been allowed either to object or say one word that could have been heard in the West.

Soon Alexander Kuprin was solemnly laid to rest. The organizations that had been busy with the living Kuprin turned his dossiers over to the archives and occupied themselves with other émigrés. And the myth was handed over to the creative unions for further refashioning. Articles about the happy life that Kuprin achieved before his death, and about his importance to socialist culture, trickled out to the West. The author was in no way responsible for any of these fabrications. The dead have no shame, but our wretched Faust is paying for his dealings with Mephistopheles to this day.

Five years later, in the spring of 1943, Yelizaveta Kuprina hanged herself in Gatchina out of cold, hunger, anguish, and the senselessness of her existence.

4. He's a classic—that's an order!

The half-century after that can be characterized as the apotheosis of Soviet Kuprin studies. Unfortunately, it came with the loss not only of any feeling for historical reality, but also of plain inhibition.

Before Kuprin's return from abroad, the Soviet press behaved with some restraint. After all, what if their operation came unstuck? What if the old man just went and turned stubborn? *Pravda* didn't announce Kuprin's departure from Paris until May 31, when he was being greeted in Moscow. While Kuprin was alive, the authors who wrote about him, as well as the "competent organs," were careful as could be, anyway: what if some foreign journalist who had known Kuprin for many years should disprove the nonsense that was being published? As for Soviet publishers, it was as if a dam had burst: different editions, cheap and made for giving as presents, children's stories, selected single-volume editions, and whole collected works—print runs in the millions.

From the numerous monographs devoted to Kuprin, articles, and commentaries to his works, the Soviet reader knew that Kuprin had been on friendly terms with the founder of socialist realism, Maxim Gorky. But it was never allowed to get around that Kuprin had broken with Gorky and his publishing house, *Znaniye* (Knowledge), because of a divergence in their views—and had composed a malicious parody of him—but that he had kept on working with Artsybashev and had been published in the magazines *Mir Bozhiy* (*God's World*) and *Russkoye bogatstvo* (*Russian Riches*), that were in opposition to Marxism. Soviet research proved that Kuprin's articles of the revolutionary period expressed joy in the changes. But they remained silent about the fact that the subject was the February Revolution. As if they had forgotten that his stories "The Phantom of Gatchina" ("*Gatchinsky prizrak*"), "The Discovery" ("*Otkrytiye*"), and "The Old Age of the World" ("*Starost' mira*") are full of skepticism. It was never mentioned that Kuprin had been arrested by the Bolsheviks and only by happy chance had escaped execution, in contrast with Gumilyov.

The "competent" authors, in their forewords and afterwords, always mentioned without fail the fact that the dead writer, although talented, "was often mistaken, but finally arrived at the only correct decision, that only the supreme genius of socialism could lead to the flowering of humanity in this world so tortured by contradictions." Or still another: "He angrily rose up against the enemies of the October Revolution, but, at the same time, had doubts about its success and its genuinely popular essence."

It turned out that Alexander Kuprin had emigrated due only to a misunderstanding: "This deed of his was not an organic one, it was by accident," in emigration he "almost ceased writing." All of this stuff about Kuprin was made up by a worthy man—Konstantin Paustovsky.[14] It should be confessed that, in comparison with the heroines of Kuprin's *The Pit* (*Yama*), Soviet authors had to sell not only their bodies but their souls as well.

From articles by the master himself, published in the West, and from the memoirs of his contemporaries, it is obvious that he "rose up" not against the enemies of the October Revolution, but against the Revolution itself, maintaining that it had not brought and would not bring anything to the people except disaster.

He perceived socialism to be a gray existence. "For the happiness of the people of the 33rd century," he wrote, "there is nothing to be gained by breaking your head." Putting it more simply, Kuprin was in favor of living people and against the idea of making them happy by force. Lenin's ideal had just begun to be realized, but Kuprin had already seen its essence: "Even if the experiment comes out unsuccessfully, if millions die, and more millions are unhappy, he—a cross between Caligula and general Aleksandr Arakcheyev—will calmly wipe his knife on his apron and say, 'The diagnosis was correct, the operation was brilliantly performed, but the autopsy revealed that the operation was premature. Let's give it another three hundred years ...'"

Communism to Kuprin was "paradise under a loaded gun." It was just that kind of paradise that he escaped from, and it wasn't just by a misunderstanding that he "turned up at his *dacha* in Gatchina, cut off from Petrograd by the Whites." It was precisely because of his recognition of the essence of the regime in the city on the Neva that Kuprin became the editor of the anti-Bolshevik newspaper *Prinevsky kray*. He emigrated not in "a state of confusion" and not "by accident," as it is written in his Soviet biographies, but utterly purposefully, to save himself from the Terror.

As soon as Kuprin withdrew from the Revolution, his work began to die down, as the critics put it. He was scolded for a lack of "vanguard world-view." And, all of his life, he had an aversion to the mob. The Revolution for him was a meaningless mass-movement and nothing else. Right after the October Revolution, he gently declared that the doctrine of the dictatorship of the proletariat had "come to pass at the wrong time." He was mistaken about only one thing: he thought that the new order wouldn't be around for long.

Kuprin's émigré period wasn't a very fruitful one for his creativity, we learn from Soviet researches. "While abroad the writer created nothing significant, and he agonizedly missed his homeland and gradually came to realize his errors."[15]

In reality, from 1923 until 1934, Kuprin published six books, wrote fifty new stories, and three novellas—novels, in fact. And besides that were his numerous articles and essays. True, in none of them does he depict Russia's past as gloomily as he did earlier.

But we understand why. Everything is relative. The journal of his travels around France that he wrote up in Paris, *Blessed South (Yug blagoslovenny)*, shows the style of a mature journalist, the kind that Kuprin had been since his youth, when, at the beginning of the century, he described a flight on one of the first airplanes. It almost cost him his life once, when, for the sake of understanding what risk and fear are in life, he walked into a tiger's cage with a cigarette in his lips—to have a smoke.

It goes without saying that in the Soviet Union they published that part of Kuprin's works that "fit." Works about Kuprin by Western authors—Gleb Struve, Alexander Dynnik, Georgy Adamovich, Stephen Graham, Lidiya Nord, Rostislav Pletnev, numerous memoirs about him, and Western publications that he was published in (although useful quotes were borrowed)—were not available.

During the famous post-Stalin thaw the liberal journal *Novy mir (New World)* spoke out against dogmatism in the evaluation of Kuprin (a sin that that magazine itself must have committed). But during the Stagnation, critics again began to put the author to shame for a realism far removed from a consistently Revolutionary ideology.

However, according to the *Literary Encyclopedia* for 1966, Kuprin had already ripened to this ideology, because he depicted the "brilliant social protest against Moloch-capitalism," and expressed "admiration for the heroism of the leaders of the Revolution," although he feared for the fate of his culture.[16] And in the article "Russian Soviet Literature as the Literature of Socialist Realism," in the third edition of the *Bol'shaya sovetskaya entsiklopediya (Great Soviet Encyclopedia)*, Kuprin was simply ranked among Soviet writers who had already, along with others, taken up the struggle for Communism.

After the Soviet Union's collapse, clever living writers dropped the struggle; the banners had already come down long before. But the dead, unspeaking Kuprin, it turns out, fights on. I wouldn't have been surprised if, following closely after Boris Pasternak and Alexander Galich, he'd been made a member of the Writers' Union of the U.S.S.R. At the end of the 1980s in Moscow only two organizations that accepted people posthumously were still around: the Writers' Union and the crematorium. But soon the lone Writers' Union itself departed this life.

Even Kuprin's personal life got adjusted to the standards of the ideological myths. He was an irritable, irascible man, independent in his opinions and intemperate, both in word and deed. Without any serious excuse, in front of guests he tossed a burning match onto the hem of his first wife's skirt. Fortunately, the woman was saved. He had a child by his second wife before he had even gotten divorced from his first.

A sinner, he was unembarrassed about bringing the heroines of his novel *The Pit* into decent society. Getting drunk, he would brawl, insult people, and become unpredictable. He loved nature—and loved siccing dogs onto cats. "He would have to go sailing," recalls Teffi, "on some sailboat or other, best of all one with pirates."[17]

Already during the war and the Revolution Kuprin had started drinking, out of ennui. Arkady Averchenko wrote about him: "In such a state you shouldn't show yourself to people, but sit still, hiding yourself like a bear in its den."[18] For many years Kuprin suffered from this wretched Russian disease, coming alive only with drink. His wife tried to give him not more than a glass of wine a day. Georgy Adamovich called this state in Kuprin a cross between haplessness and senility. For whole periods at a time, drinking would occupy the author more than politics would (which was taken into consideration by the literary types in civvies), because after all it was precisely by promising him a drink that they could extort the signatures they needed out of him.

Three years before Kuprin's return, he had expressed his attitude to Aleksey Tolstoy's earlier return to Moscow: "To leave in order to get a little medal or a cushy job, like Tolstoy did, is shameful, but if I knew that I was dying, definitely and soon was going to die, then I would return to the motherland in order to rest in my native soil."[19] Rostislav Pletnev wrote:

> Having let himself go to pieces, almost losing his memory and will he left for the U.S.S.R. with his wife and daughter in the spring of the frightful year 1937 ... he was afraid that they would remind him about his newspaper articles in *Obshcheye delo (General Affairs)*, *Posledniye novosti (Latest News)*, *Segodnya (Today)*, *Vozrozhdenye (Rebirth)*, and, especially, in *Russkoye vremya (Russian Times)*.[20]

It goes without saying that it was a slip of the tongue to say that the Kuprins left with their daughter: Kseniya showed up in Moscow only in 1958.

In Moscow Kuprin was very surprised by the advice of a debauchee-drunk whom he had taken home with him and who, after listening to the naïve old man, advised him to shoot off his mouth less. Lidiya Nord wrote the same thing in her memoirs: "Is it really true about being spied upon?" asked the author in perplexity. "But in my own house, who could it be? The servants? The sick-nurse? The doctor?" It shouldn't be out of the question that even the drunkard who recommended that the writer keep his mouth shut was not just a chance-met debauchee. After returning, the writer didn't inscribe a single line of prose nor a single note in his diary. But texts that were written for him are being cited to this day.

Nobody gave the writer any medical treatment, until he felt terrifically ill and his wife demanded a doctor. More than a year after his arrival (July 10, 1938) he was operated on, which made no sense, and possibly even shortened his life. Kuprin died on August 25.

In the Soviet press there was not even a hint that Kuprin had called for a priest before his death, in a Leningrad hospital. The consciousness of the sick man cleared up, and the writer spoke to a holy father alone for a long time. What were they talking about? Who was the priest? Surely his last will and testament was taken down and left on the table for whomever it was necessary. I would really like to find out on what shelf of what secret archive it now lies.

Later, in the writer's biographies, another explanation for his death was proposed. "The many years of Kuprin's life in emigration had a bad influence on his health, overtaxed his strength, and turned him into an old man before his time."[21] And even ". . . his separation from Russia stretched for 17 years, and finally undermined his once-vibrant health."[22]

Soviet critics declared that Kuprin, along with Konstantin Tsiolkovsky, was a founder of Soviet science fiction and Communist utopian fantasy, continued later by Aleksey Tolstoy. Maybe anti-utopian fantasy? And continued not by the courtier-author of *Bread* (*Khleb*), but by entirely different people?

In Kuprin's story "The Toast" ("*Tost*"), the action takes place a thousand years in the future. The proletarian wars of the planet Earth cause the inhabitants of other planets to look on with horror. The heroes of the story propose a toast to the martyrs of the past, to the victims of the bloody Terror:

Can't you see that bridge of human corpses that connects our radiant present with the horrible, dark past? Can't you feel that bloody river that carried all mankind to the spacious, radiant sea of universal happiness?

The clairvoyant Kuprin wrote this story during street fighting in 1905, and published it in the satirical magazine *Signaly* (*Signals*) a year later. He called the Revolution "black lightning," and Peter the Great and Ivan the Terrible—Bolsheviks. Communism for Kuprin was paradise under a loaded gun. If he did pave the way for anyone in utopian fantasy, it was for Yevgeny Zamyatin, Mikhail Bulgakov, and Orwell.

Before the Revolution Kuprin was printed far and wide by the biggest publishers in many countries. The poignancy of his slant on the facts, the visibility of his images, his coarse-juicy language, all set apart the master from the very beginning. His respect for human dignity, his defense of what we now call human rights, the unobtrusiveness of his judgements, his refined and melancholy and—I would even say—serious humor, became Kuprin's literary principles. *The Garnet Bracelet*, *Gambrinus*, *Listrigony*, and the novel *The Pit* (*Yama*), which is usually called a novella, are read and re-read to this day.

A creator of tightly-put-together short stories, Kuprin, in contrast to the majority of his colleagues, never joined the ranks of novelists for good, but created short stories almost all his life. He took something of the manner of description of details of Leo Tolstoy, something from Chekhov's brevity and precision. The last classic author of the past epoch, he developed and passed on the mastery and principles of the embodiment of literary truth, the way an author sees and mirrors it, to a whole generation of Russian authors all over the world. Caustic with his facts, the talented author fashioned his journalistic pieces tastefully, too. Kuprin could scarcely have read everything written about him in his homeland. But his punditry in the émigré press was never read by those who wrote about him in Moscow, either.

For decades, moralizing about classic authors of world literature was the essence, the definition of literary scholarship and education in the humanities in the Soviet Union. The codex of socialist realism turned grand literature into grand waste paper. Kuprin's friend, the writer Nikolay Nikandrov, who died in 1964, asked before his death to have written on his gravestone "Murdered by the Writers' Union."[23]

The scholars of Russia have in store for them the Herculean task of stripping off the thick layers of bias and cheerless monochrome from the Augean stables of their literature. A vulgar sociologism, steamrolling a writer's living oeuvre, lives on in the appraisal of writers and literary events.

I could be gainsaid: literary scholarship is a dependent science. What could you expect from it if there is no freedom in the literature itself? The library stacks have been sterilized, and God knows if we will succeed in revitalizing it. The archives of the country remind one of eunuchs who have been decreed a license to reproduce themselves. I think that the laws of socialist art were not conceived by Marx at all, but by the English physicist Dalton. Their essence is the pathological inability to differentiate between colors.

Emaciated history emerged from its torture-chamber on crutches, reeling—another rickety source for the scholar. Kuprin seems to have predicted this: "But, after all, Russian literature—however much circumstances known to everyone might deform, torture, or castrate it—has always been selfless."

The *maître* wrote these words when the Revolution was yet to come.[24] Today they sound like a testament from the Last of the Mohicans. The study of Kuprin, so easily exchanging one set of preconceived positions for others just as biased, is doomed to change again—but this time, in search of the truth.

Visiting Stalin's, Uninvited

A certain Moscow writer (I'll leave out his name to avoid offense), thoroughly successful, but at the time young and purposeful, finished a poem at the beginning of 1953. Its hero was a boy, very touchingly rendered, who goes with a package to Red Square, straight up to the Spasskaya tower. So as to forestall any more-contemporary thoughts of his possible unsavory designs, I'll make it clear right here: the boy wanted to give a present to Joseph Stalin, and in this fashion express the love of millions of children. Although "millions" is a political error. I should have said "all" children.

They don't let the boy in. That is to say, yes, please, in general, Stalin loves children like no one else. But right now let's exclude that. Grown men turn their faces to the vague heaven beyond the Kremlin walls: there, see, where the window is shining? There he stands at the helm, day and night. He's writing away. When he's not writing, he's thinking. "There, in the Kremlin, he's thinking about every single one of us." He's thinking about the fate of mankind. Even about you, little boy. Leave your present here. It'll be passed on to him when Comrade Stalin comes to the mausoleum to commune for a while with Grandpa Lenin. Did you write your name on it? There's a good boy, run along home quick as you can, now.

Here the little boy sprouts angels' wings and happily flies away. Or maybe not. Having carried out his Pioneer's duty, maybe he just makes off on his own two feet. And the Wise One in the Kremlin, breaking off from his strenuous labors for just a second, walks up to the window and, squinting in the sunlight, sees the boy off with his warm gaze. Stereotypes continue to be hypnotic: in Russian, the word "boy" almost demands to be written as *malchik*, without its soft sign after the L, just the way he pronounced it in his Georgian accent. But we won't. After all, in his linguistic treatises he never proscribed the use of the soft sign. But he could have. And nobody would have said a critical word about it.

The poem's theme wasn't exactly a hundred percent original. Take the following, for example: "Stalin often smokes a pipe, but perhaps he has no pouch. I'll sew up a wonderful tobacco pouch for him as a souvenir." A girl in my class during the war recited this poem with the word *korset* ("corset") in place of the word *kiset* ("tobacco pouch"). Another pupil said the word as *kastet* ("brass knuckles"). Where these children are now, I don't know. As far as the semantics of their recitation pieces goes, theory tells us that porridge is none the worse for a little butter. In a general sense, this very subject was given its definitive form a long time ago in the underworld-style song "Mama, I love Stalin."

Everyone was supposed to love him. Many did love him—where would you draw the line now? To this day, certain people honor him. But we're not talking of love anymore, as the perspicacious reader will have realized. Neither are we talking about poetry (toward the end of the 1970s, Colgate University Professor Richard Sylvester acquainted me with his plan for a paper on Stalin as the hero of Soviet poetry, although he's never published it, as far as I know). The frequency with which eulogies to Stalin appeared in the press of the 1930s and 1940s has been ascertained. A list has been compiled of all the epithets that were ever bestowed on him, the likes of "The Great Helmsman" or "Soviet Women's Best Friend." This much we know. So what are we in fact talking about here? Well, let's raise some entirely prosaic questions in response to that one. For starters, why did the poem's protagonists meet at the Kremlin? Where, in fact, did Stalin really live? Where was the country governed from?

Like every single Soviet citizen, he was registered to live someplace. Not in heaven. The place where he was registered was certainly the Kremlin. The gaze of progressive (and unprogressive) humanity was directed upon his registered residence, while he, like many another Soviet, lived unregistered somewhere else. Throughout his life this was the strategic secret guarded by a highly select number of persons (not counting the special services).

The majority of the people he saw on business (or whatever) were taken to the Kremlin, where he continued to appear at times, after he had moved. VIPs, especially foreign Communists arriving from abroad, were delivered in automobiles with curtained windows to where he lived. The escorts would say, "We're taking you to the Kremlin." Such a serious game. Sufficiently serious that even many years later this official myth served as the source of information even for authoritative writers. The scrupulously exact Robert Conquest, in his book *The Great Terror* (published in 1969), established that Stalin lived in a modest flat in the Kremlin.

It has to be definitively revealed that the general secretary left the Kremlin for a Moscow suburb in 1934. His apartment in the Kremlin remained as it was. In constant expectation of an attempt on his life (like Arafat today), he would never even tell his personal secretary Aleksandr Poskrebyshev and his bodyguard-chief general Nikolay Vlasik that he was going home until the very last moment. But he would nearly always go home to his secret residence. At one time this house had been intended for less-official meetings, while important foreigners were to pay their visits to the Kremlin. Then a period ensued where he refrained from traveling, and then, just like a lot of old folks, even stopped going out of his abode altogether. He even stopped communing with Lenin in his mausoleum.

In official secret papers the place was called "Out-Of-Town Site No.1." In the jargon shared by his guards, his courtiers, and the man himself, the Kuntsevo *dacha* was called "Nearest," in contrast to other dachas of his, further out. This jargon was for use in telephone conversations that might be overheard by enemies of the people. More precisely, it was located in the old village of Volynskoye, but the entire district was included in Kuntsevo. According to certain sources, a tunnel for special cars was constructed from the Kremlin to the dacha, and according to others, an entire secret subway line. It is said that Stalin traveled by the tunnel only once, and then always went by the Arbat and the Minskoye highway as far as the turn onto his personal road.

I found out about the Kuntsevo hideaway by being at this very house, that is, by paying a visit to Stalin. True, the master of the house had died half a year before. I found myself there at the end of 1953. And despite the frivolity of youth, the shock was strong enough to fix the details fast in my memory.

Later on this house was referred to in Svetlana Alliluyeva's book.[1] We'll have to compare what the author of *Twenty Letters to a Friend* of course knows better with what I, however, saw with my own two eyes. Svetlana Josephovna says that she was at the Kuntsevo house for the last time on the day of Stalin's death. Differing versions and those details that Alliluyeva forgot to mention leap out as important, and curious.

I was a third-year student in the Department of Russian history and literature of the State Pedagogical institute in Moscow on Pirogovka Street. Right now in America and on other continents there are not a few graduates of that institute—maybe we should organize a reunion. The member of our immediate group who had the responsibility for our Education-for-the-Masses events was a slender blonde girl, Nina.

More efficient than the rest of us, she got married, naturally enough, to another classmate of ours. She turned out to be hard and spoiled, with a quarrelsome character. She would argue with her husband during lectures, making the whole body of students in the auditorium—and sometimes even the professor—a party to their family quarrel. It was as if our lecture on foreign literature of the Renaissance were being given in a communal kitchen.

Always hungry, many of us would drool and gulp on breaks when she would pull a sandwich with red or white fish out of her little green lunchbox, or some kind of fruit in winter. Eight years had passed since the end of the war, but many of us in the group hadn't once eaten our fill since the beginning of it. But Nina's community activities earned our respect. She looked after our collective with excursions to the movies and museums, took care our little credit union, out of which a ruble might be made when some outstanding debt was paid. At the end of one November, Nina came up to me between lectures and asked in a whisper:

"How would you like to get on the list of people who want to visit Stalin's house?"

My eyes popped.

"More than likely it won't happen," she added hurriedly, "but there is a chance. No questions! Keep as quiet as a fish, and carry your passport with you at all times."

It remained to figure out what the deal was: rumor had it that Nina's father was the head of the household administration of the Kremlin.

The times were strange. Stalin had been bewailed eight months before. Our leaders had closed ranks in fear of disappearing one by one, and had shot the far-too-ambitious Lavrenty Beria, just in case. Secret shakeups were going on upstairs. Nikita Khrushchev broke away into the lead, but the gap between him and the rest remained easily surmountable. The head of the cultural affairs department of the Central Committee, who was also the Esteemed-Memory-of-Stalin-Secretary of the Soviet Writers' Union (as if there could be a non-Soviet writers' union), Dmitry Polikarpov, suddenly turned up, in disgrace, as director of our institute in Pirogovka.

We brightened up considerably and just barely dared to have a real student party, I and my schoolmates and later recognized poets Yuri Vizbor, Yuli Kim, and Yuri Ryashentsev (someone christened us "The Third Cousins" in a Russian pun: *chetveroYUrodnye bratya*, "the four YU-born brothers"). The percentage of "Paragraph Five" students (or Jews—after the infamous fifth question on the identity form that required a specified nationality, which Jews were in the Soviet Union) at the institute increased. Writers took to appearing at the literary faculty. I remember Konastantin Fedin, Aleksandr Tvardovsky, Ilya Ehrenburg, Mikhail Svetlov (I invited him myself), and the young Stalin Prize-winner Yuri Trifonov. The glorification of the great man by the great came to an end, although in our lectures, as previously, both of his pamphlets—on socialist linguistics and on communist economics—were abundantly quoted.

I am afraid of introducing a modern-day cynicism into my feelings about those times and distorting the picture. Not one hint of Stalin's abuses had ever been spoken. A lot was perceived as it had been before, although official writer Konstantin Simonov later recalled that they had telephoned him from the Central Committee to ask: "Who gave you permission to write that Stalin will live forever?" God had become a demigod. But a visit to the house where the demigod had lived still seemed unreal.

Nonetheless, after a couple of days our culture-agent, Nina, informed us—again on the quiet—that the tour had been scheduled and they were going to take us to the "only-just-opened closed museum." The terminology didn't occasion any perplexity, nor did its sense. Naturally a museum would be opened after

Stalin's death. After all, there were museums for other great people. It wouldn't be necessary to advertise it: a crowd would have mobbed it straightaway, like at a funeral. And just as natural was her command: "Passports! It's important for everyone to have their passports with them!" Enemies were all around.

Fluffy snowflakes were falling. Scattering the wet slush, a small bus drove up to the square beside the institute. Its top half was white, the bottom light-blue, and the whole splashed with mud. The driver checked our group pass and counted the seated passengers with a finger. There were twelve of us. The windows were covered by white curtains, but a little could be seen through the cracks. We passed by Kievsky railway station and appeared to be on the Minskoye highway. We turned left off of it, once past Poklonnaya hill, and were immediately in a thick forest. Not a house nor a human could be seen, if you didn't count the militiamen strolling along the sides of the road, accompanying us with their attentive gaze. The snow stopped falling. The short day, a gloomy one to boot, was approaching its early end.

We hadn't been driving for long. Nobody joked, nobody laughed. We were as solemnly hushed as if we were at a funeral. Unexpectedly the bus turned sharply, and suddenly it was broad daylight again. Everything was lit up by searchlights. The snow around glistened; we could see it like New Years' decoration on the sagging branches of the fir trees. The driver braked. When our eyes had adjusted to the light, it became evident that we were surrounded by officers in State Security uniform. They didn't have to ascertain who we were; they, of course, already knew. They simply began to count heads. Then the gate opened. The bus drove on in and once again came to a standstill.

Behind us was a fence of about five meters in height, dark green. Inside, at a certain distance from it, was yet another barrier, this one of barbed wire. Alongside the fence ran a narrow asphalt road, illuminated by lamps under black shades. Now you would say right off: a prison-camp zone.

Once again there were people in uniform around the bus. Two of them stepped into the aisle and gathered up our passports, peering into everyone's face and checking their names against a list. They checked under the seats, which plunged the women of the group into confusion, squeezing their knees together. The checkers went back to their guardroom, and two young men in civilian clothes with indifferent expressions came aboard and sat down at the back. We didn't move; we sat silent, waited. After a certain time, a woman of middle years, I would say sternly beautiful, clambered up the bus steps. She greeted us and spoke words of warning:

> You may not fall even a step behind the rest, you may not photograph anything, you may not write anything down, you may not talk among yourselves. Upon exiting the bus you may not bring with you any bags, bundles, or books. You may not smoke. Men must leave their hats behind on their seats.

She paused, then nodded to the driver to get going. The crowd of security types parted. Standing in the stairwell, half-turned toward us, the woman's intonation changed to that of a tour-guide.

> You now find yourselves situated on the same territory as the house in which the great leader of all of progressive mankind, Joseph Vissarionovich Stalin, lived, worked, and died. When Comrade Stalin chose this plot of land in Kuntsevo, it was a vacant spot, a barren place. The forest through which we are driving was planted by order of Comrade Stalin.

This declaration seemed improbable: the bus had been traveling for more than ten minutes (or maybe it just seemed that long) down the clean, narrow asphalt road—on which it would be impossible to pass another vehicle—through a huge, real forest. Age-old pines and firs grew now thick and now thin, but right up to the bus, brushing branches against us on both sides, showering down snow.

Later I found out that they had purged the entire district of its people, evicting particular categories of populace from the near-lying villages. A quiet, elderly woman traveled alongside an acquaintance of mine once on an airplane in America. It turned out that in the beginning of the 1930s she had been living with her neighbors in the Volynskoye village of Davydkovo. The authorities had come to her place at night, given the family a half-hour to collect their things, helped them load up, and then removed them to Kalinin province.

"Maybe they were afraid of someone shooting from our village," was that lady's comment on their banishment.

Meanwhile, the bus slowly moved ahead when our tour-guide continued.

Here ravines were dug, hills piled up, all by personal order of Comrade Stalin, who loved nature very much. You see those paths through the trees? Whenever snow fell, they would stamp them down by foot, so that he could stroll in the woods.

Now and again lights could be seen among the trees, illuminating pathways and watering-faucets sticking out of the snow. There had just been a snowfall, and in the woods there really were already-tamped-down paths. For whom? After all, the lover of strolls in the woods had already died last spring. Maybe they just forgot to change the order to the stompers?

Imperceptibly, a two-story building emerged from the gloom, painted green, with a glassed-in terrace and a courtyard cleared of snow before a typical formal entrance, alongside which the bus came to a halt. We were invited to get out of the bus and stand in one place, without moving. They counted us up again. The bus drove off, and a deathly hush straightaway filled our ears. The house, as it came clear from the explanation of our guide, had been designed by the architect Miron Merzhanov at the personal order of Stalin, and had been built in 1933-34. Some commentary is necessary here.

Merzhanov built other dachas as well in the Caucasus and the Crimea for the general secretary. As his retreat near Moscow, Stalin had earlier picked out a sumptuous spot for himself in deep woods near the Usovo railway station, and spent his summers there from 1919 until 1932. The estate, complete with gothic-style palace, was called Zubalovo after its former owner, an oil baron by the name of Zubalov. Going by his daughter's testimony, Stalin was nudged into thinking of moving out of the Kremlin by his wife's suicide on November 8, 1932 (he himself adored living in seclusion). But it is thought that another more practical consideration was his desire to detach himself from the remaining party leaders. They all lived together in the Kremlin citadel. He felt like having his own special citadel, so he built one. As to Merzhanov, he was sent to a forced labor camp and returned back in 17 years half-alive.

The forest around shone with lights. The paths outside the house were carefully cleared, the unwanted snow taken away. To the right of the entrance was a cosy little door. Comrade Stalin wasn't fond of his formal entryway, the guide explained. His car would pull right up to this door, and he would disappear inside it. What was it, anyway, I think to myself now: modesty, a revolutionary habit of secrecy, or a feeling of constant danger? Or maybe just a character trait?

We looked up at the second story. At first, there hadn't been any second story to the house. There had been a solarium on the roof. But the owner of the house loved the cool of the forest more. The second story was constructed in 1948, recalls his daughter in her book *Twenty Letters to a Friend*. The superstructure stood there to no purpose, if you don't count a single reception for a Chinese delegation. Our guide explained it to us otherwise:

"The superstructure (you see, it was smaller than the first story—a house on top of a house) was ordered to be built during the war."

In it, she said, lived the representatives of the general staff, which I will add now is highly unlikely. Perhaps they did stay overnight when the Germans were on the threshold of Moscow, but it would have been in the bunker, of course. There, in that small building, day and night they mulled over the fate of the country, and later, when they managed to overcome Hitler, the fate of the whole of Europe. Who could say now which of the ideas on the subject were his own and which ones were born in the heads of the attendant generals?

Twilight was coming on. We were taken around the outside of the house. Outside, along the glassed-in terrace, protected from the frost by bast matting, bushes were formed up in a rank, powdered over with snow. A little further on were cherry trees, pretty, no doubt, when in blossom. From her commentary it became clear that there were roses under the matting. Gardeners looked after them on the instructions of the master of the house. He didn't like to work in the garden himself. But sometimes he would pick up a knife and trim off dead twigs.

From the opposite side of the house a view opened out over a birch grove—this, too, artificially planted. There were gazebos there. In them were chaises-longues and armchairs. The master would walk from one gazebo to another. Tea would be brought there to him. The guide said:

> Before construction of the house began, they started bringing twenty- to thirty-year-old trees here from Moscow and Smolensk provinces. Right at that moment a great plan for transforming nature in our homeland occurred to Comrade Stalin.

The house was separated from the birch grove by a narrow gully that looked like a broad ditch with a brook running along the bottom. A bridge with a thick railing had been thrown across the gully. Many years later, I realized that a medieval idea had occurred to the mind of a twentieth-century man. The hill where the dacha was built had been surrounded by a gigantic moat with two bridges flown across it. The moat was filled with water coming from the river Setun, painstakingly guarded all the way from its source to Kuntsevo.

Across the bridge, passing the birch grove, we came upon some conservatories. Their glass walls and roofs were shining brightly. Inside, bunches of grapes hung from vines. The grapes had been planted under his personal supervision, the wines made according to the master's recommendations. Even in this area he was a specialist.

> The best agronomists, gardeners of the highest qualification, the guide explained simply, work here to bring to life the agricultural ideas of Ivan Michurin and Trofim Lysenko, approved by Comrade Stalin.

Without doubt they were not only of the highest qualification, but of a definite rank as well. Who else could have been there constantly, inside two circles of guards, Georgian and Russian, without a common language? Who else could have been trusted to grow vegetables and fruits for him? But the guide anyway explained that Stalin liked to eat fresh vegetables from his garden and had given instructions on how to grow them properly.

From time to time our group came to a halt. The snow would stop crunching underfoot, the guide would fall silent, and a hush would ensue. It pressed against our ears. But maybe it just seemed that way, from nervous tension. After all, it was 1953. The other world, that is, the one beyond the fence, was absent here. Living nature, artificially created, was beautiful, but it was a simulacrum. Life had stopped here in March. Time had died together with the master of the estate. There were neither birds nor squirrels in the trees. An uninhabited island. Neither entry nor exit without an escort standing behind your back. There was a sensation of being an alien from another planet, although ordinary Moscow was somewhere not very far away.

Suddenly, returning to the house along the forest path, we discovered that we were not alone. Another group, which had just come out of the "museum," was heading towards us. Ahead of them was another guide, the complete double of our own. Behind them were two twin brothers. Between them, a group of writers. I recognized Aleksey Surkov, Mikhail Bubyonnov, Vasily Azhayev, the sister of Vladimir Mayakovsky Ludmila, and next to her the author of the unforgettable poem about the boy hurrying with his present to the Kremlin.

As soon as we got up to the house, a man in a security-service uniform opened the main door. The guide entered first; the last ones, behind us, were the two in civilian clothes. It was warm inside.

"Take off your overcoats and hang them on the hooks. Tie those slippers on over your shoes ..."

Ordinary museum-style slippers with laces. If this were today, someone would surely ask if Stalin himself wore such slippers. But at that time the silence was broken only by the rustle of clothing. The sensation of being in a mausoleum.

Without a coat and in slippers, I glanced around. To the left, straight ahead, and to the right were doors to rooms. In between the doors there was an elevator. Next to it was a bathroom and a toilet. On the elevator panel were four buttons. That meant that there was one more floor above and two floors down. There was a bunker, there or somewhere else, also underground, a government communications nexus. There was no mention of the bunker where Stalin spent the dangerous months of the war in Svetlana Alliluyeva's book either.

"Upstairs," pronounced the guide, "is a film theater."

She made no mention of any downstairs. It goes without saying that no one even asked. Nowadays we know that he loved westerns and Chaplin movies, and that he would watch them at night. But most of all he loved filmstrips about himself, which could now be filed under the general heading of "Stalin Shows Himself to the People." The myths about him were composed under his unremitting personal supervision.

We were taken into a room some twenty meters in length, almost without any furniture, if a large oval table in the middle and a sofa weren't taken into account.

> On the table you can see the newspapers for the first of March, said our usherette. Mail was brought here in the morning and he looked at it himself. You can see the workers' letters about their wholehearted love for their leader and teacher. These newspapers and letters Comrade Stalin never managed to read ...

It goes without saying that the letters were of love. Of devotion. Of readiness to give their lives for him. Letters with prayers and grieving floated down a different river. Only a pure stream flowed into this abode.

We came back out into the corridor. An ordinary habitation, if one with a huge area. We passed on to the so-called dining room. In the Moscow of that time there were better and more beautiful ones in the houses of academicians, people's artists, Stalin prize-winners. The prize-giver himself lived modestly. Here was a sideboard of light-colored wood, inexpensive. Ordinary dishes inside it. In the middle of the room, there was a table under an orange cloth lampshade with tassels. A sofa with round bolsters and a high back. The ossified style of the Thirties. There was a bowl with apples on the table. On the sideboard there was an open bottle of Borzhomi mineral water and a glass. A not-very-large refrigerator of a familiar shape, one of the first Soviet ones. A not-very-tall bookcase.

Behind its glass doors were books: of course Marx and Engels, Lenin. Books lay open as examples. In them were the quotations learned by everyone in school, childishly underlined in colored pencil. Did he underline them himself? Or perhaps they were underlined "for the museum?"

"Here he had his dinner," the guide explained.

But, in reality, as it turned out later, mostly not here. Incidentally, the kitchen wasn't inside the house. After coming out of the birch grove, the tour-guide had drawn our attention to a long, covered passageway connecting the house to an annex. It held a kitchen and a dining room for his retainers: drivers, guards, waitresses, gardeners, cooks, generals of the guard, stewards of the estate. The master didn't like kitchen smells, it had been explained to us at that point. Did they remind him of his childhood with his cook-mother, which he didn't like to recall? Or did they build it that way to keep the servants at a distance, for his *privacy* (the English word has to be used, as it doesn't exist in Russian)?

"It was a rule at the house that the server who brought the food first tasted every dish ..."

The tour guide suddenly blurted this out, leaving off with no explanation, and quickly led us out of the living room to the left, to a room that seemed inappropriate in a small dwelling. The modesty of the master of the house seemed to have somewhat hypertrophied. It was a hall thirty meters long. The opposite end was curved, like in the mansions of the nobility of two centuries before. There were lots of identical windows, tightly covered by heavy white drapes that gathered on rollers up above, just like the ones in all the important institutions in the center of Moscow.

The lower part of the walls, up to about a meter and a half from the floor, was brown, trimmed with Karelian birch, looking rather stuffy. Under the windowsills there were electrical heating radiators covered by grills of the same birch. Portraits were hanging in the spaces between the windows. These were Politburo members: Georgy Malenkov, Nikolay Bulganin, Lazar Kaganovich, Anastas Mikoyan, Kliment Voroshilov, Viacheslav Molotov, Nikita Khrushchev.

Later, in his memoirs, Khrushchev would say that that hall was called "the big dining room." In the middle of the hall, down its entire length, was a table. Its surface was covered with dark-green billiard baize. Hard armchairs of light-colored wood were placed tidily around it. Along the walls were armchairs and sofas. There was a colossal carpet covering the whole floor—it seemed like the only really expensive thing there.

"We are now located in the place where the Politburo held its sessions," the guide solemnly intoned. "Comrade Stalin liked every one of those present to sit just beneath their own portrait."

Nothing disturbed us twenty-year-olds at the time. Now I read my old notes and my eyes come to a halt. What was going on with these meetings of our leaders at someone's house? What were they, members of an underground organization? Or was the general secretary was too lazy to drive to work? And what about the "sitting under the portrait" ritual?

In contrast with degenerate succeeding Politburos, at that time we knew them not only by their names but by their faces. Lavrenty Beria had been close to Stalin while he was alive. There was no portrait of Beria. Meaning that they had gotten rid of it—that was the only thing I could imagine at that point in time.

The tour guide let her hand fall onto the back of a wooden armchair that had been pulled away from the table. This seat was to one side of the table, next to a corner, not at the head of it. On the green baize in front of it lay neatly sharpened and as-yet-unused ordinary and colored pencils alongside a pad of clean, unlined sheets of paper. Beside an ashtray rested a pipe. It was well known that he had stopped smoking several months before his death. But there the pipe lay.

"Comrade Stalin loved to sit alone at this table and work."

Just to the left was a book—it wasn't hard to recognize a volume from the collected works of Lenin. On an open page a number of lines had been underscored in red pencil and something written lightly across the margin. The guide read out the inscription. Some significant banality or other. Later one of Stalin's interpreters would note that "He wrote with a cheap schoolboy's pen of those years, dipping it into a spillproof inkwell."[2]

Behind the chair at the wall there was a cabinet where he kept his papers, envelopes with his salary (which he never spent), and medicines that he took at his own discretion. For instance, he would drink iodine drops in water. Doctors could never treat him, not only because he put them all in prison, but also because instruction, as in all other spheres, had to come from him to medicine, not from doctors to him.

There was a Chinese embroidery on the wall, a big, bright tiger, as well as cheap reproductions: portraits of Maxim Gorky and Mikhail Sholokhov, and Ilya Repin's "The Zaporozhye Cossacks Write a Letter to the Sultan." Next to them were several large photographs of children. The guide commented:

"Comrade Stalin liked these pictures of Soviet children in the magazine *Ogonyok*, and asked for them to be enlarged."

I read in Ms. Alliluyeva's book that he had never even wanted to see five out of his own eight grandchildren, and it's difficult for me to explain how both these facts can be apprehended at the same time. Either he liked children only in pictures, or, even simpler, there had been no photographs of children here while he was alive.

To one side of the pulled-out chair there was a small table at the wall. Two telephones sat on it, a white one and a black one. One was an ordinary phone, the other was a hot line. Two chairs. One of them was lower than the other, with short legs.

> Comrade Stalin was not a tall man, the guide said, divulging state secrets. When he spoke on the phone, it was uncomfortable for him to sit in this sort of chair, so he ordered a carpenter to saw off its legs. His secretary sat on the big one.

That's how, by chance, yesterday's truth came to light. An ordinary chair, whose legs had been sawn off by an ordinary Soviet serf-peasant at the squire's order. This stumpy freak-chair, this dwarf-chair, this midget-chair, normal to begin with and mutilated later, was the Throne of Power, the seat of rulership by two telephones, one white and one black. The black telephone rang with secondary problems, the white one with important ones, and that was that. Or didn't ring at all, when the master dozed off.

According to the recollections of Yuri Trifonov, Aleksandr Tvardovsky was lying in the Kremlin hospital alongside Aleksandr Poskrebyshev, Stalin's secretary. On one occasion, Poskrebyshev burst into tears and said of his master: "He used to beat me up! He would grab my hair like this and hit my head against the table ... "[3] The tsar must have whacked his lackey's head off this very table.

I just mentioned the Throne of Power. The Russian capital under Peter the Great moved from Moscow to St. Petersburg, and under Lenin back to Moscow. The truth of Stalin's times was that Moscow became just a mythical capital. And the real-but-secret capital of the U.S.S.R. from 1934 to 1953 was the town of Kuntsevo, in the Moscow countryside. Western Kremlinologists should have called themselves *Kuntsevologists*, or even more precisely, *Volynologists*. If only they had known about this fact.

"In this room he spent all of his last years, almost twenty years," Alliluyeva notes in her letters. In the Thirties, when the master was younger, his comrades-in-arms had whooped it up at Nearest. A lot of his Georgian relatives came to visit (before they were wiped out). *Shashlik* was served, the men played billiards, and everybody danced to the record player that Stalin wound up himself, playing records of his choice and making everyone dance. The Caucasians would sing their doleful songs, and "the master would lead the singing in his high tenor."[4]

From other sources we know about his famous "suppers" from eleven in the evening until four o'clock in the morning, where he would force drink on everyone to loosen their tongues.[5] Not a word was said at that time by the tour guide about those jolly nighttime dinner parties around that gigantic table that the thoroughly Oriental leader had such respect for when he was younger, nothing about his favorite wine *khvanchkara*.

A Central Committee type who managed to come to Stalin's attention in his last two years wrote that age and illness came upon Stalin all of a sudden at the brink of his seventieth year.

> The process of aging became more and more noticeable: his eyes somehow lightened to the color of wet clay, his gaze became less piercing, his gait less firm. In great secrecy his friends told others that, at times, he would get schnockered, as they say, on his favorite Georgian wine.[6]

Stalin's daughter recalled that next to the big hall was a small one, the "little dining room." It wasn't shown to us, but I remember the door. I don't know where the billiard table that he liked to play on stood—that's a state secret, too. "Comrade Stalin liked folk songs," the guide said, "Russian, Georgian, and the songs of other nations. You can see the record player and his huge collection of records." So for us tourists he liked folk songs, but for himself he liked gypsy songs and Aleksandr Vertinsky, an émigré, that "degenerate bourgeois art."

Here, according to recollections that I read later, he would play his gramophone after a drinking bout and make the Politburo members dance in pairs. From the table where they held their sessions we were taken straightaway to the door next to his workplace. His bedroom. It was a small, square room with a couple of windows letting in dim light through curtains. To the left, there was an old-fashioned, high, and rather broad bed, with a wooden bedstead, tidily covered with a spread. In Russia that bed size is called a "one-and-a-half," narrower than the American double bed. The pillows had been carefully plumped up, one atop another, and covered with a doily in country fashion. Across from the bed was a clothes cupboard. Ordinary shutters, not even carved. They were open. Inside, two thirds of the space was for hangers, and a third held linen-shelves.

On the hangers in the cupboard, like a mirage, was a service jacket and military overcoat with generalissimo's shoulderboards, trousers with a wide red stripe—the accouterments of a military leader of genius, familiar to an entire generation. The designers had whipped up this unique costume for a single person. The best anonymous tailors had measured his figure, warped with physical deformities, figuring how to disguise his flaws. A gold-embroidery craftswoman had woven the pattern on his tunic. But—there was only one service tunic. He would have had enough clothing for a whole company of generalissimos.

My hand stretched out, but I couldn't go so far as to touch something. The things were worn, cleaned many times. Next to them were two ordinary dark men's suits, in which we had never seen him, either in photographs or in films. Did he wear them at home alone? while receiving guests? or did he keep them in reserve for a quick flight to Vienna or Zurich? Where had they hidden his snow-white and gold dress uniforms? Stacks of undershirts and drawers, well-washed socks wrapped up into balls, were all laid out tidily on the shelves. At the bottom, two pairs of black boots, glistening with shoe polish and noticeably worn-looking as well. And next to it, at the same wall, another bookcase. Again books by Lenin and Soviet writers. But where was Machiavelli and his other favorites and preceptors?

I remember that five years before this excursion my school history teacher had said several times that the Leader read 500 pages every day. Where did that figure come from? How could even a 500-page-a-day-reading-genius manage to get anything else done? And here it was that even half a century later the legend was still alive. "He was a voracious reader," a Central Committee official informs us. "The library in his Kremlin working quarters alone, on the evidence of his aides, numbered more than 5,000 volumes, and the one at his dacha in Volynskoye was several times larger."[7] Several times larger, that is, twenty to thirty thousand volumes—why not? But here's your "voracious reader ... " Remembering with bewilderment the wretched library that fit into a pair of small bookcases, I wonder about the tastes of this speed-reader, and about the literature awarded his prize in accordance with those tastes.

We were between the bed and the cupboard in a room as cramped as in a communal apartment. It was pitch dark outside the windows. Here, in his bedroom, were the same institutional white curtains. A black grand piano was in front of them, taking up all the available space. For what reason and when had the piano appeared at Father's house? Svetlana Alliluyeva recollected the piano, but added that she didn't know its origin. A strange forgetfulness. But his daughter did pay attention to the removal of the piano from the big hall to the bedroom, where, in fact, Stalin did not sleep. The woman escorting us then said this:

> The lid is open, as if someone has just played on it ... No, Comrade Stalin didn't play piano himself. This grand piano belonged to Comrade Zhdanov. Comrade Stalin liked Comrade Zhdanov very much and liked it when he played. When Zhdanov

died, Joseph Vissarionovich had this piano brought here. Those who came to visit here played the piano.

"Here?" someone blurted.

"No, not here. The piano was taken out into the hall."

Therefore the piano belonged to Svetlana's former father-in-law. But where was the accordion that Andrey Zhdanov also loved to play? No, there was no accordion. Meanwhile, the guide was opening a door that we hadn't noticed. It was one more exit—from the bedroom to the glassed-in terrace. Rattan summer-house furniture, wooden planters with earth for flowers, but without flowers. Cold lay over the terrace. Frost had drawn figures on the glass.

> For the last several months when our Leader couldn't walk anymore, he liked to spend his time on this terrace, the guide said. That last winter, despite the frosts, he liked to sit here for long stretches in his sheepskin coat, his hat with earflaps, and felt boots.

Chilled to the bone, we returned to the bedroom, and from there to the hall. Now the light was striking us from the left part of the building, as you went out of the bedroom. Here, on a yellowish, varnished parquet floor, stood several wooden barrels with palms, and, sticking out catercorner across the floor was a rather everyday sofa bearing no relation to the ones in the meeting hall, with round bolsters and an absurdly high, swollen back that ended in a shelf for statuettes. An ordinary couch. We had a similar one in our room before the war. It was very uncomfortable to sit on. The guide's voice rang out and then fell:

"On this couch the Great Leader of the Soviet people and all progressive mankind, Comrade Stalin, lay ill and di ..."

The unfinished word hung in the silence. The most genuine of tears filled her eyes. Nina burst into tears, and another of the girls right behind her. Finally the guide collected herself and continued more calmly.

"On the right you can see the scarlet cushions with the orders and medals awarded to him by the Party and the government."

She precisely and at length enumerated what kinds of orders, what they were for, and when awarded. Our eyes raced along after her index finger. Along the wall, covering up the fireplace, there were wreaths of paper flowers with green cast-iron leaves: from the Central Committee, from the Council of Ministers, from the Writers' Union and other organizations, as if he were just about to be buried. But students were already being guided around his apartments, allowed to peep into his cupboards. Meaning he had died, after all. But if he was dead, what was the strict guard for? Why were we being watched to make sure none of us went one step out of line? Now I remember that feeling that arose in me then. The feeling of being trapped. We had been brought here. Were we going to get out of here now? They led us to the entry hall and told us to put on our hats and coats.

"And where is his study?" someone timidly asked.

No answer was forthcoming. Later I read in Alliluyeva that his study had been designed by the architect. But the house was then rebuilt several times at the master's orders and the study disappeared, since it was unwanted.

The door was opened for us. We went out into the open air. It was dank and damp. The bus opened its door. The film wound in reverse: the forest road in the blinding searchlights, the checkpoint. The inspection and checking of our documents according to the list. But were the searchlights as blinding when he himself drove up? Or did they turn them off for him? Finally, we drove out onto the highway. A half-hour later they turned us loose at the Kievskaya metro station. We felt an emptiness at heart, and a strange sense of liberation.

To ground my impressions in some kind of normality, that winter I decided to make a pilgrimage to Kuntsevo one more time, on my own. To find the place and to see at least from the outside, from the woods, how it looked, to remember it better. I shared this intention with a friend, and he told me about a man who had gone there a couple of years before.

The man headed down the road through the woods, holding his small son's hand. They had managed to go literally several steps in the direction of the forbidden zone when a car drove up quietly and he was invited inside. At his interrogation he was asked how he had found himself on the highway. He answered sincerely that he had heard that Comrade Stalin supposedly passed this way, and he had wanted to show it to his son. The result was ten years in prison for intent to assassinate the Leader.

"Do you really want to go there?" my friend wondered.

"But Stalin is dead," I contradicted.

"You sure understand a lot! He's dead, but his *thing* lives on."

To put it in nutshell, I got too frightened to drag myself there and soon forgot about my "intent."

Stalin's daughter called the Kuntsevo house gloomy and empty. That has to be a subjective impression. It didn't seem that way to me. Bright, spacious, and, given our communal way of life, simply luxurious. Fairy-tale nature all around. So what was actually bothering me then at that time? To this day I can't explain my own feelings. I'll try to put it this way: it was as if I had gone to the theater to see some Shakespeare, but they were putting on a Soviet dramatist Anatoly Sofronov soapy play instead.

Nowadays, with the recollections of eyewitnesses and publication of materials discovered by historians, we know the state of his health and how he died in better detail. He had high blood pressure, but there was no one around to treat him. Not long before his death he had taken a steam bath, which hadn't done him any good. Khrushchev recalled that the night before his stroke there had been a big drinking bout until six in the morning.[8] And so—sclerosis of the blood vessels, a stroke paralyzing half of his body, and the loss of speech. Later on his daughter wrote "During the second part of the day on March 1, 1953, the servants found my father lying beside the table with the telephones, and demanded that the doctor be summoned forthwith."[9] I wouldn't dare argue, although the word "demanded" from the mouths of servants calls for strong doubt. Only it's curious what our tour guide said about it:

"He was found on the carpet alongside this couch. They picked him up and put him on the couch."

He was lying on the floor, a puddle spreading out under him, his eyes popping out, but they wouldn't allow any doctors to see him. They said that he was asleep, but then themselves deliberated on what was to come and how to divide up power. It is possible that he could still hear them but couldn't react. They demanded that he be undressed and taken to another room—and all this without any doctors. The record of his illness was so hush-hush that no one has ever found it. Vlasik, Poskrebyshev, his personal physician Vinogradov—had all been arrested by that moment, supposedly on Stalin's personal orders.

Flipping through the literature on the subject, I can see a lot of variant readings concerning the house in Kuntsevo, but the true details are important for a deeper understanding of Stalin. We all collect details—every little bit helps. What kind of man was he in reality, alone with himself? His tastes, his habits, his favorite occupations, his mind, his morals, his culture, as reflected in his everyday life, going by the principle of "the style is the man"? After all, this was reflected in his decisions, decisions that the whole world waited on. Describing this visit, I tried to separate what I saw with my own eyes from what I had heard and read. I noted my rough impressions in my diary that winter. Now it's necessary to add something.

"The formula-phrase 'Stalin is in the Kremlin' was made up by someone unknown," Ms. Alliluyeva wrote. We know who made it up, I can tell you that with certainty. Of course, he himself thought it up. This was an integral part of the great myth of government. Try to exchange that with the formula "Stalin is in Kuntsevo"—and there is no myth. But then the main myth-holder dies. Still, the mythocracy remains. The idea for a museum came up.

In her own words, his daughter was in this house in December of 1952, on her father's birthday. Later she recalled that her father talked to her on the phone in January or in February of 1953. After that she was called several hours before his death, when he was already unconscious. Evidently she communicated with him anyway, although in some strange fashion. Judging by a published letter of hers, the daughter couldn't just go see her father whenever she wanted. In the letter she asks permission to come to his place with her children for a two-day holiday.[10]

In her recollections, Alliluyeva writes an untruth, that she was persecuted after her father's death. By resolution of the Council of Ministers, Stalin's house was assigned to her "with services" and an "allowance" of 4,000 rubles per month.[11] While describing her father as a misanthrope, Alliluyeva forgot to mention one small detail: a house had been built for her not far away from Stalin's own. She liked to stay overnight in it whenever she was around during her father's lifetime.

Nothing was mentioned to us about her house, but an eyewitness who had been in it told how there were three or four bright rooms, comfort, and peace. Alliluyeva refused the "services," but another dacha free of charge and a car with a personal driver remained assigned to her. Stalin's daughter considered that she achieved everything thanks to her personal capabilities, and forty years later on justified her father with all her might in her last book, blaming his henchmen and the Party as a whole.[12] However, the offspring of the characters surrounding Stalin and the celebrities who flourished under the sun of Stalin's constitution are all singing the same old song today.

Svetlana Alliluyeva remembers an important detail.

> They were going to open a museum here, similar to the one in the Lenin Hills. But then the 12th Party Congress followed, after which, of course, the idea of a museum wouldn't have come into anybody's head.

I was at that museum (and not just me) more than two years before the aforementioned party congress. In the gap between Stalin's death and the opening of the museum the following took place.

On the second day after Stalin's death, Alliluyeva recalled, Beria ordered everyone out of the area of the house. They at once began to load up and cart away the furniture and things to a Ministry of State Security warehouse. The causes of Stalin's death still remain a mystery, but this isn't the place to discuss that. But if Beria had to liquidate everything associated with his master in such a hurry, a suspicion of his complicity in the general secretary's death arises. Maybe Beria, I should ask, intended to move into that estate from his house at the corner of Sadovo-Kudrinskaya and Kachalova Streets, next door to the Chekhov museum?

The servants were all told that they were to keep silent about the dacha, as if it had never existed at all. The official version announced in the press has remained mythological up till now: Stalin died "in his apartment in the Kremlin." In an article published 35 years later, Alliluyeva added: "This was done so that none of the dacha servants could complain."[13] But, come on, this isn't even a little bit serious—who would be afraid of servants' complaints? They could be ground to dust, anyway.

Some of the ones who had lived there with Stalin for twenty years had nowhere to take themselves off to. A couple of them shot themselves. Valechka, that is, Valentina Istomina, his so-called housekeeper, and in reality his devoted concubine, whom he trusted to taste all his food and sleep with him, remained alive, but they had her hidden away somewhere.

After Beria's removal from power the command was suddenly given to bring everything back, to restore the house of Comrade Stalin exactly as it had been.

At the end of the Sixties, I met a woman who had been a museum employee. She told me how in autumn of that memorable 1953 she had been given a call and invited to the reception room of the Lubyanka. The woman had said farewell to her husband and children, grabbed a little bag with some zwieback, and left.

She was received by an elderly man in a major's uniform. After checking her documents, he rather formally asked her to accompany him, as he expressed it, to "a certain place," where "we need your consultation." She was taken to Kuntsevo. The state-security major explained what the matter was:

"There has been a decision to open a museum in this house. I was with Stalin all my life, and now everything is as it was when he was here. Take a look around, please. Can it be opened to the public in this state?"

She was shown around the house. She counted sixteen rooms (we hadn't been shown all of them). There were couches in all of them. On every couch lay a Caucasian cloak.

"But where did he sleep?" she asked.

His bodyguard answered simply:

> Nobody knew in what room he slept, or when—day or night, we just had to guess. We weren't allowed to bother him. He slept with his clothes on. He would lock his door from the inside or just latch the door chain. If the servants knew where he was, they would pass food to him through the crack. But is that important at all?

"This is going to be his personal museum-house," the curator-woman explained.

> In it, everything is supposed to be set out scientifically, so that it's clear to visitors where his study is, where his bedroom is, and so on. But here it seems that all the rooms are identical. For instance, the question will surely occur to visitors 'Why did he sleep in different places?' And the tour guides should be able to explain why.

The major listened to her attentively and asked:

"Could you set out all your complaints on paper?"

"I have absolutely no complaints at all," said the curator, turning cold. "You just asked and I answered."

"So, just set them out for my report to the leadership ..."

"Well, were there any portraits there?" I asked the woman.

"What portraits?"

"Politburo members."

"No, there definitely were no portraits."

Neither are the portraits mentioned by the author of *Twenty Letters to a Friend*. Within several days the museum had started receiving visitors. Evidently, they were in a hurry to execute the order and had hurriedly locked up all the superfluous rooms. Whose idea was it for a museum? What was its purpose? Maybe it was just ritual inertia. Why did they hang up the Politburo portraits? To my way of thinking, when handing out instructions for opening the museum, the leader's comrades-in-arms were thinking not so much about his glory as about themselves. The demigod became a hemi-demigod, and the mythocracy labored on. The throne with its sawn-off legs was empty, but his drinking buddies remained right there in the cast of characters around it. And who it was who would occupy it was unclear. Not a single one of them would have refused it. But the house-of-cards palace was trembling and about to collapse in the wind. The courtiers were clinging to the skirts of the myth-holder's overcoat as if hanging on for dear life, trying not to get blown away themselves, to stay at the seat of power.

Even after his death the master's house remained the abode of a fearsome man who all of his life was afraid and who made his fear universal. But equally he made universal his puritanism, his Machiavellianism, his tastes. His Kuntsevo horizon became the horizon of the whole country, its barbed wire ensnaring everyone.

Stalin was completely capable of conducting sessions of the Politburo with their portraits instead of them. The portraits could have as actively expressed their points of view as their originals. But why would he want to look for whole days at a stretch at portraits of those whom he deeply despised and used as lackeys? Today it's clear to me: his successors themselves ordered their images to be hung in the hall and made up the legend about how the Great Leader had sat them under their own portraits. It's what Stalin had done before them: in photographs he always appeared, in hindsight, to be an appendage of Lenin's. That's how the Politburo members became the possessors of the general secretary's scepter.

Undoubtedly they wanted the power and the homage that he had raked in with his mighty hand. That's exactly why the best writers with their high-ranking secretaryships were the first to turn up at the museum (we students were allowed in after them through influence in high places). The trusty writers were supposed to continue the old tradition of doxology, but with new names.

The writer that I mentioned at the beginning, for instance, was waiting until the period of personal modesty of the new leader was over, and, as soon as an opportunity arose, he readjusted his poem about the little boy to have him now bring his present to Comrade Khrushchev at the Kremlin. He didn't succeed in republishing the poem: Khrushchev was replaced by the next leader. It was necessary to wait out the next period of "collective leadership." This talented writer wasn't put out by this and reworked the poem yet another time. The boy was going to the Kremlin to see Comrade Brezhnev. But the poem once again had no luck. The aged general secretaries began to succeed one another at such a pace that even the most brilliant of poets wouldn't have been able to keep up with the alterations. I am far from making up this story about my colleague. If a suitable situation arises in Russia, the public will be satisfied that that I'm not joking.

I'm saying this because the dwelling-places of our leaders still remain a mystery to this day. But now everybody knows that they don't live in the Kremlin. Although certain of them have their chambers there, as the writer Boris Balter used to say, in case of popular unrest. I was thinking about this while I was wandering around the White House on a tour of Washington, which seems to be easier to get into than into some elite restaurant, say. And everything inside the White House has frequently been described and photographed—you can even buy postcards showing everything there.

I don't know how many people in all and of what social strata managed to visit the estate at Kuntsevo. I would guess not a lot. I heard that the museum had been shut down several days after our visit. It was shut with the same secrecy that it had been opened with. It goes without saying that no announcement was ever made about it, and that the 20th Congress had nothing to say about it. The Congress was in session during the turbulent days when Stalin's milieu still didn't know whether to sing "Suliko" (his favorite Georgian folksong) or stomp on his ashes. They were inclined toward the latter. However, the museum could have served either of these two purposes. And, if you like, the second was lots better. But more about this later.

"There came a moment when they suddenly decided at the top to hand over the estate for a model orphanage," the lawyer Leonid Oyrikh told me. "The party stalwart Aleksandr Perov was appointed principal. Before that he had been responsible for the management of a resort on the premises. I was on friendly terms with him. It was thanks to him that I got a chance to see Stalin's dacha."

"Was there furniture there?"

No, everything had been taken out of the house, the guards discharged, even the lights had been cut off—they'd left just a watchman. Perov was really proud of his new place of work, his eyes were even burning. He put me and my wife into his *Pobeda* and took us off to see Stalin's dacha. I remember that we left the car at the gates, passed through two fences, between them German shepherds running around. We walked around the house and along the paths by flashlight. The rooms were empty. I remember that there were two barbecues in the garden: *shashlyk* for the Leader was cooked on them. At that time Perov had been told to assemble the furniture for the orphanage. It was ordered from a factory in Riga, and they had already started shipping the furniture in.

"But surely they never opened any sort of orphanage?"

"Two months later the higher authorities changed their mind, and the Kremlin household administration confiscated the keys from Perov."

Thus the new leaders still hadn't resolved the dilemma of what to do with Stalin's house. Why did neither Khrushchev nor any of them move to Stalin's ostentatious dacha? Because it wasn't an easy thing to do. Their mortal fear clung to the place. Besides, they all looked kind of chintzy against the Master's backdrop. They weren't ashamed of besmirching their own reputations—those had been muddied long ago. Neither were they afraid of public opinion. Evidently they were just uncomfortable about becoming a laughing-stock in the eyes of their colleagues.

For the leaders of the new wave, Stalin's house had achieved moral obsolescence, and simply seemed too small. Having seen the West, all of them wanted comforts of a more contemporary sort. Modesty in private life and the backpacking asceticism of terrorists, who always had to be ready to throw on their overcoats and slip off into the night, had become unnecessary. Not for them the drinking bout with dancing to the gramophone: imposing receptions in furs and fancy dress required a different architecture. The dachas of succeeding leaders were situated in inviolate woods farther from the center of town.

And the town of Kuntsevo with its vanished village of Volynskoye, visited by Gogol, and the river Setun, running along the foot of Voznesensky Forest, and the ancient village of Ochakovo, the possession of the 18th century scholar and writer Mikhail Kheraskov, and a row of adjoining villages—in a word, these ancient environs, including Stalin's estate, were all joined up to the city of Moscow by a stroke of Khrushchev's pen.

In the years after Stalin, broad Minskaya Street cut across the Minskoye highway (formerly the Mozhayskoye highway), built on the bones of hundreds of thousands of prisoners. The highway at that point was called Marshal Grechko Prospect, but possibly has been renamed again. At one point Minskaya Street was called Khrushchev highway by the local inhabitants. This new street cut across yet another deserted road going through the forest along Poklonnaya hill to Stalin's estate. The forest remained, but new construction, forbidden in the Master's time, was springing up all around.

The standardized boxes of identical buildings filled the Ochakovskaya district and the floodplain of the Setun, demonstrating the cheerless solemnity of such town planning, against the background of which even the Stalin Renaissance style looks like masterwork. In the forest on the other side of the road Kalinin's dacha is preserved, where important guests used to come, the leaders of the fraternal communist parties. They were even shown the "Kuntsevo museum" in confidence.

I found myself once again on the territory of the estate in 1976, coming on a visit to a sick journalist friend. He lay in a ward of a building where Stalin's guards had formerly been quartered. Now a multistory therapeutic department for Hospital No.1 of the Fourth Directorate of the Ministry of Health, the Kremlin branch, had been constructed there. The bus stop at the former nine-kilometer marker on Minskoye highway is modestly called "First Hospital." It isn't the most ostentatious of hospitals, although not for mere mortals. In the same ward as my friend, who had gotten there only by pulling strings, lay other man: the deputy of some ministry or other, the son of an executive member of the Central Committee, and the personal chauffeur of Blatov, Brezhnev's assistant—there you go, a national table of ranks.

Blatov's chauffeur was complaining about how the wedding party for his boss's daughter had brought on his stomach ulcer. For the party Blatov had been sent parcels from regional committee secretaries all over the country. For two weeks, the chauffeur had been dashing around between railway stations and hotels like someone possessed. And of course he had to have a drink with everybody. So his ulcer started acting up again.

The deputy minister related how the people at the top were going to get rid of all the Jews in the country. The method—expelling them all, all at once—wouldn't suit: first they had to prepare for their replacement at all of the leading branches of culture and science. And at the same time let go the superfluous Jews and hang on to the rest until their Russian replacements were ready. As the evening came on, conversation in the ward died down. The crackle of radios could be heard. All the chauffeurs and ministers were pulling out shortwave radio receivers from underneath their pillows and tuning in to the Voice of America Broadcasting in Russian.

I stepped out of the former guardhouse and ambled toward the forest. A bridge stretched across the gullies, but further on the road was cut off by the high fence so memorable from my student years. By moving the fence, they had somehow foreshortened the estate. I remembered one of the conversations in the hospital (lying in bed next to Stalin's house, the patient now and then would return to that sainted theme). The son of the Central Committee executive related that, before important Party events, they would lodge the people who composed, massaged, and agreed the texts of reports for the leadership in Stalin's house. The atmosphere contributed a lot to their creative juices.

Ten years further on I went to see an acquaintance at a home for retired filmmakers that had been built alongside that same forest. They were allowed to walk on the outskirts of the park, but not, of course, as far as the secret abode. A new reinforced-concrete fence had been raised around it, but inside, it was said, everything stood as it had before. And that's right. What if it was suddenly needed again? We'll outwait the elements, and then we'll see what to do with this national shrine.

If it were up to me, I would reopen the Stalin museum in Kuntsevo right now. True or false, it doesn't matter. The falser it is, however paradoxical, the more real it is. A museum to a man not so much a modest misanthrope as a primitive one. A national Communist theme park. A museum to the Politburo, that is, to all of them, the wielders of power in this wretched country. A museum to the triumph and mediocrity of the Soviet ideology. A museum subordinate, unlike all others, not to the Ministry of Culture, but to a corresponding department of the Lubyanka.

It would be better, of course, to secure the permission of the master of the house. After all, it is his private property. I don't know if he has forgiven us for visiting him at the pleasure of Politburo but without any invitation from him. And what if his shade, wandering at night along the pathways
tamped down in the snow, ordered his uninvited guests dealt with?

The Ruchyi Churchyard Mystery

The trip was risky. I wanted to check up on a suspicion of mine in connection with the death of Velimir Khlebnikov. We left St. Petersburg at an ungodly hour. The thick fog didn't disperse for a long time, even after the appearance of the sun. I was trying to drive the car as carefully as possible, but it was hard on the broken two-lane, in the mud left by tractors and in the smoke from trucks. Soon we caught sight of a car in the roadside ditch, smashed into a tree. Two corpses sat in it like dummies, a man and a woman. After a certain while, an overturned car, also with a dead driver. An endless stream of traffic and no roadside services.

The village of Kresttsy is on the river Kholova about two hours' drive from Novgorod in the direction of Valday and Vyshniy Volochok. Kresttsy is neither better nor worse than a lot of similar old Russian settlements: a swamp, mosquitoes, and some shacks. But the place, famous for its white Kresttsy embroidery, has been in existence there for a century and a half. The startling geometrical designs are woven in linen by the women master-weavers, and later picked out thread by thread and the openings left in the fabric. I would have liked to investigate that decayed-and-revived handicraft more deeply, but our business swallowed us up whole.

With night coming on, where could an outsider find to stay in Kresttsy? We were lucky enough to get ahold of the local folklorist-historian, a former teacher at the trade school, Pavel Gurchonok, who offered to help and even accompany us on our mission, but not, of course, at night. They took me and my wife in, heated up a bath, and fed us with what God had provided. We would go on in the morning: the road was only partly paved, but now, in August, it was dry.

I had been interested in Velimir Khlebnikov from an early age. My granny used to tell us how Khlebnikov had gotten close to my grandfather in St. Petersburg: granddad was studying at the Mining Institute and attended literature lectures at the university on the side. They were brought together by their interest in disputation and an attribute of their minds that granny called engineering-poetic. They would roam around the city chattering away and then come home hungry, and grandma, by then in the family way (she was 22), would help the servants feed them.

They both dashed off verse, although grandfather's was conservative, fluent, and on the subject of love, something that the bachelor Khlebnikov made fun of; but he showed up anyway with a fir-branch bouquet at my mother's christening (she was born on December 19, 1908, which means that the christening was a little bit later). On each branch fluttered a piece of paper inscribed with poetry. My grandfather's life finished in November 1917: the rebelling proletariat at his mercury mine in Nikitovka threw the engineer down the mine shaft, kicked his wife and two small children out of their house and burned it down. His collection of Khlebnikov's poetry, his letters, the whole of my grandfather's archive, all burned up as well.

1. The Beginning of his End

Death was hovering over Khlebnikov too. The war and the Revolution left him alive, but not for long. I think that a person like him, in similar conditions, couldn't in theory live for long. Khlebnikov's grandfather died in Jerusalem, his uncle emigrated to New Zealand. A genetic inclination to the road was in his blood, like in Pushkin's. The social storm spun him around: barracks, barges, insane asylums, freight trains, military hospitals. He dashed all over, showing up now in St. Petersburg, now in Moscow, now in Baku, now in Astrakhan, now in Kharkov. He behaved like a delinquent, phoning the Winter Palace and subjecting Prime Minister Aleksandr Kerensky to verbal abuse. And then he boasted about it to his friends—otherwise, if nobody had known about it, what would be the reason for such amusements? "A man outside everyday life," his biographer Nikolay Stepanov called Khlebnikov.[1]

In 1918, along with poet Dmitry Petrovsky, Khlebnikov composed a "Creators' Declaration" that they directed at the Council of People's Commisars, declaring that

> all creators—poets, painters, inventors—must be stipulated as being outside nations, states, and ordinary laws. They have to be given the right of travel without charge on railways and of exit beyond the borders of the Republic to all countries of the world. Poets have to wander and sing.[2]

At that time they didn't yet put you in prison for your dreams. But in reality, Khlebnikov saw and described the mortuary where they brought the corpses of those who had perished during the revolutionary commotion in Moscow. "The first capital letter of the new days of freedom," he wrote, "is so often written in the ink of death."[3] You can get a shudder from this idea of his even today.

From hungry Moscow he rushed off to Kharkov, where his friend Grigory Petnikov and the Sinyakov family lived. Khlebnikov had already served in the Red Army that had invaded Persia in an attempt to get a revolution going there. Assigned to staff guard duty, he lay around on a Caspian beach for whole days at a time, went swimming. And then he completely missed a movement of his unit. He caught up with them a month later, having wandered his fill, returning to Baku. As Vladimir Mayakovsky recalled, Khlebnikov returned from Persia "in a railway carriage of epileptics, stressed out and ragged, wearing only a patient's smock."[4]

Then the Whites entered Kharkov and starting recruiting people into their army. Before signing Khlebnikov up as a soldier they sent him to a psychiatric hospital for examination. He wrote from it to Petnikov: "Take a rare chance and send me envelopes, paper, tobacco, and some bread, and potatoes."[5] And half a year later, he informed Osip Brik, "In a nutshell, I've been lying in field hospitals, saving myself from conscription by the Whites and suffering from typhus, for four months! Terrible!"[6]

Rita Rait recalled how she caught sight of the restless, ragged, always-hungry poet, and how she and a friend sewed him trousers out of discarded duck curtains. His head had been shaved after two bouts of typhus. On April 20, Sergey Esenin and Anatoly Marienhoff came to Kharkov for a public appearance, and agreed to perform a ritual of consecration of Khlebnikov as Chairman of the Globe on stage. It was only towards the end of the rite that the barefoot Khlebnikov, on whom they had stretched a jester's white cassock, understood that his colleagues were mounting a farce for the amusement of the crowd. But he'd thought that it was serious, and got awfully upset.

He lived alone in a half-darkened room, to which people could get by clambering through a ruined terrace. In the room was a mattress without sheets, and a pillow, "the pillowcase [*of which*] served as the cache for his manuscripts and, obviously, was the only property Khlebnikov had."[7]

At the end of December 1921 Khlebnikov returned to Moscow and lived in the Moscow Institute of Art (*Vkhutemas*) student hostel. In the spring of 1922 he took part in two evening events at the All-Russian Union of Poets Club. He was trying to publish at least something, but editors couldn't take seriously the hurriedly-written scraps of paper that he pulled out of his bosom. He was taken more and more often for a crackpot.

When Khlebnikov died, Mayakovsky wrote of him (for some reason in the present tense): "In practice, Khlebnikov is a most unorganized person. In his whole life, he himself never published a line."[8] His friends David Burlyuk and Aleksey Kruchenykh pasted together fragments of his poems, sometimes mixing up beginnings and endings. He himself could never be allowed to edit his poems, because he would cross out everything and write parallel texts. Khlebnikov authorised his friends to do this strange work: you "have the right to amend the text according to your taste, shortening it, changing it, giving strength to colorless places. I insist. Let's see what comes of it."[9]

Some of Khlebnikov's last surviving letters show that, although still full of creative plans, he looks as if he's already tearing himself away from this sinful earthly life. "I have achieved the promised revolution in the understanding of time, involving fields of several sciences ..." This is from a letter to Vsevolod Meyerhold.[10]

He informed his friend the painter Pyotr Miturich about his just-discovered "basic law of time, in which negative and positive dislocations take place over a definite number of days" on March 14, 1922:

> When the future comes clear thanks to these computations, the sense of time is lost; it seems like you're standing unmoving on a deck overlooking the future. The sense of

time disappears, and it looks like a field ahead and a field behind: it becomes in its own way a kind of space.

And a little further down in the same letter is an instruction: "Wear my work's imaginary watch of mankind on your wrist, and give me the wings of your work, I am already sick and tired of the heavy tread of my present."[11]

For us he remains an lambent, wise genius; some of his poems resound with a certain illumination as natural as breathing:

> Years, people and nations
> Run away forever,
> Like flowing water.
> In the lithe mirror of nature
> The stars are a seine, we are fish,
> The gods—spectres in the dark.

Only a great poet could so simply (and sonorously, in Russian) fuse into one the varied essence of existence. But he lived like a hungry, vagrant dog, and had had enough of life, or so it seems. One hundred and six days were left in his life.

But to his mother he wrote lucidly and realistically: "As before, I'm getting a book ready in Moscow, I don't know if it will see the light of day; as soon as it's published, I'll go to the Caspian via Astrakhan; maybe everything will be different, but that's how it's dreamed of." Later a brilliant description of the city follows, as if he were seeing it today:

> You wouldn't recognize Moscow, it looks like it has suffered from a heavy illness, and now there is neither a 'Zamoskvarechye' nor teas nor samovars nor the lightness nor the richness of previous times! It looks like it has suffered a 'world fever,' and the people, with their hurried gait, stride, and faces, remind you of cities of the New World.

Khlebnikov informs his mother about his own daily life sadly:

> Life is middling for me, but in general I'm fed and warm, although I don't work anywhere. My book is my main thing, but it's stuck at page one and won't move on. There were articles about me in *Revolyutsiya i Pechat'* [*Pechat' i Revolutsiya—Y.D.*], *Krasnaya Nov'*, *Nachala*. Yakobson published a research article on me ... Around Christmas the average income of a working Muscovite was considered to be 30 to 40 billion; a wedding party [*costs*] four billion. Now everything is ten times more expensive, a pre-war ruble is worth two million, you can ride in a car for 5 million an hour.[12]

What was going on with Khlebnikov, anyway? He was known and esteemed, but in recent months he'd gotten left behind: some people lost interest, while others got frightened of the urban madman that he appeared to be, had become, or maybe had always been. He was chronically starving; malarial attacks tortured him. Pyotr Miturich remained among the few loyal to him to the end.

He had exchanged letters with Khlebnikov before this. They had discussed the "flying wing." At one point, homeless, Khlebnikov was living at Miturich's. Miturich had sent his family away from the starving city life to a village in Novgorod province. His wife, Natalya, found a job there as a teacher. Their son and daughter were with her.

This moment was important because Miturich was on the verge of divorcing his wife and marrying Khlebnikov's sister, Vera. Vera Khlebnikova was a painter as well. She had been studying in Paris for two years when she was caught up in the world war. In 1916 she got to her mother in Astrakhan via Italy, and then later moved to Moscow with her. After her brother's death she married Miturich, who had left his first wife, and bore him a son. We'll get acquainted with May Petrovich Miturich later on.

Khlebnikov, exhausted by the burdens of life, decided to go stay with his relatives in Astrakhan in May, 1922, to get rest and medical treatment. He had no money for the trip. Miturich managed by the use of his relatives' influence to sign him up on a mission for some kind of revolutionary-propaganda work involving a free trip down the Volga. Two weeks were left before departure. They decided to go off to the countryside for the period. Khlebnikov was carrying two heavy manuscript-stuffed pillowcases. The vagabond, used to sleeping overnight at railway stations, was heading for his last stop on this planet.

2. How He Died

From the Borovenka railway station they walked nearly forty kilometers through the spring slush, through forests and swamps, eaten up by mosquitoes, squelching through mud up to their knees, to the village of Santalovo. They set themselves up there in the school, a large peasant hut, or, more precisely, in the half of it reserved for the schoolteacher—Miturich's wife and children.

Khlebnikov had come here not like someone on holiday, but like citydwellers are now doing again, in order to stave off starvation: he was heeding advice to build up his waning strength on fresh air and milk. Forty-three days were left in his life. The weather became warm and sunny. Khlebnikov started feeling better.

He would walk in the woods or to the river, where he would fish with a rod or just lie in the sun, looking at the clouds. "Velimir felt well," Miturich noted. "He complained once or twice of a chill, but the shivering fits would pass quickly... But it became noticeable that Velimir was hanging around the house more, sitting at the table and writing more."[13] Khlebnikov's last verses are full of despair: the unacknowledged prophet—torn from reality, needed by no one "in the wild, headlong gallop," as he called the revolution—saw that his end was near.

And here we were now in Santalovo—all of twenty kilometers from Kresttsy. There was even some pavement left, but the village of Santalovo in reality didn't exist anymore. Its population had been scattered during collectivization, and only a few homesteads were left. The windows had been broken out of the school. Yevdokiya Stepanova had already been married in 1922. She hadn't been at Khlebnikov's funeral: her own small daughter had died just then, but she had met the visitor and remembered him. Her husband, Aleksey, helped to dig the grave. Her son, also Aleksey, was at one time the chairman of the collective farm here. They would have destroyed the church and all the memorials here but for the fact that he was careful of his mother's feelings.

"The whole village was looted and burned," witness Stepanova recalled. "What great bread we had then! And now? My husband got stabbed with a knife in 1927, and I was left with two children. During collectivization they took my horse, and it died on the collective farm."[14]

"Where a village is on a hill, there's not a crust of bread in it." But this isn't Stepanova, it's Vladimir Dal. I had read in a book by the Moscow critic Mikhail Lobanov, who visited the place at the end of the 70s, that, through a window of the school, he saw a bench propping up the ceiling so that it wouldn't cave in.[15]

"Lobanov made up a lot of it," our escort, Pavel Gurchonok, remarked. "About the memorial plaque on the wall of the school, saying that Khlebnikov died here. He described a bathhouse that hadn't been here for a long time, mixed people's names up."

We were standing alongside the place where the school had been: they had long ago torn it down for firewood; a part of the foundation and its pit remained. And there was still a depression on a hillock from the former bathhouse—covered with trash and weeds up to the waist.

Khlebnikov gave the Stepanovs some of his manuscripts as a gift, but where they are Yevdokiya Stepanova doesn't remember.

"He lived in the village for about fifteen days, " Stepanova recalled. "I was shy of him. He was all yellow. Coughing. People thought he had consumption. Nobody came to visit him and very few people would even talk to him. Pretty soon his legs gave out and he couldn't get around. Nobody was able to help him. He was feeling terrible and asked to be taken to the hospital. On June first they found a horse and cart and carried him to the hospital in the closest town, Kresttsy. He stayed there for a while, but they didn't keep him long."

Khlebnikov's last letter, his handwriting shaky with weakness, without any date on it, was from the hospital to A. P. Davydov:

> Dear Aleksandr Petrovich!
> I inform you, as a doctor, of all my medical afflictions.
> I got to the dacha in Novgorod province, Borovenka station, Santalovo village (40 versts [*19 miles—Y.D.*] from it), here I walked around on foot, slept on the ground, and lost the use of my legs. They don't work. Disorder ... (*illegible*) ... of service. They have put me into the Korostets hospital, Novgorod province, Korostets town, 40 versts from the railway line.
> I want to get well, regain the gift of walking, and get to Moscow and to my native home. How can I do it?[16]

Korostets is of course Kresttsy. And what he wrote from the hospital to the doctor in Moscow is sad.

He was in a bad way.

> Publishers pretending to be my brother come to visit me in hospital, in order to rob me of my manuscripts, publishers, waiting for my death, so as to raise a howl over the poet's coffin. And keep my poems lying on their shelves for several more years. Be damned to you all![17]

He was having hallucinations. Nobody came to visit him in the hospital, nobody had a clue where he was and what was happening to him. Whatever he wrote he would hide in his pillowcase and sleep on it. The fact that only the dead are prized is a truth that is spoken more softly and weightily by a different poet.

He got even worse in the hospital. The doctor established the obvious: bodily edema and paralysis. Three more weeks of suffering, since he didn't receive any kind of treatment at the hospital. According to other sources, he also had an open form of tuberculosis, and gangrene—but these are just conjecture. He developed bedsores, because no one was taking care of him there; it's not clear if he was even being fed. Miturich found a cart and carried the half-alive poet back to Santalovo.

They say that sea elephants leave the herd and head for the abyss when they sense their coming death. The particular decency of this man came to light in this critical moment of his life. Half a month before his death the severely ill poet asked to be carried to the abandoned bathhouse so as not to infect the dwellers in the house, especially the children.

> My husband said, Stepanova continued, 'neighbor Khlebnikov has asked to go to the bathhouse, let's carry him over.' Khlebnikov himself asked to go to the bathhouse in order not to infect the people he was staying with. They put him in the bathhouse. My husband came over and put down some straw underneath him. Before he died the sick man asked us to bring him a bunch of cornflowers.

On June 28, 1922, Khlebnikov died in the bathhouse. It's probable that it was malaria that brought him to heart and kidney failure, but that would be just our modern-day conjecture. He died, and that's that. The last word pronounced by him in this world was "Ye-e-sss ..." It's horrible to say it, but death brought the poet's chaotic life to some kind of order.

The old folks learned of it and started building him a coffin. They put him in it and immediately put the coffin on a cart and carried it off. From Santalovo, where the school and bathhouse used to stand, to the churchyard at Ruchyi was a two-hour walk. A small group of people—five men and one woman— slowly walked behind the cart on which the coffin lay. Stepanova recalled:

> My husband went to bury him. Six people accompanied the coffin. Miturich with his wife, Natalya, Vasily Ivanov, Lukin, Bogdanov, and my Aleksey. Not one of them is among the living today.

We got to Ruchyi in our car by a roundabout way. The old road past Makovskoye lake, where there had been a feudal estate on the hill, had gotten overgrown. At the foot of the hill, two small rivers, the Anyenka and the Oleshnya, flow together. Khlebnikov used to go there on his strolls; trout abounded there at the time.

The old lady Sasha took us to the church and its graveyard—Aleksandra Srodnikova. She hadn't taken part in any funerals then, but she lived nearby the church and kept an eye on the graves. The graveyard was overgrown and untended, sheltered by mighty trees from bad weather, the church in ruins, but around it all was tidy, pretty, and peaceful.

They carried the coffin to the Ruchyi churchyard, which later on came to be in the center of a collective farm. Quietly they lowered him into a grave under a pine tree, even hurriedly, without words, without ceremony, without ritual. On the pine tree Pyotr Miturich cut his name: "Velimir Khlebnikov." Later he planted a rowan and two birch trees beside the hummock. Someone from our time had put up a board with the dates of his birth and death.

We walked through the high grass, uncut, half-dried, between the graves, among which was the final resting place of the Chairman of the Globe. Khlebnikov's grave was luxuriantly overgrown with nettles, so our arms and legs swelled up with welts. And here was the tree.

The bark on the pine was weepy with sap. The surname *Khlebnikov* couldn't be seen. But the name *Velimir* in some miraculous way had not grown over, although it had blackened until you could hardly guess what it was even if you knew. Stepanova had just recently said that Khlebnikov had asked for a bunch of cornflowers to be left on his grave, and they regularly left some for him. Gurchonok was certain that this story was made up for the sake of prettiness. Even if Khlebnikov had said something about cornflowers, there was no one to pick them or bring them, never mind regularly.

Written in Pyotr Miturich's hand on a piece of paper preserved in the Central State Archive of Literature and Art is:

In the morning at 7-8 o'clock 27.VI to the question of Fedosya Chelnokova 'Is it difficult for you to die?' he answered, "Yes," and soon lost consciousness. He was breathing evenly with a weak moan, periodically taking a deep breath. His breathing and heart gradually weakened and at 9 o'clock 28.VI it stopped.

A little further on a coffin with "First Chairman of the Globe Velimir Khlebnikov" written on the side had been drawn, and it was added:

> Lowered into a grave one and a half deep in the graveyard at Ruchyi, Novgorod province, Krestinsky district, Timofeyevskaya townland, in the rear left corner at the very fence, between a fir and a pine tree. Pyotp Miturich.

Pay attention to the fact that the grave was dug shallowly: an *arshin* and a half is about three and a half feet.

Khlebnikov's legacy remained with Miturich: two dirty pillowcases stuffed with scraps of paper. He did drawings of Khlebnikov's death and sent them to the magazine *Vsemirnaya illustratsiya* (World illustration), where they were published. Most of the poet's manuscripts—which, as Maykovsky's mistress Lilya Brik wrote, he easily lost or left behind wherever he fetched up in his dog's life—disappeared.[18]

We returned from the churchyard in silence. Darkness was all around: not a light, not a passerby. In Kresttsy we made the acquaintance of a schoolteacher. She had never even heard of Khlebnikov, being busy enough already, to say nothing of the children knowing anything about him. There were none of Khlebnikov's poems to be found in the nearby libraries.

3. Death as the Road to Immortality

Khlebnikov had a sense of death. All his conscious life he thought about it. "I feel the grave heaped up over my past. My verse seems to me like someone else's."[19] More than once, the fateful number 37 that concludes the lives of great Russian poets from Pushkin on has been noticed, but no one has yet explained it. Khlebnikov's life too was sundered in his thirty-seventh year. In his autobiography, he wrote: "In 1913 I was called the great genius of modern times, which title I have kept even to the present day." Was he joking, or was he self-confidently establishing a fact?

He wrote his own epitaph, which of course was ignored. "Let them read on the headstone: 'Inspired, he dreamed of being a prophet.'"[20] No, he didn't consider himself a prophet, unlike several other self-assured Russian authors; he only *dreamed* of being one—a big difference! He called himself "a tired dissembler" and people "reasoning bees."

In 1912 Khlebnikov had asked: "Shouldn't we expect the collapse of the state in 1917?"[21] He suggested finishing the Great War by flying to the moon. Possibly it was just because of the rhyme in Russian between "war" (*voyna*) and "moon" (*luna*). The man who called himself an unconditional materialist was a pure idealist.

In a lot of ways he was just an anarchist, a tramp, homeless. Twice he was put in an insane asylum; he lived under the Reds and under the Whites. Who was he, then: a genius, a compulsive scribbler, a madman? Apparently, the one and the other, and a little of the third. I remind you of his poem "Thunderstorm in the Month of A-oo!" that seems like something a three-year-old would come up with:

> Poopoo-opo! That's thunder.
> Gam gra gra rap rap.
> Pee-peepeezee. That's it.
> Nitey-nite gzogzeezee. Lightning flash.[22]

Send a poem like that to any publisher in the world and they would turn it down flat. But, after all, Korney Chukovsky also played with sounds, for instance: "Here's a *tur*, here's an *urt*, here's an *rtle* ..." And of course Daniel Kharms with his group of the *Oberiuty* (The Union of Real Arts). And all so-called poetry of minimal expression. But the very same Khlebnikov at that moment was composing political-education doggerel for ROSTA, the Russian Telegraphic Agency:

> Wrangel is, from dawn till late,
> Plaiting puttees for his mates;
> And when the job is nicely done, he'll
> Fight to free the tsar's money.[23] *Etc.*

Sergey Gorodetsky called Khlebnikov the leader and founder of Futurism, which drove the poets crazy who were doing well at the time, wounding their self-esteem.[24] They all wanted to be conceded the founder, and that's understandable. But he was the strangest of them all.

"I wanted to find the key to the clock of mankind, to be its clockmaker and to outline the fundamentals of prediction of the future," a magazine quoted him, from the then-unpublished "Boards of Fate." At the same time the magazine informed its readership that, although Khlebnikov had predicted great success for the Soviet regime in 1922, he was among other things "a medieval seeker of the philosophers' stone, an alchemist of word and number."

Gorodetsky himself was one of the first Acmeists and organizers of the Poets' Workshop, and in Stalin's time he had to rework the text of the libretto of Mikhail Glinka's famous opera, including changing the words "Glory, glory to our Russian tsar" to "Glory, glory, to our Russian people," and occupy himself with other such dubious enterprises, in order to survive.

Cosmic utopianism was in the air; Khlebnikov was following in the footsteps of Nikolay Fyodorov. Philosophical time and fate are Khlebnikov's central motifs, but real time and real fate never afforded him enough to penetrate into these two mysteries. He tried to get to the heart of the mystery of art, but he failed—it comes across as banality: "A word has a special sound when another 'second meaning' shines through it, when it is a glass for a dim mystery covered by it, hidden behind it ...."[25] Yes, it has been known for a long time that Khlebnikov wrote that.

A great man for mixing up thoughts, Khlebnikov confounded logic, and you never know whether to delight in his impenetrable wisdom or calmly throw away yet another idiocy that you've just read. Here's an example: "Spiritual science will achieve great significance because it will be learned how one man's indolence will help the labors of many." But maybe it's neither the one nor the other, but irony, because Khlebnikov adds: "In this fashion the sluggard will be justified because his heart's work is directed towards a general increase in the joy of labor."[26]

Pay attention: in this phrase you can see the prose of Andrey Platonov. So, Khlebnikov the seer foresaw that laziness in the Soviet land would unite with labor and produce "lazibor" (*lenetrud*—his own, made-up word, to whose sense, by the way, the name Lenin is well-suited, too).

"The king of time" and "the stork fallen to thinking" is what Benedikt Lifshits called him. He was abstracted by the "highest absent-mindedness," as M. Matyushin wrote. Yuri Tynyanov said that Khlebnikov was "the new viewpoint" in the poetry of the 20th century. In his "will-be-ish" (*budetlyansky*) book *The Teacher and the Pupil*, Khlebnikov in his own words "conceived of defeating the state by means of thought." It came out in May 1912, and, as a result of calculations made in conformity with world history, the poet predicted the fall of the Russian Empire in 1917.

After the Revolution it seemed that he had been clairvoyant, but now we can see that the empire survived three-quarters of a century longer. It has fallen apart in front of our eyes, but is it to its logical conclusion? And there are no new Khlebnikovs to predict its path.

Khlebnikov tried to improve the Russian lexicon, and did so widely and with brilliance. Osip Mandelshtam wrote: "Khlebnikov takes time over his words, like a mole, but at the same time he has dug out passageways underground for the whole century ahead."[27] Cubism and general experimentation in painting undoubtedly influenced the Cubo-Futurists. However, Khlebnikov perceived the roots of this influence in folklore, and said that it was "Russian grandstanding, always hankering for its rights."[28]

A bit of a mathematical education had given Khlebnikov the idea of uniting verbal creativity with mathematics: "Wouldn't both the resourceful Euclid and Lobachevsky name the eleven imperishable verities of the root [*sic!*] of the Russian language? After all, in words they will see only traces of slavery to birth and death."[29] Leaving aside the surprising illiteracy, it is difficult anyway to find in these thoughts scientific seriousness of any kind.

But Khlebnikov's "newspeak" (*novorech*) inspires further search and experiment with language. He plays with words like a juggler of the highest order. For him an author is a "wordster" (*slovach*), a critic a "wiseyjudge" (*sudri-mudri*), a poet a "skydreamer" (*nebogryoz*) or a "song'n" (*pesnil'*), literature "writese" (*pis'mesa*). An actor is a "playist" or "playess" (*igrets* or *igritsa*) or even "temperaman" (*oblikmen*). The theater is "plaity" (*igrava*) and the cast is "peoplist" (*lyudnyak*), a performance is a "spectatery" (*sozertsinya*), a drama is a "talkety" (*govoryana*), a comedy a "jokety" (*shutynya*), an opera is a "voicety" (*golosynya*), a slice-of-life play (or soap-opera) a "lifoon" (*zhiznukha*).

I'll risk using some of these *Khlebnikovisms* transformed into English: *Yesterday I went to the plaity. They were putting on the talkety The Three Sisters by the wordster Chekhov, that wonderful writese master and fine song'n. The wiseyjudges remarked in their reviews that the peoplist put on an inspired spectatery. The temperamen and* (it's easy to fall into the teacher's method) *temperawomen unveiled a new interpretary* (*tolkovalka,* vice the old-style "treatment," *traktovka*) *by a stagedon* (*stsenoboss*) *or stagechief* (*stsenokhoz*—i.e., director, *rezhissyor*) *who feels the full skydreamerness of this lifoon.*

This is how it sounds three-quarters of a century later. Probably the time hadn't come to bring into being a language like that, and maybe will never come. We should try to continue the experiment, though, whenever the inspiration strikes. But that's just a start. Khlebnikov called into creation a "language of thought" and a "common" or "universal" language.

What are the results of the fight of the "classical myth-maker" Khlebnikov against poetic canons? Mayakovsky very precisely appraised Khlebnikov thus: he had a hundred readers in all, fifty of whom called him a compulsive scribbler, forty who read and were surprised that nothing came of it, and only ten who loved this Columbus of new poetic languages.[30] Yefim Etkind considered that "Khlebnikov's ideas have turned out to be richer than his works."[31] And here's the opinion of Aleksandr Zholkovsky: "Despite Khlebnikov's genius—but maybe precisely because of its scale and extremism—this attempt, Utopian, 'graphomanic,' has never yet met with success, even in its conception."[32]

His "Swandom of the Future" (*Lebednya budushchego*) was a state of poets and scientists, the Chairmen of the Globe, in which world harmony would be made manifest. In 1917 he and Petnikov called themselves the Government of the Globe. Together the two of them issued The Proclamation of the Chairmen of the Globe. Grigory Petnikov, a comrade-in-arms of Aleksey Gastev's, lived on into the epoch of "developed socialism."

I remember meeting with Petnikov in the Crimea in the 1960s, where he was living, having become, from age and circumstance, a correct Soviet poet. The wheel had ground him down, and to stay out of harm's way he had had to forget the sins of his youth. 1994 was the one-hundredth year since Petnikov's birth. A famous photograph of Khlebnikov (take a look, for instance, at the Shorter Literary Encyclopedia, *Kratkaya literaturnaya entsiklopediya*) in reality was shamelessly cut out of a photo of him together with Petnikov.

Khlebnikov and Petnikov tried to get Mayakovsky, Burlyuk, and Gorky to sign their proclamation, but they obviously sensed its over-the-top nature and kept their distance. And a year before that, Khlebnikov had written about himself alone: "I have gradually become chief of the globe." But later on he became more democratic, releasing the world from his dictatorship. On January 13, 1922, half a year before his death, the boss all by himself issued an "Order from the Chairmen of the Globe," which he ended with the words, "It's boring on this earth." And signed it "Velimir the First."[33]

It wasn't just for him alone that the October Revolution came along in its guise of death. But it's as if he saw it coming. He got his freedom by a costly route. Isn't this the essence of his mysterious testament, never fulfilled: "Let them read on my headstone: he wrestled with Form and lost his footing."[34] In 1920 he attended a performance of his play *A Mistake of Death* in Rostov-on-Don. In the play is a delirious dance by twelve dead men.

In contrast with Petnikov or Gorodetsky, Khlebnikov in dying remained the man he wanted to be. Had he lived further what would they have done to him? But he died and outfoxed both Agitprop and the Lubyanka. They couldn't tolerate that, so Khlebnikov's brilliant chaos was begun to be put in the order necessary for Soviet literary scholarship.

4. Posthumous games

Even after his death the fate of his works failed to be any luckier. Even Mayakovsky, who had earlier defended him, hearing of Yuri Tynyanov's and Nikolay Stepanov's intention to publish the complete collected works of Khlebnikov, jealously exclaimed, "Paper to the living!" In the 1950s Stepanov sadly related this to us, his loyal students. How painfully familiar this is in a Russian context: to share a place in Parnassus, that's all right—but to share paper, not on your life!

By all the rules, the "Utopian cosmist," "createman" (*tvoryanin*), this what-wouldn't-he-get-up-to-next poet disapproving of technology and progress, this Khlebnikov had to be rejected by socialist realism. But, in contrast to many more conformist writers, he was never subject to ostracism. I think there are two reasons for that: he hymned, however chaotically, future universal brotherhood (and there were never enough such thoughts on that mythology around), and he died young.

"We think too little about Khlebnikov as a Soviet poet," wrote Dmitry Mirsky, "even though Khlebnikov is one of the brightest examples of the enormous, fruitful influence of the October Revolution on the creative development of a great poet."[35] We have to be careful responding to the raptures of this famous literary scholar. An émigré who became a member of the British Communist Party and then a returnee to the U.S.S.R. who vanished into the labor camps, he was often contradictory in his appraisals. But such a point of view is one almost learned by rote. I would say that, to the contrary, the October Revolution consumed the poet as raw material for its own purposes.

Khlebnikov was made to fit into socialist realism in predictable ways; for instance, they often quoted his poems "The language of love rushes round the world" and "The wars have spit out your eyes" with a commentary added on, as if it were Khlebnikov's own: "Love is the essence of revolution, war the essence of the old world."[36] But even reputable academics understood that there was no other way to save the legacy of the poet from the authorities.

That he was never trampled underfoot was due to the contribution of his more-organized acquaintances: Vladimir Mayakovsky, Nikolay Aseyev, Boris Pasternak, and literary scholars devoted to the cause, foremost among them Yuri Tynyanov and Nikolay Stepanov. The politically naive Khlebnikov could have been preserved in only one way: presenting him as a fighter for the proletarian cause. That's even what Stepanov wrote: his works "express Khlebnikov's steadfast faith in the righteousness of the Revolution." Once long ago I asked an old writer-*cum*-ex-prisoner (*zek*) "Why did you voluntarily shout 'Glory be to Stalin!' even in the labor camps?" The *zek* answered: "Well, you see, at that time it was like crossing yourself when you pass by a church."

"Khlebnikov without vacillation connected his fate with that of the Revolution; it became his basic theme, the main content of his work," Stepanov declaimed.[37] And that was like crossing himself. Today we're getting more patient with that kind of remark. After all, with this wittingly-trite garnish they managed to publish many of his pieces, although of course far from all of them and not always. For instance Stepanov paraphrases Khlebnikov, in whose works "war is followed by its companions, famine, ruin, typhus."[38] It was palatable only when smothered in First World War sauce. But Khlebnikov had a different war in mind, of course: the civil war. Who started that one? Shouldn't it be clear to the reader that the famine, the ruin, and the typhus were brought on by the Bolsheviks?

Khlebnikov was Stepanov's weakness. In a time that was difficult for literature, he preserved a part of Khlebnikov's opus. While his student, I visited Professor Stepanov's home. His slightly retarded son Aleksey studied at the university with us. They lived on the Khoroshevskoye highway on the Begovaya Street corner. Their apartment didn't have a single bare wall: in the corridors, in the kitchen, even in the toilet, there were bookshelves from floor to ceiling. Stepanov's book on Khlebnikov, that he'd been writing almost his entire life, was published after Stepanov's death in a catastrophically abridged version (M. P. Yeremin was the editor), and I don't know if his manuscript has been preserved.

They tried to adapt Khlebnikov's "new mythology" and the man himself to the advantage of socialism. Khlebnikov's disapproval of Western civilization and his glorification of the providential role of Russia in unifying West and East, for instance, were stressed.[39] It has been written many times that the poet predicted the major successes of the Soviet state in 1922, when the New Economic Policy began, but these successes didn't touch Khlebnikov himself.

In the official local-history literature, as usual, they have begun to clean up the image of the poet: it turns out that he arrived at the village on an educational mission to work as a teacher, and died in hospital under doctors' supervision.[40] In another work, the myth of the paternal concern of the Soviet state began to sound even weightier: "Every possible measure undertaken by Anatoly Lunacharsky and the poet's friends could not save the sick man."[41]

5. "The Stone Woman"

Somehow we've managed to forget that the cult of death came to Russia with the Bolsheviks: "And as one we shall die in the battle for it." An admirable task, but if everybody dies, who is going to live in the bright tomorrow? Nonetheless Lenin ordered that the clock on the Kremlin's Spasskaya tower regularly play a funeral march, and every day took a walk to this music around the grave of Inessa Armand, his mistress, who for some reason had been buried in a pit together with the enthusiastic American John Reed. Could the reason have been to keep Lenin's wife Nadezhda Krupskaya from being jealous?

The new regime quickly made clear that it was easier to manipulate the dead. Lenin couldn't have suspected that his perishable body would never be buried at all; that, with its entrails drawn, they would periodically spruce it up and change its clothes, so that the leader could continue working for the new state. A campaign began to demolish traditional graveyards and transfer the remains of appropriate people to the capital.

In 1924, for rather understandable reasons, they decided to rebury Karl Marx, reposing in London, alongside Lenin. The Soviet government set aside half a million dollars for a memorial to Marx, despite the catastrophic conditions in the country. The issue seemed decided, but the grandson of the founding-proposer of Communist dogma categorically refused to give permission to transfer the remains of his famous grandfather to Moscow, and even declared that the reason for it was the Soviet leaders' betrayal of Marxism.

They tell me that reburial is accepted in all civilized countries, and there are no unified rules. I not only agree with that, but will give you examples myself. Mikhail Lermontov's grandmother, having received permission from the authorities, sent her serfs to the Caucasus to dig up her dead grandson and bring the coffin back to Tarkhany. I went down into the crypt in order to touch that coffin, and went to Pyatigorsk, where a monument stands in place of the original grave. Vasily Zhukovsky and Anton Chekhov died in Germany and were both conveyed home in accordance with their wishes. Zhukovsky is buried in the Alexander Nevsky monastery alongside Karamzin, and Chekhov is now at Novodevichy cemetery. It has happened that people's bodies have been divided up according to their wills: Chopin is buried at the Père Lachaise Cemetery in Paris, but his heart is immured in the Holy Cross Church in Warsaw.

In the 1930s a mania for the reburial of the remains of great people became a part of the Soviet government plan of monumental propaganda. In essence this campaign recalls the collectivization of agriculture, this time borrowed from the plot of Nikolay Gogol's *Dead Souls*. Instead of bringing order to cemeteries many of them were ruined, but Novodevichy, the lucky one, was enlarged and made into a showplace.

Gogol's remains were dragged out of the Danilov monastery to Novodevichy, where they built him a memorial with the inscription "From the Government of the Soviet Union." From other Moscow cemeteries they transferred the bones of Sergey Aksakov and Anton Chekhov. Then the painters Valentin Serov and Isaak Levitan, Maria Yermolova and other famous painters and actors who had not been buried where the new authorities wanted were moved there, heroes and twice-over heroes like the mythologized Zoya Kosmodemyanskaya.[42]

Remains got shifted according to rank, destroying the graves of their ideological enemies in the process. Mayakovsky's brain was removed for study, of which the newspapers wrote with pride. I saw it in a jar full of formalin at the Brain Institute, and it appears to have been preserved there to the present day. The urn with Mayakovsky's ashes, formerly located at the Donskoy crematorium, was transferred and reinterred in Novodevichy. They even reburied Mikhail Bulgakov. As for Sergey Esenin, he was kept at Vagankovskoye cemetery, because he was a drunk and a hooligan.

In 1964 Soviet agents stole the remains of the famous Latvian conductor T. Reiters, who died in 1956 and was buried near Stockholm. Reiters had emigrated, but the authorities decided to turn the dead émigré into a Soviet musician, and the Swedish authorities failed to notice the operation. A methodical processing of the relatives of distinguished émigrés was carried out by Soviet diplomats. In 1966 they succeeded in digging up in England and reburying in Novodevichy the remains of the poet Nikolay Ogaryov, who had only gotten out of the country with great difficulty. Then the relatives of Fyodor Shalyapin gave up, and as a Soviet newspaper wrote, "the municipality of Paris rendered assistance in the transfer of the remains of Fyodor Shalyapin from the Parisian cemetery of Batignole to the U.S.S.R."[43]

I remember a Soviet ambassador to France recalling in his memoirs how much effort had been spent in chasing down Alexander Herzen's heirs, while they, unaware of their social obligations, were of no help at all. In 1970 the hundredth anniversary of the death of that writer was observed, and it was eminently desirable that the great émigré return to his motherland by this anniversary and, *de facto*, recognize the lack of necessity for "external" publishing, and thereby stem the massive brain drain. But Herzen remained in Nice.

Probably émigrés visiting graves in Russia have their own opinion of reinterment, especially from one country to another, and I will be grateful for their comments. I'll only repeat a Russian folk saying: "They don't take the dead from the churchyard" (*mertvykh s pogosta ne nosyat*).

I know Novodevichy well from my childhood: I went to school next to it, and several of my friends lived in the monastery buildings. A lot of names from the cultural heritage of Russia entered my memory from those cemetery inscriptions. From the monastery there was unrestricted access to the new cemetery, the architectural center of which from 1932 became the grave of Stalin's wife Nadezhda Alliluyeva, and they chose worthy surroundings for her. In the middle of August, 1960, according to the official version, Khlebnikov's remains were taken to Moscow and reinterred at Novodevichy cemetery.

I saw Khlebnikov's grave more than once. According to the inscription, his mother, Yekaterina Khlebnikova, his sister, Vera, and Vera's husband, Pyotr Miturich, were all buried in it with him.

But now let's return to the Ruchyi churchyard, to the putative former grave of Khlebnikov. As it happens, it's not the former at all, but the real one, and it's finally time to tell the truth. The locals attest that the people who came to Ruchyi churchyard for his remains opened not Khlebnikov's grave but a neighboring one, of someone unknown. And they dug it up catch-as-catch-can—shallow as it was, in a rush, nervously, afraid of protests from the locals—threw something into a box, and then left. It can't be excluded that the locals deceived them on purpose, so that visitors wouldn't pester their guest in his grave, the man who had died here in suffering.

Aleksandra Srodnikova vigilantly kept watch so that nobody would touch Khlebnikov's grave. She firmly declared to us:

"They dug around it, but I showed up at the grave every day and saw that the grave was right as rain."

"Maybe they dug it up secretly at night?"

"No, I sleep lightly at night, nobody passed the house, nobody was hanging around the cemetery. They dug up something, found a button and a bone, took a handful of dirt, and put it all under the stone at Novodevichy in Moscow."

Yevdokiya Stepanova (with the same surname as Khlebnikov's famous biographer) had testified to the same thing before this:

"They didn't dig in the place of the grave, the real one was next to it, whole, untouched, God help him."

Sometime later I received a letter from the local historian, Pavel Gurchonok, which I necessarily cite in its entirety:

> I didn't relate some information of interest to you about the grave of Velimir Khlebnikov for the reason that to the present time we still haven't been able to edit the audio recording of conversations with the long-lived Yevdokiya Stepanova, made at her apartment and right at the poet's grave.
>
> In these recordings she categorically challenges the version of the opening of Khlebnikov's grave and his reburial in Moscow. The grave, in her words, is unviolated, and the mistake came about due to the ignorance of a certain greedy man. When the recording is at our museum I will be able to raise the issue of restoring the grave to a condition worthy of the poet's memory before the regional executive committee.
>
> During that time I met with Vasily Miturich, the son of Pyotr Miturich [*a child of his first marriage; he was living with his mother in the village when Khlebnikov died—Y.D.*], who also holds with the conviction of the truthfulness of the long-lived woman's words ... It turns out that Velimir Khlebnikov's reinterral at Novodevichy cemetery in Moscow was purely symbolic.[44]

This letter is very important as documentary evidence. Everything is understandable in it except for the "greedy man." Who was that, and why was he greedy? I think that what we have here is a family conflict that still hasn't healed over up to the present, first between the two wives, and then between the children of the two wives as well, and neither this conflict nor the remains of the poet should be stirred up.

There was one remaining person who could clear up the mystery: the son of Pyotr Miturich and Vera Khlebnikova—May Miturich. I almost found him in Moscow, but it turned out that he had gone to Japan for an extended period. I finally found him only from California, by telephone. This is what he had to say:

> The Literary Foundation of the U.S.S.R. was informed by the relevant authorities that a place had been set aside for Velimir Khlebnikov at Novodevichy cemetery. I personally transferred his remains. The first time, my nephew and I and a friend—the painter Pavel Zakharov, who had a car—drove to Santalovo on a reconnaissance, in order to clarify the situation and speak to the local people. The second time, two years later, three of us again went there to dig him up.

"And who did the digging?"

"We did the digging ourselves and left right away."

Miturich interestingly told about his job: he was a graphic artist like his father, who now did oil-paintings, since books were put together nowadays with as little input from artists as possible.

So here you are, folks: no documents, commissions, records from the opening of the grave, experts—no historian, archaeologist, criminologist, not even an impoverished representative of the local authority—nothing! And this, after all, isn't ancient times—this is August, 1960.

"On Khlebnikov's headstone," I went on asking Miturich, "in Novodevichy monastery, there are four names, aren't there?"

> Grandmother's there, that is, Velimir's mother, who died in 1936, and my mother Vera, that is, Khlebnikov's sister, who passed on before the war in 1941. The urn was at my place in a cupboard. I transferred my grandmother's and my mother's remains to the same grave, but I don't remember when. My father, as he had written in his will, wanted to lie 'at Velimir's feet.' So I reinterred his remains in the new grave, too.

"And who made Khlebnikov's memorial at Novodevichy?"

"I made that myself, too."

I decided to publish this conversation only to bring out the truth, and not in the least to reproach the artist, the poet's nephew May Miturich. On the contrary, I want to stress that it is only through the enthusiasm of individuals that Russian cultural values have been preserved, especially during the Soviet epoch.

The Mituriches—father and son—saved part of Khlebnikov's opus. The father left the manuscripts to his son, and the son kept them at his place after his father's death in 1956, and only in 1963 decided to give them to the Russian State Archives of Literature and Art. It's not the younger Miturich's fault that no commission was ever created, or if it had been created, only on paper. To have done everything lawfully and, so to speak, scientifically, wouldn't have been difficult. As it was said before, the grave was shallow, undisturbed, in the woods. But who in the Writers' Union would have had an inclination to head off to the backwoods, all the more so when Khlebnikov hadn't even been a member of that union?

So the Soviet regime did trample down the dead poet underneath it, using him like a paving stone. For Khlebnikov himself, a person with a universal language, Chairman of the Globe and Citizen of the Universe, who seemed like an ancient

Greek wise man to Mayakovsky and who considered himself living in the unknown future—the location of his grave would probably be unimportant. It's important for *us* to know the truth.

So at Novodevichy in Moscow in Khlebnikov's grave his relatives have been laid: his mother, his sister, his sister's husband—obviously, with time there will be more still. I myself am for family plots, but the tragicomic aspect lies in that the poet himself is nowhere to be found in the prestigious cemetery. And the inscription should read: "Here lie not the remains of Velimir Khlebnikov."

It's strange, anyway. Could you imagine that in Pushkin's grave, in the ground that he had purchased for himself when he buried his mother, the remains of his brother Lev would be reinterred from its burial place in Odessa (where the cemetery has been destroyed and on its territory erected a monument to Lenin with its hand in supplication extended to the West), the remains of his sister Olga, and then even her husband, Pavlishchev?

I have already had occasion to write elsewhere that the poet Alexander Griboyedov is in all probability not in his grave in Tbilisi. I won't go into the details here. Pushkin wrote how he met the coffin carrying Griboyedov's body during his trip to Erzerum (if it wasn't just a literary fantasy of the poet's). They were bringing a body in a coffin from Teheran that was supposed to be Griboyedov's, which in reality had never been found, bringing it in order to smooth over a dispute with the Russian government. So alongside Nina Chavchavadze, Griboyedov's wife, lies some Persian fanatic or criminal, possibly even her husband's murderer. But there were mitigating circumstances there.

Millions of Russian people who have died in our century don't have graves at all. And it seems that in this sense Khlebnikov has been awarded a special honor: the one poet has two graves. I hope that no adroit enthusiasts will use these lines to finish the job of reinterring his remains. Enough! The true grave should be looked after, taken care of, and the Novodevichy one should be known just as a memorial.

> My eyes amble, like autumn,
> Over faces' strange fields,
> But I want to tell you, hubs of the world,
> "We won't 'low it!"

As a teenager, composing my attempts at poetry, I would recite whole pages of Khlebnikov, and now, half a century later, I still want to quote him, even the lines that I don't understand, in the hope that maybe someday I'll get them.

Not long ago I was standing at Khlebnikov's gravestone in Novodevichy with its sullen limestone woman and, instinctively glancing around, recited some lines of the poet. In the poem "Night in the Trench" the image of this stone woman appears, standing out on the steppes like a harbinger of new, heavy ordeals, of approaching unhappiness, grief, and death:

> Vacant is the animal face
> Of the steppe goddess ...
> "Tell me, bleak limestone,
> "Whose turn is coming after war?"
> "Typhus! ...
> When that lady shows up,
> Next day the dead will not be numbered..."[45]

You shudder from the way the poet sounds in tune with modern times; you realize that Khlebnikov was yet another unnumbered sacrifice of the October Revolution. And that that was the "stone woman" who starved and sickened him, humiliated him, even changed the spelling of his name and surname (both contained letters banished in the new post-Revolutionary Russian orthography), infected him with diseases, and murdered him.

Nobody who allowed the monument to be raised to him understood this idea, and May Miturich, who made it, explained it as having something to do with archaeology. He pulled the Soviet regime's chain with this archaeology business: he broke away from their myth, composed on the bones of Khlebnikov. The poet, buried in the Ruchyi churchyard and undisturbed, was unaware that in Moscow the myth that he had composed had become reality on his mythical grave. Above the gravestone May Miturich had placed a real "prehistoric" stone woman found by archaeologists at the lake of Issyk-Kul. You scrutinize that phantasmagorical image of horror and death, overthrown by a still-more-terrible force, and the "stone woman" scrutinizes you back with her cold eyes. Uncanny!

It's uncanny as well in that Khlebnikov not only has two graves, but also two birthplaces. According to some data, it was the village of Tundutovo, according to other, Maliye Derbety in the former Astrakhan province. Not one of the many authors writing about him in the Twenties and Thirties managed simply to ask his mother, Yekaterina Khlebnikova, where she bore him—after all, the woman would be unlikely to forget that. She died fourteen years after her son.

So, let us clarify at least one fact for the one-hundred-tenth anniversary of his birthday: his remains do not lie in his official grave. And an unknown inhabitant of Santalovo or Ruchyi was lucky: he (or she?) reposes in elite Novodevichy, although not under a name they would know.

Trifonov's Fate;
or, A Good Writer in a Bad Time

1. Two ways to get abroad

Four writers by the name of Trifonov were listed in the Soviet Writers' Union: Vladimir, Georgy, Nikolay, and Yuri. But it is obvious which of them is the subject here: of course, without any doubt, the last one on the list.

It is not yet time (some of the participants still being alive) to touch upon the intimate sides of Yuri Valentinovich Trifonov's life, and I will not do that. A lot has been written about him, both analysis and memoir, and dissertations defended. But, at the same time, certain danger zones get skirted round.

These are not Aesop-like understatements of his published works, or hidden-from-the-evil-eye-till-the-time-comes manuscripts, or secret aspects of his biography. Everything in that regard is more than just in order. The press establishment at its boiling point, rattling the lid of *glasnost*, got more out of his texts than he probably thought he was putting into them in those times. His widow, the Heritage Commission, and the State Literary Archive have published almost everything. But some space on his territory, as I see it from a distance, is still fenced in, and entrance to it prohibited thus far.

At the beginning of summer of 1977, two organizations secretly connected with each other sought out Yuri Trifonov and me, and found us with no difficulty. He was phoned up by the foreign committee of the Writers' Union, and I by the KGB. When I dazedly asked "Who? Who?" a hearty voice eagerly spelled it out for me: "The Committee for State Security."

We were both at our places in the country. Trifonov was at his *dacha* in Krasnaya Pakhra; I was renting part of a house in the village of Anosino, on the Istra River, not far from Krasnovidovo, where a new country-house cooperative for writers was being built, secured through high influence with the Council of Ministers. The first payment had been made. It stank of the huge bribes that had to be paid to the leaders of the Literary Fund in order to get to the head of the line. But since my official position soon shriveled to nothing, my money was for naught.

I ran into Trifonov in a passageway between the old and the new wings of the Central Writers' House. He was in his invariable imported black leather jacket and turtle-necked sweater (literary uniform for those years). He liked to be there in the afternoon, to have lunch with the staff officials, hear the news. This time he was in a rush.

"They badgered me," he said, sullen, almost gloomy. "I have to go to America."

"Twisted your arm, eh?" I said sarcastically.

Trifonov laughed jerkily, screwing up his large, puffy lips. It was obvious that the news had aroused him. He was coming from the foreign committee. The old, crowded wing, the one on Vorovsky Street, was crammed with safes and people with expressionless faces. Personnel there established international connections (and still do) and went abroad now and again, led by the secretaries of the Writers' Union, which would get chronicled in *Literaturnaya gazeta*: "For the development of contacts between literatures, So-and-so visited Such-and-such country."

At the foreign committee, Trifonov had been informed that Kansas State University had invited him to give a series of lectures on Soviet literature. All expenses were to be paid. Not without irony, Trifonov told me that the issue had been hanging fire for a long time in the "heavenly spheres." It had been looked over by the secretariat, which had proposed sending a group of worthies including the secretary and members of the administration to the university in Kansas. Kansas refused and demanded their one particular writer. Now the foreign committee had been allowed to start the paperwork, and he had been summoned up from his *dacha*. They could not relate this secret information to him over the telephone.

Trifonov had begun the Soviet-era pre-departure routine: a medical, character references, commissions, his district committee.

"Since they've offered it to you, it's probably already been arranged," I supposed.

"Nevertheless, you never know till the very last day," Trifonov contradicted.

This was the normal, sometimes Jesuitical, boorishness of the administration.

They rang me up when I came to Moscow for a short while, before my trip to Rostov-on-Don to a playwrights' conference. I refused to meet and "converse" with them. They said that they would "pick me up" in front of everybody at the Writers' Union, and that would be even worse for me. They phoned me several times, and then sent a notification "to appear in connection with the conduct of an administrative investigation." They were trying to intimidate me, asking me which writers I was keeping in contact with. I avoided answering. Names were "produced." Trifonov was not on their list, something that I mentioned to him as well as to all my other acquaintances, who was and who was not on the list. I wanted the greatest number of people to know about it.

Things were going badly for me. In a review of magazine prose, the newspaper *Izvestiya* accused me of distorting the images of real Soviet people.[1] Immediately after that, the *Sovetsky pisatel'* publishing house struck my already-accepted material off their plans. *Sovietskaya Rossiya* and *Moskovsky rabochy* did the same. The Ministry of Culture made out that the main character of my comedy was an alcoholic, and came to a corresponding conclusion. Trifonov listened to me carefully, sympathizing, but did not offer any advice. Tact and outward composure were indispensable qualities of his.

We came out of the Writers' House together. The steward, Shapiro, the shortish and fattish little Cerberus on duty at the entrance, followed us with his eyes. The next time Shapiro saw me, I had been already been expelled from the Writers' Union, and he would not let me in anymore. "And who exactly are you?" he would ask writers, but would let the managers of vegetable distribution centers in without a murmur. Once Anatoly Markusha, a writer and the former pilot, grabbed Shapiro by the lapels and lifted him off his feet: "If you're not going to know writers on sight, I'm going to paste you to the wall." After that Markusha ranked among the leadership in Shapiro's mind, and at his appearance the steward would rise up on tiptoe and bow.

In short, in connection with Trifonov's departure, he was summoned to the Central Committee of the party, and I was summoned to the KGB. Coming out of the place, I realized that I was experiencing a sea change. Herzen talked about the condition of external slavery and internal liberation. But external slavery had also become repellent. Walking down to Kuznetsky Most Street, I reserved a telephone call to America, and then asked them to send me an invitation. Then we both had invitations to American universities and publishers. But Trifonov left for America, and I remained, a refusenik.

I recall now that we became friends in the period when he was turning from a famous writer into a good one. His prize-winning work of social realism, *The Students*, and his stories and essays about Soviet sport, were all behind him. His latent protest was ripening, and had only just poured out in *The Exchange*. Intellectuals had begun reading Trifonov.

At this moment I was rounding off my career as a journalist. Working on a newspaper had become unbearable: prohibitions and intimidation dried up your soul; lies, printed and spoken, poisoned your mind; it was shameful to see what was published. Hopelessly but stubbornly I continued to write for myself. In January 1969, I was sitting in the writers' retreat in Dubulty. For two weeks I had been dictating my story "The Gray Folder" onto an old reel-to-reel tape recorder, a story about a *Samizdat* that gets slipped onto a newspaper editor's desk. Later it became part of the novel *Angels on the Head of a Pin*—the invasion of Czechoslovakia overshadowed everything after that.

On December 11, 1969, *Moskovsky komsomolets*, which had already been known under a couple of different names (it is probably time to change again now), was getting ready to celebrate its 50th anniversary. Without a jubilee celebration, neither honors nor monetary awards could be obtained in those days, but the main thing was that the celebration was insurance against getting done in. For this 50th anniversary the newspaper had been awarded the Order of Merit. Later on, Trifonov was asked to fill out forms in advance of awards for his own 50th birthday, and the Order of Honor decorated his own breast.

But, for a while, the editors would call to mind everyone who had become anybody and who was in one way or another connected with the newspaper, writers first and foremost, of course. Those guilty of disloyalty were struck off the list at once, and the positive ones were all sent invitations.

First on the list was Mikhail Sholokhov, who had been published in the paper under the pen-name of Sholokh. They found the staffer who had taught the young member of Komsomol League Sholokhov to read and write. This turned out to be the poet Aleksandr Zharov. The wife of an editor was entrusted with getting, by whatever means, Sholokhov's congratulations on the newspaper's jubilee. The classic author was apparently on a bender, but a telegram over his name was published by the newspaper. It went: "I warmly salute your ageless youth. M. Sholokhov." This artistic text was authored by Boris Yoffe, a talented, underrated sort of man, who could do everything at the newspaper. "Implementing" the list, Yoffe rang up his old friend Yuri Trifonov (half of the people in the Moscow cultural scene were friends of Yoffe's).

They spoke for a bit, after which Yoffe wrapped up their live dialogue in officialese, writing two paragraphs and headlining it "Yuri Trifonov, State Prize Laureate." Yoffe read his composition to the "author" over the telephone, and Trifonov approved it. According to the text, the writer said: "We all came out of *Moskovsky komsomolets*." He recalls how he received his first article assignment from the editors. He wishes "that the newspaper as always will never soften its stand."[2]

"We won't give up!" rumbled Yoffe, putting a full stop on it. "How can you give up what you don't have?"

The text of his congratulations, however, did not make it into the newspaper itself. The rank of the other congratulators turned out to be higher than his. But on the day of the anniversary, they published a special issue, something like a wartime bulletin, in half-page format—for internal use, lavishly illustrated. Appeals "to serve Lenin's party tirelessly, to bring up youth in the spirit of selfless devotion to the ideals of Marxism-Leninism" and other deep thoughts were printed in the boldest type. The bulletin was passed out to the guests gathered in the conference hall, who then moved to the foyer for the banquet.

And who was not there in that crowd! Newspapermen, fiction writers, *apparatchiks*, actors, hockey players... In my whole life I have never seen a noisier drinking bout. We were drinking on windowsills, blathering in the offices, on the stairs, in the toilets. The chandeliers were wreathed in blue-gray smoke. Everyone was slipping one another copies of the paper to autograph as souvenirs. Here it is, lying in front of me, covered with the joking comments and signatures of my colleagues. This is the one I quote Trifonov from.

Yoffe brought him, stunned by the uproar, into his cubbyhole. I had not seen him since his discussion of *The Students* with us at my pedagogical institute—Trifonov had changed a lot in the intervening fifteen years, had gotten respectable. Right away we discovered we had close friends in common, the Litinskys; both of us had been upset by their incarceration. In those days we did not hold our tongues, but cursed everything and everyone almost openly. Trifonov looked over both his shoulders, his thick-lensed glasses magnifying his eyes, and from time to time laughed jerkily and somewhat artificially.

We left together. In those days I had an oldish Moskvich, and I gave Trifonov a ride home (we lived near each other on the Peschaniye Streets). I remember I called him *maêtre,* and he did not mind. I was confused by his lack of curiosity, a characteristic of shy people. It has always seemed to me, and now I am positive, that a man of letters has to be a sponge. Without any intake of information, of whatever kind, the mind dries up. With nothing but your own experiences, you get into a rut. Trifonov would answer questions, but himself asked few, which made dialogues with him very one-sided. He would come to life if the conversation touched upon his own things. He showed up at the newspaper offices when he needed to help someone with their publication. His coworkers' attitude towards him was a pious one. If he was mentioned in critical articles, it was only with the kindest of epithets.

I do not know anyone with whom he was on familiar terms. Practical jokes, role-playing, making fun of someone, were all alien to him, and would be stifled in his presence. Distance always arose between him and others. He was egotistical in his friendships, and that does not appeal to everyone. Right here I would like to make the proviso that I am writing about this (and everything else about him) without the slightest disapproval—quite the contrary: with respect for the autonomy of his lifestyle, character, and position—for everything.

By an irony of fate, in those very days when Trifonov was lecturing in America, I was being secretly expelled from the Writers' Union. My years of ostracism had begun. After his return from America, he politely inquired about my situation.

My situation was primitively simple: I would not be published in Russia, I would not be allowed to leave, and for publishing in the West, I was threatened with prison camp and loony bin. I was washing my car in my yard in order to sell it: I had nothing to live on. He stood, looking at me.

"The time of mass murders has passed," I said. "But the desecration of human dignity remains."

"That is so," he mouthed. "But it's hard over there, too. After all, I've traveled a lot."

"Worse than here?" I asked.

He did not answer.

His probity and ability to keep his silence were without any doubt. I gave him my first draft of *Angels on the Head of a Pin*, finished in 1976. He said some nice words, but wrote no notes on the margins, as we usually did for each other, although I had asked him to be hard on it: it was dangerous to leave any traces. We discussed plot twists and turns for a long time. He came to life, asking which newspaperman was disguised under this name, who under that. It turned out that he was reading it with amazing attention. His verdict was categorical.

"A death-defying act. This will never get published."

"Sofya Vlasyevna's skirt is hiked up too high?" I said, referring to the regime—*Sovietskaya vlast'* in Russian—in the dissidents' satirical personification.

He burst into whinnying laughter.

"This is another dimension entirely. It's beyond the capabilities of even clever editors," he said.

We were playing at a kind of politeness, as if nothing had happened. But something had happened. The whole thing was much more serious than it seems now. Our paths, after crossing so many times, diverged. They began to grow in opposite directions, despite personal sympathy and friends preserved in common.

On one occasion, trying to improve my decrepit health, I was running a third circuit around the children's park surrounding "Vasya," and overtook Trifonov, who was walking slowly. In the Peschany Streets district, "Vasya" was the name of the abandoned foundations of a house for general Vasily Stalin, in which it was planned to set up an indoor skating rink where his favorite hockey team, Central club of the Soviet army, could practice. A quarter of a century later, the foundations were blown up and they began the erection of a cultural recreation center for the secret Krasnoye Znamya rocket works.

Shaking Trifonov's hand, I jogged alongside him for a bit, to catch my breath.

"I should do that, too," he said, as if apologizing.

"You should swim," I contradicted him.

"Now I'll be going abroad on a trip, and in summer I'll do calisthenics at my *dacha*."

I guffawed.

"What?" he took offense.

"I meant you should go by boat. Any time we meet, you're going abroad. But me?"

"Really, that is strange..."

We spoke for about ten minutes. He did not ask about anything, and it seemed to me that he was being wary. I remember one detail. At this time, a literary workshop gathered regularly at my home. We would discuss unpublished works and *Samizdat*, even arrange concerts. I invited Trifonov.

"But these are refuseniks," he said. "Local culture and interests..."

"It's Russian culture," I amplified. "But unofficial."

He looked around, then stretched his hand out in parting.

The last time I saw him, a friend and I ran into him in the "Leningrad" cinema, not far from my home. I have always been interested in people who go to the movies by themselves. Would they not need to chat before and after it? He seemed unhealthy and pinched-looking, he'd aged, he drooped and walked slowly. At the end of March 1981, via our common friend Grigory Litinsky, the old jailbird and drama scholar, I heard that Trifonov had gone into the hospital for some tests, even though he should have had them done considerably earlier.

They operated on him right away, removing a kidney. The operation was done by a surgeon who wrote a thing or two in his spare time, who wanted very much to be ranked as a writer. People this surgeon had operated on had helped him get published. It is not clear which was his hobby, literature or medicine. They say that Anton Chekhov was a very mediocre doctor. This doctor was a mediocrity in both spheres. In the morning Litinsky called me up, and, falling silent, finally said, "Trifonov is dead." Blood clot; heart failure.

And here was the official funeral at the Writers' Union. The atmosphere was tense along the approaches to the Central Writers' House. Besides the special-division policemen, indifferent young people in sheepskin coats and in athletics jackets were strolling here and there. Why do authorities fear dead people? Whom do they guard, against what, at funerals?

A strange and absolutely unfamiliar person lay in a red coffin, surrounded by a bunch of literary hacks, in Dubovy Hall, formerly a Masonic lodge. Possibly he did not look familiar because I had never seen him without his heavy glasses, and people do not get buried wearing their glasses—really, somehow there is no reason to bury people in glasses. A portrait of a young-looking Trifonov looked down sadly from the wall upon all that was taking place. Ushers were bustling about officiously, and the farewell line moved ahead. Then came speeches by people carefully chosen for the occasion.

I was standing towards the back, with a feeling of some sort of doom, and from the emptiness in my soul distractedly slid my gaze over the crowd. At the time, could I even have been thinking that I would get to America finally, that I was going to meet Trifonov there, ten years later, and he, normally silent, would tell me about himself? But I'll tell you about that meeting later.

2. Survival technique: payment for success

By all the logic of Soviet life in those times, Yuri Trifonov could not and should not have become a writer. People like him could be whatever you like—the obedient engineer, prison camp inmate, teacher, parasite, writer-for-others (as the case was with Ioffe)—but not members of the highest echelon of that culture that he himself called a mafia.

He spent his childhood in the most elite house in Moscow.[3] A son of an enemy of the people, managing to conceal his father's name, he entered the elite Literary Institute. The very first work by the student received the Stalin Prize. At a time when "cosmopolitans"—the standard euphemism for Jews—were being persecuted, Trifonov was celebrated.

The just-dead, hounded Andrey Platonov had been sweeping the yard of the Literary Institute, but they hung a gilded medal bearing the profile of the Great Father of All Peoples on Trifonov's breast. Mikhail Zoshchenko and Anna

Akhmatova, unpublished, sat at home in expectation of arrest, and Yuri Trifonov sat at the Presidium in expectation of stepping out onto the podium and receiving applause. Against the background of his triumph, cosmopolitans were being arrested all around.

The unmasking of Stalin? Stalin's authors are in disgrace—Trifonov comes in a winner. The ideological struggle? The writer's cousin Mikhail Demin requests political asylum in the West. He scribbles anti-Sovietisms, serves at the enemy broadcasting "Voices"—it never touches Trifonov. And later—Boris Pasternak and Vasily Grossman are both driven to their deaths. Alexander Solzhenitsyn gets shown the door. The culture looks to the West for salvation. And Trifonov gets all of his work published in this stagnant time.

One cannot disagree with the accepted point of view that few authors reflected that epoch, and Yuri Trifonov in his best and best-known works was among those few. But why were others no less talented not able to speak their minds, or spoke their minds and then paid for it with destinies blown to smithereens, and sometimes even with their lives? And even if he said something negative, he would get off with a slight fright, without any consequences. "Why were the things, even the most pessimistic things he wrote, published anyway?" American students ask me now.

And indeed—why?

Trifonov's "A Neighbor's Notes" was published in the magazine *Druzhba narodov* in 1989. It was published with a footnote: "Published for the first time in the manuscript version."[4] The footnote was strange. The fact was that "A Neighbor's Notes" (that is, his recollections of Tvardovsky), written in 1972, had been published many times, but not in the author's manuscript version, as the magazine informed us.

"Notes" had been published in part in those days, for instance, in his book *Preliminary Results*. In what other "version," then? The same version, of course. Only it was in the same way that Trifonov in that very book made sarcastic fun of other authors that he did not relate to: "distilled water percolates through ten filters."[5] Unfortunately, when they got hold of the manuscript that Trifonov had not even entrusted to a typist, the editors made their obvious cuts, accompanied by various other improvements.

Trifonov confessed: he was making, as he put it, a photograph, working at "a fresco of the lives of Russians of the Sixties" for those who "come into God's world many, many years afterwards," and right there and then amplifies, "in about a hundred years."[6] Seventeen years passed—and it was published. Although the writer-nasties are referred to alphabetically as A, B, C, D, E, F, H, J, K, M, and for some reason W, at the same time a lot is said that lifts the veil.[7] Let us take note of some details that were brought to our notice by the author himself—in credit to his sincerity.

The young Trifonov unambiguously considered that everything published in the 1940s was "non-literature."[8] He himself, entering the Literary Institute in a worker's uniform, found himself among the tight-knit clan of the chosen few who were ordained by the State to create that very same "non-literature." In order to graduate from the Literary Institute, he had to write a dissertation. He worked on it for a year and a half, sometimes 15 pages a day, ending up with 500 pages in all. He did not know its genre; he considered it now a novellette, now a novel. He did not have any title for it, but he wanted to see it published.

Konstantin Fedin, his teacher, was a member of the editorial college of *Novy Mir*. Trifonov (a proletarian from a factory, an extra-mural student) put two thick folders on his desk. Fedin either did not have time or did not want to read it. Trifonov observed: "He was in a hurry to get rid of me." But how? Fedin picked up the telephone, called Aleksandr Tvardovsky, and recommended the young author without having read him, saying: "It's an interesting read."[9]

Before that the student had taken his short stories around to different editors, but nobody had wanted even to leaf through the pages. And here, surmounting several rungs of the ladder at a stroke, Trifonov, via one lofty phone call, was being personally looked at by Tvardovsky. It was not the manuscript that did it, it was the recommendation. As for the manuscript, I would say that here the process of creation of a given unit of Soviet literary product had its inception.

Trifonov was assigned to the writer Tamara Gabbe, whose task was not so much to shorten and edit his text (his "heavy and watery prose") as to define, in the process of three months of joint labor day after day, what was still missing, what it was necessary to deepen and justify. The woman hired by the magazine was in actuality his co-author, who cleaned up every line and every word of his text, on several occasions even seeking advice from Samuil Marshak and getting instructions from the editorial offices.

After Gabbe, the magazine editors themselves took over the job and labored over the novelette for a further half-year, during which machinations Trifonov himself met the entire literary elite of those days, the circle of Stalin-Prize laureates. Tvardovsky and others let him drink with them in the next-door boozer. The young author had become one of their own.

No sooner had *The Students* been published when, as Trifonov wrote, "supreme approval came down."[10] More than that: such an emotional, artistic response to the command to struggle against rootless cosmopolitanism. Critics praised the novel unrestrainedly—such activities being concerted from the center. But I remember that there was sincere interest on the part of the readership, as well. Such alien thinking was available to very few of the chosen. Something live splashed around on the pages of the novel: the sprouts of a life maturing after the war, of hope, sentimental love, student disputes, and, of course, the undoubted talent of the young author could be seen. I remember long hours of discussion at debates in both the institutes I studied in, passionate arguments. What Trifonov himself said I did not write down; unfortunately, nothing stuck in my mind.

Today those discussions would seem childish, but this was 1950, after all.

Something ambiguous remains in the incredible fact of a student receiving the Stalin Prize for Literature. Twice I carefully asked Trifonov how it had come about. He answered that he did not know himself, that it was a mystery to him, too. In "A Neighbor's Notes" Trifonov now and again shifts from one period of time to another, and it is kind of difficult to understand the logic of events, but something does get revealed, nonetheless.

Yelizar Maltsev, a classmate and friend of Trifonov's, also the recipient of the Stalin Prize for his novel *From the Bottom of My Heart*, hinted that he had heard an opinion about *The Students*: "There are too many Jews."[11] That was a lie. In general, Trifonov had evidently generated a lot of invidious rivalry both at the Institute and in the Writers' Union. The Stalin Prize was worth a great deal in benefits, glory, insurance—and an open road.

Tvardovsky, in his cups, liked to make anti-Semitic jokes in front of Trifonov. Trifonov would say nothing; such were the times. A cosmopolitan scholar in *The*

Students by the name of Kozel'sky seems to be without any taint. But still, Trifonov thought up the surname without much care. Yakov Kozlovsky, the future poet and translator, is not the greatest person in the Soviet Parnassus, but he was a classmate and friend of Trifonov's. Together they wrote the very first article of Trifonov's life, for the newspaper *Moskovsky komsomolets*—about the factory that Trifonov had been working in before. Present-day critics call it his "first short story."

In "A Neighbor's Notes" Trifonov recalls receiving the Stalin Prize thus: at the prize-awarding committee meeting, Mikhail Bubennov said: "He's the son of an enemy of the people." Stalin asked: "Is the book any good?" And Fedin once more backed up his student: "Good." They gave (that is, Stalin himself gave, who else could have?) him third prize. Trifonov supposed that Stalin recollected his father or his uncle Yevgeny, and this "was his favorite game: for children to kiss the hand stained with their fathers' blood."[12] That kiss, however much you would disown it, provided the take-off to the writer's career, with all the consequences that flowed from it.

The doors of publishing houses and magazines opened up to Trifonov. Not all doors, he would stipulate. There was "a different mafia" in the theatrical world, and a play written by him got suppressed. At home, his shelf of new editions and translations of *The Students* kept on growing. In the role assigned to him of engineer of the human soul, the young writer went to study life at the grand construction project of Communism—the Turkmen canal. There, shutting his eyes to the labor camps, he wrote what he was allowed to under the artistic title of *Quenching Thirst*.

He was saved from this hard-core literary path, strangely enough, by Stalin. He was saved by his death. The grand project was shut down, and his manuscript bogged down as well. Brought up in a family where the bookshelves carried Stalin's dedicatory inscriptions to his revolutionary grandmother, Trifonov began to figure out what was going on slowly, much more slowly than many others, and it was past time to. And his marriage to Nina Nelina, a Bolshoy Opera singer, could not but have had an effect on him as well. He must have found out that she had been bedded several times by the KGB head Lavrenty Beria. Life with her was burdened with frequent arguments, pouting, and great offense, and was brought to an end only by her strange death at the resort of Druskininkay, to where she had run away from him.

He despised the crowd that flowed past the Leader's coffin with its "meaningless sheep's animation," as he put it later. He dissociated himself from those who continued writing in "sly-wise-laudatory" style, as Trifonov himself put it. Both these quotations are from the later Trifonov. But, in those days, the multiply-refashioned novel *Quenching Thirst* was published by Vadim Kozhevnikov, editor of *Znamya*. And again it is not clear what in the text was written by Trifonov himself. The manuscript went from one magazine to another, getting covered with corrections by others many times over.

These days, that kind of pulp is unbearably boring. But, at that time, the author was going around telling others at the All-Union Congress of Writers how to do it. The magazine *Roman-gazeta*—middlebrow pulp—opened its doors to Trifonov. The mafia of producers of ersatz literature included him among their number. The novel was nominated for the Lenin Prize, but for some reason did not fill the bill. Maybe more muscular writers showed up in line for the prize ahead of Trifonov?

The brief denunciation of the cult of personality was over. *Agitprop* was once again feeding the masses on their heroic fathers' deeds. These fathers were the party bonzes of the 1920s and 1930s, sincere or hypocritical, stooges of Lenin or Stalin, the creators of the glorious empire. The publishing house Politizdat was prompted to attract writers interested in what they should not be to get down to the business of a series called "Flaming Revolutionaries." Trifonov of course had something to say—after all, his own father was one such hero.

Historians have yet to study in detail what Valentin Trifonov was really engaged in. He was not just one of the creators of the Red Army. In 1917 he organized robberies. It was under his leadership that the Bolsheviks attacked the warehouses of the Officers' Union on the Moyka, getting ahold of 4,000 rifles for the party, along with other weapons. His son himself called his father a boiler-stoker of the gigantic furnace. They burned up the economy, the culture, turned millions of people to ashes, melted the country to slag.

Valentin Trifonov turned out to be one of the main scourges of the country. First as chairman of the military tribunal of the front in the south. Then during the years of most importance to the rise of Stalin, he was chairman of the military collegium of the Supreme Court of the U.S.S.R., the very one that threw him into the furnace himself. How many people had he personally sent to their execution or to the camps?

Part of his father's archive remained at home, never taken away. But, most importantly, it will be in the state depositories, if the records have not been destroyed, that we will find out at least the total number of victims of this henchman of Stalin's. The myth in the Soviet Encyclopedia is based on his son's article, "From Youth Throughout Life," about which it is embarrassing even to speak.[13] But his father, turned back again from an enemy of the people into a party hero, helped his son to enter a particular circle of the post-Stalin elite. In the press they praised the flaming revolutionaries, but in *Samizdat* we read "My father killed Mikhoels," the memoirs of a former KGB guy.

Trifonov wrote the book *Campfire Reflection* for the Politizdat publishing house. In his memoirs he took note of its "anti-Stalin tone."[14] But the book itself is very pro-Soviet. In romanticizing his father, the hero, Trifonov elevates himself. At the same time, his father's experience taught him to be careful in his words and deeds. But in contrast to his father, the son went by normal morality and not a class-based one, a decency common to all mankind. In literary affairs anything could happen, but in his everyday life Trifonov junior did neither good nor harm to anyone, but avoided doing anything dishonest.

The sanctification of the revolution, the eulogizing of its mythological heroes—this was the task that Politizdat, the publishers of the Central Committee of the Communist Party of the Soviet Union, placed before its authors. Trifonov wrote (and it could not have been otherwise) half-truths, which is to say, half-lies. I remember how the Politizdat editors received my own book about bringing up children—I had never been exposed to such humiliation anywhere. The half-literate female editors (several of them wives of party officials) carelessly hacked up page after page any old which way. That was their directive.

Who changed what, and how much, in the texts that are now quoted by Trifonov specialists as examples of the writer's individual style? Was this an "abomination of manhandling" or a burnishing of what had already been written? Did the final product become worse or better than the one done by the author's hand? What does Trifonov look like when he is unaltered, virgin, so to speak?

Shall we ever find out what he composed himself, personally, sitting alone at the table, if everything that he created was modified for months, sometimes years, at multiple layers under the supervision of internal reviewers and dozens of editors of every rank—from the highest down to copy-readers? But without a doubt, this multilayered and inexorable control oppressed the writer's gifts, forcing him to be more careful in his expression of feelings and thoughts, to think constantly about practicability, encroaching upon his talent. Self-censorship became an integral part of his creative process.

Can you imagine a very mediocre pre-Revolutionary Russian writer being rewritten by his publishers from cover to cover? This process—and not only doctrines and heroes—is the inalienable essence of social realism. The pregnant author gives birth, so to speak, collectively. Everyone grunts together while combining his talent with the directives. We are not talking about the deficiencies of Trifonov's prose, but about the crux of a writer's activity in a country like his. His task is to chisel out an acceptable half-finished product that will be finished up by people who cannot write but who have a flair for what should be—and most importantly what should not be—in the text.

Somehow we forgot that even Alexander Solzhenitsyn began as a Soviet writer, and his text of *One Day in the Life of Ivan Denisovich* was transformed by its editors into a modified product. Solzhenitsyn burst his bonds only through *Samizdat*, when they prohibited his publication. I do not have a single book, story, or article published in the Soviet Union without that abomination of manhandling. Only in the West did we find out what publishing was all about. It meant that the editor and publisher simply read something and either liked it or did not. And if they liked it, they did not change even a jot or tittle.

The writer Yuri Trifonov lived with nursemaids from his birth to his death. Without them, he would never have managed to get published. But he recalls this not only without any indignation, but with praise for his wonderful editors. You can understand that. After all, they made him into an author with a name, not just the man by himself. And again, it's not his fault but his misfortune.

Nowadays critics write that he fought for every line. But this is only proof that every line was X-rayed, discussing what could be extracted, added, or re-done. Even what had already been published was re-filtered into new editions. Any untoward hints were scrubbed away. Unfortunately, none of the presently available published texts of Trifonov can be considered authentic—they are a collective product.

At symposiums with foreign colleagues, Trifonov was seated next to KGB writers. Trifonov himself claimed in his "Notes" that distinguished members of the Writers' Union had their own people above them who gave them support. Trifonov "suited" the powers that be, satisfied them, and that is why he traveled, so that in the West they could not say that Russian writers were being kept on a leash.

He was a fan of football and hockey—a tribute to times condemned indirectly in his books. At home he would sit at the television set for hours, watching who would score in which corner of the goal and with which foot. He preferred to talk about the same subject. And as a fan, he would go abroad to sit as a representative in the stands, cheer "for our guys," and give psychological support to Soviet sport. And when they got up to tricks with the Communists of the Federal Republic of Germany, he would be recommended to meet with the Communists in München (he spoke a little German).

According to his own recollections, his eyes were opened slowly, later than others, in secret. He read what he had not read before: Marina Tsvetayeva, Osip Mandel'shtam, Mikhail Bulgakov. He learned to imitate Ernest Hemingway. Gradually he became a different Trifonov. The combination of old and new in his collected works looks strange. But is it not strange to see a genuine talent in the role of an official Soviet writer?

There was a struggle going on between the regime and the country's intellectuals, and he, among the few exceptions, tried to stay out of it. They tried to pull him into the whirlpool of protests, but he managed to avoid it. He even substantiated his position in his last novel, *Time and Place*: "In literature, everyone answers for himself." It sounds respectable, but was it really? And where in his striving to understand and describe objective reality—the small, separate worlds of people like us—is his the civic posture of a writer of a definite time, and where is it just insurance against the danger of losing all that he had won? "The most difficult thing to do," he reflects, "is to live the way you want."

In his novel *Time and Place* (a title that could be given to almost any work by any author, by the way), Trifonov portrays someone like himself. Here his formula "the unneeded genius" appears—about unwanted people, a derivative of the "superfluous person." It goes without saying that to nourish needed geniuses and to persecute the unneeded was one of the basic tasks of the regime's ideology in the realm of culture. But Trifonov himself was not considered in any way either superfluous or unneeded by the regime.

In Russia, authors at maturity become great writers, but official recognition and readership most often exist independent of each other. He gained recognition while still a student, and his triumph was moreover both official and popular. Maybe that is what held him in check, opened up the possibility of taming him further?

He was published, accumulated fame, ascended. Many were sickened by the sycophantic games at sessions of the Writers' Union. Twice his friends involved him in signature campaigns to defend aggrieved writers. Later he recalled it with irony and a kind of squeamishness.

In 1975, for services rendered to Soviet literature, Trifonov was awarded the Order of Merit. For many people it was humiliating to cooperate with the functionaries, but for him, he participated in all of their goings-on with an air of significance. He occupied an official post, which helped him to publish what others would not have gotten away with. He wrote positive internal reviews of the manuscripts of the third-rate writers with whom he sat on the governing board, and they did the same for him. He was entirely practical, an achiever.

When his daughter graduated from her institute and he needed to make sure she was not rusticated away from Moscow like normal newly-trained youngsters, Trifonov skillfully mobilized all his connections, pushed all the necessary top buttons, and the issue was settled satisfactorily. At home or walking around, he was himself; but among other people he turned into their creature, a stranger to himself and to us. Better than many, he absorbed the rules of the game, what you could do, and to what extent. And to what extent you could do the things you could not do.

In his novel *The House on the Embankment*, for which some of the official critics reproached the writer for excessive gloom, he did not even tell the least bit of what was actually going on—even if it was in the manuscript he left for posterity.

Trifonov was trying to get published in *Novy Mir*, which was riding high at the time. But Solzhenitsyn was being published there, and they had already cooled to Trifonov long before. And then Tvardovsky bought the *dacha* of the recently deceased writer Vladimir Dykhovichny. And Trifonov (his luck, again) bought the neighboring *dacha*, which was the property of Dykhovichny's co-author, Moris Slobodskoy. There was even a connecting gate in the fence for the two co-authors, which Tvardovsky nailed shut right away, on moving in. The neighbors gradually got closer. Gardening chores mixed with literary, but it turned out that the most important thing was something else again.

The editor of *Novy Mir* developed a fondness for taking the hair of the dog at his neighbor's, who always had something in store. And Tvardovsky's wife begged him not to refuse, since he would find something somewhere anyway. Trifonov wrote—ingenuously, I would say—that "saying goodbye after a wonderful *al fresco* banquet in the garden, or on the porch with the windows open," Tvardovsky would ask, his tongue stumbling, staggering: "Why don't you ever bring us anything? Bring it over! Every page of yours is interesting to us!"[15]

So here Trifonov is, handing his manuscript over straight into Tvardovsky's hands through their communicating gate, and—as had happened with *The Students*—the fate of the manuscript was decided without any literary dogsbodies. Although, of course, they once again huffed and puffed: take something out here, put something in there. Trifonov wrote that even when they were enthusiastic about his new manuscript, they would anyway later on "get to work on it."

Alexander Solzhenitsyn gets persecuted. Tvardovsky gets kicked off of *Novy Mir*. And this was the moment when Trifonov's *Exchange* was coming out, as he himself recalled, "without a single censor's cut."[16] Everyone asked, "How did you manage to publish it?" "I suppose sad circumstances just turned out lucky for me," Trifonov would elucidate.[17] All right, it's possible. But the manuscript had been acceptable, and editors had already worked on it, of course, before the censors got to it. And there was still another reason, in my opinion.

In Trifonov's own words (not expressed out loud, but written, at home), all around him "the inedible vegetable-tops of Vsevolod Kochetov-style pseudoliterature were rustling."[18] After Solzhenitsyn's getting his comeuppance, the authorities also understood that. They needed Trifonov. "Trifonov is Solzhenitsyn for domestic consumption," it was said then in the corridors of power. He represented good literature in its moderate, loyal form. Trifonov satisfied the people on top, offering works that were talented but skillfully avoided the main sore points of society. He filled the place in literature of those who had been suppressed: Boris Pasternak, the author of *Doctor Zhivago*, Alexander Solzhenitsyn, Vasily Grossman, Yuli Daniel, Andrei Sinyavsky, and the other *Samizdat* writers.

Many intelligent and just words have been published about the virtues, psychological depths, and sincerity of Trifonov's prose. The writer's virtue lies in the fact that he, bent under the knot of circumstance, developed his own language for communicating with intellectual readers, a language of half-utterance, of avoidance of the prohibited, of hints at what was known to everyone but was forbidden in print. It is strange, however, that he, who tried to explain the mentality of the Soviet "middle class," could get by without fantasy or word-play. Mikhail Bulgakov's phantasmagoria and aphorism were not his style. He possessed no humor. And this was at a time when real life was overflowing with jokes about how official goings-on looked like soap opera, and even the figures of the leaders were parodies of themselves.

It is a sin to condemn a writer, trying to express himself in those times, who struck a deal with the powers that be for the sake of exposing himself to the reader by legal means. It is awkward to blame him for weakness, ambition, and compromise. And the more talented the author, the more you have to forgive him. But it is necessary to try to understand how writers survived in this system (and all in their different ways), to separate and pigeonhole our conscience and dishonesty, uncompromisingness and complacency, misfortune and blame. Our conformity is our historical experience. Now I read articles about the fact that there is no and never was a Soviet literature—is this the way to arrive at the truth? And what about the shelves all over the world full of Soviet books?

It was not by accident that certain Western critics did not include Trifonov among "the literature of moral resistance." In the gloomy years, he published, not including the millions-circulating readers' digest magazine *Roman-gazeta*, more than fifteen books. His works were published in the thick magazines on twenty occasions. Secretive and phlegmatic, neither a fighter nor a non-conformist, who offensively called dissidents "the so-called progressivists," he looked like an entirely Soviet successful writer—if you want, a member of the literary *nomenkla-*

tura. "The prosperous and thriving Trifonov," he was called by Mr. Zaks, the then-executive-secretary of *Novy Mir*.[19]

At the same time, from his very first book, Trifonov became to a certain degree a spokesman for the concerns of a part of society Solzhenitsyn ironically called *obrazovantsy* (half-educated people"), and for a part of the genuine intelligentsia.

The range of his themes was narrow. In the opinion of Slavic scholars in the West, he showed the unhappiness in the Soviet family—which was doing a lot, of course.[20] A man from the "stratum," as Agitprop christened the layer of the best people in Russian society, he tried to reflect what was going on in that stratum in those bad times: everyday life, past periods of history taken to the bounds of what was allowed. After all, if there were anything extra, they would praise you for your bravery and then cut you out of their editorial plan. In his *Impatience*, there is an interesting attempt to investigate the source of the Terror in Russia, but the most dangerous points of contact between the Terror and Lenin are skillfully avoided. Sitting on two chairs, he tried to tear himself away from mythology, from the Soviet mentality, and he succeeded in this somewhat.

He had to pay for his narrow range of subjects by repeating himself. The editors became inured to the repetitions, and publication was made easier, with small additions to what had gone before. Characters from *The Students* were transported on more than one occasion into other works. *The House on the Embankment* repeats a lot of what was in *The Students*. The same heroes (there was a Vadim Belov, who became Vadim Glebov), the same plot (student-professor conflict) only different, in the spirit of another time, another angle of view. His unfinished novel, *The Disappearance*, is in essence one more repetition of *The House on the Embankment*, and *The Old Man* is also a replay of an already-written topic.

In *The Old Man*, all the positive characters are Russian, and all the scoundrels, the perpetrators of lawlessness and murder, are all minorities. This primitive nationalism was encouraged by the authorities. This familiar concept, which seems unthinkable for a decent writer to use, is nonetheless present here.[21] Did Trifonov really think like that? No, he was paying for his publication. In order to survive, and then "get on the list," he voluntarily adopted their standards (or allowed himself to be adapted to them, which in practice is the same thing). For prosperity and success he paid with the loss of contact with reality. "Russia eats its fill...a test for satiety is taking place," he wrote, when everything was already falling apart.[22]

Perhaps Trifonov was never able to reach his full development properly? Would his remaining years have sufficed? Clio, the muse of history (he called her a goddess for some reason) will judge who was right and who was wrong, he wrote; and we, the sinners, create as today allows us to. You cannot be condemned for that, but not to speak up about it means to act against your own conscience.

Today it is interesting to read not only Trifonov's prose, but articles by his critics as well. It was they who made up the positive features of his characters from whole cloth, and now in just the same way they overemphasize their negative features. In his days, his critics were proving that Trifonov was creating the shining future—now they prove that he was unmasking it. He himself preferred the truth in homeopathic doses, as one of his colleagues said about him.

At the section devoted to Trifonov of the world Slavic congress held at Harrowgate in England in 1990, one of the female Soviet critics of the *glasnost'* era shouted "Trifonov specialists of the world, unite!" This idealization of Trifonov, distant from a real "time and place," takes place among Western Slavic scholars as well.[23] Evidently, the time has not yet come for an objective analysis.

He was often under the thumb of circumstance. Young writers would try to find a way to get to him, looking for help. He rarely gave it. About young authors, he wrote, "the faster you get away from them the better."[24] He even pronounced from the podium his theory that you should not give them any help, that a talented person would make his mark in literature by himself, forgetting what would have happened if Fedin or Tvardovsky had not given him a hand. But he helped the people he needed, the go-getting mediocrities with connections. In this way he set on his feet a young journalist who had been recommended to him, the son of a highly-placed father, who joined the Party very quickly, wrote a couple of stories, and published them with Trifonov's support. Several years passed, and Trifonov's protege was made secretary of the Moscow writers' organization.

One of the paradoxes of Trifonov's biography is that the writer was supported by the power of that particular third-rater, who actively drowned other literary talents. The editor of his works was a secretary of the Writers' Union, Sergey Baruzdin. Another secretary of the Writers' Union, Feliks Kuznetsov, wrote a preface to his works about the fact that they held revolutionary ideals sacred, and that Trifonov had kept his loyalty to our fathers' and grandfathers' ideals.[25] That was how they tamed him. But even in his arduously-obtained glory, Trifonov still remained a sacrifice to Moloch.

In the 1970s, no one any longer demanded belief in dogma, but an exceptional ability to adapt was called for, the gift of following the rules of ideological behavior, and these qualities were to be found in Yuri Trifonov. He turned out to be a suitable inward intellectual and outward collaborationist. His face even came to look like their faces when he was among the *apparatchiks*: significant and expressionless. The sense of danger never left him. He skillfully avoided acquaintances who could hurt him. But when a lot was being printed about the make-believe countryside, the positive proletariat, and Party heroes, he was the one who tried to comprehend the absurdity and squalor of existence for the stratum, the Soviet intelligentsia. It is in his works that we see those who had fought for happiness come to a miserable existence, full of petty worries; we see the moral collapse of the heirs of the hero-fathers.[26]

Luckily, he escaped the fate of becoming a "people's" writer, even though reckoned one of that "cartridge clip." In the capitals, the thick magazines with his novels were read to pieces. But in the city of Tver, I bought his selected works bundled together with the hard-to-get book *Home Conservation of Vegetables*. He could have come a cropper at any time, but he always held on. Under Stalin, under Khrushchev, under Brezhnev, he received in full what had passed over many. I am reading his posthumous notes—there is not one word about his own zigzags. He condemns the errors of the time. He himself was always right in those times, and that is a pity.

3. A Meeting in America

At the end of 1988 the Department of Russian of the University of California, Davis, invited me to give some lectures. At one point in a conversation with Professor Jim Gallant (in the evening, we were swimming in the swimming pool down parallel lanes) Trifonov's name got mentioned. The writer, as it turned out, had been at Davis not long before his death. The next day I recorded Gallant's recollections of the visit onto a dictaphone. With the permission of the teller of the tale, I present them here in my own translation, with whatever explanations necessary.

"I remember the day in 1977 when Trifonov flew in to Davis," recalled Jim Gallant. "It was clear, dry, and sunny. We'll get the precise date from the videocassette at Olson Library. They always register everything there properly."

Traditionally, buildings on American college campuses are named after the people who donated the funds for their construction, or after famous people who once taught there. The three-storied Olson building adjoins the "languages and literatures" building where teachers have their offices, and there are auditoriums in it. The most comfortable floor is the underground one. Here, in the language laboratories, you can watch television programs from more than a hundred countries, including, for instance, the Russian *Vremya* news program.

> Trifonov was originally invited by Kansas State University, Gallant continued. It was their idea to listen to what living Soviet writers had to say. Then he was invited to Los Angeles, and from there Professor Elena Weil (she was a Russian, and looked like a gypsy) brought him to the campus at Irvine. I told Trifonov via Elena Weil that we were offering him two lectures and wanted to record him on videotape—in those days it was something of a novelty. Trifonov demanded a huge fee. At any rate, for us, a double fee for each lecture seemed excessive. We had to strike a bargain with the department at Berkeley and share transport expenses. We agreed that our guest would give a general lecture for the university at large in the evening, and one in the television studio during the day. At eleven in the morning, I met Trifonov at Sacramento airport and took him straight to lunch.

Gallant was recalling all this unhurriedly, and I was finding the smallest details interesting. Our Davis campus lies in a golden valley. From the east and west, mountains throng the horizon. Sacramento airport is a fifteen-minute drive up route 102, and then a bit on I-5, that runs along the whole of the Pacific coast from the Mexican border through all of California, clear to Canada.

"Our guest turned out not to be very talkative. A rather strange fellow accompanied him as his interpreter, who was also amazingly quiet."

"Maybe Trifonov was just tired from his travels?"

> And maybe Elena Weil squeezed every drop she could out of him, and there wasn't anything left over for us. Bulat Okudzhava had been with her before Trifonov, and she had literally kept him to herself, like he was in prison, endlessly asking him

over and over about everything. She was just writing something about Soviet authors. I think she imprisoned Trifonov the same way, too.

This is that Gallant said. But, seriously, surely a writer would not have gotten that tired from talking to Professor Weil, even if over several days.

They arranged to have lunch at the faculty club in the park by the river. Several students who were always looking for an opportunity to hear live Russian speech showed up as well. They started discussing his program. The general lecture was planned for a wide audience, with an interpreter, and the second, more special, was to be for the teachers and graduate students who understood Russian.

I'll clear this up right away: a wide audience at Davis—if, for instance, John Updike or Kurt Vonnegut was appearing—meant several thousand students and many professors. The entrance fee was not steep, but it was not free. If a famous Russian were the guest (not necessarily a writer), there would be three or four dozen people in the best of circumstances, and, it goes without saying, they would get in for free. But the select group would be three to five professors and three to five post-graduates—in all, six to ten listeners. True, they would be those interested and grateful. After lunch, Trifonov said:

"I'm terribly tired. I've had to do so much traveling!"

"But we have an agreement," Gallant frowned. "And everything is already scheduled."

The writer was not particularly amicable, and kept silent.

"Okay," Gallant gave up. "If you can't give two lectures, we would prefer one at the television studio. We'll keep it as a souvenir."

They set out for the studio, not in the best humor. Gallant endeavored to lift their spirits. It did not matter how lunch had gone, he soothingly told his guest. The students understood that he was tired. Now they would try to ease the tension. He should cheer up, be himself. Everyone was glad to see him here. Of course, not all the students understood Russian. But it would be interesting for future generations to see him. Generally, a psychiatric session to get Trifonov into the mood. But he did not pay any heed.

They sat their guest down in an armchair, and everyone sat around him. Trifonov looked around warily. His puffy face was gloomy. He looked like a hippopotamus taken out of the water against his will and put into a cage. They turned on the stage lights. It got bright and hot.

"Well, okay. What should I do?"

"Whatever you like," answered Gallant. "Perhaps you could tell us about what you're writing? Or...maybe something about what's happening in Soviet literature?"

"That can't be!" I remarked. "A writer comes here to give a talk and has to ask what he's supposed to be doing?" Gallant recalled:

> It was strange, but he wasn't ready to give a lecture. Evidently he hadn't given any thought to what he was to talk about, even though he'd been to several universities. Surely he didn't do that everywhere? He didn't even take any advance interest in what we would want from him. And we didn't know what we could and couldn't ask. Mutual incomprehension arose, it seems to me. Meanwhile, our guest pulled a little book out of his pocket and asked again: 'Shall I begin?' I nodded...

I'll interrupt Gallant's recollections here. He and I set off for the laboratory in the Olson wing, and asked for the video recording. In the intervening years, no one had taken it out. There is a date on the cassette: November 22, 1977.[27] We took our seats in one of the viewing cubicles. The walls were painted black, there were two chairs and the television set, and nothing else. Try to feel with us the mystical circumstance in which, by pushing a button, we could summon up Yuri Trifonov's spirit. He appeared before us, sighed noisily, and asked from the screen, looking somewhere to one side, past us: "Shall I begin?"

And Trifonov began. Here is the text of his lecture. Unfortunately, I have to wring it out carefully: if I didn't, his speech wouldn't be fit to print. The writer spoke inertly, laboriously, repeating and mixing up words, without emotion. The feeling was as if everything that was happening was repellent to him.

> This is my book of essays on literature." Trifonov held up the book.[28] "The book consists of articles that have been published at various times in our newspapers. In particular, here is a small article that was published in *Literaturnaya Rossiya*. There is a column in it called 'How We Write.' It addresses a request to a selection of authors, to talk about how writers work. I don't know how it is in America, but in our country, there is a huge interest among readers in how writers go about their work, properly speaking, what is their creative *modus operandi*.
>
> I remember that in the 1920s [*proviso: not actually "remember," but read or heard that...Y.D.*] a book like that was published on several occasions. The leading

authors of the time were printed: Aleksey Tolstoy, Gorky, Zamyatin, Babel, Pilnyak—but no Bulgakov, it seems to me—Vsevolod Ivanov, Lidin, Zoshchenko, Tynyanov. Each of them wrote something individual. Some seriously, others, so to speak, approached the questions scientifically: when do you like to work most of all, in the morning, at night, or in the evening? do you smoke? Aleksey Tolstoy joked that the main thing for a writer while he's working is a loose stomach. You have to clean out your stomach. Some answered, as the Germans say, with brutal seriousness. When *Literaturnaya gazeta* asked me [*proviso: the reference above was to Literaturnaya Rossiya—Y.D.*] I couldn't joke about it, and took it all seriously.

Writers can be divided into two basic categories, it seems to me. One is graphomanes, who start to feel themselves to be writers from their early childhood and devote their lives to it. The second kind come to literature from other professions. And they are very often even more successful. Chekhov was a doctor; Bulgakov was a doctor. And certain Russians, however strange it may sound, even studied to become writers. The Literary Institute is a mysterious place. It's not clear if it's necessary or not. I studied at it, but whenever I mention it, I meet with ridicule. Did Pushkin study at the Literary Institute? Did Gorky? Well, then, what's the Institute for?

It was, most likely, the smallest institute in the Soviet Union. It was founded by Gorky in 1934. There are about 80 people there in all its class years at any one time. The academic program is the same as at a university. But, in addition to that, there are creative writing seminars. I studied there after the war. Fedin, Paustovksy, Leonov, Katayev, the poets Selvinsky and Antokolsky were there. We read our works to each other, discussed them. Was this necessary, or not? I don't know to this day.[29]

I consider myself a graphomane and would be involved in literature come what may. Soloukhin, Tendryakov, Baklanov, Bondarev, Vinokurov, Simonov, Kazakov, Yevtushenko, Akhmadulina, and so forth, graduated from this Institute. A lot of Soviet writers studied there. This is no proof of the usefulness of the Institute, but undoubtedly some good came from it. Not from the academic part: a university would have afforded a better education. There was, first of all, communication with writers, and, secondly, communication with one another. I remember that the first and second years were very fruitful. We could feel a huge internal growth. We understood a great deal. After those years, everything slowed down, of course.

I graduated from the Institute in 1949. There I started writing my diploma-piece, the novel *The Students*. It came out in 1950. Now it's as if it's not my book. But in those times it felt to me like I had become a writer. You see, it was rather difficult to withstand certain kinds of circumstances, because I received an award right away. The book was officially approved, published outside the country. Now it's as if this book doesn't exist, for me. A writer, I believe, shouldn't deny his own works, but he can get very far from them, which is what happened to me, strictly speaking. But, here, I'll read you something from my article...

Then Trifonov, without a glance at his audience, without the slightest expression, read from the book about what advice writers of the older generation had given him. Having read a bit, he tore himself from the book:

I should say a few words here. Paustovsky is a very popular writer in our country, but as a prose stylist, he's not my idol. I think that he has many weaknesses. He's too much of a romantic. But in his civic posture, and the literary circle that we inhabit, he proved himself to be a good man, and was a real teacher for many of his students.

At that point, Trifonov read another excerpt from the same book. And commented:

> I should again say a few words here. After the book *The Students*, I went through a difficult period in my life, when I no longer wanted to write as I had been writing, but couldn't find a new style or a new path. I went to Turkmenia, to the construction project, to the Kara Kum desert. Several years passed before my next book came out—a book of stories connected with this journey...

He read further about how he imitated Paustovsky in his description of detail, and then he called this literature something that "smelt of damp fences" (a quotation from Paustovsky). He explained why Paustovsky had written the way he had and how he had survived on his romanticism, far from real life. Then Trifonov struck his American audience with a revelation: a writer had to have something to say. From time to time he would stop, leaf through a few pages at random, and again read. Then he said:

"There, the excerpts are like that, as a matter of fact. It seems to me that you can understand the rather complicated difficulties that I have had to overcome."

Then, which was totally strange, Trifonov started reading aloud his own interview with himself, that had been published in the magazine *Moskva*, about his favorite literary heroes, among whom were Raskolnikov, Ostap Bender, and from the time of the Revolution and civil war, Grigory Melekhov and Aksinya. Trifonov justified his liking for these negative characters as being only because of the way they were depicted. Then the writer said:

"I could read something else, but if you don't want me to, then ask me some questions..."

Jim Gallant recalled:

> I glanced at my watch when he finished, and was at a loss. There hadn't been anything live, new, no kind of analysis of what literature was like there. Nothing that resembled a lecture or a discussion. Maybe it was too hot for him? Trifonov asked again: 'Well, shall I read any further?' and I hurriedly answered, 'That'll do, that'll do.' An awkward pause descended. A kind of disappointment, or, to put it more

softly, a perplexity. The cameras were switched off, and I asked: 'Do you want to have a look at yourself?'

At that time this was all quite extraordinary, to see yourself. There were almost no home video recorders even in America.

"No, no," their guest responded.

"I'll make a copy for you," said Gallant, so that Trifonov could be sure that he had not said something he should not have.

Their guest, however, had uttered absolutely no dangerous thing. The lecture had lasted 32 minutes. Half of this time was pauses and innumerable "so-to-speaks," "in-generals," and "properly-speakings," that I, begging your pardon, have cut out. The lecturer received an envelope with his four-fold honorarium, including the fee for the lecture he had not given: a check did not suit their guest, and one of the professors put his own cash into the envelope. Later, Trifonov, as he was supposed to, punctually turned over the greater part of the hard cash to the Soviet embassy in Washington.

Here I'll allow myself a digression about speeches by authors in general.

It is thought (both in emigration and in Russia) that a good writer should be able to give a brilliant speech full of humor and wit. But in fact the artistry, the ability, to hold an audience, to find and present impromptu ideas with good timing to listeners, however often they have been repeated, is not given to everyone. Writers who can give a good speech are few, I'll put it straightaway. But even they, as a rule, do not stick to their themes. The majority will list the names of their books with a short description of their contents. They will read old stories, not taking their eyes off the page. Some of them bring along fat manuscripts and, sitting at the table, leaf through them at length, reading unrelated bits. The audience exchanges glances in amazement, and the writer accepts this as a sign of delight. I can understand readers yawning, standing up, and walking out.

Trifonov completely lacked the gift for public speaking. However, the reason for his audience's disappointment lay at a deeper level.

There were several Russian writers' names familiar to American students. The Slavic scholars at the departments knew more, it goes without saying. For long years, American experts had considered Trifonov to be an author of the same pedigree as, say, Vsevolod Kochetov or Yuri Bondarev. But after the appearance of *The House on the Embankment*, this writer was, so to speak, lifted to another level. And it was this Trifonov that the university had invited. In other words, they expected more from him than from other Soviet visitors. It looked as if he himself was not ready for this, however, and obediently carried out his mission as a cud-chewer instead. And I say that again not in judgement upon him, but in order to understand what was going on more precisely.

Trifonov, meanwhile, again announced that he was tired and wanted to return to his hotel. Of course a room had been reserved for him in a quiet hotel on a leafy street, and Gallant gave him a lift. Although the evening's lecture had been scheduled and widely advertised, they had to post a notice on the door that it had been canceled.

Three hours later, as had been agreed, Gallant returned to the hotel. Larry Blake's restaurant was across the street from a new movie theater and was then one of the most pleasant in the town. The entire Russian department (about five people) and several émigrés were getting together at the dinner in Trifonov's honor. That morning everyone had been distressed at the curtailing of the lecture series, but now they were even glad about it: again, it would have been boring, and scarcely anyone would have shown up, anyway.

Trifonov's silent interpreter sitting next to him was not a KGB guy who everyone had assumed he was, as it turned out, but just a graduate student from Kansas. Andrzej Brzeski, an economics professor, joined the Russian department people.

"Are you a Pole?" asked Trifonov. "Where did you learn Russian?"

"In a Soviet camp near Bologoye," Brzeski smiled.

Trifonov choked. And his hosts hurried to change the topic.

Their guest kept complaining: he had had to give lectures here every day, and tomorrow another one in Berkeley. The conversation at the table continued to be circumspect, and was for that reason even more boring.

"The times were like that," Gallant excused Trifonov. "Gloomy. He was afraid to talk, and we tried not to raise any burning topics. At one time Solzhenitsyn's name escaped Brzeski's lips, and we shushed him:

"Anything but that!"

They had invited Trifonov to Davis, for a fee, to talk about the weather, as it happened. Literary America passed him by; he was not aware of it and did not try to understand it. To say nothing of émigré literature. Having eaten, Trifonov got up from the table and stretched:

"Whew, am I tired!"

"Then let's go, I'll see you back to the hotel," volunteered Gallant. "It's right next door."

On their way, the guest stopped at the movie theater.

"What is playing here?"

"*Death in the Desert.*"

"What is it about?"

"I don't know, some kind of action film."

"Wow, great! Let's go see it," he had for some reason lapsed into informal speech.

Several minutes before, Trifonov had been on his last legs, and now Gallant bought two tickets and they took their seats in the empty theater. It was a primitive movie with endless gunfire and heaps of corpses. His interpreter asked:

"Shall I translate for you?"

"Don't have to," said Trifonov. "Everything is clear, anyway."

He became almost childlike.

"See how well it was made. Wonderful!"

He was thrilled at the detail, the colors, the sound. But as soon as the screen went dark, the guest once again put on his armor.

They arrived at the hotel. A lovely, cosy room with a little balcony. Trifonov sat down on his bed and again turned into a creature locked up in a cage. Gallant reminded him that he would be picking him up in the morning, early—to take him to Berkeley.

"Why would he be so thrilled by a stupid movie?" I asked. "He, a man of intellect…"

Gallant shrugged his shoulders.

"Maybe he just wanted to take a break from conversations with dimwit Americans? Probably he was bored with us, too. He'd become a hostage to his own lectures."

If you do not count the movie, the spark of curiosity appeared in Trifonov's eyes only once. One of the university's specialists in comparative literature turned out to be a collector. As a joke, he collected translations of novels whose authors were awarded the Stalin Prize. *The Students* was among his collection. Trifonov came to life on hearing that he was an exhibit. Gallant ran to the library and made Xerox copies of *The House on the Embankment* and something else besides. He showed them to Trifonov. The writer got embarrassed, thinking that this was some kind of *Samizdat*. Gallant explained that this was copied from Soviet magazines. Then the author inscribed it: "Amicably. Yuri Trifonov." For those who have preserved books with his dedication, I will add, take a look: for everyone, without any arch philosophizing, he wrote the word "amicably."

In the morning, Gallant, Trifonov, and his interpreter sped down I-80, going west in the direction of San Francisco. His guest kept silent, and the tactful Gallant did not know what to ask him. The day before, two young fellows, Russian émigrés, had come up to Trifonov to introduce themselves. They had probably asked him naive or stupid questions—they had just wanted to speak to a compatriot, rare enough in those days. Now in the car, Trifonov suddenly asked:

"And who were those pathetic creatures?"

Gallant explained.

"Strange kids..."

"They seemed strange to me, too," agreed Gallant. "A little bit crazy... By law, Soviet Jews get to emigrate to America. One of those kids is Russian, and an anti-Semite, to boot. And it was hard to talk to him, he chattered like a machine gun."

"That's a medical term," Trifonov said, "to suffer from machine-gun speech."

"Sometimes," Gallant said carefully, "the Soviet Union just sends away people who aren't needed."

Trifonov confirmed it:

"They send trash, packing material."

"But for some people it's impossible to live there. And it's difficult for them here, too: they have to get used to the American way of life..."

In sum, they whiled away the hour it took to make the trip. And when they arrived in Berkeley, Trifonov's Slavic Department hosts took him straight off to lunch at a restaurant. Their guest appeared to come to life somewhat.

"But did he ask about anything himself?" I tried to clear it up. "About life in California, maybe? About any problems? Or did he tell any funny stories? Even one innocent Moscow joke?"

"No! Nothing is left from our encounter with him, except for the feeling of boredom. None of the writers either before or since—and we have had all kinds—ever cast such a blue funk over the proceedings."

I listened to these recollections about the lecturer-martyr and thought: to hell with it, with the guest's observation that refugees from his homeland were just packing material; maybe down deep in his soul he did not think that, and said it merely for strangers' ears, just in case. Something else was more important. Here they had invited Trifonov to Kansas State University to give six lectures in three weeks, and then kept him for three more weeks, to travel around and appear in different places. For occasions like that, Vladimir Nabokov wrote his lectures in advance, but Trifonov, who knew a few English words—what did he have to rely on?

I had a feeling like I was some sort of accomplice. Talking to Gallant, I felt guilty for my colleague after the fact. What did he fly halfway around the world for, without preparing for at least one interesting discussion? Why knock yourself out galloping from university campus to campus in order to read aloud from some old printed pages that are already on file in any American academic library?

Returning the video tape, I dropped in to the university library, keyed in "Trifonov" on the computer, went up in the elevator and took down from a shelf a brochure entitled "Extension Courses." I sat down on the floor like students do and began reading. It turned out that nearly all the oral additions that Trifonov made while reading were all contained in the book as well.

I recalled Trifonov's idea: a writer cannot deny what he had published. Why could he not, if it were shameful, wrong, or just stupid, if the burden of conscience bore down on him?

They invited the writer-lecturer Trifonov to America to hear about what was happening in contemporary Soviet literature, and he did not even say anything about what was being openly discussed. He uttered not a word on the topic he had been invited to speak on, not a hint about the real situation, in order to help Americans understand, to support people like him, after all.

And here we come to the crux of the matter. Of course it was not Trifonov who decided if he would go to America or not. An invitation usually had no significance; they would normally not even inform the person being invited about it. Sometimes it would even have a negative effect. So maybe there was a good reason to send him in particular. When Trifonov returned from the United States, an extensive interview appeared in the magazine *Inostrannaya literatura*.[30]

Trifonov said that the trip to the United States scared him, because he went on his own, and moreover without any knowledge of English. But he was afforded an interpreter there. At first he says that he was invited as a lecturer, and then, at the end, as a professor (he obviously never understood the difference, utterly essential to American higher education)—while in reality he had been neither the one nor the other. At Kansas State University, the guest held six discussions in total, about literature after the Twentieth Party Congress, of course: on revolutionary and military themes, about writers on village life, and about himself. In other appearances he discussed his works' translations into English (let us note: without any knowledge of English, it means that somebody organized the discussion and the speakers, and so on, and Trifonov would just listen while others did the talking).

In his interview, Trifonov, as he was supposed to, enumerated the horrors in America: the gloominess of the cities, the absence of pedestrians, crime, drug addiction, the flight of people from America because of the unbearable existence and "standardization of life." On the other hand, Russian wheat grows in America, and so does interest in the Russian language. However, Sllavic scholars in America are "poor devils," says Trifonov. They have to write dissertations on "loyal topics"—religion, Dostoyevsky, Chekhov—instead of writing about the sterling successes of Soviet literature.

During his trip to the U.S.A. he had not met a single American writer, and he avoided émigrés like the plague. His greatest joy there, he recalled, was his meeting in New York with an official group of Soviet writers who were staying at the same hotel. The rest of the time he was sad. "During my stay there I kept returning to the thought that this was a country of very great unrest, and sometimes excruciating anxiety," said Trifonov, and explains that life in that country was the pursuit of phantoms, and the essence of existence was fear. "America is in a state of serious and prolonged crisis."[31]

Of course Trifonov had not sent been there for the sake of squalid propaganda and then the publication of that interview. Then just what was the trip for? It happened in connection with the publication in the U.S.A. of the English translation of the book *Leonid Brezhnev: Pages From His Life*. Trifonov was sent to arouse interest in that Soviet book. In New York, he met with Brezhnev's publisher, Michael Cord. In the middle of Trifonov's interview in *Inostrannaya literatura* there was a story about how the publisher had shown the proofs of Brezhnev's book to Trifonov in delight and said how he burned with desire "to come to Moscow to hand a copy of the book to Leonid Brezhnev, just as soon as it came out."

But there remained one more task for Trifonov in his trip around America, and he touched on it several times during the interview. He was a living representative in America of the myth of Soviet literature. In the heat of the battle with dissidence he had been sent there as an exhibit. And represented himself in his appearances, as he said, as "the simple truth: real Russian literature is being created by Soviet writers, living and being 'officially' published in their own country."[32]

I'd like to believe that these words were written by some editor, but we cannot check up on that. Even if it were so, the fact remains the fact anyway that, for American money, Trifonov participated in a Soviet con game, the so-called "spirit of Helsinki" and appeared in the capacity of a fighter against *Samizdat*, *Tamizdat* (publications in Russian outside the country), and the dissident movement. In those very same days when Trifonov was being driven around California, we were microfilming manuscripts in Moscow, in order to save them from confiscation during searches, and sending them abroad.

Evidently the authorities stayed content with him, since, after returning from America, Trifonov published his interview; and he soon was sent abroad again. Here were his "House Upturned" and other stories of that cycle. Are they short stories? More likely, journalistic sketches, in which the author unmasks universal bourgeois consumerism, and the notorious American imperialism. After his death, Trifonov was vouchsafed the totally *nomenklatura*-like immortalization reserved for people who had been of special use to the regime: a Soviet ship was named the *Yuri Trifonov* in his honor.

Is it good to return to what has been forgotten? Trifonov himself thought that you could not separate the past from the present, something he wrote about in his novel *Time and Place*. "Is it necessary to call these things to mind?" he asked himself. "Dear God, that's as stupid as asking if it's necessary to live. After all, recalling and living are integral, together—can't be destroyed one without the other, and represent a certain verb that doesn't exist."

Now, thinking of Trifonov's life step by step, I ask myself: what is better—collaboration, the appearance of doctored works, "not his," not Trifonov's, or—let us say—writing for himself? Attempting to say the minimum in public, or dooming yourself to silence? As has been noted, Trifonov wrote that everything written in the 1940s, thus before his time, was "non-literature." A dangerous position for the writer, since it gives a post-Trifonov generation of writers of the *glasnost'* period the right to say the same about what was written by Trifonov.

"I'll try to explain," Gallant said thoughtfully. "He tried to do everything cleanly in literature. And everything else was excrement, without which no living creature can live."

You cannot but give American intellectuals their due: they are always ready to forgive you. And they even offer you the means to justification, so you'll feel yourself forgiven.

I think that the reason for the popularity of Trifonov's prose, his influence over his readers of that time, can be explained by the readers'—the same kind of non-dissidents as Trifonov—understanding of the difficulties of publishing a feasible maximum of the truth. This was the mutual, enforced conformity, the tactic, understood by both sides, of minor ruses of detection and extrapolation of an understated truth. But his lies were missed, forgiven, or understood as necessary by his readers.

In that very understatement, by the way, lies the reason that Trifonov, so important to Russians, still remains neither interesting nor understandable to the American and the Western reader in general. He has not been reissued for a long time, although he had good translators. An unhurried narrative of the nuances of an alien life leaves Americans cold. Trifonov in English requires constant explication—what and where and why is left unsaid, missed, or implied. It is not the author's fault, but neither is it the readers'.

Talented writer Yuri Trifonov tried to liberate himself from the compulsory Soviet mythology, but the price he had to pay was compromise. Try to understand how literature was done in those days, how an author had to be willing to stoop to get access to readers. It is just in this partial but necessary sincerity that the significance of Yuri Trifonov lies, his role in the thaw, the place firmly occupied by him in the history of Russian literature of the 20th century.

Trifonov died when he was only 56. Kidney disease does not show up overnight. Nor the need for an operation, either. Unfortunately, Trifonov only felt tired in California; his kidney problems did not show up in Davis, but in Moscow. Had it happened in America, he would have been taken to the university medical center for an operation. So he died from the low level of medical services in his native land: a blood clot from the operation. In the United States, Yuri Trifonov would have been on his feet in one day, and in a week would have recovered and would still be alive today. It is a pity that the conditional mood only works in a written text. It does not help in real life.

Notes

Pushkin, Stalin, and Other Poets

[1] A. V. Lunacharsky, "Pushkin," in *Pushkin. Polnoye sobranie sochineny* (Moscow-Leningrad, 1936), 37.
[2] A. V. Lunacharsky, ed., *Ocherki po istorii russkoy kritike* (Moscow-Leningrad, 1929), parts 1-4, 190.
[3] V. Y. Kirpotin, *Naslediye Pushkina i kommunizm* (Moscow, 1936).
[4] *Pravda*, December 17, 1935.
[5] V. Y. Kirpotin, *Pushkin. Pamyatka* (Leningrad, 1937), 147, 153.
[6] Editorial in *Pravda*, February 10, 1937.
[7] A. M. Yegolin, ed., *Pushkin. Sbornik* (Moscow, 1941), 3.
[8] *Pravda*, December 5, 1938.
[9] Speech by I. V. Stalin, November 6, 1941, in *Izvestiya,* November 7, 1941.
[10] Nina Tumarkin, "The Great Patriotic War as Myth and Memory," in *Atlantic* (June, 1991), 28.
[11] *Izvestiya*, May 26, 1943.
[12] B. S. Meylakh, *Pushkin i yego epokha* (Moscow, 1958), 4.
[13] *Izvestiya,* May 26, 1943.
[14] *Izvestiya*, June 18, 1943.
[15] We have a special collection of such inscriptions, more than 20.
[16] I. A. Novikov, *Sobranie sochineny* (Moscow, 1967), vol.IV, 448, 544.
[17] *Izvestiya,* May 27, 1945.
[18] *Izvestiya,* June 5, 1945.
[19] "Pamyati velikogo russkogo poeta," in *Izvestiya,* June 13, 1944.
[20] "Velikiye traditsii russkoy nauki," in *Izvestiya,* June 13, 1944.
[21] N. F. Pogodin, "Svershilos'!" in *Izvestiya,* May 9, 1945.
[22] "Narod-geroy, narod-pobeditel'," in *Izvestiya,* May 23, 1945.
[23] *Izvestiya,* June 4, 1945.
[24] *Pushkin. Materialy yubileynykh torzhestv* (Moscow, 1951), 5.
[25] Ibid., 6.
[26] Ibid., 13.
[27] Ibid., 17.
[28] Ibid., 9.
[29] *Trudy pervoy i vtoroy Vsesoyuznykh pushkinskikh konferentsy. 1949, 1950* (Moscow-Leningrad, 1952), 25.
[30] B. S. Meylakh, *Pushkin* (Moscow-Leningrad, 1949), 8-9, 3, 13.

[31] I. V. Stalin *Marksizm i voprosy yazykoznaniya* (Moscow, 1950), 7.
[32] *Trudy*, 23.
[33] V. A. Malinin, *Filosofskiye vzglyady Pushkina. Avtoreferat* (Moscow, 1954), 6
[34] Ibid., 4.
[35] I. K. Yenikolopov, *Pushkin v Gruzii* (Tbilisi, 1950).
[36] V. V. Yermilov, *Nash Pushkin* (Moscow, 1949), 94, 95, 61.
[37] Abridging the verbosity, ibid., 5.
[38] Meylakh,18.
[39] Ibid.,172-173.
[40] *Trudy*, 15.
[41] Meylakh, 52-53.
[42] *Trudy*, 7.
[43] Meylakh, *Pushkin i yego epokha*, 177.
[44] Yegolin, 12
[45] Yermilov, 94.
[46] V. F. Tendryakov, "Kul'tura i doverie," in *Ogonyok* (Moscow, 1990), No.88, 9.

"Hitting it Off with Pushkin"

[1] G. P. Makogonenko, *Gogol i Pushkin* (Leningrad, 1985). The inversion in the book's title (Gogol before Pushkin) reveals the author's desire to prove the importance of Gogol for Pushkin. Transpose the names and the picture becomes less tendentious.
[2] D. D. Blagoy, *Literatura i deystvitel'nost'* (Moscow, 1959), 401-422.
[3] N. Petrunina, G. Fridlander, "Pushkin i Gogol v 1831-1836 gg.," in the anthology *Pushkin. Issledovaniya i materialy* (Leningrad, 1969), vol.VI, 203.
[4] Simon Karlinsky, *The Sexual Labyrinth of Nikolay Gogol* (Harvard University Press, Cambridge: 1976), 287.
[5] P. I. Bartenev, *Rasskazy o Pushkine* (Moscow, 1925), 44.
[6] V. V. Gippius, commentary in *Gogol. Polnoye sobranie sochineny* (AN SSSR: 1938-1952), vol.X, 435.
[7] D. S. Mirsky, *A History of Russian Literature* (1958), 150.
[8] A. Pozov, *Metafizika Pushkina* (Madrid, 1967), 228.
[9] V. N. Ilyin, "Dostoyevsky i Gogol," in *Orient und Occident* (1932), Heft 10.
[10] N. L. Stepanov, Foreword in *Gogol. Sobranie sochineny v shesti tt.* (Moscow, 1952-1953), vol.I, xxii. I recall a lecture by my Professor Stepanov in the Stalin years, when he was trying to get away from the obligatory political doctrines, but he could not avoid them in his publications.
[11] V. G. Belinsky, "O russkoy povesti i povestyakh Gogolya," in *Izbrannye sochineniya* (Moscow, 1948), 79. "Pokhozhdeniya Chichikova, ili Mertvye dushi," ibid., 218.
[12] The conflict surrounding the two names that preceded the erection of the monument to Pushkin in Moscow has been given thought by Marcus C. Levitt in *Russian Literary Politics and the Pushkin Celebration of 1880* (Cornell University Press, Ithaca and London: 1989).
[13] V. I. Lenin, *Sochineniya* (4th ed.), vol.XVIII, 286.
[14] V. V. Gippius, *Gogol* (Leningrad, 1924), 40.
[15] Gippius, commentary, 436.
[16] Stepanov, in Gogol, vol.1, lxiv.
[17] B. V. Tomashevsky, *Pushkin. Kn. 2* (Moscow-Leningrad, 1961), 442.
[18] Makogonenko, 23.
[19] Petrunina, Fridlander, 197.
[20] I. P. Zolotussky, "Portret 'strannogo' geniya," in V. V. Veresayev, *Gogol v zhizni* (Moscow, 1990), 13.
[21] Blagoy, 408.

[22] P. V. Annenkov, *Materialy dlya biografii Pushkina* (2nd ed., 1873), 360.
[23] *Gogol. Sobranie sochineniy v shesti tt.*, notes, vol.VI, 360.
[24] P. V. Annenkov, *Literaturniye vospominaniya* (Moscow, 1983), 54.
[25] Ibid., 58.
[26] Abram Terts (Andrei Sinyavsky), *V teni Gogolya* (London, 1975), 328.
[27] M. A. Tsyavlovsky, "Khronologicheskaya kanva biografii," in *Pushkin. Polnoye sobranie sochineny* (Moscow-Leningrad, 1931), vol.VI, 17.
[28] V. I. Shenrok, *Materialy dlya biografii Gogolya* (Moscow, 1892), vol.I, 348.
[29] A. N. Pynin, *Gogo* (Brokhauz i Yefron, 1893), vol.XVII, 19.
[30] A. S. Dolinin, "Pushkin i Gogol. K voprosu ob ikh lichnykh otnosheniyakh," in *Pushkinsky sbornik* (Moscow-Petrograd, 1923), 184.
[31] V. Nabokov, *Nikolay Gogol* (New York, 1959), 30.
[32] See the report in *Severnaya pchela* (1854) No.175, and also in Shenrok, vol.III, 228.
[33] M. Lemke, *Nikolayevskiye zhandarmy i literatura 1826-55 gg.* (St. Petersburg, 1909), 135.
[34] *Pushkin. Polnoye sobranie sochineny*, guide, 99.
[35] Stepanov, in Gogol, vol.1, xix.
[36] I. S. Turgenev, *Sobranie sochineny* (Moscow, 1962), vol.X, 114.
[37] Tsyavlovsky, 21.
[38] P.V.Annenkov, *Literaturniye vospominaniya*, 59.
[39] Collective commentary by the collaborative team of the IRLI in *Pushkin v vospominaniyakh sovremennikov* (Moscow, 1985), vol.II, 498.
[40] A. Slonimsky, Notes, in *Gogol. Sobranie sochineny v shesti tomakh*, vol.V, 437. See also N. N. Petrunina, Notes, in *Pushkin. Pis'ma poslednikh let* (Leningrad, 1969), 386; Y. M. Lotman, *Pushkin* (St. Petersburg, 1995), 268.
[41] Nabokov, 31.
[42] P. V. Annenkov, *Vospominaniya i kriticheskiye ocherki* (St. Petersburg, 1877), 184. What was said by Pushkin was interpreted by Y. Nagibin thus: "Got to be more careful with this *khokhol* [*Ukrainian*]" (*Literaturnaya gazeta*, October 20, 1993). The sense of the expression, according to Nagibin, was that Pushkin was wary of Gogol's capturing the prose crown for himself entirely, which, to put it mildly, is thoroughly debatable.
[43] *Literaturnoye nasledstvo*, No.16-18, 600-602. This volume is one of the publications whose political orientation distorts Gogol's entire biography and "the history of their friendship."
[44] Ibid., 99; B. V. Tomashevsky, in *Pushkin. Polnoye Sobranie sochineny* (Leningrad, 1977-1979), vol.VI, 552.
[45] Gippius, Notes, 436.
[46] Makogonenko, 33.
[47] I. P. Zolotussky, *Gogol* (Moscow, 1979), 185.
[48] I. I. Panayev, *Literaturniye vospominaniya* (Moscow-Leningrad, 1950), 65.
[49] Terts, 335.
[50] A. Zholkovsky, "Bluzhdayushchiye sny," from *Istoriya russkogo modernisma* (Sovetsky pisatel', Moscow: 1992), 92.
[51] N. I. Tarasenko-Otreshkov, "Vospominaniya o Pushkine," in *Russkaya starina* (February 1908). B. Lukyanovsky, "Pushkin i Gogol v ikh lichnykh vzaimootnosheniyakh," in *Besedy* (Moscow, 1915), 43.
[52] Y. G. Oksman, Guide to *Pushkin, in Polnoye sobranie sochineny* (1931) vol.VI, 99.
[53] Ibid., 100.
[54] Nabokov, 59.
[55] Letter of January 19, 1836, *Ostafyevsky arkhiv knyazey Vyazemskikh* (St. Petersburg, 1899), vol.III, 285.
[56] Helen Muchnik, "A Long Nose Argued with Its Owner," in *The New York Times Book Review*, December 23, 1973.
[57] V. V. Veresayev, *Sputniki Pushkina* (Moscow, 1937), vol.II, 294.
[58] John Bayley, "The Frivolity of Genius," in *Times Literary Supplement*, March 4, 1994.

[59] Karlinsky, *Sexual Labyrinth*.
[60] V. E. Vatsuro, *Zapiski kommentatora* (St. Petersburg, 1994), 313-319.
[61] From P. A. Pletnev to N. V. Gogol, October 27, 1844, in *Russky vestnik* (1890), No.11, 34.
[62] Wedding certificate at IRLI. Re this: S. Krayukhin, "Rodstvennitsa Pushkina i Gogolia," in *Nedelia* (Moscow, 1984), No.22.
[63] B. I. Bursov, *Sud'ba Pushkina* (Leningrad, 1986), 126.
[64] L. A. Chereysky, *Pushkin i yego okruzheniye* (2nd ed., Leningrad, 1988), 105.
[65] G. P. Danilevsky, "Znakomstvo s Gogolem," in *Sobranie sochineny* (9th ed., St. Petersburg, 1902), vol.XIII, 121.
[66] P. V.Annenkov, *Vospominaniya i kriticheskiye ocherki*, 185.

The Poet's 113th Love

[1] M. I. Tsvetayeva, "Moy Pushkin," in *Sochineniya* (Minsk, 1989), vol.II, 290.
[2] As related by A. A. Benkstern, "Biograficheskiy ocherk," in *Al'bom Pushkinskoy vystavki 1880 goda* (Moscow, 1887), 16.
[3] M. L. Gofman, "Nevesta i zhena Pushkina," in *Pis'ma Pushkina k zhene N. N. Goncharovoy* (Paris, 1936)
[4] P. K. Guber, *Donzhuansky spisok Pushkina* (Petrograd, 1923), 43. Guber cites an incomplete list, consisting of thirty-four names.
[5] Y. M. Lotman, *Roman "Yevgeny Onegin". Kommentary* (Leningrad, 1983), 388.
[6] *Pushkin v vospominaniyakh sovremennikov* (Moscow, 1974), vol.II, 192
[7] M. L. Gofman, *Pushkin—Don Zhuan* (Paris, 1935), 46-47.
[8] Koenig, *Ocherki russkoy literatury* (1837). Translated from the German (St. Petersburg, 1862), 114.
[9] *Literaturnaya gazeta*, 20 October 1993.
[10] M. D. Belyaev, *N. N. Pushkina v portretakh i otzyvakh sovremennikov* (Leningrad, 1930), 97.
[11] V. V. Yermilov, *Nash Pushkin* (Moscow, 1949), 57.
[12] *Zvenya, III-IV* (Academia, Moscow-Leningrad, 1934), 180.
[13] A. A. Akhmatova, *Stikhi i proza* (Leningrad, 1977), 547.
[14] V. V. Veresayev, *Sputniki Pushkina* (Moscow, 1937), 419.
[15] These notes are preserved in the Jules Lacroix archive of the Arsenal library in Paris.
[16] A. F. Florovsky, *Pushkin na stranitsakh dnevnika grafini D. F. Fikel'mon* (Prague, 1959), 565.
[17] S. Bulgakov, "Zhreby Pushkina," in *Nashe nasledie* (1989), 346
[18] P. P. Vyazemsky, *Sobranie sochineny*, 521.
[19] M. I. Tsvetayeva, *Moy Pushkin* (Moscow, 1981), 127.
[20] Ibid., 132.
[21] From N.P. Ozerova to S. L. Engel'gardt from Moscow, 4 May 1830, in *Pushkin i ego sovremenniki*, vol.XXXVII, 153. In French.
[22] From A. Y. Bulgakov to his brother, 2 July 1830, in *Russky arkhiv* (1901), vol.III, 482.
[23] Sobolevsky, a friend of Pushkin. From an article by V. I. Saitov (Petrograd, 1922).
[24] From S. D. Kiselev to N. S. Alekseyev, 26 December 1830, in *Pushkin. Pis'ma* (Moscow-Leningrad, 1928), vol.II, 124.
[25] P. I. Bartenev, *O Pushkine* (Moscow, 1992), 357.
[26] From A. Bulgakov to his brother, 16 February 1831, in *Russkaya mysl'* (1902), vol.I, 52.
[27] N. M. Smirnov, "Iz pamyatnykh zapisok," in *Pushkin v vospominaniyakh sovremennikov*, vol.II, 237.
[28] Veresayev, vol.II, 25.

[29]C. Frankland, *Narrative of a Visit to the Courts of Russia and Sweden in the Years 1830 and 1831* (London, 1832).
[30]From Prince Vyazemsky to his wife, 30 May 1830, in *Literaturnoye nasledie*, vol.16-18, 806.
[31]V.I. Tumansky, *Stikhotvoreniya i pis'ma* (St. Petersburg, 1912), 310-311. This evidence is given great importance, very reasonably, by A. Shik, *Zhenaty Pushkin* (Berlin,1936), 43.
[32]*Lik Pushkina*. Speeches given at a gala session of the Bogoslovsky Institute in Paris. (Paris, 1977), 26.
[33]R. G. Shults, *Pushkin i Knidsky mif* (M_nchen, 1985)
[34]P. Ye. Shchegolev, *Duel' i smert' Pushkina* (Moscow-Leningrad, 1928), 50
[35]Appendix in *Pushkin. Pis'ma k zhene* (Leningrad, 1987), 89.
[36]A. P. Arapova, *N. N. Pushkina-Lanskaya* (Moscow, 1994), 36-37.
[37]B. I. Bursov, *Sud'ba Pushkina* (Leningrad, 1986), 414.
[38]Veresayev, 439.
[39]*Pushkin i ego sovremenniki*, vol.XVII-XVIII, 168.
[40]*Sobolevskiy, drug Pushkina* (Petrograd, 1922), 38.
[41]"Bryullov v gostyakh u Pushkina letom 1836 goda" in *Pushkin v vospominaniyakh sovremennikov*, 293.
[42]A. Pozov, *Metafizika Pushkina* (Madrid, 1967), 224.
[43]Ye. A. Dolgorukova, in the anthology *Pushkinsky prazdnik* (1974), 24.
[44]*Pushkin v pis'makh Karamzinykh* (Moscow-Leningrad, 1960), 167.
[45]*Sochineniya i perepiska Pletneva*, vol.III, 524.
[46]Cited in I. Obodovskaya, M. Dementyev, *Posle smerti Pushkina* (Moscow, 1980), 162.
[47]About this in more detail, see S. Engel', in *Novy mir* (No.11, 1966); M. A. Dementyev, "Yeshche raz o pis'makh k Pushkinu yego zheny," in *Seriya yazyka i literatury* (Izvestiya AN SSSR: 1970), vol.XXIX, No.5.
[48]*Pushkin v vospominaniyakh svremmennikov*, 185.
[49]This work was published over a year before the publication of Serena Vitale's *Il bottone di Puskin* [*Pushkin's Button*] (Milan, 1995). D'Anthes's letters discovered by Vitale afford additional confirmation, but do not change our estimate of the situation.
[50]Bartenev, 335.
[51]Veresayev, 428.
[52]S. L. Abramovich, *Pushkin v 1836 godu* (Leningrad, 1989), 262.
[53]*Russky. arkhiv*, vol.IX, 124.
[54]Ach Gallet de Kultur, *Le tzar Nicolas et la sainte Russie* (Paris, 1855), 202-203.
[55]Veresayev, 435-436.
[56]Ibid., 437.
[57]M. I. Yashin, "Khronika predduel'nykh dney," in *Zvezda* (1963) No.9, 174.
[58]Cited in D. M. Urnov, *Pristrastiya i printsipy* (Moscow, 1991), 421.
[59]V. I. Kuleshov, "Zhena poeta," in I. M. Obodovskaya, M. A. Dementyev, *N. N. Pushkina* (Moscow, 1987), 7.
[60]In V. V. Kunin, compiler, *Druz'ya Pushkina* (Moscow, 1984).
[61]Obodovskaya, Dementyev, 13. Criticism of this book in the West was by Mark Altshuller, Helena Goscilo, in *SEEJ* (1987), vol.XXXI:3, 435-437.
[62]This myth is retold in various guises in other works by these authors as well: *Vokrug Pushkina* (Moscow, 1975); *Posle smerti Pushkina* (Moscow, 1980); *Pushkin v Yaropoltse* (Moscow, 1982).
[63]D. D. Blagoy, *Tvorcheskiy put' Pushkina* (Moscow, 1967), 361-362.
[64]A. A. Kuznetsova, *Moya Madonna* (Moscow, 1987), 46.
[65]V. V. Kunin, "N. N. Pushkina," in *Druz'ya Pushkina*, vol.II, 445.
[66]V. A. Sollogub, in *Pushkin v vospominaniyakh svremmennikov*, vol.II, 306.
[67]Kuznetsova, 24, 47.
[68]V. Kozyavin, "Luchshaya shakhmatistka Peterburga," in *Nedelia* (Moscow, 1987), No.5.

[69] Kuznetsova, 115.
[70] *Vremennik pushkinskoy komissii* (1966), 11-12.
[71] N. A. Rayevsky, "D. F. Fikel'mon v zhizni i tvorchestve Pushkina," in *Izbrannoye* (Minsk, 1978), 220.
[72] Kuznetsova, 121, 133, 44.
[73] Bursov, 405, 416.
[74] This was reported without any sense of humor in *Ogonyok* (1991), No.6, 16-17.
[75] Y. L. Levkovich, "Zhena poeta," in *Legendy i mify o Pushkine* (St. Petersburg, 1994).

A Divorce for Pushkin's Tatyana, *née* Larina

[1] F. M. Dostoyevsky, *Polnoye sobranie sochineny* (Leningrad, 1984), here and elsewhere vol.XXVI, 129-142; vol.XXV, 200.
[2] V. A.Viktorovich, "K probleme khudozhestvenno-filosofskogo yedinstva 'Evgeniya Onegina'," in *Boldinskiye chteniya* (1989), 24.
[3] The author would use his own word *antisemeytism* in the text, with the Russian root *semya*— meaning family, but it could be mixed up with another word *anti-Semitism*.
[4] G. I. Uspensky, "Prazdnik Pushkina," in *Dostoevsky v russkoy kritike* (Moscow, 1956), 240. In Soviet parlance, these words mean *parasites, renegades, morally depraved people*.
[5] Y. M. Nikishov, "Dal' svobodnogo romana kak kompozitsionny priyom v 'Evgenii Onegine'," in *Boldinskiye chteniya* (1985), 49.
[6] Nabokov, *Eugene Onegin* (New York, 1964), vol.II, 228.
[7] S. Zimovets, "Molchaniye Gerasima," in *Psikhoanaliticheskiye i filosofskiye esse o russkoy kul'ture* (Moscow,1996), 52.
[8] A. A. Potebnya, "Pereprava cherez reku kak predstavleniye braka," in *Moskovsky arkheologichesky vestnik* (1867-68), vol.I.
[9] V. N. Turbin, "'Yevgeny Onegin' i my," in *The Pushkin Journal* (1993),vol.I, No.2, 205.
[10] *Perepiska Pushkina* (Moscow, 1982), vol.I, 420-421.
[11] D.Clayton, *Ice and Flame* (Toronto, 1985). Here and elsewhere: 35, 37, 57, 113.
[12] V. G. Belinsky, *Polnoye sobranie sochineny* (Moscow, 1955). Here and elsewhere: vol.VII, 425-502; vol.XII, 94.
[13] A. A. Grigoryev, *Estetika i kritika* (Moscow, 1980), 67.
[14] D. D. Blagoy, *Masterstvo Pushkina* (Moscow, 1955), 193, 194.
[15] G. A. Gukovsky, *Pushkin i problemy realisticheskogo stilya* (Moscow, 1957), 271; G. Makogonenko, *Roman Pushkina "Yevgeny Onegin"* (Moscow, 1963), 125.
[16] M. Umanskaya, "Romantizm i realizm v literature 20-30kh godov XIX veka," in the anthology *Problemy russkoy literatury* (Yaroslavl, 1966), 24.
[17] V. N. Turbin, *Poetika romana Pushkina "Yevgeny Onegin"* (Moscow, 1996), 158.
[18] V. B. Shklovsky, *Ocherki po poetike Pushkina* (Berlin, 1923), 214.
[19] G. L. Gumenaya, "Zametki ob avtorskoy ironii v 'Evgenii Onegine,'" in *Boldinskiye chteniya* (Gorky, 1977), 47-54.
[20] K. Kasama, "Homosexuality in the Works of Pushkin," synopsis read at the Third International Pushkin Conference (1995), 4.
[21] V. K. Küchelbecker, *Dnevniki. Statyi* (Leningrad, 1977), 99-100.
[22] A. Terts, *Progulki s Pushkinym* (London, 1975), 28-29.
[23] N. M. Karamzin, *Izbranniye sochineniya* (Moscow, 1964), vol.I, 600.
[24] *Literaturnoye nasledstvo* (1958), 102-103.
[25] P. A. Vyazemsky, *Zapisniye knizhki* (Moscow, 1963), 208.
[26] E. G. Babayev, *Iz istorii russkogo romana XIX veka* (Moscow, 1984), 38.
[27] Blagoy, 180.
[28] S. G. Bocharov, "Formy plana" in *Voprosy literatury*, (No.12, 1967), 118.

[29] Y. M. Nikishov, "'Yevgeny Onegin': problema zhanra, " in *Boldinskiye chteniya* (1986), 7.
[30] A. A. Akhmatova, *Stikhi i proza,* 550.
[31] D. S. Mirsky, *Pushkin* (New York, 1963), 105-106.
[32] M. A. Tsyavlovsky, *Rukoyu Pushkina* (Moscow-Leningrad, 1935), 207-208.
[33] L. N. Pavlishchev, *Vospominaniya o Pushkine* (Moscow, 1890), 49.
[34] P. I. Chaykovsky, *Ob opere i balete* (Moscow, 1960), 53.
[35] N. O. Lerner, *Muzh Tatyany* (Leningrad, 1929).
[36] Y. N. Tynyanov, *Poetika, istoriya literatury, kino* (Moscow, 1977), 52-77.
[37] Ye. S. Khayev, "Problema fragmentarnosti syuzheta 'Yevgeniya Onegina'" in *Boldinskiye chteniya* (Gor'kiy, 1982).
[38] D. P. Makovitsky, "U Tolstogo" in *Literaturnoye nasledstvo*, vol.90, 143.
[39] D. S. Merezhkovsky, *Vechnye sputniki* (3rd ed.), St. Petersburg, 1906), 41.
[40] S. Bulgakov, "Zhreby Pushkina," in *Nashe naslediye* (III, 1989), 343.
[41] A. A. Grigoryev, *Literaturnaya kritika* (Moscow,1967), 212.
[42] Turbin, *Poetika romana,* 158
[43] M. Katz, "Love and Marriage in Pushkin's *Yevgeny Onegin*," in *Oxford Slavonic Papers.* (New Series, 1984), vol.XVII, 77, and further.
[44] Ye. S. Khayev, "Idillicheskiye motivy v 'Yevgenii Onegine,'" in *Boldinskiye chteniya* (Gor'kiy, 1981), 96.
[45] C. Emerson, "Tatyana," in *Vestnik Moskovskogo universiteta.* Series 9. Philology (No.6, 1995), 31.
[46] D. Rancour-Laferriere, *The Slave Soul of Russia* (New York, 1995), 247.
[47] L. N. Tolstoy, *Polnoye sobranie sochineny.* Here and elsewhere: vol.18, 322; vol.19, 213; vol.23,12-40; vol.62, 16-269.
[48] Babayev, 133
[49] S. A. Tolstaya, *Dnevniki,* (vol.I: Moscow, 1978), 503.
[50] A. Zagorovsky, *O razvode po russkomu pravu* (Khar'kov, 1884), 282-393.
[51] R. G. Shul'ts, *Pushkin i knidsky mif* (Munich, 1985).
[52] B. I. Bursov, *Sud'ba Pushkina* (Leningrad, 1986), 414, 416.
[53] M. Lermontov, *Polnoye sobranie sochineny* (Leningrad, 1940), vol.4, 384-5.
[54] N. L. Brodsky, *Yevgeny Onegin* (Moscow, 1964), 321.

Pushkin's Hallowed Nurse

[1] See: L. B. Modzalevsky, ed., *Pushkin. Pis'ma* (Academia: 1935), vol.III, 674; L. A. Chereysky, *Pushkin i yego okruzheniye* (Leningrad, 1988), 524; John Bayley, *Pushkin: A Comparative Commentary* (1971), 50-51; Yakovleva—multiple sources.
[2] N. I. Granovskaya, *Yesli yekhat' vam sluchitsya* (Leningrad, 1989), 63.
[3] B.S. Meylakh, *Pushkin i yego epokha* (Moscow, 1958), 686.
[4] *Slovar' sovremennogo russkogo literaturnogo yazyka* (Moscow, 1954), vol.III, 596.
[5] P. V. Annenkov, "Materialy dlya biografii Pushkina," in *Sochineniya Pushkina* (St. Petersburg, 1855), vol.I, 3.
[6] A. I. Ul'yansky, *Nyanya Pushkina* (Moscow-Leningrad, 1940).
[7] Granovskaya, 97.
[8] Ibid., 104.
[9] N. S. Braginskaya, *Pushkin i yego nyanya* (Rakurs: New York, 6 June 1995).
[10] V. V. Nabokov, trans., *Eugene Onegin* (Princeton, 1975), vol.IV, 64.
[11] A. Y. Pushkin, "Dlya biografii Pushkina," in *Moskvityanin* (1852), book 2, 21-25.
[12] N. V. Berg, "Seltso Zakharovo," in *Moskvityanin* (1851), book 3, 29-32.
[13] Chereysky, 455, 524. She is given different names and different years of birth in two places in the reference work.
[14] Ulyansky, 25.

[15] O. S. Pavlishcheva, "Vospominaniya o detstve Pushkina," in *Pushkin v vospominaniyakh sovremennikov* (Moscow, 1974), vol.I, 52.
[16] Nabokov, vol.II, 362, 454.
[17] His mother was his father's great-niece: "... my grandfather ... married ... a daughter of the brother of my father's grandfather (which makes him my mother's second cousin)" A. S. Pushkin, *Avtobiograficheskiye zapiski*. Could this be why five out of eight of the Pushkins' children died, because of the consanguinity in the marriage?
[18] Thomas Shaw, *Pushkin: A Concordance to the Poetry*, vol.I, 661.
[19] P. I. Bartenev, "Rod i detstvo Pushkina," in *O Pushkine* (Moscow, 1992), 57.
[20] Nabokov, vol.II, 362.
[21] N. Kotlyarevsky, *Pushkin kak istoricheskaya lichnost'* (Berlin, 1925), 167.
[22] P. V. Annenkov, *Pushkin. Materialy dlya yego biografii* (St. Petersburg, 1873), 112-113.
[23] M. I. Osipova, "Rasskazy o Pushkine, zapisannye M. I. Semevskim," in *Pushkin v vospominaniyakh sovremennikov* (Moscow, 1974), vol.I, 423.
[24] *Lyubovny byt pushkinskoy pory* (Moscow, 1994), vol.I, 232.
[25] Annenkov (1855), 4.
[26] As deciphered by M. A. Tsyavlovsky, *Tetrad' 2371. Rukoyu Pushkina* (Moscow-Leningrad, 1935), 315.
[27] More precisely, N. O. Lerner, "Arina Rodionovna i nyanya Dubrovskogo," in *Pushkin i yego sovremenniki*, 7th ed. (St. Petersburg, 1908), 68-72.
[28] Nabokov, vol.II, 274.
[29] N. F. Sumtsov, *Sbornik v pamyat' Pushkina* (Khar'kov, 1900), 115.
[30] Kotlyarevsky, 168.
[31] A. P. Kern, *Vospiminaniya. Dnevniki. Perepiska* (Moscow, 1989), 95.
[32] Nabokov, vol.II, 452, 454.
[33] V. V. Veresayev, Sputniki Pushkina (Moscow, 1993), vol.I, 41.
[34] Kern, 285.
[35] P. Parfenov, *Rasskazy o Pushkine, zapisannye K. A. Timofeyevym*.
[36] Ye. V. Pavlova, *Pushkin v portretakh* (Moscow, 1983), 26.
[37] B. V. Tomashevsky, *Kommentarii. Pushkin. Polnoye sobranie sochineny* (Leningrad, 1977), vol.I, 443.
[38] M. V. Shevlyakov, *Pushkin v anekdotakh* (St. Petersburg, 1899), 6-7.
[39] Bartenev, 57.
[40] Annenkov (1855), 4.
[41] Y. M. Lotman, *Roman "Yevgeny Onegin". Kommentariy* (Leningrad, 1983), 384.
[42] Annenkov (1855), 3,4; (1873), 112.
[43] B. S. Meylakh, Pushkin. Ocherk zhizni i tvorchestva (Moscow-Leningrad, 1949), 57.
[44] *Lyubovny byt*, 203-204.
[45] B. S. Meylakh, *Zhizn' Aleksandra Pushkina* (Leningrad, 1974), 198.
[46] "Slava russkogo naroda," in *Pravda*, 10 February 1937.
[47] Ulyansky, 5.
[48] N. V. Kalikina, *Osnovnoye v tvorcheskom i moral'nom oblike Pushkina* (Washington, 1975), 12.
[49] Granovskaya, 59.
[50] Ul'yansky, 5.
[51] Both quotations from V. V. Kunin, "Yakovleva," in *Druzya poeta* (Moscow, 1984), vol.I, 114.
[52] Granovskaya, 60, 62.
[53] Since in the Russian *societas* there exists a *motherland*, it would be nice if the word *matriotism* could be introduced into usage; but association with the vulgarism *"mat"* (foul language) would prevent it.

[54]There is an interesting analysis of this phenomenon in D. Rancour-Laferriere, *The Slave Soul of Russia: Moral Masochism and the Cult of Suffering* (New York, 1995), 242.
[55]Nabokov, vol.II, 452.
[56]D. J. Richards, C. R. S. Cockrell, "Introduction," in *Russian Views of Pushkin* (Oxford, 1976), xi.
[57]Bayley, 50.
[58]Pavlova, 98.
[59]Kunin, 120.
[60]V. S. Bozyrev, *Po pushkinskomu zapovedniku* (Moscow, 1977), 9.
[61]V. V. Pochinkovskaya, "Shest' let v Mikhaylovskom," unpublished memoir cited in I.T. Budilin, *Zolotaya tochka Rossii*, (St. Petersburg, 1995), 18-19.
[62]Z. Kh. Gareyev, as cited in Bozyrev, 10.
[63]Kunin, 119.
[64]N. I Granovskaya, "Podruga dney yego surovykh," in *Vecherniy Leningrad*, 2 November 1971; "Risunok Pushkina. Portrety Ariny Rodionovny," in *Vremennik pushkinskoy komissii, 1971* (Leningrad, 1973), 29.
[65]N. V. Izmaylov, *Ocherki tvorchestva Pushkina* (Leningrad, 1975), 44.
[66]N. I. Granovskaya, *Yesli yekhat' vam sluchitsya* (Leningrad, 1989), 67, 96, 97.
[67]Annenkov (1855), 122.
[68]V. N. Maykov, Skazka o rybake i rybke i yeyo istoki (St. Petersburg, 1892), 3-5.
[69]Ul'yansky, 43.
[70]Annenkov (1873), 112.
[71]I. I. Pushchin, "Zapiski o Pushkine," in *Pushkin v vospominaniyakh sovremennikov* (Moscow, 1974), 109.
[72]Osipova, *Pushkin v vospominaniyakh sovremennikov*, vol.I, 426. For an example of the emended text, see Granovskaya (1989), 57.
[73]Ulyansky, 53.
[74]V. D. Svirsky, an author of textbooks on Russian literature; a personal communication made in Riga in 1985.
[75]Pushchin, 109.
[76]*Russky bibliofil* (1911), No.5, 34. There is also some commentary on the poet's serf mistresses and his nurse in her capacity of procuress in B. L. Modzalevsky, *Pushkin. Pis'ma* (Moscow-Leningrad, 1928), vol.II, 153.
[77]M. K. Azadovsky, "Pushkin i folklor," in *Vremennik pushkinskoy komissii No.3* (Moscow-Leningrad, 1937), 154.
[78]Izmaylov, 28.
[79]V. E. Batsuro, "Litseyskoye tvorchestvo Pushkina," in *Pushkin. Stikhotvoreniya litseyskikh let* (St. Petersburg, 1994), 387.

The Dangerous Jests of Albert Robida

[1]A. Robida, *Dvadtsatoye stoletiye: elektricheskaya zhizn'* (St. Petersburg, 1894), 7-8. See further: Robida. There are many stylistic faults in the book, made evidently by the translator, and many proofing errors as well. In the quotes cited, they have been corrected as far as possible, as long as it doesn't change the sense of the text.
[2]Robida, 25.
[3]Ibid., 28.
[4] "King of the Apes," "Around the World in 80 Days," "The Four Queens," "In Search of the White Elephant," "His Highness, the Ruler of the North Pole." (Paris, 1882)
[5]Robida, 313.
[6]Ibid., 243-244
[7]Ibid., 102.

[8] John Clute and Peter Nicholls, eds. *The Encyclopedia of Science Fiction* (Orbit, 1993), 1014.
[9] Robida, 16-17.
[10] Ibid.
[11] Ibid., 22-23, 70.
[12] Ibid., 265.
[13] Ibid., 76.
[14] Ibid., 196.
[15] Ibid., 253.
[16] Ibid., 130.
[17] Ibid., 133.
[18] Ibid., 140.
[19] Ibid., 143.
[20] Ibid., 213.
[21] Ibid., 144.
[22] Ibid., 238-239.
[23] Ibid., 200.
[24] Ibid., 216.
[25] Ibid., 298.
[26] Ibid., 248.
[27] Ibid., 127.
[28] I. Il'f and Ye. Petrov, "Zapisniye knizhki," *Sobranie sochineny* (Moscow, 1961), vol.V, 189.
[29] Robida, 207.
[30] Ibid., 237.
[31] Ibid., 186.
[32] Ibid., 170, 171.
[33] D. Ziberov, "Alber Robida—shutnik i mechtatel," in *Nedelya* (Moscow, 1973).

The Overt and Covert Lives of Konstantin Ventzel

[1] K. N. Ventzel, notebook, 1933-1935. Archive of the Academy of Pedagogical Sciences (now the Russian Federation Academy of Education). Stock No.23, inventory No.1, page 14, sheet 39. In further references, only page and sheet numbers (whenever sheets are numbered) are indicated for his manuscripts.

[2] Ventzel, diary, 1878, page 7, quotation on sheets 19-38.

[3] *Deyateli revolyutsionnogo dvizheniya v Rossii. Bibliograficheskiy slovar' ot predshestvennikov dekabristov do padeniya tsarizma* (Moscow, 1933), vol.3, issue No.1, 557.

[4] Ventzel, *Iz perzhitogo, peredumannogo, perechuvstvovannogo i sdelannogo*. Autobiographical sketch, 1932. Page 1, sheet 106. In further references, *Iz perezhitogo...*

[5] Ventzel, copybook with prison notes, 1885. Page 7.

[6] Letter to Ventzel from V. G. Korolenko of May 9, 1889, in *Sobranie sochineny*, vol.10 (Moscow, 1956), 111.

[7] *Iz perezhitogo...*, sheet 336.

[8] Ventzel, "Etika, pedagogika i politika," in the magazine *Vestnik vospitaniya*, No.3 (1906). Cited from manuscript, page 1, sheet 360.

[9] Ventzel, "Nravstvennoye vospitaniye i svoboda," in the magazine *Svobodnoye vospitaniye*, No.4 (1908), 52.

[10] *Iz perizhitogo...*, sheet 360.

[11] Ventzel, *Nuzhno li obuchat' detey nravstvennosti* (1912). Page 31, sheets 20-24.

[12] *Iz perizhitogo...*, citations on sheets 405-462.

[13] Ventzel, *Unichtozheniye tyurem* (Moscow, 1917), 1.

[14]Ventzel, "Sotsializm i vospitaniye," in *Svobodnoye vospitaniye*, No.1-3 (1918). Cited from manuscript page 1, sheet 101.

[15]Ventzel, *Teoriya svobodnogo vospitaniya i ideal'nyy detskiy sad* (Moscow, 1923), 24-25.

[16]Ventzel, in *Svobodnoye vospitaniye*, No.1-3 (1918), 24.

[17]N. K. Krupskaya, *Pedagogicheskiye sochineniya* (Moscow, 1957), vol.I, 140.

[18]*Bol'shaya sovetskaya entsiklopediya*, 1st ed. (Moscow, 1928), vol.X, 240.

[19]P. P. Blonsky, *Izbrannye pedagogicheskiye proizvedeniya* (Moscow, 1961), 43.

[20]Ventzel, "Provozglasheniye prav rebyonka," in *Svobodnoye vospitaniye*, No.1-3 (1918). Cited from manuscript, page 31, sheet 109.

[21]*Iz perezhitogo...*, sheets 467 and 476.

[22]Ventzel, diary, 1917. Page 39, sheet 183.

[23]S. Vinokurov and T. Pchel'nkov, *Vidnye russkiye pedagogi v Voronezhskom kraye* (Voronezh, 1972), 23.

[24]*Voronezhskaya kommuna* newspaper, No.28 (1922).

[25]Ventzel, copybook with notes, Voronezh, 1921. Page 46, sheet 17.

[26]Ventzel, *Revolyutsiya i trebovaniya nravstvennosti*, manuscript collection of articles from Voronezh, undated. Page 32, quotation from sheets 5-27.

[27]Ventzel, diary, 1917. Page 39, sheets 107-108.

[28]A. V. Lunacharsky, *Osnovy prosvetitel'skoy politiki sovetskoy vlasti* (Moscow: Rabotnik Prosveshcheniya,1924), 6.

[29]*Byulleten' IV Vserossiyskogo syezda zavgubono, 3 dekabrya 1923*, No.6, 14.

[30]*Izvestiya*, November 5, 1922, and March 22, 1923.

[31]*Na putyakh k novoy shkole* magazine, No.7-8 (1923), 5-6.

[32]Ventzel, diary notes, 1925. Page 14, sheet 13.

[33]*Iz perzhitogo...*, sheets 52 and 67.

[34]*Bol'shaya sovetskaya entsiklopediya*, 2nd ed. (Moscow, 1951), vol.VII, 468.

[35]*Pedegogicheskaya entsiklopediya* (Moscow, 1966), vol.III, 801.

[36]*Sovetskiy entsiklopedicheskiy slovar'* (Moscow, 1979), 211.

[37]V. Zenkovsky, *Russkaya pedagogika v XX veke* (Paris, 1960), 16. (First edition of book: Belgrade, 1933).

[38]*Bolshaya sovetskaya entsiklopediya*, 3rd ed. (Moscow, 1971), vol.IV, 1550.

[39]Ventzel, copybook with notes, from Voronezh, 1921. Page 46, sheets 27 and 27 *verso*.

[40]Ventzel, diary, 1884. Page 7.

[41]Ventzel, diary, 1925. Page 14, sheet 2 *verso*.

[42]Ibid., sheet 24 *verso*.

[43]Ventzel, diary, 1930. Page 16, sheet 3 *verso*.

[44]Ventzel, *Moi zamechaniya po povodu teorii dialekticheskogo materializma, 1929-1935*. Page 63, quotations from sheets 2-40.

[45]Ventzel, *Tri revolyutsii* (1923). Page 54, sheets 2 and 20.

[46]Ventzel, *Etika i pedagogika tvorcheskoy lichnosti* (Moscow, 1912), vol.II, 589.

[47]Ventzel, *O vnutrennem rabstve* (1925-1934). Page 59, sheets 4 and 5.

[48]Ventzel, *Religiya tvorcheskoy zhizni. Problema religii v svete osvobozhdeniya ot tsepey nevidimogo rabstva* (1923). Page 53, sheet 390.

[49]Ventzel, *Tri revolyutsii* (1923). Page 54, sheet 20.

[50]Ventzel, *Osvobozhdeniye rebyonka* (Moscow, 1906), 5.

[51]Ventzel, diary, 1936-1937. Page 16, sheet 8.

[52]Ventzel, *Evolyutsiya nravstvennykh idealov* (unfinished manuscript). Page 75, quotations from sheets 75-105.

[53]V. S. Solovyov, *Dukhovnye osnovy zhizni. Sobranie sochineny* (Petrograd, 1917), vol.III, 288.

Alexander Kuprin: from Midden to Mantelpiece

[1] V. I. Lenin, *Polnoye sobranie sochineny*, 5th ed., vol.XXII, 280.
[2] *Bol'shaya sovetskaya entsiklopediya*, 3rd ed., vol.V, 359.
[3] V. Vorovsky, "A. Kuprin," in *Literaturno-kriticheskiye statyi* (Moscow, 1956). The articles in the collection have been cleaned up and amended since their original appearance in the 1920s.
[4] This is a curious and little-studied fact. I found out about it from my colleague Professor Mark Steinberg.
[5] Letters of Kuprin, in K. N. Batyushkov and F. D. Batyushkov, *Kuprin* (Vologda, 1968), 168.
[6] *Ogonyok*, No.36 (1945), 9.
[7] *Literaturnaya entsiklopediya*, A. Lunacharsky, ed. (Kommunisticheskaya akademiya: Moscow, 1931), vol.V, 746. This was withdrawn from Soviet libraries in the Thirties by Stalin's censors.
[8] K. A. Kuprina returned to Russia twenty years afterward and there wrote the book *Kuprin—moy otets* (*Kuprin—My Father*). The manuscript was emended to such an extent that it is useless as a source of information.
[9] N.A. Teffi, "Moya letopis," in *Vremya i my*, No.111, 237.
[10] S. I. Fonskaya, *Dom v Golitsyne* (Moscow: 1967).
[11] *Literaturnaya gazeta*, June 5, 1937: "Kuprin: otryvki vospominaniy"; *Izvestiya*, June 18, 1937; "About the author," in Alexander Kuprin, *The Garnet Bracelet* (Moscow, no year indicated), foreign edition.
[12] A. Kuprin, "Moskva rodnaya," in *Kosomolskaya pravda*, October 11, 1937.
[13] Ibid.
[14] K. G. Paustovsky, "Potok zhizni," in *A. I. Kuprin: Sobranie sochineny* (Moscow, 1957), vol.I, 8, 27.
[15] N. N. Fonyakova, *Kuprin v Peterburge-Leningrade* (Leningrad, 1986), 4.
[16] *Kratkaya literaturnaya entsiklopediya*, vol.III, 910.
[17] Teffi, 231.
[18] As cited in A. Dynnik, *Kuprin: ocherk zhizni i tvorchestva* (Lansing, 1969), 87.
[19] Ibid., 99.
[20] R. V. Pletnev, *Istoriya russkoy literatury XX veka* (Englewood, 1987), 28.
[21] P. N. Berkov, *Kuprin* (Moscow, 1956), 161.
[22] L. V. Krutikova, *Kuprin* (Leningrad, 1971), 115.
[23] A. V. Khrabrovitsky, from a personal communication in Moscow, 1985.
[24] *Zhurnal-zhurnalov* (St. Petersburg, 1916), No.15, 5.

Visiting Stalin's Uninvited

[1] S. I. Alliluyeva, *Twenty Letters to a Friend* (London, 1967). Further on in the text there are references to Alliluyeva's pronouncements on pp.17-23.
[2] V. Nekrasov, "Ya byl ryadom so Stalinym," in *Novoye russkoye slovo*, Oct. 28, 1994.
[3] Y. V. Trifonov, "Zapiski soseda," in *Druzhby narodov* (No.10, 1989), 39.
[4] The diary of M. A. Svanidze, *Stalin v obyatiyakh semyi* (Moscow, 1993), 169-170.
[5] S. A. Mikoyan, "Asketizm vozhdya," in *Ogonyok* (No.15, 1989), 29.
[6] V. Nekrasov, "Zakat khozyayina," in *Novoye russkoye slovo*, Oct. 24, 1994.
[7] Ibid.
[8] See *Ogonyok*, No.37, 1989.
[9] S. J. Alliluyeva, "Dva poslednikh razgovora," in *Moskovskiye novosti*, No.42, Oct.12, 1990.
[10] *Stalin v obyatiyakh semyi*, 104.
[11] Ibid., 104-105.
[12] S. J. Alliluyeva, *Kniga dlya vnuchek* (New York, 1991), 160-161.

[13] Alliluyeva, "Dva poslednikh razgovora."

The Ruchyi Churchyard Mystery

[1] N. L. Stepanov, *Velimir Khlebnikov. Zhizn i tvorchestvo* (Moscow, 1975), 176.
[2] D. V. Petrovsky, *Povest o Khlebnikove* (Moscow, 1926), 45.
[3] *Sobranie proizvedeniy Velimira Khlebnikova v pyati tomakh pod obshchey redaktsiey Y. Tynyanova i N. Stepanova* (Leningrad, 1928-1933). Cited below as Khlebnikov, volume, and page number.
[4] V. V. Mayakovsky, *Sobranie sochineny* (Moscow, 1978), vol.XI, 155.
[5] Khlebnikov, vol.V, 315.
[6] V. Khlebnikov, *Neizdannye proizvodeniya* (Moscow, 1940), 384.
[5] R. Rayt, "Vse luchshiye vospominanya," in *Uchenye zapiski Tartusskogo universiteta*, issue N°184, *Trudy po russkoy i slavyanskoy filologii* (Tartu, 1966), vol.IX, 267.
[8] Mayakovsky, vol.XI, 155.
[9] *Yezhegodnik Rukopisnogo otdela Pushkinskogo doma, 1974* (Leningrad, 1976), 17.
[10] Khlebnikov, vol.V, 318.
[11] Ibid., 324.
[12] Ibid., 325-326.
[13] P. V. Miturich, *Vospominiya* (manuscript).
[14] Y. L. Stepanova, from conversation notes.
[15] M. P. Lobanov, *Razmyshleniye o literature i zhizni* (Moscow, 1982), 220.
[16] Khlebnikov, vol.V, 236.
[17] Notebook. Khlebnikov, vol.V, 274.
[18] L. Y. Brik, *Almanakh "S Mayakovskim"* (Moscow, 1934), 78.
[19] Khlebnikov, vol.V, 270.
[20] See the article "'Yunosha' Khlebnikov i 'vzrosly' Platonov," about Khlebnikov's artistic foresight, by I. M. Yefimov, in *Novoye russkoye slovo*, July 9, 1993.
[21] Khlebnikov, vol.V, 179.
[22] Khlebnikov, vol.V, 73.
[23] Khlebnikov, vol.V, 82.
[24] S. M. Gorodetsky, "Velimir Khlebnikov. Nekrolog," in *Vsemirnaya illyustratsiya*, issue N°III (Moscow, 1922).
[25] There is an interesting commentary in Barbara Lönnqvist, "Chlebnikov's 'double speech,'" in Chap.6 of *Velimir Chlebnikov: Myth and Reality* (Amsterdam, 1986), 291.
[26] Russian State Archives of Literature and Art (R.G.A.L.I.), stock 527, list 1.
[27] O. E. Mandelshtam, *Sobranie sochineny* (1971), vol.II, 247.
[28] Khlebnikov, *Neizd.* On manuscript rights, 323.
[29] Ibid.
[30] Mayakovsky, vol.XI, 151.
[31] Ye. G. Etkind, "Zabolotsky i Khlebnikov," in *Velimir Chlebnikov: Myth and Reality* (Amsterdam, 1986), 544.
[32] A. K. Zholkovsky, "Grafomanstvo kak priyom," ibid., 585.
[33] Khlebnikov, vol.V, 165-167.
[34] V. Khlebnikov, *Proza* (Moscow, 1990), 4.
[35] D. P. Mirsky, *Literaturno-kriticheskiye statyi* (Moscow, 1978), 223.
[36] M. Polyakov, "Khlebnikov. Mirovozzreniye i poetika," in *Khlebnikov. Tvoreniya* (Moscow, 1986), 34.
[37] Stepanov, *Khlebnikov*, 186.
[38] Ibid., 188.
[39] For example, Polyakov, *Khlebnikov. Tvoreniya*, 13.
[40] A. Zhavoronkov, E. Tikhonova, V. Tyurin. *Pisateli na Novgorodskoy zemle*

(Novgorod, 1960), 103.
[41] E. G. Istomina, *Kresttsy* (Novgorod, 1968).
[42] Zoya's mother, thriving at the time, was my neighbor. The poor woman had been turned into a hysteric, for years repeating endlessly the tribune's official version of how the fascists had hanged her heroic daughter, and then crying out a hail in honor of whoever was at the top.
[43] *Vechernyaya Moskva*, Oct. 29, 1984.
[44] Personal archive.
[45] Khlebnikov, vol.I, 182 and 174.

Trifonov's Fate: or, A Good Writer in a Bad Time

[1] V. Stepanov, "Syuzhety zhurnalnoy prozy," in *Izvestiya*, 16 August 1974.
[2] *Moskovsky komsomolets*, special ed., 11 December 1969.
[3] "In apartment 137 of entrance No. 7 lived Valentin Trifonov, as a result of whose affair with the daughter of his second wife Yuri Trifonov was born." From A. Kolesnikov, "A Continent on a Quayside," in *Novoye russkoye slovo*, 4 September 1992. Comment on this affair, something to make you shudder, I'll leave to the reader.
[4] Y. V. Trifonov, "A Neighbor's Notes," in *Druzhba narodov*, No. 10, 1989, p. 7; *passim*. Prepared for publication by Trifonov's widow, O. R. Miroshnichenko.
[5] "Notes," 36.
[6] Ibid., 37.
[7] Ibid.
[8] Ibid., 7.
[9] Ibid., 8.
[10] Ibid., 13.
[11] Ibid., 12.
[12] Ibid., 17-18.
[13] *Great Soviet Encyclopedia*, 3rd ed., vol.XXVI, 1977, 681. See also the anthology *Komissary* (Moscow, 1967).
[14] "Notes," 24.
[15] Ibid., 25.
[16] Ibid., 33.
[17] Ibid., 35.
[18] Ibid.
[19] M. Popovsky, *Journals*. Manuscript.
[20] T. Papera, "Trifonov: His Heroes and Their Family Life," *IV World Congress for Soviet and East European Studies. Abstracts*. (Harrowgate, 1990), 99. And the book by the same author.
[21] On this subject: I. Yefimov, *Vremya dobra* (Tenafly, 1993), 172-174.
[22] Y. Oklyanskiy, *Yuri Trifonov. Portret-vospominaniye* (Moscow, 1987), 171.
[23] For example, see: Carolina De Maegd-Soëp, *Trifonov and the Drama of the Russian Intelligentsia* (Ghent, 1990). In this book, Trifonov is simply equated to Leo Tolstoy and Chekhov.
[24] "Notes," 8.
[25] Y. Trifonov, *Rasskazy i povesti* (Moscow, 1971); F. Kuznetsov, "V borbe za cheloveka," in *Sobranie sochineny v chetyryokh tomakh* (Moscow, 1985), vol.I.
[26] This analysis: from Wolfgang Kasack, Dictionary of Russian Literature since1917 (New York, 1988), 424-425.
[27] Y. Trifonov, *Literary Reminiscences* (Olson Laboratory, U.C. Davis) Tape 23074-1.
[28] *Predvaritel'nye itogi* (Moscow: Sovetskaya Rossiya, 1975), 102 pp.
[29] In the *glasnost'* period articles began appearing to the effect that the Literary Institute "had become a refuge for militant hacks and ignorant alcoholics." See, for example: S.D. Artamonov, F.G. Biryukov, "Nuzhen li Litinstitut?" in *Literaturnaya gazeta*, 9 February 1990. Incidentally,

those categories of people have always been there, just as there have always been talented students.
   [30]Y. Trifonov, "Intervyu o kontaktakh. Beseda s Ye. Stoyanovskoy," in *Inostrannaya literatura*, No.6, 1978, 243-251.
   [31]Ibid., 247.
   [32]Ibid., 251.

Bibliography

Abramovich, S. L. *Pushkin v 1836 godu.* Leningrad: 1989.
Akhmatova, A. A. *Stikhi i proza.* Leningrad: 1977.
Alliluyeva, S. I. *Kniga dlya vnuchek.* New York: 1991.
------. "Dva poslednikh razgovora." *Moskovskiye novosti* No.42 (October 12, 1990).
------. *Twenty Letters to a Friend.* London: 1967.
Altshuller, Mark, and Goscilo, Helena. *Slavic and East-European Journal* (vol. XXXI, 1987).
Annenkov, P. V. *Literaturniye vospominaniya.* Moscow: 1983.
------. *Vospominaniya i kriticheskiye ocherki.* St. Petersburg: 1877.
------. *Pushkin. Materialy dlya yego biografii.* St. Petersburg: 1873.
------. "Materialy dlya biografii Pushkina." In *Sochineniya Pushkina.* St. Petersburg: 1855.
Arapova, A. P. *N. N. Pushkina-Lanskaya.* Moscow: 1994.
Artamonov, S. D., and Biryukov, F. G. "Nuzhen li Litinstitut?" *Literaturnaya gazeta* (February 9, 1990).
Azadovsky, M. K. "Pushkin i folklor." In *Vremennik pushkinskoy komissii No.3.* Moscow-Leningrad: 1937.
Babayev, E. G. *Iz istorii russkogo romana XIX veka.* Moscow: 1984.
Bartenev, P. I. *O Pushkine.* Moscow: 1992.
------. *Rasskazy o Pushkine.* Moscow: 1925.
Batyushkov, K. N., and Batyushkov, F. D. *Kuprin.* Vologda: 1968.
Bayley, John. "The Frivolity of Genius." *Times Literary Supplement* (March 4, 1994).
------. *Pushkin: A Comparative Commentary.* 1971.
Belinsky, V. G. "O russkoy povesti i povestyakh Gogolia" and "Pokhozhdeniya Chichikova, ili Mertvye dushi." In *Izbrannye sochineniya.* Moscow: 1948.
------. *Polnoye sobranie sochineny.* Moscow: 1955.
Belyaev, M. D. *N. N. Pushkina v portretakh i otzyvakh sovremennikov.* Leningrad: 1930.
Benkstern, A. A. "Biograficheskiy ocherk." In *Albom Pushkinskoy vystavki 1880 goda.* Moscow: 1887.

Berg, N. V. "Sel'tso Zakharovo." *Moskvityanin.* (1851).
Berkov, P. N. *Kuprin.* Moscow: 1956.
Blagoy, D. D. *Tvorchesky put Pushkina.* Moscow: 1967.
------. *Literatura i deystvitelnost.* Moscow: 1959.
------. *Masterstvo Pushkina.* Moscow: 1955.
Blonsky, P. P. *Izbrannye pedagogicheskiye proizvedeniya.* Moscow: 1961.
Bocharov, S. G. "Formy plana." *Voprosy literatury* (No.12, 1967).
Bolshaya sovetskaya entsiklopediya, 3rd ed. Moscow: 1971.
------, 2nd ed. Moscow: 1951.
------, 1st ed. Moscow: 1928.
Bozyrev, V. S. *Po pushkinskomu zapovedniku.* Moscow: 1977.
Braginskaya, N. S. "Pushkin i yego nyanya." *Rakurs.* New York: June 6, 1995.
Brik, L. Y. *Almanakh "S Mayakovskim".* Moscow: 1934.
Brodsky, N. L. *Yevgeny Onegin.* Moscow: 1964.
Budilin, I. T. *Zolotaya tochka Rossii.* St. Petersburg: 1995.
Bulgakov, A. Y. Letter to his brother, February 16, 1831. *Russkaya mysl.* Vol. II. (1902).
------. Letter to his brother, July 2, 1830. *Russky arkhiv.* Vol. III. (1901).
Bulgakov, S. "Zhreby Pushkina." *Nashe naslediye.* (No.III, 1989).
Bursov, B. I. *Sud'ba Pushkina.* Leningrad: 1986.
Byulleten IV Vserossiyskogo s"yezda zavgubono. (No.6, December 3, 1923).
Chaykovsky, P. I. *Ob opere i balete.* Moscow: 1960.
Chereysky, L. A. *Pushkin i yego okruzheniye.* 2nd ed., Leningrad: 1988.
Clayton, D. *Ice and Flame.* Toronto: 1985.
Clute, John, and Nicholls, Peter, eds. *The Encyclopedia of Science Fiction.* Orbit, 1993.
Danilevsky, G. P. "Znakomstvo s Gogolem." In *Sobranie sochineny,* 9th ed. St. Petersburg: 1902.
De Maegd-Soëp, Carolina. *Trifonov and the Drama of the Russian Intelligentsia.* Ghent: 1990.
Dementyev, M. A. "Yeshche raz o pis'makh k Pushkinu yego zhene." *Seriya yazyka i literatury.* Vol. XXIX, No.5. Izvestiya AN SSSR, 1970.
Deyateli revolyutsionnogo dvizheniya v Rossii. Bibliograficheskiy slovar' ot predshestvennikov dekabristov do padeniya tsarizma. Moscow: 1933.
Dolgorukova, Y. A. *Pushkinsky prazdnik.* 1974.
Dolinin, A. S. "Pushkin i Gogol. K voprosu ob ikh lichnykh otnosheniyakh." In *Pushkinsky sbornik.* Moscow-Petrograd: 1923.
Dostoyevsky, F. M. *Polnoye sobranie sochineny.* Leningrad: 1984.
Dynnik, A. *Kuprin: ocherk zhizni i tvorchestva.* Lansing: 1969.
Emerson, C. "Tatyana." *Vestnik Moskovskogo universiteta.* Series 9. Philology No.6, 1995.
Etkind, Y. G. "Zabolotsky i Khlebnikov." In *Velimir Chlebnikov: Myth and Reality.* Amsterdam: 1986.

Florovsky, A. F. *Pushkin na stranitsakh dnevnika grafini D. F. Fikelmon.* Prague: 1959.
Fonskaya, S. I. *Dom v Golitsyne.* Moscow: 1967.
Fonyakova, N. N. *Kuprin v Peterburge-Leningrade.* Leningrad: 1986.
Frankland, C. *Narrative of a Visit to the Courts of Russia and Sweden in the Years 1830 and 1831.* London: 1832.
Gippius, V. V. *Gogol. Polnoye sobranie sochineny.* Vol. X. AN SSSR, 1938-1952.
------. *Gogol.* Leningrad: 1924.
Gofman, M. L. "Nevesta i zhena Pushkina." In *Pis'ma Pushkina k zhene N. N. Goncharovoy.* Paris: 1936
------. *Pushkin—Don Zhuan.* Paris: 1935.
Gogol, N. V.. *Sobranie sochineny v shesti tomakh.* Vol. VI. Moscow: 1952-1953.
Gorodetsky, S. M. "Velimir Khlebnikov. Nekrolog." *Vsemirnaya illyustratsiya,* No.III. Moscow: 1922.
Granovskaya, N. I. *Yesli yekhat vam sluchitsya.* Leningrad: 1989.
------. "Risunok Pushkina. Portrety Ariny Rodionovny." In *Vremennik pushkinskoy komissii, 1971.* Leningrad: 1973.
------. "Podruga dney yego surovykh." *Vecherny Leningrad* (November 2, 1971).
Grigoryev, A. A. *Estetika i kritika.* Moscow: 1980.
------. *Literaturnaya kritika.* Moscow: 1967.
Guber, P. K. *Donzhuansky spisok Pushkina.* Petrograd: 1923.
Gukovsky, G. A. *Pushkin i problemy realisticheskogo stilya.* Moscow: 1957.
Gumennaya, G. L. "Zametki ob avtorskoy ironii v 'Yevgenii Onegine'." *Boldinskiye chteniya.* (1977).
Ilf, I. A., and Petrov, Y. P. *Sobranie sochineny.* Moscow: 1961.
Ilyin, V. N. "Dostoyevsky i Gogol." *Orient und Occident.* Heft 10, 1932.
Istomina, E. G. *Kresttsy.* Novgorod: 1968.
Izmaylov, N. V. *Ocherki tvorchestva Pushkina.* Leningrad: 1975.
Kalikina, N. V. *Osnovnoye v tvorcheskom i moral'nom oblike Pushkina.* Washington: 1975.
Karamzin, N. M. *Izbranniye sochineniya.* Moscow: 1964.
Karlinsky, Simon. *The Sexual Labyrinth of Nikolay Gogol.* Cambridge, Mass.: Harvard University Press, 1976.
Kasack, Wolfgang. *Dictionary of Russian Literature since 1917.* New York: 1988.
Kasama, K. "Homosexuality in the Works of Pushkin." Synopsis read at the Third International Pushkin Conference, 1995.
Katz, M. "Love and Marriage in Pushkin's *Yevgeny Onegin.*" *Oxford Slavonic Papers.* New Series: Vol. XVII, 1984.
Kern, A. P. *Vospiminaniya. Dnevniki. Perepiska.* Moscow: 1989.
Khayev, Y. S. "Problema fragmentarnosti syuzheta 'Yevgeniya Onegina'." *Boldinskiye chteniya.* (1982).

------. "Idillicheskiye motivy v 'Yevgenii Onegine'." *Boldinskiye chteniya.* (1981).
Khlebnikov, V. *Proza.* Moscow: 1990.
------. *Neizdannye proizvodeniya.* Moscow: 1940.
Kirpotin, V. Y. *Pushkin. Pamyatka.* Leningrad, 1937.
------. *Naslediye Pushkina i kommunizm.* Moscow: 1936.
Kiselev, S. D. Letter to N. S. Alekseyev, December 26, 1830. In *Pushkin. Pis'ma.* Vol. II. Moscow-Leningrad: 1928.
Koenig. *Ocherki russkoy literatury* (1837). St. Petersburg: 1862.
Kolesnikov, A. "Kontinent na naberezhnoy." *Novoye russkoye slovo* (September 4, 1992).
Komissary. Moscow: 1967.
Korolenko, V. G. *Sobranie sochineny.* Moscow: 1956.
Kotlyarevsky, N. *Pushkin kak istoricheskaya lichnost'.* Berlin: 1925.
Kozyavin, V. "Luchshaya shakhmatistka Peterburga." *Nedelya.* Moscow: No.5, 1987.
Kratkaya literaturnaya entsiklopediya. Vol. III.
Krayukhin, S. "Rodstvennitsa Pushkina i Gogolya." *Nedelya.* Moscow: No.22, 1984.
Krupskaya, N. K. *Pedagogicheskiye sochineniya.* Vol. I. Moscow: 1957.
Krutikova, L. V. *Kuprin.* Leningrad: 1971.
Kuleshov, V. I. "Zhena poeta." In *N. N. Pushkina.* Moscow: 1987.
Kultur, Ach Gallet de. *Le tzar Nicolas et la sainte Russie.* Paris: 1855.
Kunin, V. V. "Yakovleva." In *Druzya Pushkina.* Moscow: 1984.
Kuprin, Alexander. "Otryvki vospominany." *Literaturnaya gazeta.* June 5, 1937.
------. "Moskva rodnaya." *Kosomolskaya pravda* (October 11, 1937).
------. *The Garnet Bracelet.* Moscow: [*no year indicated*].
Kuznetsov, F. "V borbe za cheloveka." In Trifonov. *Sobranie sochineny v chetyryokh tomakh.* Vol. I. Moscow: 1985.
Kuznetsova, A. A. *Moya Madonna.* Moscow: 1987.
Küchelbecker, V. K. *Dnevniki. Statyi.* Leningrad, 1977.
Lemke, M. *Nikolayevskiye zhandarmy i literatura 1826-55 gg.* St. Petersburg: 1909.
Lenin, V. I. *Polnoye sobranie sochineny.* 5th ed.. Vol. XXII.
------. *Sochineniya.* 4th ed.. Vol. XVIII.
Lermontov, M. *Polnoye sobranie sochineny.* Vol. IV. Leningrad: 1940.
Lerner, N. O. *Muzh Tatyany.* Leningrad: 1929.
------. "Arina Rodionovna i nyanya Dubrovskogo." In *Pushkin i yego sovremenniki,* 7th ed. St. Petersburg: 1908.
Levitt, Marcus. *Russian Literary Politics and the Pushkin Celebration of 1880.* Ithaca and London: Cornell University Press, 1989.
Levkovich, Y. L. "Zhena poeta." In *Legendy i mify o Pushkine.* St. Petersburg: 1994.

Lik Pushkina. Speeches given at the Bogoslovsky Institute. Paris: 1977.
Literaturnoye nasledstvo. Nos. 16-18; 58.
Lobanov, M. P. *Razmyshleniye o literature i zhizni.* Moscow: 1982.
L_nnqvist, Barbara. "Chlebnikov's 'double speech'." In *Velimir Chlebnikov: Myth and Reality.* Amsterdam: 1986.
Lotman, Y. M. *Pushkin.* St. Petersburg: 1995.
------. *Roman "Yevgeny Onegin". Kommentary.* Leningrad: 1983.
Lukyanovsky, B. "Pushkin i Gogol v ikh lichnykh vzaimootnosheniyakh." In *Besedy.* Moscow: 1915.
Lunacharsky, A. V. "Pushkin." In *Pushkin. Polnoye sobranie sochineny.* Moscow-Leningrad: 1936.
------, ed. *Literaturnaya entsiklopediya.* Moscow: Kommunisticheskaya akademiya, 1931.
------, ed. *Ocherki po istorii russkoy kritiki.* Moscow-Leningrad: 1929.
------. *Osnovy prosvetitel'skoy politiki sovetskoy vlasti.* Moscow: Rabotnik prosveshcheniya, 1924.
Lyubovny byt pushkinskoy pory. Moscow: 1994.
Makogonenko, G. P. *Gogol i Pushkin.* Leningrad: 1985.
------. *Roman Pushkina "Yevgeny Onegin".* Moscow: 1963.
Makovitsky, D. P. "U Tolstogo." *Literaturnoye nasledstvo,* No. 90.
Malinin, V. A. *Filosofskiye vzglyady Pushkina. Avtoreferat.* Moscow: 1954.
Mandelshtam, O. E. *Sobranie sochineny.* Vol. II. Paris: 1971.
Mayakovsky, V. V. *Sobranie sochineny.* Vol. XI. Moscow: 1978.
Maykov, V. N. *Skazka o rybake i rybke i yeyo istoki.* St. Petersburg: 1892.
Merezhkovsky, D. S. *Vechniye sputniki,* 3rd ed. St. Petersburg: 1906.
Meylakh, B. S. *Zhizn' Aleksandra Pushkina.* Leningrad: 1974.
------. *Pushkin i yego epokha.* Moscow: 1958.
------. *Pushkin. Ocherk zhizni i tvorchestva.* Moscow-Leningrad: 1949.
Mikoyan, S. A. "Asketizm vozhdya." *Ogonyok* (No.15, 1989).
Mirsky, D. P. *Literaturno-kriticheskiye statyi.* Moscow: 1978.
Mirsky, D. S. *Pushkin.* New York: 1963.
------. *A History of Russian Literature* 1958.
Miturich, P. V. *Vospominiya.* Manuscript.
Modzalevsky, B. L. ed. *Pushkin. Pis'ma.* Vol.I-II. Moscow-Leningrad: 1928.
Modzalevsky, L. B. ed., *Pushkin. Pis'ma.* Vol. III. Moscow-Leningrad: 1935.
Moskovsky komsomolets (Special ed., December 11, 1969).
Muchnik, Helen. "A Long Nose Argued with Its Owner." *The New York Times Book Review* (December 23, 1973).
Na putyakh k novoy shkole, (1923).
Nabokov, V. V. *Eugene Onegin.* New York: 1964-1975.
------. *Nikolay Gogol.* New York: 1959.
Nekrasov, V. "Ya byl ryadom so Stalinym." *Novoye russkoye slovo* (Oct. 28, 1994) and "Zakat khozyayina" (Oct. 24, 1994)..

Nikishov, Y. M. "'Yevgeny Onegin': problema zhanra." *Boldinskiye chteniya.* (1986).
------. "Dal' svobodnogo romana kak kompozitsionnyy priyom v 'Yevgenii Onegine'." *Boldinskiye chteniya.* (1985).
Novikov, I. A. *Sobranie sochineny.* Moscow: 1967.
Nusinov, I. M. *Pushkin i mirovaya literatura.* Moscow: 1941.
Obodovskaya, I., and M. Dementyev. *Posle smerti Pushkina.* Moscow: 1980.
Oklyansky, Y. *Yuri Trifonov. Portret-vospominaniye.* Moscow: 1987.
Oksman, Y. G. Guide. *Pushkin. Polnoye Sobranie sochineny.* 1931.
Osipova, M. I. "Rasskazy o Pushkine, zapisannye M. I. Semevskim." In *Pushkin v vospominaniyakh sovremennikov.* Vol. I. Moscow: 1974.
Ostafyevskiy arkhiv knyazey Vyazemskikh. St. Petersburg: 1899.
Ozerova N. P. Letter to S. L. Engelgardt, May 4, 1830. *Pushkin i yego sovremenniki.* Vol. XXXVII.
Panayev, I. I. *Literaturnye vospominaniya.* Moscow-Leningrad: 1950.
Papera, T. "Trifonov: His Heroes and Their Family Life." *IV World Congress for Soviet and East European Studies. Abstracts.* Harrowgate, 1990.
Parfenov, P. "Rasskazy o Pushkine, zapisannye K. A. Timofeyevym." In *Pushkin v vospominaniyakh sovremennikov.* Vol.1. Moscow: 1985.
Paustovsky, K. G. "Potok zhizni." In *A. I. Kuprin: Sobranie sochineny.* Vol. I. Moscow: 1957.
Pavlishchev, L. N. *Vospominaniya o Pushkine.* Moscow: 1890.
Pavlishcheva, O. S. "Vospominaniya o detstve Pushkina." In *Pushkin v vospominaniyakh sovremennikov.* Vol. I. Moscow: 1974.
Pavlova, Y. V. *Pushkin v portretakh.* Moscow: 1983.
Pedagogicheskaya entsiklopediya. Moscow: 1964.
Perepiska Pushkina. Moscow: 1982.
Petrovsky, D. V. *Povest o Khlebnikove.* Moscow: 1926.
Petrunina, N. N. Notes. *Pushkin. Pis'ma poslednikh let.* Leningrad: 1969.
Petrunina, N., and Fridlander, G. "Pushkin i Gogol v 1831-1836 godakh." In *Pushkin. Issledovaniya i materialy.* Vol. VI. Leningrad: 1969.
Pletnev, P. A. Letter to N. V. Gogol, October 27, 1844. *Russky vestnik* (No.11, 1890).
------. Sochineniya i perepiska, St. Petersburg, 1885.
Pletnev, R. V. *Istoriya russkoy literatury XX veka.* Englewood: 1987.
Pochinkovskaya, V. V. "Shest' let v Mikhaylovskom." Unpublished memoir cited in Budilin, I. T. *Zolotaya tochka Rossii.* St. Petersburg: 1995.
Pogodin, N. F. "Svershilos!" *Izvestiya* (May 9, 1945).
Polyakov, M. "Khlebnikov. Mirovozzreniye i poetika." In *Khlebnikov. Tvorenya.* Moscow: 1986.
Popovsky, M. *Dnevniki.* Manuscript. New York, 1990.
Potebnya, A. A. "Pereprava cherez reku kak predstavleniye braka." In *Moskovsky arkheologicheskiy vestnik. Vol.* I. 1867-68.

Pozov, A. *Metafizika Pushkina*. Madrid: 1967.
Predvaritelnye itogi. Moscow: Sovetskaya Rossiya, 1975.
Pushchin, I. I. "Zapiski o Pushkine." In *Pushkin v vospominaniyakh sovremennikov*. Moscow: 1974.
Pushkin, A. Y. "Dlya biografii Pushkina." *Moskvityanin*. Book 2, 1852.
Pushkin. Materialy yubileynykh torzhestv. Moscow: 1951.
Pushkin. Pis'ma k zhene. Leningrad: 1987.
Pushkin v pis'makh Karamzinykh. Moscow-Leningrad: 1960.
Pushkin v Yaropoltse. Moscow: 1982.
Pynin, A. N. "Gogol." In *Entsiklopedichesky slovar'. Izdateli F. A. Brokhauz i I. A. Yefron*. St. Petersburg: 1891-1907. Vol. XVII. (1893).
Rancour-Laferriere, D. *The Slave Soul of Russia: Moral Masochism and the Cult of Suffering*. New York: 1995.
------. *Out from under Gogol's Overcoat: A Psychoanalytic Study*. Ardis, 1982.
Rayevsky, N. A. "D. F. Fikelmon v zhizni i tvorchestve Pushkina." In *Izbrannoye*. Minsk: 1978.
Rait, R. "Vse luchshiye vospominanya." *Uchenye zapiski Tartusskogo universiteta*, issue No.184, *Trudy po russkoy i slavyanskoy filologii*. Vol. IX. Tartu: 1966.
Richards, D. J., and Cockrell, C. R. S. *Russian Views of Pushkin*. Oxford: 1976.
Robida, A. *Dvadtsatoye stoletiye: elektricheskaya zhizn*. St. Petersburg: 1894.
Saitov, V. I. *Sobolevsky, drug Pushkina*. Petrograd: 1922.
Shaw, Thomas. *Pushkin: A Concordance to the Poetry*. Columbus, O.: Slavica Publishers, 1985.
Shchegolev, P. Y. *Duel' i smert' Pushkina*. Moscow-Leningrad: 1928.
Shenrok, V. I. *Materialy dlya biografii Gogolya*. Moscow: 1892.
Shevlyakov, M. V. *Pushkin v anekdotakh*. St. Petersburg: 1899.
Shik, A. *Zhenaty Pushkin*. Berlin: 1936.
Shklovsky, V. B. *Ocherki po poetike Pushkina*. Berlin: 1923.
Shults, R. G. *Pushkin i Knidsky mif*. München: 1985.
Slonimsky, A. Notes. *Gogol. Sobranie sochineny v shesti tomakh*. Vol. V. Moscow: 1952-1953.
Slovar' sovremennogo russkogo literaturnogo yazyka. Moscow: 1954.
Smirnov, N. M. "Iz pamyatnykh zapisok." In *Pushkin v vospominaniyakh sovremennikov*. Vol. II. Moscow: 1985.
Sollogub, V. A. *Pushkin v vospominaniyakh sovremennikov*. Vol. II. Moscow: 1985.
Solovyov, V. S. *Dukhovnye osnovy zhizni. Sobranie sochineny*. Vol. III. Petrograd: 1917.
Sovetskiy entsiklopedicheskiy slovar'. Moscow: 1979.
Stalin, I. V. *Marksizm i voprosy yazykoznaniya*. Moscow: 1950.
------. Speech on November 6, 1941. *Izvestiya* (November 7, 1941).
Stepanov, N. L. *Velimir Khlebnikov. Zhizn i tvorchestvo*. Moscow: 1975.

------. Foreword, in *Gogol. Sobranie sochineny v shesti tomakh.* Vol. I. Moscow: 1952-1953.
Stepanov, V. "Syuzhety zhurnalnoy prozy." *Izvestiya* (16 August 1974).
Sumtsov, N. F. *Sbornik v pamyat' Pushkina.* Kharkov: 1900.
Svanidze, M. A. Diary. *Stalin v obyatiyakh semyi.* Moscow: 1993.
Tarasenko-Otreshkov, N. I. "Vospominiya o Pushkine." *Russkaya starina* (February 1908).
Teffi, N.A. "Moya letopis." *Vremya i my* (No.111).
Tendryakov, V. F. "Kultura i doveriye." *Ogonyok* (No.88, 1990).
Terts, Abram (Andrei Sinyavsky). *V teni Gogolya.* London: 1975a.
------. *Progulki s Pushkinym.* London: 1975b.
Tolstaya, S. A. *Dnevniki.* Vol. I. Moscow: 1978.
Tolstoy, L. N. *Polnoye sobranie sochineny.* Vols.18, 19, 23, 62.
Tomashevsky, B. V. In *Pushkin. Polnoye sobranie sochineny.* Vol. VI. Leningrad: 1977-1979.
------. *Kommentarii.* In *Pushkin. Polnoye sobranie sochineny.* Vol. I. Leningrad: 1977.
------. *Pushkin. Kn. 2.* Moscow-Leningrad: 1961.
Trifonov, Y. V. "Zapiski soseda." *Druzhba narodov* (No.10, 1989).
------. "Intervyu o kontaktakh. Beseda s Y. Stoyanovskoy," *Inostrannaya literatura,* (No.6, 1978).
------. *Rasskazy i povesti.* Moscow: 1971.
Trifonov, Yuri. *Literary Reminiscences.* Olson Laboratory, U.C. Davis: Tape 23074-1.
Trudy pervoy i vtoroy Vsesoyuznykh pushkinskikh konferentsiy. 1949, 1950. Moscow-Leningrad: 1952.
Tsvetayeva, M. I. "Moy Pushkin." *Sochineniya.* Vol. II. Minsk: 1989.
------. *Moy Pushkin.* Moscow: 1981.
Tsyavlovsky, M. A. *Rukoyu Pushkina.* Moscow-Leningrad: 1935.
------. "Khronologicheskaya kanva biografii." In *Pushkin. Polnoye sobranie sochineny.* Vol. VI. Moscow-Leningrad: 1931.
Tumansky, V.I. *Stikhotvoreniya i pis'ma.* St. Petersburg: 1912.
Tumarkin, Nina. "The Great Patriotic War as Myth and Memory." *Atlantic* (June, 1991).
Turbin, V. N. *Poetika romana Pushkina "Yevgeny Onegin."* Moscow: 1996.
------. " 'Yevgeny Onegin' i my," *The Pushkin Journal* (Vol. I, No.2, 1993).
Turgenev, I. S. *Sobranie sochineny.* Vol. X. Moscow: 1962.
Tynyanov, Y. N. *Poetika, istoriya literatury, kino.* Moscow: 1977.
Tynyanov Y. and N. Stepanov, eds., *Sobranie proizvedeny Velimira Khlebnikova v pyati tomakh.* Leningrad: 1928-1933.
Ulyansky, A. I. *Nyanya Pushkina.* Moscow-Leningrad: 1940.
Umanskaya, M. "Romantizm i realizm v literature 20-30kh godov XIX veka." In *Problemy russkoy literatury.* Yaroslavl: 1966.

Urnov, D. M. *Pristrastiya i printsipy.* Moscow: 1991.
Uspensky, G. I. "Prazdnik Pushkina." In *Dostoevsky v russkoy kritike.* Moscow: 1956.
Vatsuro, V. E. "Litseyskoye tvorchestvo Pushkina." In *Pushkin. Stikhotvoreniya litseyskikh let.* St. Petersburg: 1994a.
------. *Zapiski kommentatora.* St. Petersburg: 1994b.
Ventzel, K. N. *Evolyutsiya nravstvennykh idealov.* Unfinished manuscript. In the Archive of the Russian Federation Academy of Pedagogical Sciences. [*All Ventzel manuscript materials thus located unless otherwise indicated.*]
------. Autobiographical sketch. *Iz perzhitogo, peredumannogo, perechuvstvovannogo i sdelannogo.* 1932.
------. Diary. 1936-1937.
------. Notebook. 1933-1935.
------. Diary. 1930.
------. *Moi zamechaniya po povodu teorii dialekticheskogo materializma, 1929-1935.*
------. Diary. 1925.
------. Diary notes. 1925.
------. *O vnutrennem rabstve.* 1925-1934.
------. *Tri revolyutsii.* 1923.
------. *Teoriya svobodnogo vospitaniya i idealny detsky sad.* Moscow: 1923a.
------. *Revolyutsiya i trebovaniya nravstvennosti.* Manuscript collection of articles. Voronezh. 1923b.
------. *Religiya tvorcheskoy zhizni. Problema religii v svete osvobozhdeniya ot tsepey nevidimogo rabstva.* 1923c.
------. Copybook with notes, from Voronezh. 1921.
------. "Sotsializm i vospitaniye" and "Provozglasheniye prav rebyonka." In *Svobodnoye vospitaniye.* (No.1-3, 1918).
------. *Unichtozheniye tyurem.* Moscow: 1917a.
------. Diary. 1917b.
------. *Nuzhno li obuchat detey nravstvennosti.* 1912a.
------. *Etika i pedagogika tvorcheskoy lichnosti.* Moscow: 1912b.
------. "Nravstvennoye vospitaniye i svoboda." *Svobodnoye vospitaniye.*(1908).
------. *Osvobozhdeniye rebyonka.* Moscow: 1906.
------. "Etika, pedagogika i politika." *Vestnik vospitaniya* (No.3, 1906). Cited from manuscript.
------. Copybook with prison notes. 1885.
------. Diary. 1884.
Veresayev, V. V. *Sputniki Pushkina.* Moscow: 1993.
------. *Sputniki Pushkina.* Moscow: 1937.
Viktorovich, V. A. "K probleme khudozhestvenno-filosofskogo yedinstva 'Yevge-niya Onegina'." *Boldinskiye chteniya.* (1989).
Vinokurov, S., and Pchelnkov, T. *Vidnye russkiye pedagogi v Voronezhskom kraye.* Voronezh: 1972.

Vitale, Serena. *Il bottone di Puskin*. Milan: 1995.
Vokrug Pushkina. Moscow: 1975.
Vorovsky, V. "A. Kuprin." In *Literaturno-kriticheskiye statyi*. Moscow: 1956.
Vyazemsky, P. A. *Zapisnye knizhki*. Moscow: 1963.
------. *Sobranie sochineny*. St. Petersburg: 1878-1896.
------. Letter to his wife, 30 May 1830. *Literaturnoye nasledie*. (No.16-18).
Yashin, M. I. "Khronika predduelnykh dney." *Zvezda* (No.9, 1963).
Yefimov, I. M. *Vremya dobra*. Tenafly, N.J.: 1993.
------. "Yunosha Khlebnikov i vzrosly Platonov." *Novoye russkoye slovo*. (July 9, 1993).
Yegolin, A. M., ed. *Pushkin. Sbornik*. Moscow: 1941.
Yenikolopov, I. K. *Pushkin v Gruzii*. Tbilisi: 1950.
Yermilov, V. V. *Nash Pushkin*. Moscow: 1949.
Yezhegodnik Rukopisnogo otdela Pushkinskogo doma, 1974. Leningrad: 1976.
Zagorovsky, A. *O razvode po russkomu pravu*. Khar'kov: 1884.
Zenkovsky, V. *Russkaya pedagogika v XX veke*. Paris: 1960. [*1st ed.: Belgrade: 1933.*]
Zholkovsky, A. K. "Bluzhdayushchiye sny." In *Istoriya russkogo modernizma*. Moscow: 1992.
------. "Grafomanstvo kak priyom." *Velimir Chlebnikov: Myth and Reality*. Amsterdam: 1986.
Zhavoronkov, A., E. Tikhonova, V. Tyurin. *Pisateli na Novgorodskoy zemle*. Novgorod: 1960.
Ziberov, D. "Albert Robida—shutnik i mechtatel." *Nedelya* (No.6. Moscow: 1973).
Zimovets, S. "Molchaniye Gerasima." In *Psikhoanaliticheskiye i filosofskiye esse o russkoy kulture*. Moscow: 1996.
Zolotussky, I. P. "Portret 'strannogo' geniya." In *Gogol v zhizni*. Moscow: 1990.
------. *Gogol*. Moscow: 1979.
Zvenya. Moscow-Leningrad: Academia, 1934.

Index

Abramovich, Stella, 83
Adamovich, Georgy, 233, 234
Agitprop, 12, 27, 284, 308, 315
Akaky Akakiyevich, 51
Akhmadulina, Bella, 321
Akhmatova, Anna, 58, 92, 109, 146, 304
Aksakov, Ivan, 149
Aksakov, Sergey, 288
Aldiss, Brian, 180
Aleksandrina. *See* Goncharova, Aleksandra
Alliluyeva, Svetlana, 242, 249, 252, 253, 255, 257, 259, 260, 289
Amis, Martin, 180
Andropov, Yuri, 160
Angelina, Pasha, 150
Annenkov, Pavel, 20, 34, 36, 37, 42, 44, 92, 137, 139, 142, 143, 149, 151, 158
Antokolsky, Pavel, 321
Anzhelika, 55
Apraksin, Fyodor, 132
Arafat, Yasir, 241
Arakcheyev, Aleksandr, 232
Arapova, Aleksandra, 86
Arina Rodionovna. See Yakovleva, Arina
Artsybashev, Mikhail, 231
Averchenko, Arkady, 234
Azadovsky, Mark, 162
Azhayev, Vasily, 249

Baklanov, Georgy, 321
Balter, Boris, 263
Bartenev, Pyotr, 32, 63, 68, 81, 92, 136, 147, 148
Baruzdin, Sergey, 317
Bayley, John, 49, 152
Bekleshova, Aleksandra (Alina), 75, 128
Belchikov, Nikolay, 22, 23
Belinsky, Vissarion, 6, 32, 51, 103—105, 118
Bellona, 176

Benckendorff, Aleksandr, 27, 64, 71, 73, 82, 125
Berdyayev, Nikolay, 208
Beria, Lavrenty, 22, 243, 251, 260, 307
Bilibin, Ivan, 224
Birkerts, Sven, 180
Blagoy, Dmitry, 31, 93, 105
Blatov, 265
Blonsky, Pavel, 184, 194
Bogdanov, 277
Bolshevism, 6, 33, 189, 192, 193, 195, 204, 205, 219, 222, 231, 236, 286, 308
Bondarev, Yuri, 321
Boratynsky, Yevgeny, 68, 77, 103, 119
Botkin, Vasily, 104
Braginskaya, Nadezhda, 133
Brezhnev, Leonid, vi, 263, 265, 317, 329
Brik, Lilya, 7, 279
Brik, Osip, 271
Bryullov, Aleksandr, 60
Bryullov, Karl, 76, 123
Brzeski, Andrzej, 324
Bubennov, Mikhail, 249, 307
Bubnov, Andrey, 211
Bulgakov, Aleksandr, 62, 63
Bulgakov, Mikhail, 236, 288, 311, 314, 321
Bulgakov, Sergey, 60, 69, 70, 84, 115
Bulganin, Nikolay, 251
Bulgarin, Faddey, 40
Bunin, Ivan, 223, 224, 229
Bursov, Boris, 51, 75, 96, 126
Bykov, Nikolay, 50
Byron, George, v, 23, 99, 124

Caligula, 232
Carlyle, Thomas, iii
Catherine II, 96
Cervantes Saavedra, 43
Chaadayev, Pyotr, 24
Chateaubriand, F.-A., 101
Chatsky, Aleksandr, 113

Chavchavadze, Ilya, 25
Chavchavadze, Nina, 292
Chekhov, Anton, 10, 236, 260, 283, 287, 288, 302, 321, 328
Chekhovs, N. and M., The, 187
Chelnokova, Fedosya, 278
Chernov, Aleksandr, 226, 228
Chernyshevsky, Nikolay, 32
Chicherina, Olga, 146
Chicherina, Varvara, 146
Chkalov, Valery, 25
Chopin, Frederic, 287
Chukovsky, Korney, 280
Chulkov, Mikhail, 149
Clayton, Douglas, 103, 105, 115
Clio, 316
Clute, John, 170
Cockrell, C. R. S., 152
Communism, vi, 7, 17, 168, 180, 181, 186, 232, 233, 236, 307
Conquest, Robert, 241
Constantine, Grand Duke, 86
Cord, Michael, 329
Cubo-Futurists, 282
Cyrano de Bergerac, 167

D'Anthes, Georges-Charles, 13, 26, 57, 67, 80—84, 86, 88—91, 93, 122
Dal, Vladimir, 145, 275
Dalton, John, 237
Daniel, Yuli, 314
Danilevsky, A. S., 39, 41, 51
Dauge, A., 187
De la Rue, 36
De Staël, Madame, 111
Decembrists, 6, 13, 23, 33, 150
Delvig, Anton, 35, 91, 143, 144
Dementyev, M. A., 92
Demin, Mikhail, 304
Derzhavin, Gavriil, 19
Dewey, John, 188, 202, 203
Dick, Philip, 179
Diderot, Denis, 19
Dobrolyubov, Nikolay, 102
Dolgorukova, Yekaterina, 76
Don Juan complex, 162
Don Juan list, 53, 71, 75, 125, 126
Don Quixote, 192
Dore, Gustave, 167
Dorida, 55
Dostoyevskaya, Anna, 98

Dostoyevsky, Fyodor, iii, iv, 19, 69, 99—106, 112, 116, 118, 119, 122, 221, 328
Druzhba narodov, 304
Druzhinin, Aleksandr, 20
Dubovikov, A., 35
Dubrovsky, Vladimir, 153
Durylin, S., 187
Dykhovichny, Vladimir, 313
Dynnik, Alexander, 233
Dzhabayev, Dzhambul, 150

Edgeworth, Maria, 142
Ehrenburg, Ilya, 243
Emerson, Carol, 116
Engel, S., 79
Engels, Friedrich, iv, 19, 205—208, 250
Erasmus, 213
Erotomania, 162
Esenin, Sergey, 271, 288
Etkind, Efim, 283

Fadeyev, Aleksandr, 20, 26, 225
Fanny, 55
Faure, S., 188
Fedin, Konstantin, 243, 305, 307, 316, 321
Fet, Afanasy, 20, 120
Ficquelmont, Dolly, 60, 71, 78
Filipyevna, 142
Flammarion, Camille, 167
Flaubert, Gustave, 106
Fonskaya, Serafima, 225—227
Fortunatovs, Y. and A., The, 187
Frankland, Colwell, 69
Freud, Sigmund, 149
Futurism, v, 280
Fyodorov, Nikolay, 281

Gabbe, Tamara, 305
Galich, Alexander, 233
Galkin, I. S., 18
Gallant, Jim, 317—320, 322—327, 330
Garin, 179
Gastev, Aleksey, 283
Gippius, Vasily, 32, 33, 45, 50
Glasnost', 316
Glinka, Mikhail, 9, 10, 281
Gnedich, Nikolay, 49
Goethe, Johann Wolfgang, v, 52
Gofman, Modest, 53, 54, 55, 86
Gogol, Nikolay, iii, 31—52, 80, 96, 132, 173, 265, 287, 288
Golitsyna, Yevdokiya, 56, 121, 162

Index 361

Goncharova, Aleksandra, 75
Goncharova, Natalya. See Pushkina, Natalya
Goncharova, Yekaterina, 83
Gorbachev, Mikhail, 160
Gorbunov-Posadov, Ivan, 187, 190, 193, 194
Gorky, Maksim, vi, 5, 7, 10, 14, 156, 219, 231, 252, 284, 321
Gorodetsky, Sergey, 280, 281, 284
Gorokhov, Captain, 14
Graham, Stephan, 233
Granovskaya, N., 133, 141, 157
Griboyedov, Aleksandr, 19, 113, 292
Grigoryev, Apollon, 105, 116, 153
Grimm, Brothers, 149
Grossman, Leonid, 63, 304, 314
Gukovsky, Grigory, 105
Gumennaya, G., 105
Gurchonok, Pavel, 269, 275, 278, 290

Hannibal, Maria, 121, 133, 146, 162
Hannibal, Osip, 148
Hekkeren, Baron, 50, 80, 82, 84, 90
Hemingway, Ernest, 311
Herzen, Alexander, 288, 298
Hitler, Adolf, 9, 10, 25, 94, 247
Hugo, Victor, v, 173

Ilf, Ilya, 179
Ilyin, V., 32
Inber, Vera, 16, 17
Inostrannaya literatura, 328
Iskra, 218
Istomina, Valentina, 260
Ivan the Terrible, iv, 236
Ivanov, Vsevolod, 321
Iveriya, 25
Izmaylov, Nikolay, 157
Izvestiya, 11, 14, 187, 212, 297, 337

Kaganovich, Lazar, 251
Kalashnikova, Olga, 161
Kalinin, Mikhail, 265
Kalma, Anna, 226
Kapterev, Pyotr, 196
Karamzin, Nikolay, 106, 287
Karamzina, Sofya, 70
Karamzina, Yekaterina, 56, 76, 78, 162
Karenin, Aleksey, 119, 121
Karenina, Anna, 118, 119, 120, 129
Kasama, K., 106
Kashpirovsky, 173

Katayev, Valentin, 229, 321
Katenin, Pavel, 27, 111
Katz, Michael, 116
Kazakov, Yuri, 321
Kazantsev, Aleksandr, 180
Kerensky, Aleksandr, 270
Kern, Anna, 97, 110, 144, 145
Kharms, Daniel, 280
Kheraskov, Mikhail, 265
Khitrovo, Yelizaveta, 56, 162
Khlebnikov, Velimir, v, 269—286, 289—293
Khlebnikova, Vera, 289
Khlebnikova, Yekaterina, 289, 294
Khlestakov, Ivan, 37
Khlyustin, Semyon, 84
Khrushchev, Nikita, 243, 251, 258, 263—265, 317
Kim, Yuli, 243
Kireyevsky, Ivan, 69
Kirillova, Lukerya, 132
Kirpotin, Valery, 6—8
Kiselev, Pavel, 53, 63
Klechkovsky, M., 187
Kochubey, Vasily, 157
Koenig, 55
Koltsov, Aleksey, 96
Komsomolskaya pravda, 227
Kornilov, Konstantin, 194
Korolenko, Vladimir, 186
Korolev, Fyodor, 202
Kosmodemyanskaya, Zoya, 288
Kotlyarevsky, Nestor, 136, 143
Kozhevnikov, Vadim, 308
Kozlov, Nikita, 145
Kozlovsky, Yakov, 307
Krasnaya Nov, 273
Krestovsky, Vsevolod, 117
Krispin, 45
Krivtsov, Nikolay, 62, 68
Kropotkin, Pyotr, 188
Kruedener, Amalia, 71
Krupskaya, Nadezhda, 184, 193, 203, 211, 221, 287
Krylov, Ivan, 19, 40
Kultur, Ach Gallet de, 85
Kunin, V.V., 94
Kuprin, Alexander, 217—225, 227—237
Kuprina, Kseniya, 142, 223, 234
Kuprina, Yelizaveta, 223, 227, 230
Kuprina-Iordanskaya, M. K., 220
Kurochkin, Arkhip, 140
Kutuzov, Mikhail, 10

Kuznetsov, Felix, 317
Kuznetsova, Agniya, 93
Küchelbecker, Wilhelm, 106

Lacombe, Estelle, 172
Lanskaya, Natalya. *See* Pushkina, Natalya
Lanskoy, Pyotr, 68, 87—89
Larin, Dmitry, 101
Larina, Olga, 40, 55, 75, 100—103, 109, 111, 115, 134, 140, 144
Larina, Tatyana, 55, 79, 83, 99—124, 127, 128, 137, 142, 143, 146
Lazari, Andrzej, iv
Leibnitz, Gottfried, 19
Lemke, Mikhail, 40
Lenin, Vladimir, iv, 6, 9—11, 18, 19, 22, 32, 165, 168, 169, 171, 192, 194, 197, 202, 203, 205, 207, 218, 219, 223, 226, 232, 239, 241, 250, 252, 253, 255, 260, 262, 281, 286, 287, 292, 299, 308, 315
Lensky, Vladimir, 95, 100—102, 105, 106, 109, 115
Leonov, Leonid, 321
Lepeshinsky, Panteley, 194
Lermontov, Mikhail, 19, 127, 287
Levitan, Isaak, 288
Levkovich, Yanina, 73
Lidin, Vladimir, 321
Literaturnaya gazeta, 35, 56, 59, 229, 296, 321
Literaturnaya Rossiya, 320
Litinsky, Grigory, 302
Lobanov, Mikhail, 275
Lorrice, George, 181
Lorrice, Philoxene, 170—172, 177, 179
Lotman, Yuri, 42, 54, 149
Lukin, 277
Lunacharsky, Anatoly, 6, 189, 200, 219, 220, 286
Lunin, Mikhail, 86
Lysenko, Trofim, 31

Machiavelli, Niccolo, 255, 262
Makarenko, Anton, 184, 211, 225
Makarov, M., 107
Makogonenko, Georgy, 31, 33, 45, 105
Maksimovich, M. A., 40
Malenkov, Georgy, 251
Maltsev, Yelizar, 306
Mandelshtam, Nadezhda, 98
Mandelshtam, Osip, 282
Manuylov, Victor, 16
Marette, Arsene, 171

Marienhoff, Anatoly, 271
Marinetti, Filippo, v
Markov, Georgy, 93
Markusha, Anatoly, 297
Marshak, Samuil, 306
Marx, Karl, iv, 19, 168, 169, 197, 204—208, 237, 250, 287
Marxism, 193
Maslov, Pyotr, 189
Masson, Olga, 55
Matveyev, Fyodor, 133
Matveyeva, Arina. *See* Yakovleva, Arina
Matyushin, M., 281
Mayakovskaya, Ludmila, 249
Mayakovsky, Vladimir, iii, iv, v, 7, 9, 11, 271, 272, 283—285, 288, 292
Maykov, Valeryan, 158
Melgunov, Sergey, 189
Merezhkovsky, Dmitry, 115
Merzhanov, Miron, 246
Meyerhold, Vsevolod, 272
Meylakh, Boris, 13, 21, 23, 132, 150
Mickiewicz, Adam, 76
Mikoyan, Anastas, 251
Mikula Selyaninovich, 132
Mill, John, 186
Minsky, Dmitry, 20
Mironova, Masha, 55
Mirsky, Dmitry, 32, 109, 285
Mir Bozhiy, 231
Miturich, May, 274, 290, 291, 293
Miturich, Natalya, 274, 277
Miturich, Pyotr, 272, 274, 277—279, 289, 290
Moliere, 168
Molotov, Viacheslav, 251
Montessori, Maria, 188
Morozov, Mikhail, 221
Morozov, Pavlik, iii
Moskovsky kaleydoskop, 107
Moskovsky komsomolets, 298, 307
Moskva, 322
Muchnik, Helen, 49

Nabokov, Vladimir, 38, 43, 48, 102, 105, 113, 116, 134—136, 142, 145, 152, 327
Nabokova, Vera, 98
Nachala, 273
Nadenka, 55
Nagibin, Yuri, 56
Napoleon, 13
Nashchokin, Pavel, 32, 54, 63, 70, 81, 85
Natasha, 55

Index

Nazism, 10, 176
Nelina, Nina, 307
New Economic Policy, 286
Nicholas I, 49, 71, 78, 85—91, 98, 126, 132
Nicholls, Peter, 170
Nietzsche, Friedrich, 220
Nikandrov, Nikolay, 236
Nikashidze, I., 187
Nikolay Pavlovich. *See* Nicholas I
NKVD, 16, 22, 57, 211, 224—226
Nord, Lidiya, 233, 235
Nostradamus, 166, 181
Novy Mir, 313, 315

O'Donoghue, 142
Obodovskaya, I. M., 92
Obrazovantsy, 315
Obshcheye delo, 234
Odoyevsky, Vladimir, 41, 45
Ogaryov, Nikolay, 288
Ogonyok, 252
Oksman, Yulian, 41, 46, 48
Okudzhava, Bulat, 318
Okunkov, 194
Olenina, Anna, 66, 67, 91, 92
Olminsky, Mikhail, 189
Onegin, Eugene, 83, 99—129, 135, 137, 142, 152
Orina Yegorovna (Pakhomovna), 142
Orlov, Mikhail, 112
Orthodox Church, iv, 12, 120, 132
Orwell, George, 175, 182, 236
Osipova, Maria, 160
Osipova, Praskovya, 56, 64, 75, 126, 138—140, 143, 157, 158, 162
Oyrikh, Leonid, 263
Oyslender, Aleksandr, 25, 26
Ozerova, Nadezhda, 62

Pamyat, 183
Panteleyev Brothers, The, 166
Pasternak, Boris, 91, 233, 285, 304, 314
Paustovsky, Konstantin, 231, 321, 322
Pavlishchev, Lev, 44, 111, 158
Pavlishchev, Nikolay, 141, 292
Pavlishcheva, Olga, 133, 135, 136, 139, 292
Pavlov, Ivan, 10
Pechat' i Revolyutsiya, 273
Pechorin, 126, 127
People's Will, 185
Perov, Aleksandr, 264
Pertsov, Pyotr, 68
Perventsev, Arkady, 14

Peter the Great, iv, 14, 23, 94, 132, 142, 153, 236, 253
Petnikov, Grigory, 271, 283, 284
Petrovsky, Dmitry, 271
Pirogov, Lieutenant, 41
Pisarev, Dmitry, 103
Platonov, Andrey, 281, 303
Plekhanov, Georgy, 10
Pletnev, Pyotr, 35, 36, 38, 42, 43, 50, 63, 64, 72, 77, 79, 87, 124, 127
Pletnev, Rostislav, 233, 234
Pogodin, Nikolay, 18
Pokrovsky, Mikhail, 189
Poletika, Idalya, 88
Polikarpov, Dmitry, 243
Politburo, 6, 251, 254, 262, 266, 267
Polyansky, 194
Populists, v
Poskrebyshev, Aleksandr, 241, 253, 258
Posledniye novosti, 234
Potebnya, Aleksandr, 103
Potemkin, Vladimir, 224
Pozner, 194
Pozov, A., 32
Pravda, 7, 8, 150, 189, 203, 230, 340
Prinevsky kray, 232
Pugachev, Yemelyan, 153
Pushchin, Ivan, 143, 159, 161
Pushkin, A. Y., 134
Pushkin, Alexander, iii, iv, v, 2, 5—162, 270, 279, 292, 321
Pushkin, Grigory, 125
Pushkin, Lev, 135, 292
Pushkin, Platon, 136
Pushkina, Maria, 50
Pushkina, Nadezhda, 145
Pushkina, Natalya, 38, 42, 53— 59, 62, 64—89, 91—98, 107, 109, 113, 121—123, 125, 126, 161
Pushkina, Sofya, 58, 61, 65—67, 91
Pypin, A., 37

Radishchev, Aleksandr, 19
Radshe, 23
Rait, Rita, 271
Rantsov, V., 166, 168
Raskolnikov, Podion, 322
Rau, F., 187
Rayevskaya, Maria, 92, 157
Rayevsky, Nikolay, 96, 112, 138
Razin, Stepan, 149
Reed, John, 287
Reiters, T., 288

Rembrandt, 176
Repin, Ilya, 10, 252
Repnin, Nikolay, 84
Revolution, 6, 8, 9, 15, 152, 155, 168, 169, 189, 193, 194, 197, 198, 202, 203, 209, 210, 215, 219, 220, 222, 223, 225, 230, 231—236, 237, 270, 282, 284, 285, 293, 322
Richards, D. J., 152
Robida, Albert, iv, 165—182
Robin, P., 188
Roman-gazeta, 308, 314
Romanov, Konstantin, 132
Rousseau, Jean-Baptiste, 186
Roza Grigoryevna, 161
Rozanov, Vasily, 20
Russky invalid, 39
Russkoye bogatstvo, 231
Russkoye vremya, 234
Ryashentsev, Yuri, 243
Ryleyev, Konstantin, 23
Rylsky, Maksim, 11

Saburov, Yakov, 107
Saltykov-Shchedrin, Mikhail, 93
Samizdat, 2, 298, 310, 326, 329
Schtirner, Max, 209
Schultz, Rostislav, 71
Sechenov, Ivan, 10
Sedykh, Andrey, 223
Segodnya, 234
Selvinsky, Ilya, 321
Serov, Valentin, 288
Serova, Valentina, 224
Severnye tsvety, 144
Shakespeare, William, 52, 258
Shalyapin, Fyodor, 288
Shapiro, 297
Shatsky, Stanislav, 184, 194
Shaw, Thomas, 135
Shchedrin. *See* Saltykov-Shchedrin, Mikhail
Shcheglov, Nikolay, 72
Shchegolev, Pavel, 72, 84, 92, 161
Shenrok, Vladimir, 37
Shevlyakov, M., 147
Shklovsky, Victor, 105
Shleger, L., 187
Sholokhov, Mikail, 252, 299
Shulgin, 194
Shvarts, Dmitry, 137
Simonov, Konstantin, 20, 224, 243, 321
Sinyakovs, The, 271

Sinyavsky, Andrei, 37, 46, 106, 314
Skvortsov-Stepanov, Ivan, 189
Slavophiles, v, 152, 149
Slobodskoy, Moris, 313
Smirnov, Nikolay, 64
Smirnova, Aleksandra, 71, 76
Sobanskaya, Carolina, 55, 56, 58, 59, 110, 162
Sobolevsky, Sergey, 54, 63, 68, 76, 78, 91, 161
Socialist Realism, vi, 233
Sofronov, Anatoly, 258
Sofya Astafyevna, 58
Sollogub, Vladimir, 71, 84
Sologub, Fyodor, 20
Soloukhin, Vladimir, 321
Solovyov, Vladimir, 20, 216
Solzhenitsyn, Alexander, 304, 310, 313—315, 324
Somov, Orest, 144
Sotsvos, 203
Sovremennik, 46, 47, 48, 96
Spencer, Herbert, 185
Srodnikova, Aleksandra, 278, 289
Stakhanov, Aleksey, 150
Stalin, Joseph, iii, iv, v, vi, 5, 7—26, 94, 132, 150, 184, 209, 212, 224, 225, 229, 233, 239—266, 281, 285, 289, 303, 304, 306—309, 317, 326
Stalin, Vasily, 301
Stepanov, Aleksey, 277
Stepanov, Nikolay, 270, 284, 285
Stepanova, Yevdokiya, 275—277, 289, 290
Struve, Gleb, 233
Sulphatene, 173
Surikov, Vasily, 10
Surkov, Aleksey, 249
Suvorov, Alexander, 10
Svetlov, Mikhail, 243
Svinyin, Pavel, 44
Svobodnoye vospitaniye, 187
Swift, Jonathan, 167
Sylvester, Richard, 240

Tamizdat, 329
Tchaikovsky, Modest, 112
Tchaikovsky, Pyotr, 9, 10
Teffi, Nadezhda, 234
Telegraph, 41
Tendryakov, Vladimir, 26, 321
Terekhova, 194
Terras, Victor, iii
Third Rome, The 12

Tikhonravov, N., 49
Tolstaya, Sofya, 98
Tolstoy, Aleksey, 234, 235, 321
Tolstoy, Leo, 9, 10, 15, 51, 114, 115, 118—120, 129, 179, 187, 189—191, 196, 198, 211, 236
Tomashevsky, Boris, 13, 33, 147
Trifonov, Georgy, 295
Trifonov, Nikolay, 295
Trifonov, Valentin, 308
Trifonov, Vladimir, 295
Trifonov, Yevgeny, 307
Trifonov, Yuri, vi, 243, 253, 295—331
Trotsky, Leon, 9, 17
Tsvetayeva, Marina, 62, 92, 311, 336
Tsyavlovsky, Mstislav, 37, 42, 110, 141
Turbin, Vladimir, 116
Turchaninov, 155
Turgenev, Aleksandr, 22, 49, 84, 91, 145
Turgenev, Ivan, 19, 42, 57, 220
Tvardovsky, Aleksandr, 243, 253, 304—306, 313, 316
Tynyanov, Yuri, 105, 113, 281, 284, 285, 321
Tyutchev, Fyodor, 71

Ulyanov, Vladimir. *See* Lenin, Vladimir
Ulyansky, A. I., 133, 141, 150, 158
Umanskaya, M., 105
Updike, John, 319
Ushakova, Yekaterina, 53, 58, 91, 92
Ushakova, Yelizaveta, 53, 66, 67
Uspensky, Gleb, 103
Uvarov, Sergey, 40, 41

Vasilchikova, Aleksandra, 37, 81
Vasilevskaya, Tatyana, 184
Vatsuro, V., 50
Veltman, Aleksandr, 45
Ventzel, Konstantin, 183—216
Ventzel, Vera, 213
Veresayev, Vikenty, 20, 49, 58, 67, 68, 75, 84, 88, 92, 145, 158
Verne, Jules, 167
Vertinsky, Aleksandr, 254
Vestnik inostrannoy literatury, 169
Vigel, Philipp, 50, 59
Vilyanova, Fevroniya, 63
Vinogradov, Vladimir, 258
Vinokurov, Yevgeny, 321
Vizbor, Yuri, 243
Vladimov, Georgy, 183
Vlasik, Nikolay, 241

Volin, Boris, 221
Voltaire, F. M., 19, 173
Vonnegut, Kurt, 319
Voronsky, Aleksandr, 220
Voroshilov, Klimenty, 7, 251
Vorovsky, Vatslav, 218—220, 296
Vozrozhdenye, 234
Vrevsky, Boris, 95
Vronsky, Aleksey, 118—120
Vsemirnaya illustratsiya, 279
Vulf, Aleksey, 95, 138, 143, 159, 161
Vulf, Anna, 140
Vyazemskaya, Vera, 54, 75, 78, 81, 110
Vyazemsky, Pavel, 60, 82
Vyazemsky, Pyotr, 22, 40, 48, 49, 58, 63, 64, 69, 71, 81, 91, 100, 106, 108, 137, 139, 144

Weil, Elena, 319
Witt, Ivan, 59
Wrangel, Baron, 280
Writers' Union, 93, 219, 222, 225, 233, 237, 243, 257, 291, 295—297, 300, 303, 306, 311, 312, 316

Yakim, 51
Yakobson, Roman, 273
Yakovlev, Rodion, 132
Yakovleva, Arina, v, 24, 131—152, 154—162
Yakovleva, Ulyana, 135
Yakubovich, 39
Yazykov, Nikolay, 64, 143, 144, 158, 159, 160
Yeremin, M. P., 286
Yevtushenko, Yevgeny, 321
Yoffe, Boris, 299

Zakharov, Pavel, 290
Zaks, 315
Zamyatin, Yevgeny, 182, 236
Zavadovskaya, Elena, 71
Zelenko, A., 187
Zenkovsky, Vasily, 202
Zharov, Aleksandr, 299
Zhdanov, Andrey, 255, 256
Zheleznov, Mikhail, 76
Zholkovsky, A., 46, 283
Zhukovsky, Vasily, 32, 35, 37, 39, 40, 42, 43, 46, 48, 51, 60, 77, 85, 91, 287
Zolotussky, Igor, 33, 45
Zoshchenko, Mikhail, 303, 321
Zubkov, Vasily, 61, 139

STUDIES IN SLAVIC LANGUAGES AND LITERATURE

1. Peter I. Barta and Ulrich Goebel, **The Contexts of Aleksander Sergeevich Pushkin**

2. Mark J. Elson, **A Diachronic Interpretation of Macedonian Verbal Morphology**

3. Colin Partridge, **Yuri Trifonov's Moscow Cycle: A Critical Study**

4. Gareth Williams, **The Influence of Tolstoy on Readers of His Works**

5. A.D.P. Briggs, **A Comparative Study of Pushkin's** *The Bronze Horseman*, **Nekrasov's** *Red-Nosed Frost*, **and Blok's** *The Twelve*: **The Wild World**

6. Edward E. Ericson, Jr., **The Apocalyptic Vision of Mikhail Bulgakov's** *The Master and Margarita*

7. Peter E. Barta (ed.), in collaboration with Ulrich Goebel, **The European Foundations of Russian Modernism**

8. János Pilinszky, **Metropolitan Icons: Selected Poems of János Pilinszky in Hungarian and in English**, Emery George (ed. & trans.)

9. N.V. Gogol, **РЕВИЗОР/The Government Inspector: A Comedy in Five Acts**, M. Beresford (ed.) with English Introduction and Notes

10. Wendy Rosslyn, **Anna Bunina (1774-1829) and the Origins of Women's Poetry in Russia**

11. Nina A. Efimov, Christine D. Tomei, Richard L. Chapple (eds.), **Critical Essays on the Prose and Poetry of Modern Slavic Women**

12. Lauren G. Leighton (compiler), A **Bibliography of Alexander Pushkin in English: Studies and Translations**

13. Juras T. Ryfa, **The Problem of Genre and the Quest for Justice in Chekhov's** *The Island of Sakhalin*

14. Yuri Druzhnikov, **Contemporary Russian Myths: A Skeptical View of the Literary Past**